Understanding
Media Industries

Understanding Media Industries

SECOND EDITION

TIMOTHY HAVENS
University of Iowa

AMANDA D. LOTZ
University of Michigan

New York   Oxford
OXFORD UNIVERSITY PRESS

Oxford University Press is a department of the University of Oxford.
It furthers the University's objective of excellence in research,
scholarship, and education by publishing worldwide.

Oxford   New York
Auckland   Cape Town   Dar es Salaam   Hong Kong   Karachi
Kuala Lumpur   Madrid   Melbourne   Mexico City   Nairobi
New Delhi   Shanghai   Taipei   Toronto

With offices in
Argentina   Austria   Brazil   Chile   Czech Republic   France   Greece
Guatemala   Hungary   Italy   Japan   Poland   Portugal   Singapore
South Korea   Switzerland   Thailand   Turkey   Ukraine   Vietnam

For titles covered by Section 112 of the US Higher Education
Opportunity Act, please visit www.oup.com/us/he for the
latest information about pricing and alternate formats.

Published by Oxford University Press
198 Madison Avenue, New York, New York 10016
http://www.oup.com

Oxford is a registered trademark of Oxford University Press

Library of Congress Cataloging-in-Publication Data
Havens, Timothy.
   Understanding media industries / Timothy Havens, University of Iowa,
Amanda D. Lotz, University of Michigan.
      pages cm
   Includes bibliographical references and index.
   ISBN 978-0-19-021532-3 (alk. paper)
 1. Mass media. I. Lotz, Amanda D., 1974- II. Title.
   PN90.H38   2016
   302.23--dc23
                                                    2015010701

Printing number: 9 8 7 6

Printed in Canada
on acid-free paper

BRIEF CONTENTS

—

CONTENTS

—

PREFACE

Understanding Media Industries guides students through an introductory exploration of the complex and rapidly evolving media industries in the United States. The origins of this book are in the classroom. It grew out of our introductory media industries courses, which we've taught at various universities, in classrooms large and small, each of us for nearly two decades. In these courses, we found that existing textbooks tend to have *either* thematic and conceptual consistency *or* a thorough and nuanced understanding of the complexities of media industry operations, but none achieve both. Rather than simply cobble together an array of material from media economics, political economy, and more concrete explanations of actual industry practices (usually in collections with a chapter focused on various industries), we wanted to provide this material with a center—a core conceptual framework particularly crucial in an introductory class. Research and perspectives on media industry operation have grown tremendously in recent years, yet we have also found that frameworks of study or distinctive theoretical approaches often remain lacking.

The Unique Approach of This Book: Industrialization of Culture

Among the key challenges of designing a media industry class are the variation among industries and national contexts and the impermanence of information as industry practices and structures change constantly. Consequently, we felt a conceptual framework would be the most valuable contribution we could make to the existing literature, with the idea that such a framework would provide a map for students becoming aware of media industries for the first time. In designing it, we interrogated many of the previously unexamined assumptions that have driven our own scholarship and findings. Rather than the prescriptive form we associate more with the creation of "models," we believe our "framework" brings a looser, yet productive, order to the variation characteristic of media industry operation and a language for speaking about media industries in a manner that has wide application.

Thus, after many long discussions about vocabulary and the relationships among media industries and their practices, we developed the Industrialization of Culture framework that provides the core organization of this book. The framework is a synthesis of many ideas that are now well established in media studies; its innovation is primarily its articulation and explanation of these ideas. Our primary goal was to allow for the complexity of media industry operation while nevertheless making these operations understandable at a conceptual level. For example, we sought to explain different payment schemes and how they can affect media content, while not providing a detailed listing of every variation of advertising or direct payment that can be found in contemporary media industries. We hope to offer a starting point that introduces novice students to the basic processes and components of media-making while setting forth a vocabulary and set of relationships (the framework) that more advanced students can use to begin to make applications.

The book introduces and explains the Industrialization of Culture framework, which identifies the key areas and aspects of media industries that must be considered when analyzing how media industries function and why they do the things they do. The last two chapters of the book examine two dynamics—digitization and globalization—that are causing significant changes in media industry operation and explore how prior norms of operation are changing in every level of the framework.

We openly acknowledge it is impossible to write a concise text that explains all media industries everywhere. Thus we try to be succinct and provide only enough examples to make the point—allowing instructors to introduce further applications in their teaching or through assignments. We rely heavily on the framework as an organizing force in the hope that it provides a malleable tool for instructors that can be applied to a variety of teaching and media contexts. Certainly, valuable intellectual insights will come from identifying limitations of the framework and contexts in which its components have less explanatory value.

Scholars in a range of fields study media and their industries, and as a result there is considerable variation in the assumptions, methods, and goals of different types of research. The approach we take might be best described as that of "media studies." As media studies scholars, we believe that media and media industries are important because of their central role in the production and circulation of culture. We are interested in understanding the interaction between commercial industry realities (regulations, profit-maximization strategies, pricing, and so on) and the products of media industries (films, TV shows, music, video games, magazines).[1] We seek to develop understandings of the media industries that make it clear they are "complex, ambivalent, and contested";[2] we find that claims and theories about "the media" that suggest uniformity and consistency in their operation are simply not realistic.

Certain conditions may encourage media companies to perform in certain ways, but situations are often far more complicated than most grand theories about the media industries imagine. We are much more intrigued with exploring the situations that lead media companies to react or behave in unique or unexpected ways that force us to reexamine our basic assumptions. This is not to say that we would describe our approach as noncritical; rather, we acknowledge the considerable capital and power of global media industries but believe it productive to consider how their complexities and inconsistencies create opportunities for critical intervention. We are generally wary of the influence of commercial media culture on society, though we are by no means willing to dismiss commercial media outright. Unlike analysts we would characterize as "free marke-teers," who believe that commercialization inevitably leads to a vibrant "marketplace of ideas" that best serves democratic societies, we begin with the assumption that capitalist societies are inherently unequal, as certain groups have more money and power than others. Commercial media systems consequently tend to suffer from the same kinds of inequities that permeate capitalist democracies.

Features of This Book

• **Ongoing Support Material.** Instructors can access the Instructor's Guide by visiting Understanding Media Industries' Ancillary Resource Center, at http://oup-arc.com/havens-lotz/register/, which includes applications of material discussed in the text, as-signment and class activity ideas, and additional readings and media. Because some-thing is always changing in the media industries, we'll add new applications on the ARC. If you'd like to be notified of new material, follow the book at @HavensLotzUMI or be added to our announcement list by emailing us at understandingmediaindustries @gmail.com.

• **Discussion Questions.** At the end of each chapter we include some application and discussion questions. We offer questions that are less about rote recall of information and instead provide the basis for group discussions. Many ask the students to begin from their own interests and experiences in such a way as to be useful as writing exer-cises as well. Whether your course is a large lecture with smaller discussion sections or a smaller, discussion-driven class, we hope you will find these useful.

• **Application Materials.** Application materials are noted in footnotes. These are gener-ally short videos, audio stories, or print illustrations of the concepts being discussed, as well as a question that indicates how we see this as an application of the book's material. Look to the online portal for newer applications as the media industries evolve, and we welcome suggestions you find helpful as well.

• **Suggestions for Further Reading.** Each chapter also includes suggestions for further reading. For the most part, our suggestions are established books that provide greater depth on the topics necessarily skimmed in this book. These are designed to be useful as a starting point for student research for assignments. Any of these books would also provide an excellent source for a book report. We also include a longer list of readings at the conclusion of Chapter 2. Here we list a number of publications that offer overviews of specific industries, sorted by industry. These sources will be helpful for students who want to learn more about a particular industry.

New in the Second Edition

Those familiar with the first edition will find the core features remain, with some reor-ganization and update throughout. The most significant changes include

• **A substantively revised introductory chapter** (Chapter 1) that introduces media industries and why they should be studied. Some material that explains the changing economic and societal conditions that contribute to the current state of the media industries, which was previously included in a later chapter, now appears here.

- **The first chapter from the first edition (Key Concepts in Media Industry Studies) has been moved** to Chapter 2. This chapter now includes a discussion of the Industrialization of Culture Framework, as well as updated examples and material relocated from later chapters.
- **Chapter 8 (Auxiliary Practices) has been eliminated** and major sections and concepts from that chapter have been moved to other chapters, especially Chapter 7 (Creative Practices) and Chapter 10 (Globalization) in the new edition.
- **Chapter 9 (The Growth of the Symbolic Economy) has been removed.** Elements of this chapter, which dealt with larger changes in postindustrial economies, have been integrated throughout the book, in particular Chapter 1 (Understanding Media Industries), Chapter 5 (Economics Conditions of Media Production), and Chapter 9 (Digitization).
- All chapters received a thorough revision and updating. We continually scour changes in legacy and emerging media and have endeavored to include these developments in our revisions for this new edition. However, because these developments often introduce as many questions as answers, we have prioritized the more conceptual elements of emerging technologies, practices, and industries. The state of any industry can never quite be captured in a textbook, so we encourage students to keep abreast of reportage about the media industries for the most current developments.

Acknowledgments

We'd like to thank many colleagues who have shared ideas with us throughout the drafting process, particularly Alisa Perren, Aswin Punathambekar, Douglas Schules, Serra Tinic, Courtney Brannon Donoghue, Patrick Burkart, Daniel Faltesek, and Joe Turow. Also, sincere thanks to our anonymous reviewers as well as Jennifer Holt, University of California, Santa Barbara; Vicki Mayer, Tulane University; Paul Mihailidis, Hofstra University; Susan Moeller, University of Maryland; Kimberly Ann Owczarski, University of Arizona; Ann Savage, Butler University; and Sharon Sharp, California State University, Dominguez Hills, for their many thoughts and helpful suggestions. Also, we owe considerable debt to our outstanding editorial assistants, Jimmy Draper, Kitior Ngu, and Annemarie Navar-Gill. Our thanks as well to Paul Longo for far exceeding the duties of an editorial assistant. We hope you enjoy this book! We welcome suggestions and comments.

We'd also like to thank the reviewers whose comments helped make this edition better:

Charlene Simmons	*University of Tennessee at Chattanooga*
Karen Petruska	*University of California, Santa Barbara*
Sharon Sharp	*California State University–Dominguez Hills*
Andrew Ó Baoill	*Cazenovia College*
Melody Sands	*Shawnee State University*
Cheryl D. Jenkins	*University of Southern Mississippi*
Max Utsler	*University of Kansas*

Stephen Rendahl	*University of North Dakota*
Megan Mullen	*University of Wisconsin–Parkside*
Tim Anderson	*Old Dominion University*
Randy Nichols	*Bentley University*
Ann M. Savage	*Butler University*
Amy Sindik	*Central Michigan University*
Daniel M. Shafer	*Baylor University*
Mara Einstein	*CUNY–Queens College*
Janet Johnson	*The University of Texas at Dallas*
Kyle Conway	*University of North Dakota*
Ethan Tussey	*Georgia State University*
Erin Copple Smith	*Austin College*
Max Hohner	*Arizona State University*
Dorothy Kidd	*University of San Francisco*
Nicholas Boston	*Lehman College of the City University of New York*
Jillian Baez	*CUNY–College of Staten Island*
Stuart Moulthrop	*University of Wisconsin–Milwaukee*

Timothy Havens

Amanda D. Lotz
Twitter: @DrTVLotz

Notes

1. See also Timothy Havens, Amanda D. Lotz, and Serra Tinic, "Critical Media Industry Studies: A Research Approach," *Communication, Culture and Critique* 2 (2009): 234–253.
2. David Hesmondhalgh, *The Cultural Industries*, 2nd ed. (Thousand Oaks, Calif.: SAGE, 2007), 4.

CHAPTER 1

Understanding Media Industries

Key Takeaways:

Understand the factors that differentiate the "product" of media industries from other industries and their importance for society

Understand the roles of individual agency and ideology within the media industries and how these forces produce diverse and varied products

Understand how the rise of the information economy and transitions from mass production to mass customization have changed norms of the media industries

In an episode of the animated series *South Park* titled "Gnomes," we meet an entrepreneurial group of gnomes who steal underwear for profit. They explain their business plan with the slide shown in Photo 1.1. None of the gnomes is sure what "Phase 2" is, but they are certain that others know and, more important, that profit can be generated from stolen underpants.

The wisdom, or folly, of the Underpants Gnomes—their belief that they can somehow turn stolen underpants into hard cash—is similar in some ways to the commercial media industry's efforts to generate profits from cultural endeavors. The process of

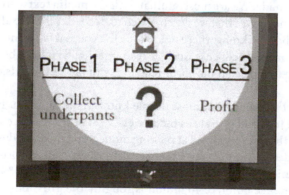

Photo 1.1 A gnome on *South Park* explains their business model.

building and maintaining an industry on the commercial exploitation of cultural expression is a challenge; and the uncertainty of "Phase 2" seems particularly relevant in the present era, when the integration of social media and traditional media industries makes amazing things possible, but business models remain elusive. Unlike other industries that produce goods and services, such as the food industry, tax preparation services, or the automotive industry, none of us *needs* the kind of popular entertainment that the media industries largely provide. And for generations, cultural activities, especially the kinds of domestic amusements that characterize the majority of our media consumption today, were nonprofessional, spontaneous, and free of charge. Today's media industries, in contrast, are multibillion-dollar global enterprises that are crucial as economic drivers and cultural arbiters to the societies that consume their goods even though media consumers are left with little but their memories afterward.

The fact that media do not fulfill essential human needs is often called the "nonutilitarian" feature of media. Yet, while we may not *need* media in the sense that we need food, many people nevertheless see media as central to their lives. In addition, many philosophers and politicians see the media as crucial to the proper functioning of a democratic society because democracies require public forums for discussion as well as the availability of news and information, which media commonly provide. Media are widely available to the public in industrialized societies, and people choose to spend significant amounts of their leisure time and money on media, again underscoring their importance.

To begin our investigation of media industries, this chapter first explains how media industries play important social roles by reviewing some of the events and situations that have led to close scrutiny of media industries. We then move into developing concepts and vocabulary that will be used throughout the book, including the concept of **agency**. Finally, the chapter identifies key issues affecting the media industries in the twenty-first century.

UNDERSTANDING MEDIA INDUSTRIES

Despite the fact that most of us have spent many hours of our lives consuming media—perhaps as much as half of our waking hours—we probably know very little about how and why media are made. We are most familiar with the **media texts**—the shows, songs, films, magazines, and games that we watch, listen to, read, or play. We also may be quite savvy users of media. We know where to look for the content we want and have established elaborate rituals of media use, such as reading news headlines between meetings or classes, listening to music on the go, or relaxing with favorite television shows in the evening.

The one aspect of media that most people know the least about, however, is how they are organized into and operate as industries. Most of the media consumed worldwide are created by businesses aimed at making money, and media industries have been very profitable indeed. In 2012, for example, *Advertising Age* reported that the top 100 media companies in the United States brought in more than $340 billion in net revenue.[1] As a reference point, $340 billion is roughly the gross domestic product of countries such as Thailand, Denmark, or Malaysia. A comparison of revenue (income) and profit (income minus costs) of major US media industries in Table 1.1 further emphasizes the relative economic power of media industries.

Media economist Gillian Doyle provides a valuable explanation of the activities of media industries: "The general aim is to make intellectual property, package it and maximize revenues by selling it as many times as is feasible to the widest possible audience and at the highest possible price."[2] We may tend to think of the creative aspects first, but Doyle's observations about making "intellectual property" and maximizing profits are crucial to understanding media industries. Though the normal functioning of the media industries may be outside of our general awareness, understanding them is an important component of being an educated citizen and consumer in today's world.

The focus on studying industries that produce intellectual property is a way of distinguishing between media industries and what are often called telecommunications or technology companies. These industries, including companies such as Cox Cable, Google, and Apple, are often confused with the media industries, but they are distinct because they primarily provide the technological infrastructures and interfaces through which we access media content. But they generally do not *create* media content themselves. Of course in an age of technological convergence and consolidation of media ownership, the distinction between companies that produce content and those that provide the means to access it is blurring. When Comcast acquired NBC Universal in 2011,

Table 1.1 US Media Industry Revenue

INDUSTRY	2014 REVENUE	2014 PROFIT	MAJOR COMPANIES
Content			
Major label music	$7.6B	$450M	Universal, Sony, Warner
Newspaper	$31.6	$1.3B	Gannett, News Corp., Tribune
Magazine	$38.2B	$1.5B	Advance, Time Inc.
Broadcast networks	$38.2B	$2.6B	Disney, NBCUniversal, Fox
Film production	$33.8B	$2.6B	Fox, Disney, NBCUniversal
Cable networks	$56B	$5.7B	Disney, Time Warner, NBCUniversal
Social networking	$8.6B	$533M	Facebook, LinkedIn, Twitter
Internet search	$22.4B	$3.4B	Google, Yahoo!, Microsoft
Internet publishing/ broadcasting	$27.3B	$6.5B	Google, Facebook, Apple
Distribution and Aggregation			
Film theaters	$14.9B	$641M	Regal, AMC, Cinemark
Film distribution	$2.1B	$97.5M	RLJ Entertainment
Wired telecomm	$129.9B	$7.4B	AT&T, Verizon, CenturyLink
Cable providers	$84.9B	$15.5B	Comcast, Time Warner, Cox
Wireless	$234B	$19B	Verizon, AT&T, Sprint

Source: 2014 IBISWorld Market Industry Reports (December 19, 2014).

for example, it simultaneously became both one of the major providers of media content *and* the major cable delivery company in the United States.

Why then do we maintain a distinction between companies that provide content and those that provide access? The answer is because companies that produce media content share some basic features and face some basic challenges that companies involved in other industries do not—even those that provide very similar kinds of services, like home cable service. So even though Comcast generates revenue from multiple industry sectors, only those sectors that produce and distribute media content are relevant for our study here. In the same way that we don't closely attend to Disney's theme park industry even though it is a major revenue source for the media giant, we do not attend too much to industries and organizations that provide the nuts and bolts of the technological infrastructure over which today's media content travels.

Similarly, companies based on broadcasting interpersonal communication such as Twitter and Facebook are related but distinct from companies primarily structured around creating intellectual property. Even though Facebook is over a decade old, we remain in the early days of social media, and its relationship to traditional media and business models continues to evolve. By the time you read this, some new company will likely have come along that will test the distinction we feel we can draw based on existing companies. Although many social media companies rely on advertising in a manner similar to the business models used by intellectual-property creating media companies, much of this book deals with the complicated nature of creating intellectual property that is different from the user-generated tweets and updates common on social media—though, of course, much of social media is related to sharing and discussing the intellectual property of the media industries we discuss. Consequently, we incorporate discussion of social media intermittently as it is relevant to discussing industries based on intellectual property. These distinctions are certainly difficult to draw resolutely; indeed, an entity such as YouTube arguably is a platform for industrially created intellectual property, amateur-created intellectual property, and the more interpersonal communication of broadcasting "yourself."

Why Study Media Industries?

By analyzing how media industries operate, we can better appreciate how and why the content we interact with comes to be created. Perhaps in other classes you have studied how the media can have social and cultural consequences. Studying media industries also intersects with these questions, but we begin looking at media goods earlier in the process, before they reach audiences, often before they are even created. Two key questions in the study of media industries are *how* and *why* media goods are created in the first place.

In most of the world and in most media industries, media today are created primarily for profit, and, for some observers, this is all we need to know. **Commercial media**, some argue, operate like any other commercial industry. Though it is true that most media industries are rooted in such profit motives, we argue that this is only part of the story. In the process of making money, the media industries create goods that also contribute to dialogues and discussions about important issues in society, to the enabling or disabling of democracy, and to helping us formulate key ideas about the world around us that we take to be natural and inherent.

Think about other industries: packaged food, automotive, furniture. These businesses contribute to what might be termed "material culture"—the objects of culture that surround us in our daily lives—and may have meaning for us. Goods such as our clothes, cars, or our portable devices do communicate something about us and the cultures we live in, but this is not their primary function. Media industries also produce meaningful cultural products, but there is something different about the role media play. In the process of conducting their business, the media industries circulate ideas, attitudes, and information in society, whether they mean to or not. Their products are important in framing civic discourse and perceptions of different cultures in ways that can affect public policy, elections, and our everyday lives—things like how we measure "success," what we think a family looks like, and attitudes about gender roles. Even though many media industries operate with the goal of making money, they are simultaneously significant cultural and political institutions. Balancing these two realities is necessary, and it is probably the most difficult aspect of engaging in serious and fair examination of the media industries.

Media industries warrant understanding for several reasons: first, they are increasingly important sectors of the American and world economies; second, they contribute to political discussions, debate, and our views of the world; and third, they contribute to our everyday lives in ways that are sometimes obvious and sometimes subtle.

Defining Media Industries

The following pages offer you many ways to classify media based on various industry characteristics. When people say "the media," they often mean something far more specific, such as news outlets, television news outlets, or the local television news station in their community. A crucial part of understanding media industries requires that we identify precisely what media or medium we are talking about when examining a specific issue. One of our key tasks here is to illustrate the great variety of conditions and practices that lead media outlets to behave in certain ways.

That said, this book would be far too long and heavy if we took an encyclopedic approach to explaining each aspect of every relevant media industry. Instead, throughout the book we discuss the economic, regulatory, industrial, organizational, and creative practices that shape many media industries. Our main examples of media industries include television, radio, film, magazines, music, video games, and newspapers. These industries have been experiencing pronounced change since the mid-1980s as a result of changes in the overall economy and the effects of **digitization** and **globalization**. Whereas we might have distinguished these "old" media from "new" media just a few years ago, it is increasingly the case that such distinctions are nebulous. As we discuss throughout the book, new technologies and the possibility of digital media distribution may be changing how we receive media, but the media themselves—print, video, and audio entertainment and information—continue to thrive. Rather than suggest blogs are some sort of "new" media form, for instance, we explore how the print media industry worked both before and after the possibility of digital distribution.

Significant discrepancies also exist within any one industry. The economic norms of the magazine industry vary considerably among magazines that are entirely advertiser supported, those paid for exclusively through reader subscriptions, and others that blend advertiser and subscriber financing. Similar variation can be found in the television industry among broadcast television (advertiser-supported networks such as NBC, ABC, and CBS), "basic cable" (channels such as ESPN, TNT, or USA, which receive subscription fees and advertiser-support), and "premium cable" (channels such as HBO and Showtime supported through subscription alone); and an entity such as Netflix may not be a "channel" at all but closely resembles premium cable from an industrial perspective. In addition, in the case of the economics of financing production costs, independent films secure financing differently than films produced by the Hollywood studios, and this too has implications for the films' creative storytelling. To deal with this complexity, we provide a framework (introduced in the next chapter) that identifies key operating conditions and business practices that influence the functioning of media industries even though there is considerable variation in media industry practices across industries and national contexts.

Media Industries in Society

Communication technologies have fascinated politicians, business people, philosophers, and poets since their earliest incarnations in the late nineteenth century. These observers tend to veer between utopian hopes about the capacity of media to enhance democracy and cultural understanding to fearful condemnations that media are brainwashing the masses and destroying individuality. Such extremes may seem normal to us in an era of instantaneous, global communication, but it is important to remember that the hopes and fears that communications technologies engender have a much longer history. We can see traces of these fears as far back as the nineteenth century, when Rudyard Kipling wrote of deep-sea cable technology that connected the United States with Great Britain in 1897:

> *They have wakened the timeless Things;*
> *they have killed their father Time;*
> *Joining hands in the gloom, a league from the last of the sun.*
> *Hush! Men talk to-day o'er the waste of the ultimate slime,*
> *And a new Word runs between: whispering, "Let us be one!"*[3]

Here we see effusive praise and hope for a technology—the deep-sea cable that allowed telegraph communication between Britain and the United States—that most of us today would consider pretty mundane. Yet this sentiment is quite similar to modern anxieties about how mobile phones and social media may be altering communication patterns and social norms. The point in either context is that communication technologies stir deep human passions, and, for this reason, the organizations that operate them and the cultural products that they circulate have long been objects of concerns for society.

The utopian versions of communication technologies received a significant boost with the introduction of radio broadcasting in the early decades of the twentieth century. Broadcasting permitted a single transmission to reach hundreds, even thousands, of listeners with the same message at the same time. In many ways, this development was the beginning of twentieth-century **mass media**, or media designed to distribute information and entertainment to mass audiences. Once again, philosophers and poets saw this ability to reach unprecedented numbers of people as an opportunity to increase understanding and democracy. Politicians, meanwhile, saw a chance to bring their perspectives and arguments to large swaths of the voting public. And businesspeople saw great opportunities to reach across the nation with their promotional messages. Though most media have become more narrowly targeted to **niche audiences** in the past few decades, media still serve important functions in society. The targeting of narrower, specific audiences and people has led to messages tailored to a greater variety of tastes and raised questions about the role of media in societies that share fewer and fewer common cultural experiences. One of the main observers of niche media, Joseph Turow, writes that they are responsible for "breaking up America."[4]

An equally powerful sense of fear has persisted alongside the soaring hopes about the democratic potential of the media—whether mass or niche—as a result of their unknown persuasive powers. Various anecdotal accounts of the powerful effects of radio broadcasting on listeners' perceptions and actions abounded as these technologies emerged, perhaps most notably in relation to the 1938 broadcast of Orson Welles' radio adaptation of the H. G. Wells novel *The War of the Worlds* (1898). Reportedly, after hearing this broadcast, which was performed as a series of news flashes that interrupted "regular" programming, thousands of listeners fled in horror from New York City as "Martians" invaded. Although the accuracy of these reports is debated, the incident still served as a warning about the persuasive powers of the relatively new medium of radio broadcasting. Moreover, the broadcast took place in the midst of Nazi movements in Germany and elsewhere that strove to influence citizens' opinions and actions through mass **propaganda**. Radio became a favored tool for Nazi propaganda, as were films and parades, again adding to widespread fears about broadcasting's social influence.

This example from the early years of radio illustrates that the media industries and the goods they produce have typically been treated differently than other industries because of widespread perceptions that their "products" possess the potential for great social good and harm. For this reason, governments have tended to regulate the media industries differently, and the relationship between commercial forces and the media industries has been more controversial than in most other industries. Take, for instance, the automobile industry. Though numerous individuals and groups protest the commercial control of the media industries, the public at large accepts a commercial automobile industry without question because cars are not seen as having the kinds of social and political potential that media products do.[5]

All Media Matter in the Public Sphere

Understanding exactly how media industries—particularly commercial industries—influence society and politics has been a matter of some debate. Many observers distinguish between entertainment and information services, with the latter typically identified as more serious and important for the proper functioning of democratic societies. This perspective emerges from the belief that noninformational media are "only entertainment" and thus unlikely to play a significant role in shaping attitudes about political and social issues. We disagree strongly with this position and later sketch out our reasons for those beliefs. First, however, let us examine information-oriented media industries and their special social and legal status.

The idea that information is central to the proper functioning of democratic societies dates back to the days of the American Revolution and earlier. The unique status of informational media was enshrined in the Constitution of the United States, which guarantees "freedom of speech, or of the press," and this idea of a free press has, more recently, been recognized as a universal human right by the United Nations.

The presses of eighteenth- and nineteenth-century America differed significantly from what we today associate with newspapers, though they somewhat reflect contemporary cable news channels; in particular, they were more frequently a place for extreme partisanship rather than objective news. One newspaper, for instance, persistently referred to President Rutherford B. Hayes—whose election victory many people doubted—as "his Fraudlency," while another called Andrew Jackson's wife a "whore" on numerous occasions.[6] Despite these excesses, press freedom enjoyed protected legal status because of the widespread recognition that vigorous, even vulgar, debate is necessary if democratic governments want to try to respond to and represent the interests of the public at large.

The German social theorist Jürgen Habermas coined the phrase **public sphere** to refer to the unique space for public debate that the mass media can provide in modern societies. His ideas have been clarified, critiqued, and expanded by a large number of other theorists over the years, but the basic concept has remained and become quite popular, even outside academia. He argues that functioning democracies need to create a public space for the expression and debate of important social ideas and that the mass media provide one powerful, *potential* vehicle for such discussions. For this reason, most public sphere theorists agree that media industries need to be free of substantial control by either governmental or business interests if they are to fulfill their public sphere functions properly. Indeed, whether niche media fulfill that function remains a matter of some deliberation.

Notice that we included interference from both government and commercial forces as possible threats to the vibrancy of the public sphere. In the United States, we are more likely to think about the dangers of government influence on the press—or what we have called a governmental mandate—than about the dangers of commercial influence. This may have to do with the history of enemy propaganda during World War II, greater faith in the democratic potential of free markets than is observed in most other nations, or a host of other reasons. Regardless of its origins, however, in the cases of both government and commercial forces, the concern is that **journalistic objectivity** in investigating and reporting stories might be compromised by meddling institutions that stand to gain or lose from whether and how stories are reported. Indeed, numerous examples of interference in editorial integrity and decision-making litter American history, some of which we recount in the pages that follow.

The metaphor of the public sphere has also been extended to include entertainment media based on an argument that entertaining content is also significant in forming our

worldviews and perspectives about society. Its main emphasis, however, has been journalism, and most discussions about the public sphere tend to either ignore or short-
shrift thorough discussions about entertainment. Instead, most scholars who work with
entertainment media draw from the theories of Raymond Williams and Stuart Hall,
who identified the important role of all forms of popular culture in both enforcing and
contesting dominant belief systems. The field of media studies does not only assess
media's degree of independence from government or industry but also identifies the
ideologies media incorporate and those groups whose interests are affirmed.[7]

The term "ideology" conventionally carries derogatory connotations of overly
politicized attitudes toward subjects or issues that are seen as apolitical. Because critical
analysts—such as those approaching the study of media industries as we do—believe
that no topics or areas of human endeavor are free from political considerations, ideology is a far more neutral term in our vocabulary, referring simply to the worldviews that
lie behind and give meaning to those endeavors. We think of ideologies as lenses that we
use to interpret the world around us. Just as with contacts or magnifying glasses, ideologies that structure our belief systems influence *what* we see, and what we see influences
how we understand the world. Whether or not we recognize them, all of us believe in
countless ideologies, some of which are well thought through, others of which we may
be almost completely unaware.

The focus on ideology in media studies comes from ideas derived from conventional theories of Marxism, which try to examine how we come to understand the world,
our place in it, and our relationships with others, as well as whose interests are served
and ignored by those understandings. **Dominant ideology** is the term used to refer to
the social common sense of our time, and the capacity to define that common sense can
be a powerful political tool. Moreover, most media scholars believe that the media are
important purveyors of social common sense.

We can begin to gain a clearer idea of what this social common sense is and the role
that both informational and entertainment media play in constituting it if we think
about contemporary definitions of terrorism in the United States. Without getting into
explosive political debates, we think it safe to say that, in some instances, one person's
"terrorist" is another's "freedom fighter." How do we come to believe that a particular
incident is the work of terrorists rather than freedom fighters? Certainly the way in
which news media and government sources frame and explain an attack has a lot to do
with it, but it also matters whether the person fits our general idea of what a "terrorist"
looks like or what "terrorist" causes include. And, more likely than not, some of our
ideas about what terrorists look like come from entertainment media as well as news
coverage of real-world events.

The terrorism example makes reference to contemporary politics, but ideology is
also political in a much broader sense; it influences our ideas about what societal groups
we do and don't belong to, as well as the traits of those groups. In these instances, scholars typically evaluate media based on whether they support or challenge social inequities. For instance, African American women in 2013 earned only 64 cents for every
dollar earned by a white male. Though we cannot attribute the entire wage gap to media
representations, the prevalence of images of African American women in music videos

as sex objects as well as their infrequent portrayal as lead characters occupying professional roles may well contribute to a mindset that understands these earning differences as either natural or unimportant. Where the scholarly analysis of media content tries to identify the ideologies present in media such as film, television, music, or print, a primary focus of media industries research is on the processes whereby various ideologies become embedded into media content, how they are framed, and how they are organized, silenced, privileged, or dismissed vis-à-vis other ideologies.

The previous pages explain why we believe media, and particularly the industrial practices involved in their creation, are important to study, as well as some of the basic assumptions with which we approach our studies. The next section of the chapter develops the key concepts of agency and ideology, which are central to understanding the roles and abilities of individuals who are responsible for making and circulating media content and our understanding of the many ways "power" operates in the creation of media. This book is concerned with not only explaining what media industries do and how they do it but also with how what they do and how they do it matters. Agency and ideology are central concepts for understanding how their practices matter.

AGENCY AND IDEOLOGY IN MEDIA INDUSTRIES

The question of the ideologies present in media content brings us quickly to debates about the autonomy or **agency** of the people who work in the media industries. To put the matter bluntly: Are they talented individuals expressing their creative visions for clear political and ideological ends, or are they merely cogs in corporate machines trying to satiate the masses by producing media full of ideological messages that maintain the interests of those in power? Given the lack of evidence for either of these extreme positions, it is safe to say that most observers today think that the truth of the matter lies somewhere in between, but little agreement exists on how we can assess autonomy and its consequences.

Some scholars argue that creative workers internalize the worldviews of the corporations they work for by the time they achieve a degree of autonomy. This includes journalists at major news outlets who wield editorial authority as well as comedy and drama writers and producers who quickly learn what types of shows and characters are likely to be developed by networks. In addition, these powerful creative and editorial workers are among the most elite members of society, and they consequently tend to share similar worldviews—worldviews also consistent with the elite owners and executives of the corporations for whom they work. In other words, while these creators may not simply be cogs in the corporate machine who reproduce the ideologies that serve corporate interests, their ideological orientations may not fall very far from the corporate tree.

Take the example of CNN anchor Don Lemon, an African American commentator who made headlines in 2011 when he revealed he is gay. He has since become a sort of champion for causes of oppressed minorities. However, his privileged status as a highly paid broadcaster emerged when discussing problems in the African American community after the verdict in the Trayvon Martin case, where an unarmed black teenager was killed by a vigilante in 2012.

In a now infamous opinion segment, Don Lemon repeated and agreed with the conservative critique of black families. Some of the discussion on the conservative side of the political spectrum focused on how the shooter's fears were warranted by the large number of black male criminals in the United States—a situation blamed on the breakdown of the black family. The idea that the breakdown of the black family is the cause of criminality is highly controversial and has generally been rejected by research that finds poverty and oppression are the main causes of black male criminality. Although Don Lemon had a *reputation* as a champion of the underdog based on previous causes and his status as an out, gay, black man, his income and social class status led him to a perspective common among affluent, white, elite journalists and news executives. This is the class status shared by nearly all professional journalists and most all decision makers in media companies, which is why we might expect a common outlook.

At the same time, in order for media content to become popular—and therefore profitable—it cannot merely rehearse ideologies that serve the interests of society's elites, because elites make up a tiny fraction of the American society and might consume very different media than those targeted by the content they develop. Media industries consequently design content targeted toward perceived audiences—what we later explore as the "constructed audience"—as a strategy for commercial success. This recognition of the need to target broad and diverse audiences allows the creation of media with a wider range of ideological positions than if only the elites involved in making media were targeted.

We focus in this section on three main theoretical principles that explain our perspective on how much autonomy—or agency—media workers have. The first principle is what we call **circumscribed agency**, a concept that conceives of the people who work in commercial media organizations as agents with some degree of individual autonomy, even though their autonomy is delimited by a range of forces including the cultures from which they come, the conventions of the media in which they work, and the priorities of their organizations and superiors. The second principle is ideological uncertainty, which suggests that no matter how much media creators may try to control the ideological content they produce, it is impossible to preordain the impact of media content on society. The final principle identifies the influence of the cultures of production within which media workers exist. The relative isolation of media producers from audiences while being entrenched in professional cultures that establish norms of quality and characteristics of media goods lead media creators to reproduce norms and ideologies unintentionally.

Agency in Media Organizations

As desirable as it may be to make blanket claims about how media industries operate and how people who work in these industries behave, we find it impossible to make such claims. There is a great deal of variation in media industry operation—so much so that we are hesitant to even make claims that would assert certain things consistently circumscribe the agency of media workers. Additionally, countless factors can play into particular situations—whether the media company has been performing well or is just trying to stay afloat, whether the company is building toward long-term goals or focused on quarterly stock prices, whether the company is a well-respected entity or is in the process of rebranding its identity—and the possible list of issues is endless. Rather than claiming certain situations allow for greater or lesser agency, we identify a number of factors to consider when assessing the agency of an individual or company.

First, why would you want to assess the agency of a media worker? One of the consistent critiques, particularly of commercial media industries, is of the sameness and predictability of their content. In the next chapter we discuss some of the reasons for this sameness, but one of the motivations behind developing the framework for understanding media industries presented in the next chapter is because we have often found that when media do something unexpected or boundary defying, it is often because of the initiative or persistence of an individual or an uncommon corporate culture, yet few conventional theories about media industry operation attend to individual media workers. Certainly, most of the time, media workers follow organizational norms and **industry lore**—the supposed but untested "rules" about what audiences desire and what will or won't be commercially successful. But the concept of circumscribed agency and factors that tend to allow for greater agency is a crucial perspective for those interested in intervening in media industry norms.

Organizational Cultures and Norms

Most basically, the cultures we work and live in—and the norms of that culture—can circumscribe agency. In cultures that value consensus (whether the culture at large or the culture of your workplace), you will be afforded greater agency if you are seen as a consensus builder than if you are one who constantly tries to go against the pervading opinion or seem to be "all about you." Similarly, if the culture of your workplace is one in which people work long hours and respond quickly to email at all hours of the day, not participating in that behavior may decrease how you are regarded and lead you to be afforded less agency.

When Comcast bought NBCUniversal, it ushered in a substantial change in corporate culture that increased the creative autonomy of people working at NBC, and the network subsequently jumped from fourth to first place in terms of audience ratings for 18- to 49-year-olds in the next season. Prior to acquisition by Comcast, NBC had cycled through numerous senior executives, which led workers throughout the organization to be nervous about their own positions and obsessed with office politics. When Comcast hired a new chairperson of entertainment, Bob Greenblat, it guaranteed him a much longer contract and he, likewise, installed new management and management teams with greater longevity. The result was that both the businesspeople and the management at NBC could stop worrying about their jobs and start focusing on creating popular programs.[8]

The conventions of the particular media industry can also circumscribe agency. Journalistic media entities that derive value from breaking news might not have the time for the many layers of management and oversight that are common to the processes of developing a film or television show. This urgency can lead to greater agency because timeliness depends on allowing reporters and editors to make decisions, rather than having decisions evaluated by multiple levels of upper management.

The priorities of the organization one works for, as well as the management style of one's superior, can also circumscribe agency. Some companies seek a steady and conventional path to success, while others emphasize originating the next big thing. Such different emphases circumscribe agency differently. Likewise, some management styles emphasize careful hiring but then give workers great latitude in hopes it allows for big successes (though it can also result in big failures); other styles require workers to seek constant and regular supervisor approval in order to mitigate against big failures. No single norm can be found across media industries or within a particular one. The top management often can influence company leadership style, but big differences still might be evident in a single company under different management teams.

Finally, agency can be circumscribed by the different identities of workers and how they correspond with power relations in society. In some cases, being a young worker might be valued and might afford you more agency, particularly in a media company trying to produce products that appeal to similarly young audiences. In other cases, youth might be seen as a liability and as connected with a lack of experience. In addition to age, education, economic background, gender, and ethnicity all might play a role in circumscribing agency, even if media employers advertise policies emphasizing the workplace as an equal opportunity environment.

The Ideological Uncertainty of Media Content

Just as the complexity and variation of media industries prevent simple and consistent theories of circumscribed agency, it is also the case that industry workers who create content cannot control the political ideology of the programs they produce. We note this fact because those unfamiliar with media industry operation sometimes make the simple assumption that media are commonly created with a particular political aim or agenda. Though this is occasionally the case, in a commercial media system, creating content that is commercially successful consistently overrides any ideological aim.

Even when an ideological aim exists, the body of media studies research has illustrated that audiences interpret messages and content according to their own experiences and perspectives, which might not be consistent with that of the creator. Further, the creation of most of the media we generally think of as the output of the media industries requires vast staffs of individuals. Though there might be a final authority for a particular piece of media—a film's director or a magazine's editor-in-chief—that individual makes decisions based on the limited array of options and suggestions of many others that make it impossible to assert it is the vision of any single individual.

Cultures of Production

Our final point in this discussion of worker agency is that the culture of production itself everything from the degree of input consumers have into the creative process to the broader cultural traditions with which individual workers operate influences the degree of autonomy that creative workers exercise. Though this varies considerably by media industry, much media content requires significant development before any audience feedback can loop back into the production process in a meaningful way. The case of film represents one extreme; once a film is complete there is little to be done in response to critiques of the film. Certainly, a hit film might lead to a sequel, and that sequel might respond to aspects audiences found unfavorable, but film producers—as well as video game makers and record producers—are fairly isolated from audience opinion because the project is complete before audiences are given an opportunity to weigh in.

Media that are continuous, such as a magazine or a television show, are a bit different. A magazine editor may note an outpouring of critique in letters to the editor and seek to adjust the content of the magazine in future issues, just as fan response to a television show plotline may lead writers to make adjustments in subsequent storylines. Sometimes concerns about content even lead to viewer protest and advertiser boycott aimed at demanding changes in content. Though such instances are rare, awareness of this possibility does factor in to creative thinking, and concern about advertiser's actions does affect the creation of media.

In addition to audience feedback, cultural traditions affect creativity. Take the case of music. Anyone who has learned to play an instrument through formal instruction knows that mastering scales is crucial. Scales help you learn how notes should sound in relation to one another and which notes and chords do and do not go together, and they allow you to anticipate developments and changes in a musical piece. At the same time, conventional scales privilege certain types of music and musical expression that predominate in Western music but are sometimes absent in music from other parts of the world, including the preference for harmony and consonance. By the time you become a concert virtuoso or composer, you will have internalized these structures so thoroughly that it will be nearly impossible to play or write music without them.

Though the aesthetic dimensions of the music example are clear, it can be more difficult to see how this process works with regard to ideology, because the ideologies of music are generally more subtle and intuitive than the ideologies of other media content. Still, if we think about how various artists, cultural institutions, and schools privilege certain types of musical expression over others and how musical practices from foreign or nondominant groups can become suppressed because they don't fit dominant models, we can begin to gain a sense of how what might seem to be objective, conventional, and natural ways of expressing oneself can, in fact, be political.

When it comes to popular media, a wide range of conventions typically restricts both aesthetic and ideological creativity. Genre, a French word that simply means "type," is one of the main restrictions; popular media must generally fit conventional genre definitions in order to be made in commercial media systems. Genres help guarantee that new media content will find an appropriate and willing audience and make the job of marketing it easier because the new media good can be situated among previous goods. For instance, band members who decide to release a death metal album are not only choosing to work in a conventional genre but are also typically choosing to write music for suburban, white, male teenagers and young adults.

Conventions often carry the *illusion of quality* (what is perceived as the "best"), *professionalism* (this is what professional media look like), or *inevitability* (this is just how media are). Particular ways of doing things, such as the editing of a situation comedy or norms of composing music, come to be seen as the only way of doing things—or the way that professionals do them. As you might suspect, these technical or aesthetic issues always have ideological dimensions to them even if they are often subtle, are easy to ignore, or might not seem obviously relevant to power relations in society. For instance, in Hollywood films of the 1940s, it was conventional to shoot dialogues between male and female leads with a low camera angle that made the man look tall and powerful and a high camera angle that made the woman look short and vulnerable, thereby reinforcing patriarchal gender roles common in that era.

Professional organizations can also circumscribe the autonomy of media professionals. One of the clearest examples of this influence comes from organizations such as the Society for Professional Journalists, which publishes a code of ethics that members are supposed to follow and which influences both what stories journalists report and how they report them. In most media professions, however, such official "codes" are less common and less specific. Instead, the main sway that professional organizations hold over members comes through trade journals and conventions that reward and teach industry-wide "best practices." Though these best practices are primarily technical and aesthetic in nature, as we have already suggested, they also operate as bearers of ideology.

With the key concepts of agency and ideology established, we turn now to setting the scene for our look at media industries in the twenty-first century. This final section of the chapter explains a bit of economic history that is crucial for appreciating the contemporary uncertainty and innovation across media industries. To appreciate the specificity of the dilemmas current college students will face as they work in or simply consume media in coming years, it is necessary to understand that the whole economy—not just media—underwent sizable adjustments in the 1980s through the early 2000s. One of these transitions was what we call the rise of the information economy, which is a way of describing the relative growth in the sector of the economy within which media industry work is typically placed. The second transition has also swept many industries in addition to media—that is, a shift from the strategy of mass production and its associated practices to mass customization and its practices. The next section explains these transitions in greater detail.

UNDERSTANDING MEDIA INDUSTRIES IN THE TWENTY-FIRST CENTURY

The final two chapters of this book focus on two "dynamics of change" that currently bring yearly, even monthly, adjustments to how media industries have long operated. These dynamics of change are the technological capability of **digitization** and the expansion of media industries to normally operate as global rather than domestic entities, or what we refer to as **media globalization** here. In this last section of the chapter, we provide some context of how media industries have operated in the past—particularly the quite recent past—in order to make clear how and why the developments of digitization and globalization have been so profound.

Though digitization and globalization continue to disrupt many existing norms of operation that we address in the book's final chapters, the media industries have recently completed a similar "dynamic" of change, a transition that might be best described as the rise of **information economy** and the emergence of **mass customization.** In order to prepare our study of media industries in the twenty-first century, this section explains the significant developments that altered the operation of the media industries during the last three decades of the twentieth century. These alterations in many ways connect with the continued changes being realized because of digitization and globalization but are better understood to have preceded these developments.

The Rise of Information Economy

Media industries are just one part of the global economy, and the rise of the information economy and the emergence of mass customization are developments bigger than the media industries. Rather, these developments refer to changes in the overall economic organization and practices of many Western industrialized countries, the rise of other national economies, and how they all interrelate. So please keep in mind that the first part of this story is larger than the media industries and describes a change in the relative importance of the media industries in Western national economies.

The rise of the information economy generally refers to the transition in the composition of national economies, such as that of the United States, so that the reliance on jobs in sectors such as the manufacturing of physical goods are diminished, while a new sector, the information economy, becomes more central. The range of industries included in the "information economy" is an issue of debate among some, though we use the term generally. What is relevant to a study of the media industries is the growth in the economy and expanded reliance on jobs that involve some sort of "symbolic manipulation," for example, jobs in which one designs, computes, and rearranges words, images, and/or sounds. Others have used the terms "knowledge economy," "creative industries," and "creative economy" to likewise describe the sector of jobs involving the production, collection, processing, analysis, and presentation of information and entertainment.*

How drastically has the US economy changed? In 1950 nearly one-quarter of all workers in the United States were employed in factory work, operating machinery or performing day labor. That percentage had dropped to less than 15 percent by the year 2000. By contrast, the number of jobs in information technology is forecast to grow by nearly 25 percent by 2016. Figure 1.1 illustrates these changes.

Though many of these information economy jobs are in industries such as software engineering or communications network management that are broader than "media industries", increasingly they also require expertise in computerized presentation software and audio and video editing to make presentations to clients, managers, and stakeholders. To put this another way, while media production students used to pursue jobs mainly in broadcasting or in-house corporate videos, today companies of all descriptions require people with these skills. At the same time, competition among job seekers is becoming more intense. This simultaneous growth in both the availability of media

---

*This video from *The New York Times* helps explain the changes in the global organization of labor that this section emphasizes. How does the explanation provided by the video relate to workers in media industries? In the development of media technologies? http://www.nytimes.com/video/business/100000001299945/the-iphone-economy.html

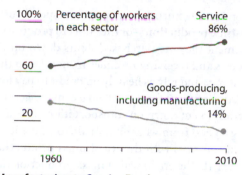

Figure 1.1 Shift from Manufacturing to Service Employment

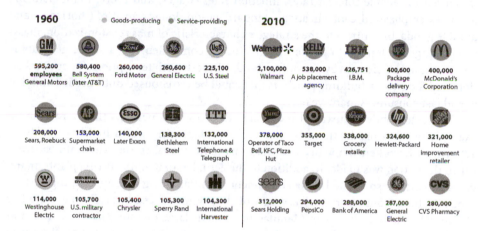

Figure 1.2 Shift in Types of Companies that Dominate US Employment

industry jobs and competition for those jobs means that media workers today have different labor norms than media workers of previous generations. Figure 1.2 presents a comparison of the top employers in 1960 with those of 2010 to illustrate the changing employment opportunities in the United States.

The Emergence of Mass Customization

The other key development is the emergence of **mass customization**, a strategy that focuses on producing commodities that are more tailored to local market conditions. Mass customization—in comparison to **mass production**—calls attention to the fact that these commodities are still produced in factories for large numbers of people, not crafted for individual consumers, but that they are more varied and targeted to buyer preferences than traditional mass-produced goods. A good example here is the shift in computers initiated by Dell in the mid-1980s. Before Dell, computer buyers had minimal choice in the features of their computers and chose among a few models. Dell revolutionized this market by allowing customers to choose particular processors, memory allocations, and other features based on their specific needs and preferences.

A number of other manufacturing practices correspond to the strategy of mass customization. **Just-in-time production**—or the effort to produce goods as close as possible in time to the moment they are purchased—cuts down on the lag time between incurring production costs and receiving revenues from sales so that companies do not have to hold large inventories and rely as heavily on credit to pay for the period between making a good and earning revenue from it. Likewise, many companies have also tried to decentralize production to cut down on transportation costs as well as decrease the lag time of transporting a good from where it is made to where it is sold.

Mass customization contrasts with the era of **mass production** that drove economies following World War II. The era in which mass production dominated was a time of predictable and consistent economic growth—particularly in the United States—which led to reliable interest rates, inflation rates, wages, and more. Manufacturing practices emphasized centralization, standardization, long-term profit horizons, and durable goods. In contrast to the strategies characteristic of mass customization, mass-produced goods tended to locate manufacturing components in a single geographic area, achieved efficiencies by providing standard goods with few options for customization, and focused on building products that could be warehoused until needed and that would last consumers many years.

The automobile industry of the twentieth century is perhaps the quintessential example of mass production. Automobile manufacturing was a highly centralized activity, with workers living in close proximity to massive factories where almost every car in the nation was made. In addition to the actual auto manufacturing plants, many parts suppliers also located their component manufacturing nearby, creating further centralization. Consumers in every part of the country faced basically the same few choices when purchasing a car. Manufacturers made large investments in research and design, factories, materials, wages, transportation, and advertising before their new models ever turned a single penny of profit. And the efficient operation of assembly lines meant creating many cars that might not be immediately sold. Finally—and perhaps most important—manufacturers generally produced high-ticket items that were designed to last for many years; at the time, durable goods like cars were the main economic engines of the American economy.

Importantly, it is not the case that the 1950s were a time of only mass production and now only mass customization exists. There has been a *general* transition—again because of changes in the broader global economy—but the key here is to be able to identify strategies of both mass production and mass customization and understand their consequences. In fact, many of the developing norms in the consumer electronics industry responsible for devices such as smartphones and tablets provide some evidence of a return to mass production, though an era in which this production is based in China and other East Asian countries.

Long Downturn

So what happened in the 1970s to disrupt the mass production, mass distribution, and mass consumption of the postwar era? Mainly, the stability of the postwar economy began to erode. The immediate precipitating event was the 1973 oil crisis, during which oil-producing countries in the Middle East refused to sell oil to the United States because of its support of Israeli military forces in the Yom Kippur War. This seemingly isolated event caused oil and gas prices in the United States to spike, forcing an already weak American economy into a deep recession. What came to be known as "stagflation"—stagnant economic growth combined with currency inflation—caused interest rates to more than double by 1974. Interest rates had generally hovered between 4.5 and 5.0 percent throughout the 1950s and 1960s, but rates near or above 10 percent became commonplace after the oil embargo.

These high interest rates slowly worked to undermine strategies of mass production. High interest rates made it much more difficult and risky to pour massive amounts of money into product development and production and then wait months or years before seeing a return on those investments, leading innovative industries to rely more on just-in-time production. At least as important as the substantial increase in interest rates was their unpredictability, which made profits similarly unpredictable. Even as recently as the mid-2000s, as interest rates dropped to near zero, they have nevertheless remained rather erratic, keeping firms skittish about borrowing too much money for too long a period.

As is often the case with major economic adjustments, it took years for changes in the way that firms operate to percolate through the economy. Forty years later, however, many of the changes that began in 1973 have taken root, become commonplace, and encouraged greater use of strategies characteristic of mass customization.

Media Industries and Mass Customization

A fair question at this point is: So what does all of this have to do with media industries? Remember, we are setting up a context for understanding the twenty-first-century media industries, and to do this, it is important to know that the media industries too transitioned from mass production to mass customization norms during the final decades of the twentieth century.

The mid-twentieth century—the 1950s into the 1970s—was a period of mass production, mass distribution, and mass consumption in American culture, and the media, particularly television, played a central role in holding this system together with the glue of mass advertising that helped create consumer demand for mass-produced products around the country and the world. Large corporations of this era invested massive amounts of capital upfront to produce goods and waited months, even years, before they recouped those investments.

Many legacy media industries developed amidst norms of mass production. The television and film industries were centralized in Hollywood and funded mainly through large, upfront capital investments, not unlike the norms of automobile manufacturing. Shows and movies tended to be standardized and aimed at common cultural tastes and sensibilities. This was the era of mass entertainment, when "everyone" in the country flocked to the same movies or switched on the same programs, leaving the impression that the nation as a whole possessed similar tastes, experiences, and aspirations, even if this impression was predicated on the exclusion of many, particularly women and citizens of color.

The recording industry, too, was organized along mass production principles at the time. Although a number of independent labels and publishers thrived and often introduced the most innovative musical acts and movements—including those such as Motown, R&B, and rock—most popular musical recordings were financed with long-term profit windows in mind, and they were nationally distributed by the major record labels. The major labels employed a large number of musicians in their studio bands and also contracted with popular musical acts who were limited to recording only with that label. Vinyl albums and later electromagnetic tapes were pressed in large factories and distributed nationwide to retail outlets. Again, much of the cultural output of the music industry under the logic of mass production reflected the preferences of a general, national listening audience, rather than the cultural tastes of subgroups.

By the 1960s, though, the magazine and radio industries had already begun to adopt principles of mass customization. Magazines were targeted to general, mass interests in the early decades of the twentieth century, but by mid-century the magazine and radio industries had begun targeting specific demographics and shifted their focus from a general readership or listener to formats built around particular interests, such as classical music or fashion, due in large part to competition from television. Foreshadowing more recent events across the media industries introduced by the specific targeting enabled by digital distribution, some of the most successful magazine formats began to focus on subjects that have persistent, cyclical turnover, such as fashion, gossip, or the entertainment industry.[9]

The newspaper industry was perhaps the only media industry not organized in terms of mass production in the postwar period, due largely to the particularly local emphasis of this medium. Certainly, some of the largest national newspapers, such as *The New York Times,* published a good deal of general-interest national news and centralized both news gathering and newspaper publishing activities in particular locations—not unlike the automobile industry. Even these newspapers, however, contained a large amount of local news, and they published different editions in different parts of the country by mid-century. Most newspapers around the country have been predominantly local enterprises, reporting on local stories and featuring local advertising. In this sense, the newspaper industry has not gone through a comparable transition to mass customization, because the news*paper* industry (that is, the version of this medium actually printed on paper) was significantly disrupted by digital distribution. The era of mass customization did not emerge in a paper form of print distribution but in blogs and online versions of print media.

Mass customization in the media industries began in the magazine industry and slowly spread across almost all media. Though just-in-time production is one component, arguably the most significant indication of the transition from mass production to mass customization in media industries is the transition from business built on designing media goods for a mass audience to designing goods for niche audiences. Mass customization begins with the identification of niche audiences and the development of media goods specifically targeted at those narrow audience targets—whether based on demographics (features such as gender, age, race) or different attitudes and interests (specific hobbies, beliefs). The magazine industry is perhaps the most evolved when it comes to creating niche media, though cable, and most certainly digital sources such as YouTube channels, indicate more recent attempts. If we look, for instance, at magazines targeted at pregnant women—already a pretty well-defined niche audience—we find *Fit Pregnancy* for women interested in maternity fashion and staying in shape during pregnancy; *Pregnancy* magazine, aimed primarily at first-time mothers; *Pregnancy and Newborn*, aimed at both pregnant women and new mothers; and *American Baby* for new and expectant mothers primarily in the 18- to 34-year-old demographic. And this is only a partial list.

In the media industries, mass customization practices such as just-in-time production are also evident in the collapsing of **distribution windows** so that consumers can access the newest films, television programs, and games through a range of different **platforms** at the same—or nearly the same—time. For example, the media conglomeration of Comcast and NBCUniversal spans media production and distribution so that blockbuster movies produced by Universal can be released in the theaters and on Comcast's pay-per-view cable and streaming platforms at the same time, a move that some observers see as the norm of the very near future. In fact, many of these changes in release windows have already taken place, as we discuss in Chapter 8. They permit distributors and producers to recoup their production investments as quickly as possible, rather than waiting for profits to trickle in over months or years as each new window opens.

We can see how both niche media and collapsing release windows take advantage of changes in the technological conditions that the media industries face, in particular digitization and the increased access to all sorts of media it makes possible. Digitization allows distributors such as Comcast, Netflix, or ESPN to deliver any media content via any distribution technology at the same time. Together, these conditions have led to an explosion of new distribution channels for media content, many of which rely on broadband, WiFi, or mobile data networks, to deliver television, movies, games, magazines, newspapers, music, and more. With an increasing number of media outlets and increasing flexibility in how we receive their content, niche audiences have become easier to identify and target. We explore digitization in more detail in Chapter 9.

At the moment, we simply want to note how changed technological conditions enable this shift to niche media. In addition, we want to point out that changes in technologies did not change industrial practices on their own. Instead, they were part of a sustained effort by large corporations, including those that dominate the media and telecommunications industries, that were seeking to adjust to the new opportunities and perils of a changed economic environment. We come back to mass production and mass customization throughout the book to explain a variety of norms of media industry operation, and to how digitization and globalization further have required media industries to reinvent their practices and business models.

QUESTIONS

1. How do media industries differ from more conventional industries that produce goods and/or services? List as many differences as you can. One former Federal Communications Commission chairperson called television a "toaster with pictures" as a

way to rationalize why the media industries should be no more regulated than any other industry. In what ways might this assessment be correct? In what ways is it incorrect?

2. Why are news media important for democracies? Why might *entertainment* media be equally important? Can you think of reasons why some people might *not* think entertainment media are important for democracy? What are they?

3. Take one of your favorite media goods (e.g., a song, a game, a film) and look closely at its credits. How many companies and people were involved in bringing this good to you? Are you able to describe what role each of them played in its production and distribution? Think about how this example demonstrates the "circumscribed agency" of its creators.

4. In your own words, try to describe the differences in the practices of mass production and mass customization. What caused the emergence of mass customization? How did this transition affect the media industries?

5. Consider media content you consume often. In what ways does it reflect—through its content, production, and so forth—the era of mass customization in the media industries? Can you explain why it is the product of mass customization? What audience niche do you think it appeals to and why?

NOTES

1. Bradley Johnson. "100 Leading Media Companies 2012," *Advertising Age* 83, no. 35 (2012): 36.
2. Gillian Doyle, *Understanding Media Economics*, 2nd ed. (London: SAGE, 2013), 20.
3. Rudyard Kipling, *The Seven Seas*, 11th ed. (London: Methuen & Co., 1907), 10.
4. Joseph Turow, *Breaking Up America: Advertisers and the New Media World* (Chicago: University of Chicago Press, 1998).
5. When the US government took significant control of that industry in 2009, it was not because of the social importance of the products it creates but rather because of the economic importance the industry has in national and local communities.
6. Roy Morris Jr., *Fraud of the Century. Rutherford B. Hayes, Samuel Tilden and the Stolen Election of 1876* (New York: Simon & Schuster, 2003); Jon Mecham, *American Lion: Andrew Jackson in the White House* (New York: Random House, 2008).
7. The term "ideology" is both ambiguous and controversial, so we want to explain what we mean by it, and we ask that you keep in mind that how your instructors in this or other classes use the term may differ somewhat.
8. Cynthia Littleton. "Bob Greenblatt Leads NBC Back to No. 1," *Variety*, May 19, 2014. http://variety.com/2014/tv/news/bob-greenblatt-nbc-jimmy-fallon-ratings-1201185518/ (accessed January 12, 2015).
9. David Hesmondhalgh, "Flexibility, Post-Fordism, and the Music Industry," *Media, Culture & Society* 18 (1996), 469–488.

CHAPTER 2

The Industrialization of Culture Framework and Key Economic Concepts

---

Key Takeaways:

Understand the general features of the Industrialization of Culture framework

Understand the various economic features that distinguish media industries

Understand the variety of strategies media industries have developed in response to the peculiarities of media as commercial goods

---

Just as the last chapter focused on preparing the book's investigation of the media industries by explaining the broad relevance of having a rich understanding of media industry operation, and of how recent adjustments in the international economy have affected the media industries, this chapter aims to offer some additional concepts and context. First, however, we introduce the Industrialization of Culture framework that organizes the book and sets the context of its investigation by explaining key developments that have prepared the media industries to operate as they do. The remainder of this chapter then presents a variety of economic peculiarities that cut across the media industries and some practices that have developed in response.

THE INDUSTRIALIZATION OF CULTURE FRAMEWORK

We organize the book using the Industrialization of Culture framework because it will still be relevant whether you read this book when it first comes out or pick it up 5, 10, maybe even 20 years after publication. The media industries are incredibly dynamic, norms vary in different media sectors, and even those norms vary from country to country, so the framework offers a foundation—think of it as a set of tools—that should be helpful regardless of the specific industry or context that you need to understand now or in the future.

The framework we use for explaining the operation of media industries features three different levels of influence particularly related to the making of media. At the

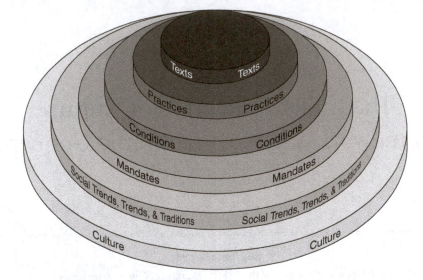

Figure 2.1 Industrialization of Culture Framework

base of the framework illustrated in Figure 2.1, are the contextual features of Culture and Social Trends, Tastes, and Traditions. These are present to remind us that these industries and the people who work in them exist in a context that shapes what they do.

The first level of the actual Industrialization of Culture framework addresses the **mandate** of the media outlet under analysis, or the organization's foremost goals—its reason for operating. The second level of the framework examines the various **conditions** under which the media industries operate, which are typically broader than an individual company and regulate the behavior of an entire media sector. Finally, the third level addresses the day-to-day **practices** of the organizations and individuals who work in the various media industries. In order to represent this framework in two dimensions, we must place one of these levels first, but we do not propose a consistent hierarchy of importance among them. Instead, each of the levels influences all of the others.

We begin with the assumption that *in theory* media industries could create just about anything, from the most abstract expressions of high art to the most offensive forms of pornography. Those bottom, contextual levels of "Culture" and "Social Trends, Tastes, and Traditions," identify the range of social and cultural resources that media producers might possibly draw on when creating media goods. Every culture possesses cultural and aesthetic traditions, such as common genres, themes, and myths that shape the kinds of media content a media producer is likely to imagine, even before the opera-tions of the media industries begin to influence the process. In addition, political tradi-tions, such as freedom of the press in the United States and the opposite condition common in authoritative regimes, affect how journalists envision their jobs and the kinds of stories they seek out. Each of the ensuing levels of the framework shapes the media content until we wind up with the actual media that are produced and circulated within society.

Notice that culture forms the base for the entire Industrialization of Culture framework, suggesting how culture influences the industries' mandates, conditions, and practices. We use the term **culture** in two related senses throughout the book: first, in an aesthetic sense, to refer to the content that the media industries produce, such as films, newspapers, and the like; second, in an anthropological sense, to refer to the specific social practices, values, mores, and hierarchies associated with a particular group of people. The anthropological sense of culture explains why some nations favor public or commercial mandates, why they enact particular laws governing the types of content that can be broadcast, and a whole host of other conditions and practices. More commonly, however, we use the anthropological definition of culture to address the ways in which the people who work at all levels of the media industries exist within industrial cultures that shape their views of themselves, the media they produce, and the audiences they engage.

Our use of the term "culture" in the framework also includes members of the public in a variety of different roles that relate to the media industries: as members of political pressure groups, as consumers of commercial products, as audiences for media, and as citizens. Groups of citizens banded together can influence the regulatory conditions of the media industries, as well as the industry's economic conditions through advertiser boycotts. As consumers, members of the public are divided into demographic groups by the advertising industry and persuaded, often through commercial media outlets, to buy products. Although media audiences do not get direct input into the practices of the media industries, commercial media producers always have audiences in mind when making production decisions. In a sense, the audience functions as a ghost that haunts every level of our framework. Thus, although we don't focus much on how audiences consume media, what importance media plays in their lives, or the economics of media consumption for audiences, the acknowledgement of culture in our framework accounts for the variety of ways that members of the public influence media industry operations.

Mandates

The first level in the Industrialization of Culture framework asks, "What is the mandate of the media industry?" A mandate is the primary goal or the reason for being of the media industry—and this contributes significantly to how the media industry is likely to behave and what content it is likely to produce. Almost all large-scale media operations today function under a **commercial mandate**. Such media primarily value the earning of profits and thus make decisions based on the perceived consequence of the profitability of content, whether such content is sold directly to audiences or supported by advertisers. With the exception of the Public Broadcasting System and National Public Radio, nearly all media of nationwide scale in the United States operate with a commercial mandate. Commercial media systems tend not to be democratic—in other words, some audiences are considered more valuable than others. As a result, some people—typically those who are younger and/or have higher incomes—enjoy far greater choice in the media content designed for them.

There are exceptions to media with a commercial mandate, as we explain in more detail in Chapter 3. Various **noncommercial mandates** include public, community, alternative/do-it-yourself, and governmental mandates. Media operating with these mandates primarily value something other than commercial profits. In the case of public systems such as the British Broadcasting Company and the Public Broadcasting System, that priority is serving the needs of the citizens of the nation that support those media outlets with tax money or contributions. Media with a community mandate are similar, but they exist to serve far more specific groups, as in the case of community radio or a community newsletter. Media produced with an alternative, or do-it-yourself, mandate often seek to fill a void in existing media outlets or are primarily vehicles of self-expression for creators. Finally, media produced with a governmental mandate are characterized by tight governmental control over content and are typically run by authoritarian regimes. In fact, most authoritarian regimes of the past century have exhibited this tendency to use media outlets as mouthpieces; such media systems continue to persist in China, and efforts by the Egyptian government to limit information about uprisings in 2011 also illustrated a governmental mandate.

Conditions

The next level in our framework encompasses what we call conditions. Conditions, such as regulation, economics, and technology, are larger than any individual entity and organize how media industries can operate. **Regulation** functions as a condition—often particular to a specific country and industry—that encompasses the legal rules within which media companies operate. There are many different types of regulation that govern media industries, but most can be categorized as regulations on content, industry structure, or technical standards. Media industries face some of the same regulations that every industry in the United States faces, such as antitrust rules; however, we emphasize those regulations that have developed to deal with the particular social and political features of media.

Economic norms provide another significant condition that affects how media industries operate. Economic considerations include how the ownership norms of a specific media industry might affect the content it produces. Two of the most significant changes in media industries over the past few decades have been the steady **conglomeration** of many different kinds of companies under a single corporate umbrella, and the **consolidation of ownership** into a handful of global companies. At the consumer level, economic matters such as norms for funding media production and whether consumers pay for media through subscriptions, by direct transaction, or by consuming advertisements also play important roles in media industry economic norms.

Finally, the available **technology** contributes considerably to defining the possibilities available to media industries. Technology can affect how professionals produce media and change a media industry from previous norms, as in the case of digital publishing and recording equipment. Technology can also affect the distribution of media, as in the case of Internet music distribution that expanded piracy and ended the dominance of the album as the primary unit of music sale, which in turn forced adjust-ment of traditional music industry economic models. Technology also governs how we access media, enabling us to freely move content among various devices, which has led to entirely new ways of using media.

One final point about each of these conditions is that they rarely operate indepen-dently. That is, changes in one of the conditions typically alter each of the others.

Practices

The final level of our framework encompasses the myriad of individual and organiza-tional roles performed by people who are responsible for the day-to-day operation of media industries and the content they produce. We designate these as practices, an umbrella term that can include a broad range of workers and activities. In one of the clas-sic textbooks about media systems, Joseph Turow identified at least 13 different "power roles" that describe the duties and activities of media industry workers (see Table 2.1).[1]

For the sake of clarity, we have organized these roles into two distinct types of prac-tices: **creative practices and distribution and aggregation practices**, although there are also roles that don't neatly fit into these categories as well.

Creative practices encompass the tasks and workers involved in the making of media. Distribution and aggregation practices include workers and activities that bring finished media goods to the audience. We can also identify a variety of other practices not well described as creative or distribution/aggregation practices—such as audience measurement and employment representation by guilds, unions, agents, and lawyers, which comprise numerous other practices that exist somewhat outside the central media industries. We generally refer to these as **auxiliary practices**. Such roles are too varied to address in a general overview textbook, but we offer examples of such roles in discussions of the others.

Table 2.1 Turow's "Power Roles" of a Mass Media Industry

Set conditions of media-making	Authorities
Make, fund media	Producers
	Creators
	Investors
	Clients
	Auxiliaries
	Unions
	Facilitators
Make media available	Distributors
	Exhibitors
	Linking pins
Consume, respond to media	Publics
	Public advocacy groups

HOW DOES THIS FRAMEWORK WORK?

Our framework is intended to be *multidirectional*, by which we mean that each level influences the others. In most instances, we imagine the Industrialization of Culture framework functioning sort of like an old-fashioned pinball machine, in which every individual ball, or media project, travels a unique path through the playing field. Forces as varied as the skill of the player, the various objects that each ball encounters, and a bit of chance lead to the ball's varied paths and trajectories. In our metaphor, illustrated in Figure 2.2, the particular culture within which a media industry operates determines the placement of the bumpers, spinners, chutes, flippers, and special bonuses that each ball (or idea) must negotiate.

The large bumpers that deflect the balls and determine their speed and trajectory might represent the "Mandates" in our framework. The other bumpers, spinners, ramps, and chutes also alter a ball's speed and direction in dramatic ways and represent "Conditions." Finally, the players themselves, who demonstrate varying degrees of skill when operating the plunger and the flippers to initiate and redirect each pinball, represent the "Practices" of the industries and the people who work in them.

For example, if we used this pinball metaphor to understand a hypothetical new television news magazine program, we'd start by considering its mandate. Imagine this show airs on Fox Broadcasting, which is owned by the media conglomerate News Corp. that owns, among other things, the *Wall Street Journal*, Fox News Cable Channel, and 20th Century Fox studio, and is headed by James Murdoch. Fox has a commercial mandate, and the purpose of this show is producing commercial profits, so we can imagine a strong bumper push toward creating content that is commercially successful. Of course a news show can be commercially successful in lots of different ways (e.g., by maintaining a reputation for the highest quality, by reinforcing the worldview of a particular segment of the audience, by emphasizing things that are interesting even if not that important), so that commercial mandate alone doesn't tell us everything.

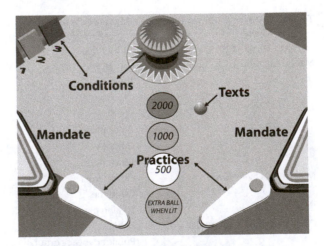

Figure 2.2 The Process of Cultural Creation as a Pinball Game

For example, the range of News Corp. holdings illustrates that the company has found ways to be profitable with a lot of different kinds of content. Fox Broadcasting has tended to be an irreverent and younger skewing media outlet for the company, so since the show is being developed for this arm of the News Corp. conglomerate, we might imagine the company would design a news show for that audience—one quite different from its other news audiences. Because Fox is a broadcaster, the news show would have to fulfill broadcasting regulatory norms—which are different than cable—another flip across the pinball board; and Fox is mostly advertiser-supported, so needing content that would appeal to advertisers—rather than drawing subscribers in—likewise sends the ball in a certain direction.

Maybe Fox designs the show so that people don't have to watch it at a certain time but can view it on any screen technology. This aim for technological flexibility would affect the show and make it different from a show meant for television-only consumption. Then what if Fox hired Anderson Cooper away from CNN and gave him the authority to make the kind of news show he'd always wanted for young people? The personal imprint of Cooper would make the show different than if Fox hired Jon Stewart or, for a very different show yet, Chelsea Clinton. The point here is that the primary creative decision-maker can affect media content in a manner like the deflection of a ball in the game—even if all the other aspects of the framework remain the same.

Even though the framework is the same every time, each ball—or each idea for a song, news story, film, TV show, or game—travels a unique path through the playfield, making the impact of the mandate, conditions, and practices on each bit of content and on industry operation uncertain. Any thorough analysis of how a particular media product comes into being must account for the ways in which all of the conditions and practices represented in the framework influence one another and the final product, and these insights are not inevitably transferrable to other media goods, industries, locations, or historical periods.

The discussion of media systems' mandates, conditions, and practices offered here is meant as a quick introduction to these concepts. The next chapters focus on each level and their components in much greater depth to better explain what they are and why they are important to understanding the operation of media industries. First, however, we need to introduce some basic concepts of media industry economics that cut across the media industries and the levels of our framework.

Photo 2.1A, 2.1B, 2.1C Hypothetical talk show hosts

KEY ECONOMIC ASPECTS OF THE MEDIA INDUSTRIES

As we noted in the previous chapter, conventions of genre, camerawork, editing, scale progression, band composition, and so on are commonly observed in popular media industries, just as journalism, likewise, has equally numerous and rigid conventions. To some extent, these conventions ensure quality, but more than that, they help diminish the economic risk that commercial media organizations face. Along with a host of other adaptive strategies, "conventions" help to make commercial media production more predictable—or, at least, they help media executives to feel that the business is more certain. Small and independent media organizations—and those with noncommercial mandates—engage in these adaptive strategies selectively. However, because many of the strategies develop from fundamental attributes of the media commodities themselves, these strategies can help smaller businesses and nonprofits reduce costs and stretch resources. In this section, we trace both distinctive attributes of media commodities and some of the adaptive strategies that the industry has developed to help combat their challenges.

Fundamentals of Media Commodities

Economist Richard E. Caves identifies some of the particularly challenging aspects of media industry operation that make them financially riskier than many other industries.[2] First, he recognizes an issue he calls "**nobody knows**," which describes how much more difficult it is to predict what media industry products will succeed than it is in most other industries. Countless times, media producers have developed films, albums, games, and so on with every characteristic of a previously successful one, only to see the new one fail. Just as often, an idea that has never before succeeded unexpectedly draws record crowds. Although every industry faces financial risks, the unpredictability of cultural commodities' success prevents many of the tactics that reduce risk and uncertainty in other industries from being effective.

One of the unique aspects of the commercial media industries is the high level of **sunk costs**. If you are making a movie, for instance, you need to spend the entire budget of millions of dollars before you have any sense of whether it's any good. Consequently, media industries typically have what are called high **first-copy costs** and relatively low **marginal** or **reproduction costs**. In other words, nearly all of the money that goes into media production must be spent to shoot the film, record the album, or make the show (first-copy costs). After that, the cost of distribution—or getting the content to millions of homes, theaters, or retail outlets—is comparatively low (reproduction costs).

Due to high sunk costs and low reproduction costs, economists consider most media as **public** or **semipublic goods**. Despite what the name suggests, public goods are not things that are good for the public but rather commodities that are not destroyed or used up in the process of consuming them. An expensive dinner is an example of a **private good**, because once you've eaten it, no one else can enjoy it. By contrast, when you watch a television show or see a film, it typically doesn't prevent someone else from also doing so.

To understand the peculiarity of media industries on this point, compare them with the automotive industry. Carmakers also have extensive first-copy costs, as millions of research and development dollars are required to design a new car model. Although those expenses can be amortized over the millions of cars built in that model, each car still has substantial marginal costs—the steel, glass, materials, and labor necessary to build each car. The result is a private good: when you buy or lease a car, no one else can benefit from the labor and goods required to manufacture it. In contrast, the cost of burning a CD or DVD or distributing a television show by broadcast or digitally online is comparatively insignificant compared to the cost of making the original version. Moreover, that content may be consumed by millions of fans, all of whom can enjoy the music, program, or film without preventing anyone else from doing so as well.

The high sunk costs associated with media production create their own challenges for media companies because larger production budgets do not always lead to greater revenues. Producers can always spend more money on a product—perhaps in more costly special effects or in paying for a bigger star—but those expenditures are less guaranteed to pay off than in many other industries.[3] For example, in crafting a chair, a furniture maker might face a choice between using pine, a light and fairly inexpensive wood, or oak, a dense and more expensive wood. The furniture maker knows the decision to use oak will make it a stronger chair and that consumers will recognize that strength and be willing to pay more for it. Media consumers, by contrast, typically pay the same amount for media products (a ticket to a first-run film costs the same regardless of its production cost). Instead, media producers must try to calculate how many more people might see a film if more expensive special effects are used or whether it is shot on a sound stage or on location, and whether those additional people will provide enough additional revenue to balance the cost.

An issue related to the questionable benefits of additional costs is the **A-list/B-list issue**.[4] Selecting talent for media goods defies norms that govern the economic decisions of many other industries. A relatively unknown actress may offer just as good of a performance as an established star with a salary 10 times higher, but sometimes featuring the star is what makes people see the film—though it is impossible to know whether the film will gross the difference in salary as a result. Unlike the example of furniture construction, in which oak will always be sturdier than pine, the popularity of actors and directors can wane without cause, or an actor who had previously offered top performances may turn in below-par work or experience some sort of celebrity scandal just before the film is released. It is very difficult to assign value to the status of creative staff in the media industry in a manner similar to tallying the production costs of many other industries.

Sometimes the products of the media industries also require a long period before they begin returning profits. In the case of television production, for instance, it has been commonplace for studios to lose money on network shows for the first three to five years, and some movies do not begin to turn a profit until they are released on DVD or for in-home streaming. On the other side of the equation, companies may continue earning profits on a media good for decades after production is completed, a phenomenon known as the **ars longa,** or the long economic life of media industry products.[5]

For instance, Apple Records, a label founded by the Beatles in 1968, continues to receive revenues when a consumer buys one of its Beatles CDs today, and CBS Corporation, which holds the license to the 1950s television show *I Love Lucy*, reports that it continues to earn more than a million dollars a year from continued licensing of the show around the world.

Finally, the creative products that the media industries produce lead to what might be considered irrational behavior in other industries. Many of the creative workers who supply the lifeblood of the media industries pursue their crafts with an **"art for art's sake"** attitude. Indeed, there are many who work in these industries whose primary incentive is to make the types of shows, music, games, or movies that are likely to make the most money, but there are also many who would willingly give up some of the profits in order to have more control over the production, to make the story they really want to tell, or to work on a schedule that better matches their creative process. As a result, those involved in the media industries often do not behave in the same profit-centered manner as workers in most other commercial industries.

Media Industry Responses to Risk

In response to the particular economic conditions that distinguish the media industries from other commercial endeavors, practitioners have developed a number of strategies to balance or compensate for the challenges. Here we first list a series of strategies with brief detail and then examine two others more extensively that are particularly important for understanding contemporary industry norms.

Media industries engage in **intentional overproduction** in an effort to offset inevitable miscalculations against a broad repertoire; this is a strategy that attempts to compensate for the unpredictability of success—defined earlier as "nobody knows." For example, David Hesmondhalgh notes that "nearly thirty thousand music albums are released in the U.S. each year, of which fewer than two percent sell more than fifty thousand copies."[6] Record industry executives are well aware that most albums—98 percent by Hesmondhalgh's figures—won't achieve wide sales, and, in response, they are faced with choosing among a few strategies to try to achieve profitability.

An alternative strategy to intentional overproduction would be to produce fewer albums and put far more resources into them. Instead, most media industries spread budgets widely knowing most of their offerings will fail because they lack reliable tools for predicting hits and failures. The film industry, for example, draws a bit from both strategies—it allocates its production budget variably, putting far greater resources behind some films—those that a studio believes likely to be **blockbusters** if successful—instead of allocating production dollars equally across all films. Even still, at least a few films with blockbuster budgets fail to find audiences and end up losing studios millions of dollars.

Some hope that the increasing information about audiences' media use and behavior provided by digital technologies and services will offer new tools to "know better." For example, the video streaming service Netflix has argued that its vast databases of what subscribers watch, how long they stay tuned, and how quickly they consume episodes enabled them to "predict" the success of the highly serialized original production

House of Cards and allayed concerns about the risk of producing new episodes of *Arrested Development*. Though media industries—like other industries—are now able to gather much more data about consumers, the use of such big data doesn't really solve the "nobody knows" principle with regard to new products.

Another practice, which has begun to erode in some sectors of the industries, is the creation of **artificial scarcity**. For decades, film viewers have accepted that they must go to a theater if they want to see the newest films, that they'll have to wait six months to a year to rent or buy a copy of the film, and that they must wait even longer to have the opportunity to view it on television. Long before the advent of the VCR, residents of small and rural towns accepted that films would "open" in big cities and that they'd have to wait weeks or months for the films to reach local theaters. There is nothing natural about such practices; rather, they indicate a strategy by which the industry attempts to create scarcity in order to stretch the life of creative goods and allow **price differentiation**, a practice that describes why it costs about $15 to see a movie right now in the theater but only a few dollars if you wait a few months for it to be available on iTunes, a video on demand service, or as part of a subscription fee paid to a service such as Netflix. These efforts to create price differentiation through artificial scarcity are part of the process of distribution windowing, which we explore in more detail in Chapter 8.

Another strategy widely used in media industries is that of **bundling**. Selling songs packaged together as an album or news stories together as an issue of a newspaper are examples of bundles. Many subscriptions provide access to a bundle of goods—all the content licensed to Netflix, for example, or all of the issues of a magazine for a year. One of the most pervasive bundles is found in television—90 percent of people with television pay a cable or satellite provider for a bundle of channels, and each of those channels is basically a bundle of programs. Bundling may be valuable to both industry and consumers in some instances, particularly where bundles provide a more efficient form of distribution. When cable first launched, providing a bundle of channels was valuable because people were attracted to the service for different reasons—some for sports programming from ESPN, others for CNN's news, others yet for MTV's pop culture videos. Digital distribution has changed the norms and made it possible to efficiently distribute content without bundling it. Digital distribution enabled the transaction of single songs in the recording industry, and the television industry now faces similar concerns as viewers have grown frustrated by pricey bundles in an era in which alternative ways to distribute content exist.

Ownership and Conglomeration Strategies

The media industries have also adapted to some of the complicated features of their enterprise by making use of a variety of strategies related to ownership. This section first explains some of the ownership strategies most evident in the media industries and then details the adoption of these strategies in the past 30 to 40 years, the time period we identified in the last chapter as the "Long Downturn" and transition to mass customization. Although the strategies we review here are also common outside the media industries, the particular risks and opportunities associated with the media industries make these ownership strategies particularly attractive. In addition, given the longstanding connections between media and the functioning of democracy, concerns about negative implications for democracy arising from consolidation of ownership in the media industries is particularly worrisome for many observers and activists.

Conglomeration and consolidation of ownership defer the risk created by the uncertainty of media goods' success by placing media production within massive, often diversified corporations. **Conglomeration** refers to the integration of previously distinct sectors of media industries under a single corporate umbrella. The Walt Disney Company, for example, was once merely a film studio, but it has since expanded into broadcast and cable television, magazine publishing, radio and recorded music, and even book publishing, as well as a number of sectors not traditionally identified as media—such as theme parks and toy merchandising—though clearly these enterprises also relate to the media industries' function of creating intellectual property. Before the 1980s, each media industry was quite distinct and generally dominated by a small **oligopoly** of large corporations. These companies tended to experience both hits and flops with a certain level of consistency—and managed risk by hoping the hits offset the flops. Conglomerating further helped manage risk by adding other types of products into the corporation.

Media conglomerates are able to diversify their profit centers and spread risk by developing multifaceted corporate networks that include holdings in production and distribution and span a broad range of media and entertainment services such as film, television, magazines, books, sports teams, and entertainment parks. In this way, conglomerates can both subsidize less successful business segments with more successful ones and reduce overall risk by combining media ventures with less risky, nonmedia ventures. Media law scholar Tim Wu notes that the ability of one significant failure—as in the case of United Artists' legendary failure *Heaven's Gate*—to destroy a studio motivated media companies to grow to a scale and diversity so that a single failure would not produce such dire consequences.[7] Disney's *The Lone Ranger* (2013) provides a recent example of this. Despite losing $190 million on the film, Disney profits were the same for 2013 as they'd been the previous year, illustrating how broad conglomeration can allow a company to absorb a massive failure.

Concentration, or consolidation of ownership, is another industry strategy that is often noted in concert with conglomeration. According to David Hesmondhalgh, concentration of ownership "refers to the extent to which a market or industry is dominated by the largest businesses."[8] Since the Long Downturn, media businesses in the United States have become both much more *consolidated* (meaning fewer competitors), as well as *conglomerated* (because the same few owners that have consolidated the industry are also highly conglomerated entities with a wide range of media and other holdings). Although the terms "conglomeration" and "consolidation" are often conflated, much of the concern about shifts in ownership patterns in recent years centers more on consolidation than conglomeration. Consolidation more precisely describes the concentration of many media industry operations into the hands of just a few companies.

We often think of consolidation as a recent development brought about in the wake of the Long Downturn and the deregulatory policies that allowed consolidated ownership beginning in the 1980s (see Chapter 4), and that is the case for media industries such as radio and television, but similar sizable shifts in ownership occurred in the newspaper industry at the beginning of the twentieth century. Between 1910 and 1930, the number of cities with competing local papers fell from 689 to 288; by 1960, only 4.2 percent of cities with a daily newspaper had a competitive local market. Consolidation of the newspaper industry was already apparent by 1933, when the six most powerful chains controlled about one-quarter of the daily circulation in the United States.[9]

Some recent policy research has identified that cross-ownership in which a company owns various media should be less of a regulatory concern in the digital era but that concentrated ownership is more problematic. Policy scholar Des Freedman makes a case that the resources of large-scale organizations are needed for comprehensive public service, and this may well be the case for contemporary media with commercial aims as well.[10]

Conglomeration can refer to two different organizational strategies: **vertical integration** and **horizontal integration**. Vertical integration describes the attempt to control every stage of a media good's development, from production through distribution and sales. For example, the music industry has become highly vertically integrated since the 1990s, as major music distributors have bought up record labels that record and produce music, manufacturing companies that press CDs, and retail and online outlets from which people buy music. Indeed, a key challenge of digital distribution and the dominance of iTunes in this area is that the labels must give up some of the revenue from sales they previously controlled. Of the $0.99 or $1.29 you pay for a song on iTunes, about 40 percent stays with Apple. If the labels were more vertically integrated so that consumers would come to a site with Sony recording artists who are owned and managed by Sony music, that share of revenue would stay with the conglomerate—illustrating the value of vertical integration.

Horizontal integration describes the conglomeration of various companies at the same level of the value chain—or companies that do the same thing. An industry that is a **monopoly** illustrates the most extreme example of horizontal integration. For instance, a company integrating horizontally might seek to purchase multiple production studios. Horizontal integration reduces or eliminates competition, which allows the entity to charge higher fees or control terms. The distribution of cable and broadband services features extensive horizontal integration. Most US residents can choose only one local cable service provider (companies such as Comcast, Cox, and Charter). If you are unhappy with its service or rates, there is little you can do other than switch to a satellite provider—an imperfect competitor as of 2015 because satellites were still technologically unable to provide Internet service. Rural homes often don't have even that choice, as cable is often unavailable, which has also made high-speed broadband difficult for rural homes to access.[11]

A key business logic behind conglomeration and consolidation is a desire to take advantage of **economies of scale**. Economies of scale operate in many industries, but they are particularly important to media industries because of the high first-copy costs and the "public good" nature of their products. Economies of scale are achieved when the average cost of a commodity decreases with expansion of output. In media industries, economies of scale explain why we have a network television system. In the early days of radio, television's predecessor, local entities and communities developed their own stations and filled the hours with programs. The local reach limited potential sponsors to those in the local community, and developing a full day of programming for every station was costly. The reach of the broadcast signal was limited by geography, which meant hundreds of stations around the country arguably duplicated each other's efforts. The network system—in which one centralized entity creates programming that is distributed to stations throughout the country—allowed broadcasters to take advantage of economies of scale. With the ability to deliver hundreds of thousands of listeners to advertisers—instead of hundreds or thousands—networks could sell advertising to national corporations and aggregate the money spread across the programming budgets of 200-some stations nationwide into one high-end production.

Many of the entities that distribute media over the Internet today similarly rely on economies of scale. The ease and low cost of digital distribution makes it possible to reach national and even international audiences. With such reach, narrow audience tastes can be effectively turned into commercially successful markets. For example, a low-budget Web series can become profitable and draw sponsors even if reaching a small and narrow audience—as was the case of *The Guild* (2007–2013). Many of the success stories, though, begin as unfunded experiments.

Here's another example that might bring home the concept of economies of scale. Universities often use this principle in lecture classes. Instead of capping classes at 30 students, lectures often enroll 100 or more students. The lecturer might deliver the exact same presentation, whether speaking to 30 students or 130, but the university is able to meet the credit needs of—and collect tuition dollars from—100 more students. As is true for media industries, we see the advantage that can be gained by economies of scale from the university's perspective, but it is important to note that there is also a downside in both of these cases. In amassing large audiences, media often have to sacrifice some of the specificity that makes content so attractive to particular audiences, just as lecturers and students lose the intimacy of one-on-one conversations when enrollments multiply.

In addition to economies of scale, media industries consolidate in order to take advantage of **economies of scope** as well. Economies of scope refer to the decreased costs of production that come from producing a wide range of products; the efficiencies can include sharing research and development costs across multiple products and taking advantage of integrated or related marketing campaigns. The basic organization of film studios and recording labels illustrate the value of economies of scope—these organizations can more efficiently create multiple films than if each film were independently produced. Conglomerates can leverage the popularity of particular characters, stories, and setting across multiple different media. For instance, Time Warner holds the rights to the *Lord of the Rings* franchise, including the blockbuster films. Prior to the release of *The Hobbit: The Battle of the Five Armies* in December 2014, Warner Bros. Interactive Entertainment, a subsidiary of Time Warner, released the videogame *Middle-Earth: Shadow of Mordor*, which takes advantage of the popularity of the film, its setting, and its characters in order to popularize the game. Importantly, the game also helps cross-promote the movie.

Going back to our earlier discussion about how the media possess the possibility of operating as a democratic public sphere, you can probably see why so many people might have concerns about changes in media ownership structure. Monopoly power not only raises the specter of media organizations failing to fulfill their public sphere function, but, perhaps more insidiously, it can mean that they maintain the *illusion* of providing a democratic public sphere while bombarding the public with one-sided or inaccurate ideas and information. Due to these concerns, various media-reform movements have agitated—and sometimes succeeded—in both local and national politics to try to halt or reverse policies that favor media consolidation.

So have the media industries generally become more conglomerated and consolidated, and, if so, why? Ben Bagdikian begins his revised edition of *The New Media Monopoly* with some stunning descriptions of the level of conglomeration and consolidation of the media industries evident by the early 2000s. For instance, he notes that by 2003 five men controlled the range of media that had been run by 50 men just 20 years earlier.[12] In their expansive and detailed third edition of *Who Owns the Media*, published in 2000, Benjamin M. Compaine and Douglas Gomery note that the top five firms in the recorded music industry account for 80 percent of the market and that in theatrical film, six studios account for 90 percent of the box office receipts.[13] By 2005, two of the five music firms had merged, resulting in the "big four" controlling all but 18 percent of the global music market. Similarly, Hollywood studios continued to control 90 percent of the market in 2012.[14] In recent years, many have expressed concern about the oligopolies and even monopolies that control access to media production. Our distribution services are just as concentrated as content producers. Verizon and AT&T dominate mobile phone service in the United States, while many homes have access to only one high speed broadband service provider.

Radio ownership consolidated considerably after the passage of the **Telecommunications Act of 1996**, which eliminated limits on how many stations could be owned nationwide. The anticonglomeration activist group Free Press reports that before 1996, no company owned more than 65 radio stations nationwide, but after the act's passage, Clear Channel corporation expanded to own nearly 1,200.[15] In television, Free Press reports that "between 1995 and 2003, ten of the largest TV-station owners went from owning 104 stations with $5.9 billion in revenue to owning 299 stations with $11.8 billion in revenue."[16] And the situation is little different in print. According to Free Press, "Since 1975, two-thirds of independent newspaper owners have disappeared. Today less than 275 of the nation's 1,500 daily newspapers remain independently owned, and more than half of all U.S. markets are dominated by one paper."[17] Even in newer media industries such as gaming, the gaming console industry operates as an oligopoly among three main companies (Sony, Microsoft, and Nintendo). The publication of games is also highly consolidated among a few companies, with the added hurdle that game designers need to license their games with the various console companies.[18]

As you can see, a fair amount of evidence exists that media industries have become more conglomerated and consolidated in recent years. What remains much less certain, however, is what this means for the operation of media industries and our understanding of them. There are generally two schools of thought on this issue. One position might be loosely described as "conglomeration equals homogenization." Scholars and media critics including Robert McChesney and Ben Bagdikian have extensively chronicled conglomeration and consolidation as we note here and often tie in examples indicating the dangers inherent in these ownership configurations. Importantly, it is not simply a matter of what these conglomerates own directly; rather, conglomeration is also relevant when you consider the complex, interconnected webs that consolidate power, such as connections among corporate boards of directors and conglomerate owners of media (particularly those with holdings outside of media), and how the commercial mandate of news entities can require them to placate advertisers and sponsors in ways that can significantly compromise the provision of news.

The other school of thought on the consequences of conglomeration and consolidation on the operation of media industries is not directly opposed to thinkers such as McChesney and Bagdikian; rather, this camp would suggest (and your authors fall into this category) that we do not yet know enough, do not have enough case studies beyond news production, and do not have a way to explain the prosocial outcomes that conglomerated media industries sometimes produce to make decisive statements about the internal operations of these conglomerates. Many in the conglomeration-equals-homogenization camp tend to rely on frameworks of media industry operation that place much more emphasis on ownership as the deciding factor of what industries do than does the Industrialization of Culture framework. In their thinking, the routines of companies and agency of individuals that we allow for in our exploration of "practices" are unimportant because they believe that workers consistently serve the needs and will of the conglomerate. These insights are based largely on a range of anecdotes because little in-depth or exhaustive research on the internal operation of media conglomerates really exists. It can also be argued that conglomerates are too vast to operate in the single-minded and concerted manner proposed.

Although it makes sense that conglomerates would operate with extensive self-interest, their scale is often simply too great for such coordination to occur. Conglomerates are organized into units and divisions, and the individuals who work in them are much more concerned about the needs of their unit or division than beholden to the broader conglomerate as a result of how reward and evaluation are structured. For example, performance is typically measured at the level of a single division (e.g., whether the home video division made its sales goals, etc.), which means that workers tend to place the performance of their division above that of the conglomerate. This has tended to prevent the conglomerations from achieving **synergies** that conglomeration is intended to create.

A Time Warner employer relayed a story that illustrates the unpredictability of synergy and how corporate structures can discourage it. When the broadband service arm of Time Warner sought to use the Road Runner character from the Warner Bros. Looney Tunes franchise as its name, the Warner licensing division initially allowed it only with an exceptionally high licensing fee. Eventually this was worked out, and Road Runner became the trademarked name of the Time Warner broadband service, but abstract ideas such as synergy don't always recognize the divisional self-interest that would lead one division to try to exact a high license fee from another arm of the same conglomerate.

Synergy was a big buzzword of the mid-1990s through early 2000s that described the efficiencies and advantages that were imagined possible through conglomeration; basically, it is the idea that the combination of two entities can be greater than the simple sum of their parts. In a few cases, synergies could be found in successful cross-promotional efforts. **Cross-promotion** describes a conglomerate's ability to market content developed for one sector of the media conglomerate throughout the other media sectors in its organization, as described in the previous example of the *Lord of the Rings* films and video games. This kind of conglomerate cross-promotion, in which each new version of conglomerate-owned intellectual property not only makes money in each different media form but also drives sales of all other versions of the property, is an illustration of synergy.

In other media industries and instances, anticompetitive behaviors certainly do arise. The major Hollywood movie studios, for instance, own theaters around the world and often give their own and other Hollywood films privileged access to their screens, and we could list many other practices that arguably abuse the power that comes from conglomerated and consolidated ownership. The point, then, is that the ownership consolidation we've seen in the media industries over the past couple of decades has certainly enabled different arms of the conglomerate to operate in anticompetitive ways. The analysis of whether, how, and how frequently these things happen, however, requires a more nuanced assessment of particular industries, organizations, and instances.

In recent years, the key trend in media ownership has not involved continued acquisition or growth among conglomerates so much as it has involved a tension between publicly and privately held media companies. **Publicly held** companies are those that anyone can buy stock in and consequently have a responsibility to stockholders to protect their investment. They are also subject to a variety of government regulations that require disclosure of financial details and adherence to particular accounting rules. **Privately held** media companies are typically managed by a family and are not subject to the same disclosure rules. Analysts of the business performance of media companies have noted a number of cases of private media companies thriving in the uncertain times of the past decade and suggested that the daily assessment of public company performance via fluctuations in stock prices has prevented publicly held companies from developing strategies likely to allow for innovation over the long term. A trend of companies buying back publicly held stock or seeking to take publicly traded companies private emerged in the media industries in the early 2000s but did not become especially widespread. Media scholars have not yet thoroughly investigated this trend, but it does appear to be a development of some consequence that might mark the next stage in the evolution of dominant trends in media ownership. Media industries were first most commonly local family businesses before developing into broad, publicly traded global media conglomerates. Assessing who owns a media company and whether it fits the dominant ownership trend of its industry at the time are important considerations in applying the Industrialization of Culture framework.

Given the range of thinking among media scholars on the subject of media owner-ship and consolidation, you may be wondering what to make of this situation or what knowledge you can take away. It is clear that who owns what can be very important to the operation of media industries. What remains contested is how important ownership is. For some scholars and approaches to the study of media industries, ownership is a crucial and primary indicator of how an entity will operate. It is the position of the au-thors and the Industrialization of Culture framework that ownership is meaningful, but it is only one of many factors that figure into how media industries operate and what they are likely to create. Returning to our pinball metaphor, ownership may be one bumper that sends the ball forcefully in one direction, but, despite the potential of that forceful push, the ball could deflect in a number of directions when it hits the next ob-stacle, or it may be the case that the ball only glances the bumper, and the ownership bumper has little effect on the media good.

Formatting

Another strategy used by media industry workers to combat the uncertainty of audience behavior is composed of a variety of techniques that emphasize features of media con-tent known to succeed in the past that might generally be called **formatting**. Perhaps the best explanation for why commercial media tend to produce content far more simi-lar than different results from the perception that known and familiar media tend to be more popular, or at least easier to promote, than media that are more atypical.

Think of formats as the media industries' effort to follow a formula to achieve suc-cess, and the main formulas are derived from past successes. Although we may think of a formula as a precise calculation, such as what you would encounter in a chemistry class, here we use "formula" much more loosely. We consider formatting to include the reliance on known attributes in design and production of media content. Formatting might include using *known stars or creative workers*; *known products*, such as sequels or serials; *known formats* such as genres; and *standard features*. Before considering these examples of formatting in greater depth, it is crucial to acknowledge that formatting is often a good business strategy, given that media industries can be characterized by the dictum that "nobody knows." Formatting remains far from foolproof, however. As we will see, formatting might increase the odds of a media product succeeding—or at least of not failing—but there are also countless cases of media products that precisely follow known formatting that fail nevertheless.

One of the most obvious examples of formatting involves the practice of using **known talent**, or those actors, directors, writers, and producers who have succeeded in the past or with whom audiences are familiar and regard positively. In many ways, the entire "star system" that characterizes the most successful workers in media industries results from the industry's belief that those who have succeeded in the past are likely to succeed again. With some creative goods, industry workers hope that audiences are so committed to the previous record of an individual that they will purchase, view, read, or listen to a new product simply because that person is involved. Actors identified in Hollywood as members of the "A-list" may not be the most skilled (although in some cases they are), but they earn this distinction because they have established a fan base that consistently turns out for new movies, no matter the subject or reviews. Sometimes the star power of one individual alone can lead a movie to be profitable, although star performer power can be less reliable in other types of media. For example, there have been many cases of A-list stars failing; sometimes star performer power isn't enough to overcome other features of a poorly conceived story, weak promotion, or bad buzz.

Although star performers quickly come to mind as a form of known talent, all sorts of creatives might be used in this way. We often hear of a new film by J. J. Abrams, a new novel by J. K Rowling, a new series by Shonda Rhimes, or a new album produced by Pharrell Williams. Any time you see media promoted by emphasizing the individuals involved in its creation, it can be seen as a case of formatting. Being J. J. Abrams or Pharrell Williams might also be crucial to securing the funding of a studio, network, or investors in order to create a media product, but it isn't a ticket to success. Most of those who have achieved high-profile successes have also experienced widely noted failures. A few failures often won't significantly diminish a reputation, however, partly because those who have succeeded in the past are given so many subsequent opportunities that there are bound to be failures.

Another, also very simple use of formatting relies on **known products**. In film, we often see this in the form of sequels. Many noted the summer of 2012 as a particularly safe film season, as the schedule included sequels *The Dark Knight Rises, Madagascar 3, Men in Black 3,* and films with intellectual property known from other products, such as *The Avengers* (known from television show) and *The Amazing Spiderman* (film reboot, comics). The sequels offered the third installment of stories about established characters and settings, and, unsurprisingly, all had strong releases. Film sequels are a common and accepted practice that allows a measure of certainty. Another example of using known products involves taking a successful media product and reproducing it in another industry—for example, making the Harry Potter and *50 Shades of Gray* books into films. In television, **format sales**—or the sale of the features of a show successful in one country to be reproduced in another country—has become a common way to better predict success. The live singing competition of *American Idol* was uncommon in the United States during the earliest days of reality television when it arrived in 2001, and most thought it had little chance of success. Fox relied on its prior massive success in several other countries as an indicator that it would likely perform well in the United States as well—so the success of a format in a different country can also be a way to minimize risk.

Television has many other ways of incorporating formatting. The television spin-off involves taking an established character from one show and creating a new show around him or her. In the magazine industry, formatting can be seen as a way to expand the brand of an existing title, such as launching *Teen Vogue* based on market familiarity with *Vogue.* This strategy is also common among video games, where many successful games have sequels produced.

Another example of formatting is that of using **known formats**. Using known formats involves reproducing much more general, existing media products. For example, the launch of Oprah's magazine *O* reproduced the well-established women's service magazine format (as well as featuring the known talent); Fox News reproduced the established cable news channel format but gave it a conservative slant. "Format" is a term most commonly used in the radio industry to describe the type of music a radio station plays, such as adult-contemporary, Top 40, or country. Identifying the format of a media product is probably the first thing you do to describe what it is, and concepts that seem new often come from combining various existing formats (a cop show that is a musical) or creating a product for a different audience (a fashion magazine for men).

In other media, we apply this concept of known formats when we use the term **genre**. Most generally, media genres describe content that is similar in general ways—such as the film genres of romantic comedy, action, or horror. The ability to gather and manipulate data about viewer preferences has led to far more refined understandings of genre. Netflix uses its information about who is watching in combination with what people watch, how quickly, and so on to support its recommendation engine. An *Atlantic* reporter studying Netflix's genres in 2014 determined that the service had 76,897 different genre categories that it used to recommend films and television as specific as "Emotional Independent Sport Movies," "Spy Action and Adventure from the 1930s," and "Dark Suspenseful Sci-Fi Horror Movies."[19] Media industries rely on familiar formats and genres because audiences prefer recognizable products and recognizable products also tend to be easier to promote.

Another formatting strategy can be identified in the **standard features** that develop in media industries. There is nothing that says a feature film must be between 90 and 180 minutes, that television shows are either 30 or 60 minutes (minus time for commercials), that stories perceived as most important will be at the top of a newspaper or news site, or that pop songs should be three to five minutes long. Similarly, film and television stories do not need to be presented in the conventional three-act narrative structure and don't have to end with resolution, although most do. These are examples of the standard features of media content that have been normalized in US society, mostly during an era in which media circulated in a physical form that required these norms. Notably most media now created outside the industry and distributed digitally—thus free from the distribution constraints that created many of these norms—reproduce these established norms. It is important to reflect on how norms accepted by a culture shape the types of stories told or increase the chances of some being told more often than others.

In some ways, what US television viewers accept as a taken-for-granted norm—that television series return new episodes about established characters and situations—is also a formatting strategy. Many of television's early series were called "anthology series" and featured an entirely new story each week, much like going to see a different play. This was especially true in the United Kingdom, where the British Broadcasting Company still features a large number of single-episode television plays, many of them penned by famous writers. The use of serial features—such as the same cast, setting, and story norms, even if the actual story resolves each week—is also an example of formatting.

Relying on formatting offers media industry workers helpful, yet unreliable, tools for dealing with the considerable uncertainty of their industries, but formulas have other consequences as well. Foremost, the reliance on formatting goes a long way toward explaining the significant similarity of media products. Perhaps the biggest criticism by those who argue for structural changes to the way media industries operate is their complaint that commercial media products are "all the same." We, however, are hesitant to make such sweeping condemnations and wish to acknowledge that even subtle differences can be meaningful. The formulaic conventions of media industries—and our acculturation to these conventions—do make change and difference difficult for those foremost concerned with commercial success. Ideas that seem too far "outside of the box," whether because of an unconventional length, an irregular central character, or even just an actor who doesn't match dominant beauty standards, simply don't receive the funding needed to come into existence. Creators have also exhibited considerable creativity and ingenuity working within the constraints of these common format expectations as well. Many excellent films, albums, television series, and so on accomplish artistic and commercial success working within these formats or by deviating from them slightly and in a manner that makes the audience rethink what they thought they knew about the format. For example, once every few decades a film makes people rethink everything they knew about the horror genre, and this happens with the Western as well. Those rules that seem most ironclad can generate some of the most fascinating responses.

CONCLUSION

This chapter has introduced the basic concepts, vocabulary, and frameworks that you will need to assess and understand contemporary media industries. The Industrialization of Culture framework, in particular, offers you a tool for analyzing a wide array of media productions, organizations, technologies, strategies, and policies, as well as much more. In addition, you have learned the fundamentals of media commodities themselves and how they pose particular challenges and opportunities for companies seeking to profit from them. These fundamentals hold true regardless of the size of the media organization or its mandate as a commercial or nonprofit entity. However, the specific ways in which organizations attempt to deal with these fundamentals can differ substantially based on the size of the organization or its mandate.

Finally, we addressed a number of strategies that larger media organizations employ as a way to deal with the central challenges and opportunities related to creating media commodities. These strategies tend to cut across different sectors of the media industries and are prevalent in large commercial print media, television broadcasting, film studios, and game publishers. Furthermore, these strategies of risk minimization explain a good deal of the media environment we live in today, including the large number of reruns available on television, the duplication of news stories across multiple newspapers and websites, and the release patterns of blockbuster films.

Before moving on to the remaining chapters of the book, you may want to pause here and spend some time going back over the vocabulary in this chapter. These are fundamental words and phrases—many of which are used in the industries—that will reappear throughout the book. Having a basic knowledge of these terms is crucial for understanding media industries.

QUESTIONS

1. Using the Industrialization of Culture framework, discuss some of the issues in a specific media industry where you might like to be a creative worker. Consider, for instance, if certain conditions might affect whether you can actually create media you have in mind. What practices might challenge your creative control of your project? How will your mandate influence how you approach its production?

2. Think about one of your favorite media goods in relation to the Industrialization of Culture framework. Can you identify the mandate under which it was created? How might various conditions and practices have affected its content? Identify a few of the specific features, such as a sitcom character's development or the cover of a magazine, and imagine how its path through the framework's metaphorical pinball machine might have led it to turn out the way it has.

3. Why do you think we emphasize culture as the background that structures media industry operations rather than emphasize it exclusively as the music, books, and other goods that are created by media industries? How does this definition change how you think about the term "culture" or how you think about the ways that media industries operate?

4. Pretend you are the head of a music corporation that wants to expand through vertical integration. How would you go about doing this? Which aspects of the music industry would you want to control? Similarly, what plans would you pursue if you wanted to horizontally integrate? What are the benefits of each approach to conglomeration?

5. Given the additional revenue possible by pushing consumers to buy songs from a record label's own site, why do you think labels continue to allow iTunes to sell their music instead of developing their own sites?

6. Think of a media good—a song, movie, or other media good—that you recently purchased or paid to experience. What were some of the economic risks involved in making that good? Now identify ways in which the media industry attempted to minimize those risks. Do certain risks seem like they might be harder to minimize than others?

FURTHER READING

We but glance the surface of the theoretical foundations of media industry studies. More detailed and comprehensive assessments can be found in David Hesmondhalgh's *The Cultural Industries*, 2nd ed. (Thousand Oaks, Calif.: SAGE, 2007). Despite its age, Joseph Turow's *Media Systems in Society: Understanding Industries, Strategies, and Power*, 2nd ed. (New York: Longman, 1997) remains an accessible text for dealing with many of the issues covered here and also attends in greater depth to the book publishing industry. Another framework or model for connecting the operation of media industries and the content they create is the "circuit of culture" that can be found in Paul du Gay and colleagues, *Doing Cultural Studies: The Story of the Sony Walkman* (London: SAGE, 1997). Julie D'Acci updates this framework in "Cultural Studies, Television

Studies, and the Crisis in the Humanities," (pp. 418–446) in *Television after TV: Essays on a Medium in Transition*, edited by Lynn Spigel and Jan Olsson (Durham: Duke University Press, 2004).

The subfield of critical media industry study and production studies has grown considerably in recent years; also see John Thornton Caldwell's *Production Culture: Industrial Reflexivity and Critical Practice in Film and Television* (Durham: Duke University Press, 2008) and "Cultural Studies in Media Production: Critical Industry Practices" in *Questions of Method in Cultural Studies*, edited by Mimi White and James Schwoch (Malden, Mass.: Blackwell, 2006, pp. 109–153); *Media Industries: History, Theory, and Method*, edited by Jennifer Holt and Alisa Perren (Malden, Mass.: Wiley-Blackwell, 2009); and *Production Studies: Cultural Studies of Media Industries*, edited by Vicki Mayer, Miranda Banks, and John Caldwell (New York: Routledge, 2009) for a variety of perspectives. The authors develop their own perspective in more detail in Timothy Havens, Amanda D. Lotz, and Serra Tinic's "Critical Media Industry Studies: A Research Approach," *Communication, Culture and Critique* 2 (2009): 234–253.

We are unable to go into considerable detail or provide examples from all media industries in the pages here. Those seeking more detailed information about a particular industry might consult a number of books that offer chapters focused on the basic industrial features of various industries: *Media Economics: Theory and Practice*, 3rd ed., edited by Alison Alexander and colleagues (Mahwah, N.J.: Lawrence Erlbaum Associates, 2004); and *Who Owns the Media?: Competition and Concentration in the Mass Media Industry*, edited by Douglas Gomery and Benjamin M. Compaine (Mahwah, N.J.: Lawrence Erlbaum Associates, 2000). Also, general introductions to media often provide helpful overviews, such as Joseph Turow's *Media Today: Mass Communication in a Converging World*, 5th ed. (New York: Routledge, 2013).

Some books or scholarly articles about particular industries that we've found helpful detail include

1. Film: Edward Jay Epstein, *The Hollywood Economist 2.0: The Hidden Financial Reality Behind the Movies* (New York: Melville House, 2012) and *The Big Picture: Money and Power in Hollywood* (New York: Random House, 2006); Janet Wasko, *How Hollywood Works* (Thousand Oaks, Calif.: SAGE, 2003), Jason Squire, *The Movie Business Book*, 3rd ed. (New York: Fireside, 2004), Alisa Perren, *Indie Inc.: Miramax and the Transformation of Hollywood in the 1990s* (Austin: University of Texas Press, 2013), Jennifer Holt, *Empires of Entertainment: Media Industries and the Politics of Deregulation, 1980–1996* (New Brunswick, N.J.: Rutgers University Press, 2011).

2. Television: Amanda D. Lotz, *The Television Will Be Revolutionized*, 2nd ed. (New York: New York University Press, 2014); Todd Gitlin, *Inside Prime Time*, rev. ed. (Berkeley: University of California Press, 2000); Bill Carter, *Desperate Networks* (New York: Broadway, 2007).

3. Video Games: Aphra Kerr, *The Business and Culture of Digital Games: Gamework and Gameplay* (Thousand Oaks, Calif.: SAGE, 2006); Mia Consolvo, "Console Video Games and Global Corporations: Creating a Hybrid Culture," *New*

Media and Society, 8, no. 1 (2006), 117–137; Nick Dyer-Witheford and Greig de Peuter, "'EA Spouse' and the Crisis of Video Game Labour: Enjoyment, Exclusion, Exploitation, Exodus," *Canadian Journal of Communication* 31 (2006), 599–617.

4. Music: Steve Knopper, *Appetite for Self-Destruction: The Spectacular Crash of the Record Industry in the Digital Age* (New York: Free Press, 2009); Keith Negus, *Music Genres and Corporate Cultures* (New York: Routledge, 1999).

NOTES

1. Joseph Turow, *Media Systems in Society: Understanding Industries, Strategies, and Power*, 2nd ed. (White Plains, N.Y.: Longman, 1997), 26.
2. Richard E. Caves, *Creative Industries: Contracts between Art and Commerce* (Cambridge: Harvard University Press, 2008).
3. Ibid.
4. Ibid.
5. Ibid.
6. David Hesmondhalgh, "Ownership Is Only Part of the Media Picture.", November 29, 2001; http://www.opendemocracy.net/media-globalmediaownership/article_46.jsp (accessed August 31, 2010).
7. Tim Wu, *The Master Switch: The Rise and Fall of Information Empires* (New York: Vintage, 2011), 217–219.
8. David Hesmondhalgh, *The Cultural Industries*, 2nd ed. (London: SAGE, 2007), 309.
9. Joseph Turow, *Media Today* (New York: Routledge, 2008), 309, 312.
10. Des Freedman, *The Politics of Media Policy* (Cambridge: Polity Press, 2008), 114.
11. In some parts of the United States, competition with cable from telco companies such as AT&T or Verizon exists, but it tends to only be in the most lucrative markets.
12. Ben Bagdikian, *The New Media Monopoly: A Completely Revised and Updated Edition with Seven New Chapters* (Boston: Beacon Press, 2004), 3.
13. Benjamin Compaine and Douglas Gomery, *Who Owns the Media? Competition and Concentration in the Mass Media Industry*, 3rd ed. (Mahwah, N.J.: Routledge, 2000).
14. James B. Stewart, "When Media Mergers Limit More Than Just Competition," *The New York Times*, July 25, 2014; http://www.nytimes.com/2014/07/26/business/a-21st-century-fox-time-warner-merger-would-narrow-already-dwindling-competition.html (accessed February 10, 2015).
15. http://www.stopbigmedia.com/chart.php?chart=radio (accessed October 21, 2008).
16. http://www.stopbigmedia.com/chart.php?chart=tv (accessed October 21, 2008).
17. http://www.stopbigmedia.com/chart.php?chart=pub (accessed October 21, 2008).
18. Aphra Kerr, *The Business and Culture of Digital Games: Gamework/Gameplay* (Thousand Oaks, Calif.: SAGE, 2006), 55–58.
19. Alexis C. Madrigal, "How Netflix Reverse Engineered Hollywood," *The Atlantic*, January 2, 2014; http://www.theatlantic.com/technology/archive/2014/01/how-netflix-reverse-engineered-hollywood/282679/ (accessed January 24, 2014).

—

CHAPTER 3

Media Industry Mandates

Key Takeaways:

Understand the different mandates that commonly drive the operation of media companies

Appreciate the various ways the funding of media, whom they are meant to serve, and how their success is assessed lead to differences among media products and industrial practices

Make connections between the mandate of a particular medium and the content it produces

For well over a decade now, many city governments, citizen groups, and grassroots media organizations have dreamed of creating municipal broadband networks to provide citywide high-speed Internet in public spaces to every member of the community at little or no cost. Likewise, many communities seek for home Internet service to be available and affordable to all members—and that systems be state of the art. One way to ensure such universal service is for municipalities to provide Internet service in the same way they provide and service roads, libraries, and schools. In addition to providing networks for emergency communications and widespread access to information services, such municipally delivered services promise to help bridge the **digital divide**, or the gap between those who have access to high-speed broadband communication—and all the information and entertainment access it allows—and those who do not.

Chances are good, however, that whatever city you live in, you have only minimal community Internet access and few options other than commercial Internet service providers, despite the fact that such networks have been technologically possible for years. The reason your community probably lacks municipally delivered broadband is because of funding and political obstacles that have slowed, and in some cases all but killed, these initiatives. The core problem involves an ongoing debate about what mandate should govern broadband access.

This issue first emerged in relation to providing WiFi access throughout cities, but since the widespread deployment of smartphones and extensive use of cellular data plans, it has also spread to concern about building public utility networks to provide home, wire-based Internet access. Finding public funding for such Internet infrastructure requires tax money, and few city governments have shown a willingness or ability to increase taxes or redirect tax money from other sources. Established commercial Internet providers such as cable and telecommunications companies and their trade associations have even lobbied the legislatures of several states to enact laws prohibiting municipal systems.

Much of the fastest and most affordable Internet access around the world has been created in places in which the city government has financed the costs of building and implementing the system or relied on other private–public partnership models. For example, the city of Stockholm, Sweden, built a wholesale fiber network covering the entire city by raising funds through municipal bonds. It now leases the fiber network to retail providers who service the residents of Stockholm directly for very reasonable prices (less than $30 a month). Similarly, the city of Bristol, Virginia, utilized federal grants and bonds to create its own broadband network, which is managed by its public utility company, Bristol Virginia Utilities. This utility company provides broadband, telephone, and cable services to about 65 percent of the residents of Bristol.

Many of the companies that have fought free, municipal WiFi and the building of municipal Internet utilities exist as monopoly service providers. According to data published in 2013, only 34 percent of US households have a choice of providers that offer broadband-speed Internet connections—leaving most of the country with little recourse in accessing this increasingly essential service.[1] Frequently, these commercial companies have been derelict in updating capacity in more rural and less lucrative areas while also fighting to make sure these communities cannot build alternatives. Internet service providers have spent millions of dollars introducing legislation in state legislatures making municipal services illegal. Companies such as Comcast have greatly expanded city-wide WiFi availability in the communities in which they operate; however, only those who pay fees to Comcast for home Internet service can access the WiFi nodes (despite the fact Comcast uses routers in the homes and businesses of its subscribers to provide the service).

The clash among users, commercial providers, and city governments over municipal WiFi and Internet service demonstrates the challenge of determining the mandate for any particular media industry, as well as the different outcomes that each mandate encourages. In an age when we—as both citizens and consumers—rely on Internet access to perform many basic daily functions, questions of the accessibility of the Internet and whether adequate pressure for innovation exists on largely monopoly providers become vital to the operation of businesses, schools, and government.

The ongoing saga of municipal WiFi and municipal Internet service demonstrates the difference between commercial and noncommercial mandates, as well as the strengths and weaknesses of each. Public mandates, the most common type of noncommercial mandate, are more effective than commercial mandates at serving public needs—particularly those needs that are unrelated to business activities. A free public WiFi system, for instance, might allow a local bicycle co-op to promote its summer group riding schedule through its splash page, or a nonprofit group to announce a call for volunteers, even though neither organization may have the funds necessary to purchase Internet access and pay to advertise these messages. In a commercial system, by contrast, these organizations might need to place advertising on local newspaper or other media sites and hope the community has adequate Internet access and happens upon these messages.

Public media do cost money, however, and they are typically supported by individual or corporate taxes. Commercial mandates, by contrast, often do not require tax money, and they serve certain kinds of needs particularly well, including those of businesses and affluent individuals or groups. Their ability to serve the needs of other people is spottier because their primary motivation is to make as much money as possible. Mandates, then, shape the operation of media industries in many ways, including whether and how various segments of the public are served, the kinds of content that the industry produces, the organization of the industry (whether it is a monopoly, an oligopoly, or competitive), and the role that the industry plays in business and civic life.

*   *   *

Those who study and discuss the media often overlook the mandate of a media industry because it's easy to take for granted. In many ways, the mandate encompasses the purpose of the media industry—its very reason for being—and, in most cases, the mandate was established so long ago that it seems unalterable. Nevertheless, as the municipal-broadband controversy reminds us, there is nothing inevitable about the mandate of any media industry, and the creation of the mandates of our established media industries often generated similar controversy.

As you'll recall from Chapter 2, we delimit two categories of mandates—commercial and noncommercial—with various subcategories of noncommercial mandates such as public, community, alternative/do-it-yourself (DIY), and governmental. We divide the mandates in this way because, for the most part, those media that are relevant to a discussion of *media industries* operate with a commercial mandate in the United States. Media operating under a commercial mandate are thus emphasized throughout the book, but we want to make clear at the outset that other options exist. We often juxtapose other mandates as examples in subsequent chapters in order to offer a reminder that what seem to be given and natural practices of media industries—or "just the way things are"—are in fact a result of a deliberate decision that the media should operate with a commercial mandate. Thus it isn't the case that we see or hear what we do in our media because "media industries just are that way." Rather, we find that content because cultivating profits is the foremost goal of most media.

The vantage point of looking back through history allows us to better see the processes through which mandates are established. Consider the example of US broadcasting. Students of radio history are often surprised to learn that when the technology we now know as radio first developed, inventors and users conceived of it as a technology akin to a mobile phone. In the first decades of the 1900s, inventors and amateurs constructed the radio sets that they used to send and receive signals across long distances. Most thought the technology, often called "wireless," was most similar to the telegraph or telephone because it provided a wireless means to send a signal from one place to another. (At first, radio transmissions were in Morse code, similar to telegraph messages, and the ability to transmit voice, as over the telephone, came later). In these early years, then, users perceived radio as a **point-to-point** medium that could be used to send a message from one person to another, not the broadcast medium capable of sending a message from one source to many receivers that we know it as today.

Gradually, entrepreneurs and businesses realized that radio's greater potential existed in using it as a mass medium rather than as a wireless point-to-point form of communication; and, once this happened, the struggle to establish its mandate began. Up until World War I, the dominant use of "radio" in the United States was by young boys and other amateurs who built their own radios and used the devices to try to receive distant signals. These so-called DXers, or "distance fiends," would tape maps to their walls and use pushpins to record all the locations from which they received signals. During this time, and throughout the 1910s, radio also emerged as a valuable means of communication among ships. By the late 1910s, increasing incidents of interference between the use of radio for shipping communication and amateurs sending and receiving signals emerged and contributed to the sense that official policies for radio needed to be instituted. These policies became part of the establishment of the medium's mandate.

To jump to the end of this abbreviated story, there was no natural reason for the mandate that eventually resulted, and the United States and Great Britain reached very different outcomes when faced with comparable situations. In the United States, an agreement between the military and the corporate interests that had been developing radio led to the demise of radio as an amateur's hobby and set up radio with a commercial mandate, while reserving other frequencies for exclusive military use. In contrast, in Great Britain the government took responsibility for developing and organizing radio, and there—as in most similarly industrialized countries—it took on a public mandate.

Before we further detail the various mandates, we'd like to make a few points very clear. First, *we can often identify multiple mandates for media outlets, although one is typically primary*. Most national systems use a combination of commercial and public media, and it can often be difficult to distinguish between them. Many of the shows aired on the US public broadcaster known as the Public Broadcasting System (PBS) are imports from the United Kingdom and Canada that have been produced originally for commercial entities in those countries. And, at times, even US commercial media—typically broadcasters—behave in ways suggesting more than just commercial profit motivation: every commercial broadcast and cable television channel in the United States forewent commercial interruptions for a week after the September 11, 2001, attacks in order to air constant news. So we see that, in practice, media industries constantly blend and merge these mandates, though they can be primarily defined in one way.

In addition, *certain media industries, particularly the broadcasting industries, tend to be more influenced by these mandates than others; thus most examples of noncommercial mandates are in broadcast media*. Much of the world outside of the United States has a rich history of public broadcast media, and the United States is an odd case where a commercial system was selected at the start. Popular music and video game industries, by contrast, are typically commercially funded regardless of where in the world they are located. In addition, a number of industries—including broadcasting, film, and even some kinds of music—are subsidized in whole or in part by federal governments in an effort to protect their nations' cultural industries. Canada, for example, has numerous subsidies for both English-language and French-language media industries, including television, film, music, publishing, and video games. Around the globe, it is now the case that, at an industry level, most countries feature broadcasting industries that blend commercial and noncommercial mandates. Other media industries are typically dominated by a commercial mandate.

WHAT ARE COMMON MANDATES?

Throughout history and around the world, media can most basically be categorized as commercial or noncommercial. The differences between these mandates emerge through considering three questions: *Who pays for media, whom does it serve,* and *what determines "success."* In many ways, the last two questions are contingent upon the first, so perhaps the first question one should always ask when beginning to assess a media industry is: Who pays for it?

Commercial Media

When asked who pays for a commercial system, many students' first impulse is to say "advertisers," and that answer is partly correct. We are often told that here in the United States we enjoy the "free" television offerings of NBC, CBS, Fox, the CW, and ABC thanks to the advertisers that pay for the commercials in the programs, just as nearly all our radio enjoyment comes to us for "free." Although we don't have to pay a specific fee to watch an episode of *Scandal* when ABC broadcasts it over its television network, we—this time as consumers—do still pay for it. All of the marketing and advertising budgets that companies spend to buy advertising comes from consumers who pay inflated prices for goods to cover advertising expenses. So the answer to who pays in the commercial system is: you. How much money is spent on advertising? In 2013 advertisers spent $140 billion in the United States, while global advertising spending was estimated to reach $517 billion.

Of course advertising is just one way of funding commercial media. Most commercial media blend advertising and payment from consumers—for example, most newspapers and magazines require a small payment to receive their products while earning the majority of their revenues from advertisers. Still other media derive almost all of their funding from consumers, as when you pay for a ticket to see a movie, buy an album or song, or purchase print or television media that have no advertising. Finally, we typically pay for media services through monthly fees, such as those you pay for your mobile phone or Internet service. We'll explore these variations in ways of charging for commercial media in Chapter 5 as part of the economic conditions shaping media industry operation. For now, it is just important to note the many ways commercial media industries earn profits from their users and audiences.

The next question in assessing mandates is: Whom does the media outlet serve? Commercial media serve those likely to make them most profitable. Media supported by advertising are categorized as **dual product markets**. This economic concept refers to the two different commodities exchanged. As audiences, we often think of media companies designing products for our needs and "selling" us the content, but, in reality, we are the ones being sold. In the somewhat graphic language of the advertising industry, the goal of most media is to "sell eyeballs." Magazines, television networks, and newspapers design a media product and market it toward various audiences (the first market). Their economic model, however, does not rely on those audiences paying for those media (as is the case in the recording and film industries, which rely on direct pay rather than advertising). Rather, those magazines, television networks, and newspapers profit by selling the audiences they gather with their media content to advertisers. This leads these media to design content in very particular ways. On some level, they are concerned with creating good content that audiences enjoy and appreciate, but they are mostly concerned with creating content that gathers the audience that advertisers seek and, in most cases, while trying to avoid controversy. Many social media companies such as Facebook and Twitter likewise aggregate eyeballs and attempt to profit by selling access to them and the information about them to advertisers.

How media implement their commercial goals—or the central strategy these media use—has changed over their history. In the past, both the magazine and television industries relied on creating media products that gathered large and "broad" audiences. Both industries now seek to reach more narrowly focused audiences with products that are geared toward particular demographics or attitudes.

As a result, commercial media systems tend toward certain kinds of content and ways of portraying people and stories. Much advertiser-supported media is designed to reach a particular **demographic**—or narrow subsection of the population—because advertisers desire certain types of customers. In the television industry, this most desired demographic is described as 18- to 34-year-olds with college educations who have household incomes greater than $75,000 per year—distinctions drawn from basic Nielsen Media Research categories of income and age. Commercial media also tend to avoid content likely to disturb advertisers—which might mean avoiding news stories critical of the practices of an advertiser or of members of the media company's board of directors.

It may seem cynical, but almost every facet of commercial media production comes back to a question of what those most valued consumers desire. Of course no media company ever knows for certain what theme, story, or format will be a hit. This creates a lot of uncertainty and possibility for creativity in the production process (remember "**nobody knows**"), and it accounts for much of the variety that does exist. The various factors noted in Chapter 2 that make media industries different from many others prevent them from being able to consistently manufacture "hits" and allows some degree of artistic experimentation and risk taking. In some cases, the desire to reach affluent audiences leads to high-quality media products. Though top journalistic outlets are motivated by commercial goals, the desire to attract audiences that are educated and affluent can lead to rigorous and sophisticated reporting in an effort to become established as the most reputable information source.

Finally, what determines success for commercial media? For the media companies, the answer is profits. This can lead to somewhat varied strategies, depending upon the economic model of the media entity—subscription media succeed when their subscriptions increase and few people cancel subscriptions, advertiser-supported media seek to attract the most of whatever consumer their advertisers most covet, and direct-pay media such as film seek to entice as many people as possible to come out and see movies or buy pay-per-view specials.

Two more important things to remember: even in the United States, no medium operates as a perfect free market. The government imposes some regulation on every medium, whether it is as limited as preventing monopolies and disallowing obscene speech or more nuanced regulations related to broadcast license requirements. Years of media operation have proven that some regulation of media industries is required in order to obtain various prosocial goals and expectations. And a gentle reminder: many of you reading these pages are likely young and on your way to being the educated and affluent media consumers that many advertisers most desire. If this is true, when assessing the strengths and weaknesses of a commercial media system it is important to remember that you are better served than most others. Remember to account for how you would feel about a commercial media system if you weren't considered desirable by advertisers. Take a moment the next time you are talking with someone over the age of 60 about the media they use and whether they feel they see their lives and stories reflected. Ask them to note characters in film or television who they can identify with or whether the stories they find in newspapers or magazines seem relevant.

Noncommercial Media
Public Mandate Media

"Who pays" is actually a trick question, as the answer is almost always "you," regardless of the mandate. How the media industry receives that payment varies, however. You typically pay for a public media system through taxes. That is, a public system gathers funding from those who belong to a nation-state or municipality and then pools those funds to provide a media service for those citizens. The classic example of this has been the case of the BBC, and we should note from the outset that broadcast television and radio are the media that most commonly pursue a public mandate. In Britain, citizens are charged an annual fee for their television sets. In 2015 this fee was 145.50£ for a color television (about $225) and 49£ for a black-and-white set ($75). The government collects this money and then allocates it to the BBC, which uses that funding to develop programming for its various radio and television channels and, increasingly, its streaming services. In 2014 the BBC's operating expenses were the equivalent of roughly $7.1 billion.[2]

In a public system, then, you—as a citizen of the country—pay for media service, and in return the media system is charged with serving you, its citizenry. How does it do this, and how do we determine whether it does so successfully? A group of people may all be citizens of a country, but they likely have vastly different needs and interests, which make such a mandate challenging. Take a much smaller scale example—imagine if your university had a media service funded through your tuition dollars (this may be the case for many of you). That campus media system is likely charged with serving the needs of the university community, but chances are that even just on your campus, there is no one student need that makes determining what should be included in that media programming easy. How should station managers decide what types of shows to develop—should they offer entertainment or "service programming" that provides news about campus? Who should the programming entertain? Should the programming focus on the needs of commuters or of campus residents? How should it balance the many interests of a diverse student body and the broader academic community?

When you consider how challenging it might be to develop a media service that adequately serves just the range of students on your campus, it becomes easy to see how difficult it is to develop and maintain a media system that serves the needs of an entire country. One way public mandate media try to fulfill this charge is through offering a diversity of programming. Certainly, the media system cannot meet *all* the needs of *all* its citizens *all* of the time, but program directors can try to construct program schedules that meet the needs of many different groups at some point in a program day, week, or year. Take a moment and think about how you would carry out this mandate if you were the programming director for your campus radio or television station. In some cases, public media are vibrant enough that they are able to offer multiple channels, and this helps meet the needs of varied constituencies tremendously. For instance, in The Netherlands, different political and religious groups run the public service television system, and each controls its own channel or a portion of a channel's broadcast schedule. In other cases, representatives of major civil groups in the country serve on a public service oversight board that determines policy and personnel.

Assessing audience needs also provides a challenge for media with a public mandate, and programmers must weigh choices like: Should they present programs with casts representative of the makeup and viewpoints of the entire country? If so, how should they go about doing this? Creating balance can be very difficult to accomplish. Should the "balance" exist in each program—such as making sure an equal number of conservative and liberal commentators and guests can be found in each show, or is it better to create separate shows or entire channels with distinctly conservative or liberal perspectives? What about representing a nation's varied ethnic, religious, class, and age diversity? Certainly it is impossible to encompass a nation's diversity within the cast of every single show, and, given that, how do you make sure you depict the various realities of people in a nation? And public media's goals aren't simply a matter of serving a nation's varied constituencies. Media policy scholar Des Freedman explains, "Public broadcasting's main goal is not to sell audiences to advertisers or subscription broadcasters but to engage viewers and listeners in a dialogue about public life."[3] Can you think of media in your life that engages you in this way?

We noted at the outset that most countries now feature "some combination" of these mandates. Most countries around the world began their broadcasting histories with public broadcasting systems (the United States is a rare exception), but nearly all now have **mixed mandate systems** in which a vital public system remains but a commercial system has developed alongside it. In many cases, public broadcasters actually run commercials and generate a good deal of their revenue from them, like the Irish broadcaster RTÉ (Raidió Telefís Éireann), which obtains about 55 percent of its revenue from advertising.

Programmers for public media in countries with mixed mandates sometimes focus their resources particularly on those underserved by the commercial media since commercial media tend to serve certain groups very well but often provide little or no services for other groups. The question of whether public media in a mixed-mandate system should spread its resources across the population or focus more effort on those unserved or underserved by the commercial media is complicated and important. The development of media industries with mixed public and commercial components leads programmers of public systems to make different decisions about how they operate than if there were no commercial sector.

Given the diverse needs of its population, a public system typically assesses its success by trying to answer the question of whether the needs of its public are being served. This might mean continuing to schedule some shows that don't have large audiences but that reach a particularly underserved community. In Slovenia, for instance, public radio broadcasters air programming in a variety of minority languages, including Italian and Hungarian, to serve small ethnic groups that would not otherwise have access to such programming.

Another tricky aspect of noncommercial media involves how to evaluate their success. In the United States we are so accustomed to thinking of success in terms of which media content gathers the most viewers or listeners—and therefore earns the most advertising dollars—that it can be quite difficult to conceive of an alternative measure of success. Rather than quantity of viewers, success might be a matter of simply making alternative content available. The CEO of Finnish broadcaster YLE explained that he identified a success for his service in the cultural discussion about race that took place after the service aired a television movie in which it cast a black actor as a historical figure that many found controversial. His sense of success wasn't tied to how many people watched or whether critics deemed it to have high artistic value but from the fact that the broadcast provoked cultural conversation about a difficult and important aspect of society.

Not all public mandate media are comparable. For example, US students are probably most familiar with PBS. While PBS is certainly different than commercial media, it is also not nearly as robust as the public mandate media available around the world. PBS is a national entity that helps produce programming and facilitates connections among the 356 locally owned and run PBS stations around the country. Annual per capita funding of PBS in 2012 was $1.49, compared with public media funding of $83 in Great Britain and $28 in Canada—thus, by measures of funding alone, it is clear that the US system is not at all comparable with those elsewhere.

Instead, US stations are largely reliant on viewer and foundation donations, though they also receive funding from a variety of other sources. Roughly 15 percent of the budget comes from the federal government, 17 percent from state and local governments, 11 percent from public and private universities, and 41 percent from private funders (26 percent subscribers and 15 percent corporations).[4] As policy scholar Patricia Aufderheide notes, "U.S. public television is a peculiar hybrid of broadcasting systems. Neither completely a public-service system in the European tradition, nor fully supported by commercial interests as in the dominant pattern in the United States, it has elements of both."[5] Thus we'd remind our readers with familiarity only with US media that their experience with public mandate media is likely atypical compared with the rest of the world.

You may have noticed a heavy reliance on broadcasting examples throughout this section and this chapter. This is because broadcast media (radio and television) are overwhelmingly the type of media that tend to operate under a public mandate. Government support of media can be found in other industries; for example, many national governments subsidize a range of cultural activities, such as films and recorded music. Even though there are bureaucratic institutions that decide which films receive public funding, the complexity, reach, and visibility of those organizations are far less than those of a public broadcaster and are not as extensive as what we'd consider typical of a public mandate. Most such film boards don't produce, distribute, or promote the films they fund; they simply provide financial assistance. We discuss the particularity of why broadcasting often uses a public mandate more in Chapter 4. Even though this is a mandate rarely found outside of broadcasting, it is crucial to understand the goals and distinctions of a public system, if for no other reason than to help us imagine alternatives to the dominance of the commercial mandate.

Although we acknowledge a range of noncommercial media that includes public, community, alternative/DIY, and governmental mandates, the most substantial alternative to commercial media (particularly from a media industry focus) is a public mandate. We freely acknowledge that the distinctions that we make among community and alternative/DIY are fairly nuanced and, perhaps, debatable; it is difficult, however, to speak in generalizations about these other types of noncommercial mandates, because questions such as who pays and who is served tend to be particular to the media outlet.

Community, Alternative/DIY Mandate Media

Media with a community, alternative or DIY mandate are arguably quite similar to public media, but they differ in scope. Instead of aiming to serve the citizenry of a nation, they might aim to reach a neighborhood or a specific group within a city. Still, they differ from media with a public mandate because the public mandate can also produce some of the same problems as commercial media in their elaborate bureaucracies. These subcategories of media are difficult to discuss in generalities because they really can't be distinguished by the questions of who pays, whom they serve, and how to judge success. In all cases, the answers to these questions are specific to the case under consideration.

Community, alternative, and DIY media are typically paid for through donations, and they might receive some governmental support. There might even be commercial support, as in the case of cable service providers offering up money for the local access stations that exist on their services. (Notably, they don't offer much money and do this only as part of the franchise agreements struck with local communities. A franchise agreement is a contract between a municipality and cable system. They are typically quite long [12–15 years] and allow the service to be the only cable-based service in the community.) The difference is that these types of media are meant to serve a much narrower and specific population, or they might exist only to serve the creator's desire to share a message.

Examples of community media include low-power FM (LPFM) radio stations in the United States. These stations are authorized for use as noncommercial educational

stations and are authorized to operate only up to 100 watts, which allows an approximately 3.5-mile radius of service. Many of these are very small, even personal operations, but although the stations reach a small radius of broadcast listeners, they can
reach a much larger audience by streaming live on the web. A feature story about LPFM
in *The New York Times* cited examples of such stations, one in St. Paul, Minnesota, that
focuses on the Hmong people in the city and one in Oregon focused on the issues of
farm workers.[6]

Other examples of community media are those shows produced for local access
cable channels. The content of these channels can be all over the map—from still camera
shots of city council or school board meetings to local talk shows with decent production values. Community media might exist to serve the needs of a niche population, or
they might just exist because of a few people with the time and inclination to provide it.

'Zines (short for "fanzines") are often cited as an example of alternative or DIY
media. These are self-published print media (similar to magazines or newsletters) with
a small circulation—typically photocopied—on any imaginable topic. Most are self-
financed and designed as a tool of expression contrary to the established commercial or
public media. 'Zines might be considered a precursor of blogs. The ease and affordability
of personal websites and aggregators, such as YouTube, enable the distribution of alternative and DIY media in the digital age. Again, the goal of these media is often primarily self-expression and may be thought of as a hobby.

The widespread availability of computerized media-production tools and broadband Internet access for distribution has led to growing popularity and awareness of
media with community or alternative/DIY mandates and has also led to the development of what some observers call the **prosumer**, a portmanteau that incorporates the
words "producer" and "consumer."[7] Some hoped the emergence of digital communication technologies would diminish the control media industries have in the making and
circulating of cultural goods and enable a robust prosumer culture.

Many have discussed YouTube as a site of alternative, DIY, or independent video
distribution. Indeed, YouTube makes video content available far beyond that typically
found in commercial or public counterparts, though YouTube is such a multifaceted
aggregator that it is difficult to assign the site a mandate. Videos made by commercial
media entities that use YouTube as a redistributor and earn money for both the creator
and YouTube through advertising comprise some of the most viewed YouTube content.
But YouTube also provides distribution for lots of amateur content that is simply created
because it is a hobby for the creator or out of hopes of being discovered and finding a
way into the mainstream commercial industry. Many of these videos likely produce no
commercial revenue for the creator. Still others use YouTube as a primary distributor of
commercial content—particularly those who develop video content for audiences with
more demographic specificity than perceived as profitable for cable channels or broadcast networks.

We would, however, qualify the perceived revolutionary nature of these developments in two ways. First, while a growing number of people are creating their own
media content and sharing it with others, this remains a small fraction of the *commercial* media activity that goes on. Second, media consumers have always been able to

"talk back" to media companies in various ways, and the ability to become involved in the production process does not undermine the economic power of large conglomerates, nor does it fundamentally change the relationship between large commercial producers and individual consumers.

Although media with community, alternative, and DIY mandates are often very important to the people involved in them, we do not feature media with these mandates prominently in the following chapters. These media outlets indeed provide meaningful content options, and their content can sometimes bubble up into more established media outlets with public and commercial mandates, but given our focus on the operation of commercial media industries, there is less to say about community, alternative, and DIY media because they function so deliberately outside the industrial norms of a commercial mandate. It may be, as supporters of media with these mandates argue, that community, alternative, or DIY media will one day revolutionize commercial and public media. Such a revolution has not yet taken place, however, and media with these mandates continue to exist largely at the fringes of the media industries—a fact that does not necessarily diminish their importance for users, readers, or listeners.

Governmental Mandate Media

Government funding is a commonality among public and governmental media, but governmental-mandate media exist primarily to serve the needs of the government in power rather than the public. Often the societies that have media with governmental mandates also have authoritarian governments. Few purely governmental media systems remain today, and authoritarian governments often derive their power through force, so the funding for media systems may come from assets that have been seized from citizens, from taxes, or from the proceeds of goods the government sells to other countries.

The mandate to serve the government can lead to many different outcomes. A government might, for instance, fund a diversity of programming and viewpoints. But it more commonly has been the case that authoritarian governments use media systems to advance the singular view of those in power. The governmental media system, therefore, would be considered successful when the views of the government are transmitted to the people. In other words, rather than the goal of informing or uplifting the citizenry, as is the goal of public-mandate media, or serving the desires of consumers as in the commercial model, the purpose of media outlets in a governmental system is to propagandize citizens with the beliefs the government desires for the citizenry to hold and neutralize dissent. Historically, Nazi-era Germany has served as an example of the most egregious—and successful—governmental media system in the modern era, because of its supposedly successful efforts to spread Nazi sentiments throughout the German citizenry. In fact, the reason that many Americans remain distrustful of government-funded media systems is because of lingering memories of the Nazi and Soviet systems.

Much like public-mandate media, governmental-mandate systems require a good deal of capital to finance. Given the fact that most of the large economies in the world are located in nations that are, at least nominally, democratic, the challenges of funding large, modern media systems have prompted many authoritarian regimes to adopt some of the principles of commercial media systems, although the content of these commercial media operators remains tightly controlled. The film industry in Myanmar, formerly Burma, is a case in point. Though far from a cinema powerhouse, the Burmese film industry does have a long and relatively active history that dates back to the 1920s. When the military junta took over the country in 1962, it effectively took over the film industry, but it began privatizing the industry again beginning in 1989. A single private company, Mingalar Ltd., controls the majority of the theaters in the country and plays only films approved by government censors. Moreover, independent cinema producers are required to submit scripts to censors before they begin shooting. The government even gets involved in movie casting, preventing film stars who were active in the democracy movements of the 1980s and 1990s from appearing in films, and the older films of prodemocracy directors are likewise banned.[8] Limits on speech began to recede with the end of military rule in 2010, but a board of censors still must approve films.

Myanmar is one of the more extreme examples of an authoritarian state, but the tendency of nondemocratic governments to privatize the media while retaining control is a widespread phenomenon. Governments throughout Asia, the Middle East, Africa, and Latin America adopt similar measures. In Kuwait, government censors edit imported television programs before airing them. In China, Internet companies go to great lengths to filter search engine results and web page access in line with the desires of the Chinese government. The challenges of maintaining governmental media were on display in several Middle Eastern countries that experienced uprisings that were part of the "Arab Spring." Many have researched the role of social media in sharing information among the populations of countries that had long received limited access to information through legacy broadcast and print media because of governmental control of media systems.

Quite often, the main goal of governmental media systems is the maintenance of social harmony, though the goal of maintaining harmony and eliminating dissent frequently go hand in hand. An incident in Thailand demonstrates how authoritarian governments exercise their power over the media system to maintain social harmony. In late 2007 and early 2008, a controversy erupted over the popular Thai soap opera *Songkram Nang Fah* (The Air Hostess War), which featured steamy and catty storylines about Thai Airways flight attendants. Offended by the portrayals of its members, the flight attendants' union petitioned the Thai Ministry of Culture to cancel the series. Although the series continued for a few months, it is unclear whether the Ministry did convince the series' producer to tone down the more offensive elements.[9] For American audiences, such a controversy is not remarkable, because numerous groups frequently lodge complaints about portrayals on commercial television. But the involvement of the federal government is probably surprising: after all, in a commercial media system, aggrieved groups seek to prompt advertisers, not the government, to put pressure on producers of controversial programs.*

---

*This link connects to a radio story about the Chinese government cracking down on "excess entertainment." What type of content is being removed? How is this an example of a governmental mandate? http://www.pri.org/stories/2012-01-04/china-cracks-down-excessive-entertainment

Table 3.1 Mandates Chart

	COMMERCIAL	NONCOMMERCIAL	GOVERNMENTAL
Who pays for media?	You	You	You
Who does it serve?	Consumers	The people	Government
What determines "success"?	Profits	The effectiveness with which the people's needs are served	The effectiveness with which the government's views are transmitted to the people
Example	Disney, *The New York Times*, NBC	BBC, LPFM, community newspapers	Nazi-era Germany

Table 3.1 provides a quick reference for differentiating among the mandates we discuss.

MANDATES IN ACTION

It is important to note that these basic categorizations of mandates and quick descriptions of who pays, who is served, and how success is determined are rarely as simple or clear-cut as their categorization suggests. In practice, there is much greater variety and complexity, but this notion of a mandate and its basic characteristics provide a starting point. As we noted in Chapter 2, we provide a framework that moves from mandates through conditions and practices in order to help make sense of what seem to be the hundreds, and maybe thousands, of factors that contribute to determining the operation of a media industry and the products it creates. These mandates offer just a first step, or deflection of the pinball, that the Industrialization of Culture framework allows. Even though we begin with mandates, we don't view them as **deterministic**. Deterministic approaches often try to explain the behavior of media industries through one aspect—typically something like a belief that the commercial mandate of a media industry to make profits will lead it to operate only in a particular way, or that the capabilities of a technology will lead it to be used only in a certain way. In the following discussion we explore the very different products that have been created by media industries despite a common mandate. It is impossible to provide a detailed example of all of the various forms a commercial or noncommercial media entity may take, but let's return to the opening example of how US radio became established under a commercial mandate for a deeper understanding of this case.

This link provides an example of how the Chinese government doesn't have to monitor content but how media industry workers have internalized perceptions of acceptable content and censor on their own. http://www.pbs.org/newshour/rundown/self-censorship-on-chinese-tv-an-american-comedians-experience/

Establishing the Mandate of US Broadcasting

The origins of commercial US radio in the 1920s may seem like a history lesson with little contemporary relevance, but keep in mind that the beginning of radio is actually the beginning of broadcasting—which is a distinctive form of media because of its reliance on using a public asset for signal transmission. In fact, the negotiations that established the norms for radio created standards shifted only slightly upon the invention of television. Some new technologies invented in the past century—particularly those that enabled the emergence of cable channels—required some adaptations in these early norms, but for the most part the broadcast policies and practices that continue to organize US radio and television can be traced to the 1920s and early 1930s. In addition, when the Federal Communications Commission began regulating Internet communications in the 1990s, one of the major questions it needed to face was whether the technology was similar to broadcasting, and could therefore be highly regulated, or whether it was closer to print, and therefore enjoyed greater Constitutional protections.

First, let's briefly consider the paths not chosen at the outset of US broadcasting. The United States could have followed the route taken by most countries that developed radio at this time and organized it with a public mandate. This would have meant establishing an agency charged with making radio available for the people of the country. This body would have likely organized the spectrum (the naturally occurring electromagnetic space used to transmit broadcast signals) and endeavored to create radio programming to meet the needs of all citizens. What happened in the United States was quite different. At this time, amateurs, the military, and industrial entrepreneurs all had different ideas in mind for how radio should be employed. Amateurs used broadcasting as a hobby, and most spent their time with the medium trying to receive distant signals rather than listening to programming. The military was devising uses slowly, and although it didn't prove vital to their operations, it mainly wanted to control broadcasting in case future use developed. Finally, the entrepreneurs, who we might say ultimately won out, sought to profit from the technology—although the system in place now was not what many initially had in mind. All these groups could have shared the spectrum; yet, in the end, the best frequencies were reserved for military and government use, and others were allocated to the burgeoning broadcast business.[10]

As well as negotiating among these groups with different intentions for radio, the agency governing the establishment of radio under a public mandate would have faced challenging questions regarding whether to develop a locally or nationally based system given the geographical breadth of the United States, and also the question of how radio should be used to serve the public. Notably, PBS, which was developed in the 1960s, faced many of these challenges and continues to deal with them today.

As we noted, Britain is one of the many countries that did choose to develop broadcasting with a public mandate at this time. Historians of the BBC have developed rich accounts of exactly how these questions and debates evolved over the decades in the British system. Some felt that broadcasting should be used as a tool for cultural uplift and focused on developing programming such as theater and opera that they believed would enrich the tastes of its citizenry. At other times during its history, some have argued that the BBC also needed to provide programming that appealed to more popular tastes, such as soap operas and comedies; in its long history, the BBC has offered all of these types of programming.

Another mandate available to those establishing US radio was a governmental system. While this may seem an impossible fit in a democratic system, the military was one of the main users of radio in its early years, and some felt that radio should be placed in military hands.[11] It is difficult to imagine how differently radio might have developed in this case. It may not have been made available to the general population at all but instead would have been used exclusively for military communication. Or, more likely, radio might have been used as a propaganda force and featured programs with themes and messages that specifically served military or government ends.

But neither the public nor governmental mandates were long considered in the United States, and although US broadcasting quickly headed down the path of a commercial mandate, it took at least a decade from the agreement that established its commercial focus until radio began to be widely available. Although a commercial mandate had been selected, some experimentation and negotiation were required to figure out how to actually finance programming and how the involved entities could gain profits from it. For one, there was considerable resistance to commercial messages in radio's early days. Radio did not start out with the type of commercials common today; rather, a single company paid for the costs of making a show and was announced as a show's sponsor (e.g., there was a program called *Lux Radio Theater*—Lux was a brand of soap). In the early years, even discussing the attributes of a product, or "hard selling," was considered unseemly, so companies sought to encourage inferences among consumers or to curry favor with consumers through techniques of indirect advertising. In one famous case, Cliquot Club, the manufacturer of club soda and other beverages, sponsored performances by the Cliquot Club Eskimo Orchestra—an orchestra not comprised of actual Eskimos but of musicians who posed for publicity photos in parkas to help indirectly communicate Cliquot's desire for consumers to associate their product with something "cool" and "refreshing."[12]

The **sponsorship model** dominated US broadcasting during the radio years and into the early years of television. We discuss the particulars of the relationships among types of commercial funding and the production of programming in later chapters. For now, we want to leave you with the understanding that nothing happens "naturally" in the operation of a media system; there is never one right way the media should or must operate. Rather there are many different interests, often of those in power—whether the power of government or the power that comes from controlling capital—that lead to certain outcomes eventually coming to seem natural. In the 1920s, it seemed most unnatural that a company would promote the features of its product in the midst of entertainment programming. Over years of gradually incorporating subtle advertising messages into content, that expectation of programming being free of commercial messaging eroded to allow for the hard sell of later sponsors that extolled the virtues of products during the show. Later, the pretense of sponsorship was eliminated for the inclusion of the type of commercial messages we are familiar with today. Now we find our entertainment content again infiltrated with sponsored messages and **product**

placement in addition to pods of commercial messages. This product placement seemed quite jarring and unnatural in the early 2000s, but for those who never knew media without product placement, it, too, might seem unexceptional and quite natural.

For a somewhat different context and case of an evolving mandate, consider again the development of the Internet. This project began as a governmental effort to develop an interconnected system of computers that could survive a nuclear war; commercial use was explicitly forbidden. Once access to the Internet extended beyond government research centers, it quickly took on a new life as it became a central communication technology for both business and pleasure, as well as an interconnected marketplace that is very commercial indeed. Given the many different uses of the Internet, we find it impossible to characterize it with a single mandate—though we might consider different websites and consider how existing mandates do or do not apply. It is certainly the case that the present version of the Internet that many of us cannot imagine living without bears little resemblance to what its inventors and innovators imagined—as was true of radio as well.

LIMITS OF MANDATES

Although these mandates and their various mixed versions are helpful starting points for understanding characteristics of media industries, they tell only part of the story. With their particular funding norms, goals, and measures of success, mandates lead to some trends and likely outcomes; the reason we offer a framework with multiple levels, however, is because many other factors intervene and can lead to similar outcomes in systems with different mandates or different outcomes within a singular mandate.

As an example of the former, consider the case of the popular Netflix drama, *House of Cards*. Many of you might be familiar with the US version of this show, which chronicles the saga of national politicians seeking power and revenge in modern-day Washington, DC. *House of Cards*, however, was first developed in Britain and was a success there for the BBC. Although the US and UK versions do differ somewhat—particularly in that many more episodes were produced in the United States—we can view this as an example of a public and a commercial system producing the same show. Understanding how this happened and why the US and UK versions developed in the manner that they did cannot be explained by mandate alone but requires that we examine the various conditions and practices that contributed to the different shows.

As another example of the limitations of mandates, consider the great variety of programming produced in just one mandate. CBS's septuagenarian news and public affairs show *60 Minutes*, MTV's *Catfish*, and HBO's *Game of Thrones* are all products of a commercial media system, yet they are very different shows. The variation among them can be understood by examining the media industry that produced them, but we must dig deeper than the mandate of that system.

The broadcasting industry has been particularly present in this chapter as a result of the features that make public and governmental mandates more common to broadcasting than any other media industry. Even in countries such as Britain that have a long and established public broadcasting system, most other media operate under a commercial mandate. Given that many of the media industries around the world function with a commercial mandate, it is necessary to now turn to the conditions that contribute to the variation in content produced by commercial media industries.

QUESTIONS

1. What are the societal implications of relying solely on a commercial media mandate? Can you imagine any other metrics of success other than profit within the commercial mandate? Thinking of the United States in particular, how has the dominance of a commercial media mandate encouraged innovative programming? Where has it fallen short?

2. Can you imagine a scenario where public broadcasting competed with commercial media for advertising dollars? What might that do to the types of content produced on the public broadcasting channel? Would it be possible for the channel to maintain its original mission of serving the citizenry if it also had to secure significant funding from corporations? Why or why not?

3. Given what you have learned about public mandates, develop a programming model for PBS. What types of programming will allow it to most effectively fulfill its mandate? Will you impose quotas for types of programming (e.g., public affairs, children's shows), and how will your entertainment programming differ from that of television with a commercial mandate? What problems do you hope to address or solve with your programming? What problems or concerns appear too difficult to fix?

4. Funding is a pressing concern for both National Public Radio (NPR) and PBS, which rely heavily on audience donations and money from the government. But the US government allocates a significantly lower amount of money to public broadcasting than governments in Britain, Germany, and Canada, among others. How do you propose that we fund NPR and PBS: taxes, pledge drives, corporate investments, co-productions, product sales, advertisements? What are the advantages and limitations of these sources of revenue? Might some of them change PBS's or NPR's mandate and/or influence their content?

FURTHER READING

For more reading on establishing the commercial mandate of US broadcasting, see Erik Barnouw's *Tube of Plenty: The Evolution of American Television*, 2nd rev. ed. (New York: Oxford University Press, 1990); Susan Smulyan's *Selling Radio: The Commercialization of American Broadcasting: 1920–1934* (Washington, D.C.: Smithsonian, 1994); Robert Waterman McChesney's *Telecommunications, Mass Media, and Democracy: The Battle for the Control of U.S. Broadcasting, 1928–1935* (New York: Oxford University Press, 1993); and Susan Douglas's *Inventing American Broadcasting: 1899–1922* (Baltimore: Johns Hopkins University Press, 1987).

More on US public broadcasting can be found in Laurie Ouellette's *Viewers Like You? How Public TV Failed the People* (New York: Columbia University Press, 2002), and Glenda R. Balas's *Recovering a Public Vision for Public Television* (Lanham, Md.: Rowman & Littlefield, 2003). For more on community media, see Kevin Howley's *Community Media: People, Places, and Communication Technologies* (Cambridge: Cambridge University Press, 2005); Ellie Rennie's *Community Media: A Global Introduction* (Lanham, Md.: Rowman & Littlefield, 2006); and *Understanding Community Media*, edited by Kevin Howley (Thousand Oaks, Calif.: SAGE, 2009).

For books exploring media systems and their mandates outside of the United States, see Fred S. Siebert's *Four Theories of the Press: The Authoritarian, Libertarian, Social Responsibility, and Soviet Communist Concepts of What the Press Should Be and Do* (Urbana: University of Illinois Press, 1956); Daniel Clark Hallin and Paolo Mancini's *Comparing Media Systems: Three Models of Media and Politics* (Communication, Society, and Politics series) (Cambridge: Cambridge University Press, 2004); and Michael Tracey's *The Decline and Fall of Public Service Broadcasting* (Oxford: Oxford University Press, 1998).

NOTES

1. Jon Brodkin, "Why YouTube Buffers: The Secret Deals That Make—and Break—Online Video," *Ars Technica*, July 28, 2013; http://arstechnica.com/information-technology/2013/07/why-youtube-buffers-the-secret-deals-that-make-and-break-online-video/

2. http://www.bbc.co.uk/annualreport/2014/executive/finances/licence_fee.html

3. Des Freedman, *The Politics of Media Policy* (London: Polity, 2008), p. 147.

4. Patricia Aufderheide, "Public Television," in *Encyclopedia of Television*, 2nd ed., Horace Newcomb (New York: Fitzroy Dearborn), 1854–1857.

5. Ibid., 1854.

6. Kirk Johnson, "From a Porch in Montana, Low-Power Radio's Voice Rises," *New York Times*, September 8, 2009, http://www.nytimes.com/2009/09/08/us/08radio.html?_r=1 (accessed February 24, 2010).

7. Alvin Toffler, *The Third Wave* (New York: Bantam Books, 1989).

8. Aung Zaw, "Celluloid Disillusions," *Irrawaddy* 12, no. 3 (March 2004), http://www2.irrawaddy.org/article.php?art_id=924 (accessed February 12, 2010).

9. Andrew Buncombe, "Cabin Crews Protest Over Thai Massage Soap Opera," *The Independent*, January 22, 2008, 24.

10. Susan J. Douglas, *Inventing American Broadcasting, 1899–1922* (Baltimore, Md.: Johns Hopkins University Press, 1989); Robert B. Horwitz, *The Irony of Regulatory Reform* (New York: Oxford University Press, 1989); Robert W. McChesney, *Telecommunications, Mass Media and Democracy* (New York: Oxford University Press, 1993).

11. Erik Barnouw, *Tube of Plenty: The Evolution of American Television*, 2nd rev. ed. (New York: Oxford University Press, 1990), 20.

12. Susan Smulyan, *Selling Radio: The Commercialization of American Broadcasting: 1920–1934* (Washington, D.C.: Smithsonian, 1994), 79.

CHAPTER 4

—

Regulation of the Media Industries

Key Takeaways:

Understand various types of media industry regulation, including those imposed by governments as well as formal and informal self-regulation

Appreciate the many ways content regulations and structural regulations affect how media industries operate and what they create

Understand who the main domestic and international regulators are and what authority they have

Understand how the informal regulations of the free market shape media industry operations and content

Understand how digitization has led to new regulatory debates and organizations

One crucial event fundamentally altered what was a thriving and vital US film industry and forced a transformation of nearly all of its standard industrial practices. What emerged after this event was a film industry that again became thriving and vital, although many of its creative, distribution, and **economic norms** changed. This event is commonly known as the **Paramount Decree,** and we begin with it here as an illustration of the enormous implications that regulatory conditions can have on the operation of media industries.

The Paramount Decree refers to the outcome of *United States v. Paramount Pictures, Inc.,* a 1948 anti-trust case decided by the Supreme Court. Although only Paramount is mentioned, all of what were then known as the "Big Eight" film studios had their businesses at stake in this case. In short, before the Paramount Decree, eight studios dominated the film industry and controlled all aspects of film creation, distribution, and exhibition—perhaps offering the most extreme version of **vertical integration** ever achieved in a media industry. This meant that a studio created films using directors, writers, and actors who were all on staff or contracted to the studio and then distributed the films to theaters that the studios also owned. The studios didn't own all theaters, but they enforced challenging terms for the independently owned theaters through a practice known as **block booking**. In order for an independent theater to get the big new studio film with top talent, it also had to agree to take another block of films selected by the studio that were much less desirable. This was a brilliant arrangement for the studios as it allowed them to control competition by determining when films were screened, in what location, and for how long, producing demand for their films through the creation of **artificial scarcity**.

This degree of control over the film industry came under scrutiny as an unfair trade practice, and legal proceedings against the studios began in 1938. The studios managed to draw out the battle for a decade, but after losing in the Supreme Court and being found in violation of the Sherman Anti-Trust Act, the studios divested themselves—or sold off their ownership share—of their theaters.

As a result of this regulatory action—in this case, a judicial decision—the film industry experienced a complete overhaul and had to adjust many of its practices in response to the new competitive environment. The creative output of the industry also changed as a result, as the studios could no longer rely on forcing mediocre films on theaters. The loss of guaranteed exhibition through self-owned theaters led the film studios to create fewer but higher quality movies, as there were few takers for the low-quality works that had flourished because of block booking. This regulatory change also required substantial adjustments in the economic norms and conventional financial practices of the industry.

Quite accidentally, the 1948 decision coincided with the launch of television in the United States, which also required the film industry to adapt its norms. This new technology threatened to draw away audiences, as those who could afford to purchase sets now had a new in-home entertainment option. When television first emerged and aired all-live content, it proved to be a significant competitor for film. However, within a decade, as television began to rely less on live programming and instead found "tele-film" lucrative, the television and film industries became crucial partners.

The film industry has adapted to many other changes since 1948. Over the long term, the studios gradually reduced their reliance on income generated from the first domestic theatrical screening of films and produced more and more revenue from international distribution, the home rental market, licensing of films to television networks, and other distribution windows—a process we describe more fully in Chapter 8. The film industry of 2016 bears little resemblance to the film industry of nearly 70 years earlier, even though the major studios again have become part of massively conglomerated media entities. The Paramount Decree is but one event in a long industry history, but it is one that nevertheless indicates how regulatory conditions can alter the content of media even when content is not being directly regulated. This single regulatory action contributed to a complete reinvention of the economics, studio operation, and nature of film art.

*   *   *

This chapter focuses on **regulation**, or the laws, guidelines, and policies that govern how media industries produce, distribute, and exhibit their products. These regulations are commonly imposed by the nation in which the media operate, but they also can be transnational—as is the case with international treaty agreements. For our purposes, regulation encompasses the creation of laws and rules governing the operation of media industries and the enforcement of those laws, which often requires the creation of specific regulatory bodies.

In addition to the mandates discussed in the previous chapter, the functioning of all media systems are further determined by several structural conditions that establish a playing field of options for media industries or, rather, often remove some ideas and ways of creating them from the realm of possibility. The film industry in the previous example, for instance, operated with a commercial mandate both before and after the Paramount Decree, even as changed structural conditions profoundly altered the business of film as well as the films themselves. Structural conditions such as regulation, economics, and technology are broad forces—typically larger than any one company—that organize how media systems and industries can operate. As in the case of mandates, none of these conditions are natural or inevitable, despite how obvious they may seem, but have developed for complicated reasons that may no longer even be relevant.

We can begin to understand regulation by exploring three interconnected questions:

1. Who regulates?
2. What is regulated?
3. How do regulations affect the products of the media industries?

One of the most common regulators is the "state," which here refers primarily to national governments. In most cases, the state does not directly regulate media, but rather it sets up a particular body to manage certain media or enact policy initiatives. Some regulations established nearly a century ago remain in place today, while others have been eliminated or adjusted over time. Some media industries—particularly broadcasting—face regulations that are specific to some aspect of their operation. Almost all media industries, though, face two types of **governmental regulation** enforced by the state: either **content regulations** or **regulations on industry structure**. In addition, technological regulations are important in certain industries, such as telecommunications and broadcasting, but we do not attend to those substantially in this chapter. The vast majority of technological regulations cover technical minutia that few people in the industry, with the exception of engineers, even understand. Arguably, a third category of regulation—**access**—is becoming more relevant because of the transition to digital media that are sometimes less widely available than their analog counterparts. Access regulations and policy are not new, but historically they have been more relevant to point-to-point technology such as telephony. The growing importance of the web as a medium for distributing and sharing media content has led to the need to reassess regulations regarding access to media.

Traditionally, media industry textbooks like ours have primarily focused on governmental regulations enforced by official bodies. While we, too, consider these in fair depth, we want to stress from the outset the need for a broader conceptualization of regulation. Often, forms of **self-regulation**, both formal and informal, most stringently regulate media industries. Many of these are addressed in Chapter 7's discussion of creative practices, in which we explore how individuals impose informal, yet consequential, limitations based on their internalized belief systems, norms, and organizational routines.

The variation in regulatory structures in different countries—and even among different types of media within a single nation—makes the regulation of media industries and their products an expansive topic, and we can only begin to address some of the most common or most important types of regulation. We must first note that in the United States, the First Amendment is a necessary starting place for considering the regulation of most media. The guarantee that "Congress shall make no law . . . abridging the freedom of speech, or of the press" provides most media with substantial protection regarding the content media industries produce. Consequently, many issues regarding the regulation of content come back to issues of constitutionality and key provisions handed down by the Supreme Court regarding matters of indecency, obscenity, and "clear and present danger." As a result of First Amendment protections, many media industries (film, magazines, newspapers, music) do not face substantially different government regulations than most other industries. The key exception here is broadcasting, and we explain the specificity of broadcast regulation in the next section.

Although media industries may not face substantial state enforced regulation, they are still very much "regulated" by an array of assumptions and perceptions about the nature of their products. This is particularly true of media operating with a commercial mandate. In this case, commonly held beliefs by media workers—about what audiences want, what might worry advertisers, and what might succeed (by commercial measures)—impose strict regulation on the possible range of media products created.

WHY IS BROADCASTING DIFFERENT?

Broadcasting—encompassing aspects of both the radio and the television industries—is the most heavily regulated form of media in the United States and most other countries, and it is also the most likely to operate outside of a commercial mandate. This extra regulation results from some of the inherent features of broadcasting. Whether we mean the transmission of voice only, as in the case of radio, or voice and video, as in the case of television, or even newer efforts to broadcast voice, video, and data, broadcasting involves using the radio waves of the electromagnetic spectrum to transmit the signal (Figure 4.1), and the use of the electromagnetic spectrum yields particular treatment.

Radio waves are a naturally occurring resource, and as inventors identified their uses, it quickly became clear that some sort of organization of the spectrum and set of rules governing who could transmit where would be needed in order for anyone to receive the benefits of using it. An oft-told—and perhaps embellished—tale recounts how the chaos of the unorganized radio spectrum led to confusing and contradictory reports about the Titanic disaster.[1] Supposedly, many amateur operators reported receiving signals and gave false accounts of survivors, and others in official capacities claimed that they were impeded from communicating important information because of the amateurs' interference. This situation resulted from the lack of regulation at the time about what part of the spectrum an operator could use and the absence of a regulatory body to enforce the few rules that did exist. The result was chaos: without assigned locations on the spectrum, signal interference was inevitable and could make deliberate communication impossible. As the commercial norm of broadcasting was established and the

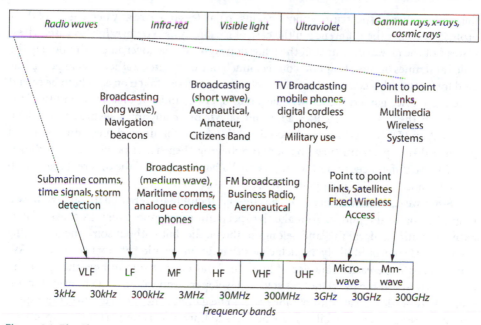

Figure 4.1 The Electromagnetic Spectrum.

Federal Radio Commission (the precursor to the **Federal Communications Commission** [**FCC**]) was created, only licensed broadcasters were permitted to use the airwaves, and, because they were licensed, they were situated on a specific part of the spectrum to prevent interference. This is still the case today. If the radio station you listen to is 107.1 FM, those numbers identify the position of the radio spectrum that the station uses (107.1) and the sector of the spectrum (FM). The question of why broadcasting is different, then, comes back to the spectrum. In the United States, *policymakers identified the spectrum as a national good that belongs to the people*; but without some oversight, no one would get any benefit from this good because we might all be transmitting overlapping signals. Or, more likely, because most of us don't have the time or inclination to use our spectrum, we are better served by the government organizing the spectrum for us and allowing other parties to purchase or borrow it. Those who simply borrow spectrum—radio and television broadcasters—are charged with serving the public interest. This is the exchange involved (in theory at least) in obtaining a broadcast license in the United States: A station (radio or television) applies to the FCC (which represents the public) for a license, and if the necessary conditions are met, the FCC allows the station to use the airwaves so long as it operates in the **public interest, convenience, and necessity.** The station does not have to pay to use the spectrum frequency. In being licensed by the FCC, it effectively "borrows" the spectrum that belongs to the public in exchange for agreeing to supply a service that benefits the public.

Radio and television stations have been among some of the most profitable industries in the United States; indeed, broadcast licenses have often been referred to as "a license to print money." Station owners are able to make great profits through their use of the publicly owned spectrum without having to pay fees or share any percentage of their profits. Consider the difference in the case of a cable system owner. In this case, wires, instead of the airwaves, transmit the television signals. The government did not lay the miles and miles of cable that now connect much of the country; rather, that expense was paid for by the cable company out of its net revenues or was taken on as debt to be repaid once the service gained subscribers, began to operate, and achieved profitability. Conversely, in the cases of satellite radio and television, companies such as Sirius XM, DirecTV, and Dish Network developed the ability to exploit unused spectrum space and purchased the spectrum they operate on, relieving them from public interest obligations. These differences in how we access media have supported the different regulation of the broadcast, cable, and satellite industries to date.

Since we can't see the spectrum, it is often difficult to understand its value or how it might belong to the public. To make the spectrum seem more tangible, think of it as akin to a national park: the land belongs to the public, but without someone managing the space, there would likely be such chaos that no one would get any use out of it. We can perhaps more easily conceive of how this land has value than how the spectrum does. Certainly, if the parkland was sold to developers who would build houses or commercial properties, great sums of money could be gained. The spectrum functions quite similarly. The government allows broadcasters to borrow certain parts of the spectrum in exchange for serving the public. Other parts of the spectrum have been sold off—at this point chiefly to wireless communication providers and satellite companies. These companies paid billions of dollars to effectively own certain parts of the spectrum. Since they bought their spectrum, they are not mandated with the same requirements of serving the public.

There is one additional important point for understanding the regulation of broadcasting. Even though we often think of broadcasters—particularly in the case of television—in terms of national networks such as NBC, ABC, Fox, or CBS, the FCC has no direct jurisdiction over these networks. Rather, the FCC has regulatory power over the individual stations that make up the network, or its **affiliates**. This is because the FCC gains its regulatory power by managing the licenses that each broadcast station must apply for and maintain regardless of whether they affiliate with a network or remain independent.

For example, when you hear about the FCC levying a fine, it is against individual stations in particular **markets**, not against the network itself. The FCC also only fines stations if a listener or viewer in the station's market complains and it finds the complaint appropriate. Consequently, it is usually the case that stations in a few cities may be fined, but many others go without penalty for airing the exact same content. Ideally, this allows for variance in community standards around the country. These fines do affect the network, because the network typically owns its largest and most profitable stations, such as those in markets including New York, Los Angeles, Chicago, Philadelphia, and Dallas. These stations, known as **owned and operated stations (O&Os)** in the business, guarantee a steady stream of revenue for national networks, whose business is more volatile. It is essential to remember, however, that the FCC directly regulates only broadcast stations, not the networks.

Perhaps we have belabored the distinction of broadcasting, but this distinction is a crucial and often overlooked part of media policy. For as long as we have been teaching about media industries, there has always been some policy issue that comes back to this distinction. In recent years, considerable attention has been devoted to questions of "indecency" on television—whether sexual content, vulgar language, or violent portrayals. Even though many of us now simply think of television—not of broadcast networks as distinct from cable channels—broadcasting is very different from a regulatory perspective. In recent debates, legislators have threatened to apply the same rules regarding content that govern broadcasters to cable channels. While the legislators are certainly within their rights to make such rules, it would be highly inconsistent with existing precedent and policy for any court to uphold such rules for cable.*

Additionally, we mustn't forget that broadcasters still make millions of dollars in profits using something that belongs to "us." It is through the use of the people's airwaves that much of the regulation regarding both content and industry structure has been justified. This is also why we should reasonably expect more from broadcasters; we should never think of them as simply "businesses" like any others because they are businesses that we underwrite by allowing them free use of spectrum.

We spend much more time attending to broadcast examples in this chapter because of the more significant influence that government-enforced regulation has for these media. We also, however, attend to laws and regulations regarding **copyright**, industry structure, and First Amendment protections that structure the behavior of media such as newspapers, films, and magazines, as well as regulations imposed internally by self-regulating bodies such as the Motion Picture Association of America's rating system.

WHO REGULATES?

Just as the governance structure of every country is a bit different, so, too, is there wide variety in who regulates media industries. Some countries spread powers over a broad range of commissions and bodies, while others try to centralize them in just a few. Certainly, in media systems with a public mandate, there is a significant amount of decision-making power concentrated in the body that oversees the operation of the national broadcasting system.

Governmental Bodies

In the United States, the FCC oversees many media regulations and is the governmental agency charged with managing telecommunications policy. It particularly has oversight of broadcasting (radio and television) and telephony (wired and wireless). Over the years it has also taken on considerable regulation of the cable industry. **The Federal Trade Commission (FTC)** regulates many aspects of the Internet and the advertising

---

*This link provides a story that discusses the lack of clarity about what can be said on broadcast networks versus cable networks. Based on the vocabulary in this chapter, how would you categorize the rules about acceptable and unacceptable language on US television? http://www.npr.org/2013/09/10/218525978/what -the-is-up-on-cable-these-days

industry. Media companies are also subject to the regulations faced by any other industry. The FTC and Department of Justice, for example, oversee the practices of all industries and ensure that companies do not develop unchecked or monopoly power.

Agencies such as the FCC and FTC carry out the policies enacted by the legislative and executive branches (e.g., major policies such as the **Telecommunications Act of 1996**) but also derive considerable power through their ability to make rules and selectively enforce them. The FCC comprises four commissioners and a chairperson, all appointed by the president and confirmed by the Senate. The FCC can develop and enact policies, but these can be "checked" by both the legislature and the judiciary. For example, in January 2014 the US Court of Appeals for the District of Columbia struck down the FCC's **net neutrality** regulations, which required Internet service providers to treat all of the traffic that comes across their networks equally, regardless of its content or origin, because the FCC did not have the authority under rules passed by Congress to make such a regulation.[2] Throughout 2015, the FCC developed new policy that reclassified the Internet in a way that would allow the FCC to regulate it. As this edition went to press, various companies had filed lawsuits contesting this policy too. Table 4.1 lists major legislation enacted by Congress that lays out the rules and regulations of media that the FCC must enforce.

Although the *making* of policies and regulations may be limited to Congress and their enforcement to the FCC, many other groups can *influence* policy. Perhaps those with the strongest influence are the **lobbyists** that represent the telecommunications industries. Most sectors of the media industry—particularly broadcasting and telephony—have industry associations that represent their interests to the FCC and Congress. Groups such as the National Association of Broadcasters (NAB), National Cable and Telecommunications Association, Motion Picture Association of America, and Recording Industry Association of America have deep pockets filled by the dues of their members. They use these funds to lobby the FCC and legislature to make sure new policies help rather than hinder their businesses. The watchdog group the Center for Responsive Politics reported that the telecommunications industry spent between $50 and $70 million per year lobbying Congress and regulators in the first half of the 2010s, while the television, movies, and music industries spent nearly $120 million in 2013.[3] The National Cable and Telecommunications Association ranked fifth in spending among all industries on lobbyists in 2013, while Comcast, a company whose interests are represented by the National Cable and Telecommunications Association, ranked seventh on its own. Such industry organizations also influence policy by testifying before Congress.

Certainly we, too, as voters and as consumers of media products, play a role. The FCC regularly invites "public comment," and legislative representatives often receive letters from constituents regarding policies. Unfortunately, the public is rarely organized, nor does it have the extensive funding of industry lobbyists. Not-for-profit groups such as the Consumers' Union and Free Press have developed considerable clout in recent years and do their best to represent the interests of the average citizen and to make sure changes in policy don't happen without public awareness. The media reform

Table 4.1 Major Congressional Regulatory Acts Affecting the U S Media Industries

YEAR	ACT	PROVISIONS
1912	Radio Act of 1912	• Mandated the licensing of all radio stations in the United States
1927	Radio Act of 1927	• Established the Federal Radio Commission, which had the power to grant and renew radio licenses and to assign bands and frequencies on the electromagnetic spectrum (thus reducing congestion and chaos)
1934	Communications Act of 1934	• Granted FCC the ability to assign frequencies, set rates and fees, establish standards, and mandate universal access for telecommunication services
1984	Cable Communications Policy Act	• Created guidelines for federal, state, and local regulation of cable companies • Mandated limits on local franchise fees to be charged to cable companies, offered minimal regulation of rates (basic cable only), established subscriber privacy protections, and sought to provide for a diversity of voices by mandating that cable companies set aside some bandwidth for unaffiliated programming
1992	Cable Television Consumer Protection and Competition Act	• Led to the creation of "must-carry" rules for cable companies (i.e., the requirement that they provide access to local TV broadcast stations at no charge) • Strengthened rate regulations on cable companies by granting franchise authorities (generally local municipalities) the ability to regulate rates for basic cable
1996	Telecommunications Act of 1996	• Facilitated deregulation within the telecommunications and media industry by • Opening up competition among local telephone providers • Loosening cross-media ownership rules (e.g., the elimination of network–cable ownership restrictions) • Increasing the national audience share limits of individual station groups from 25 percent to 35 percent • Extending broadcast license terms from 5 to 8 years; made renewal requirements less stringent

movement has grown more vibrant in recent years, but it often remains no match for the media industries' resources. Even though telecommunication policy affects all of us every day—from regulations regarding the bills we pay for services to the content different media outlets offer us—we rarely get involved in these issues or even form a position on a policy in the same way we might have a personal position on the death penalty or health-care policy.

Although we, the public, are often at a disadvantage in affecting media regulation because we lack the millions of dollars to spend on lobbyists and are often too busy with the demands of day-to-day life to organize and make our opinions known, even small acts can make a big difference. In January 2012, hundreds of popular websites went "dark" for the day to protest proposed legislation in the US Congress called the Stop

Online Piracy Act (SOPA). SOPA would have made it illegal for any site to link to or advertise with any website that contained pirated content. Protesters claimed that SOPA might criminalize the legal streaming of copyrighted content under the Digital Millennium Copyright Act and block access to entire web domains because of the presence of a single copyright infringement. Protestors included major websites, including Google and Wikipedia, effectively shutting down the Internet for one day and leading to millions of complaints, emails, and petitions by regular Internet users. While this popular protest did not immediately kill the legislation, it did effectively sound the death knell for SOPA, which languished for a while in committee before being withdrawn.

More recently, the issue of **net neutrality** drew considerable focus as the FCC reconsidered how it classifies the Internet, which would enable it to make rules governing how data traveling over the Internet could be treated. Though the populace rarely attends to media policy issues, the FCC received a record 3.7 million comments in response to its proposed rule-making, comments that overwhelmingly favored regulation that would ensure an open Internet.

The lesson here is that the public can play a crucial role in the regulation of media industries, and there are many points in the decision-making process where we can have a voice. It is also the case, however, that the deck is considerably stacked against us, as the companies that are regulated can devote much more time and money than can the public-at-large to making sure the policies advantage them.

International Regulations

In most of the world, broadcasting is regulated primarily on a national level, although some national regulatory bodies do cooperate with one another. Perhaps the most robust of these transnational regulatory groups is the European Platform of Regulatory Authorities, which includes 56 regulatory bodies in Europe. Although it does not have authority over the independent national regulators, it does serve as a clearinghouse and a kind of think-tank where members can work collaboratively on developments in broadcast regulation. Similar kinds of regulatory consortia exist in smaller regions of Europe, such as the Central European Regulatory Forum, as well as in Africa. These transnational regulatory consortia help their members deal with a range of extra-national issues in broadcasting, such as how and whether to restrict foreign media imports, as well as issues facing national regulatory bodies more generally. The African Communication Regulation Authorities Network, for instance, ran a series of conferences on how African nations might deal with the costs of transitioning to digital television.

While industries devoted to media content, such as broadcasting, cable television, film, and gaming, tend to be regulated primarily on a national level, the telecommunications infrastructure industries that deliver voice, video, and data services to the public typically face substantial international regulations in addition to national and local ones. Because the communications infrastructure has been international ever since the British began laying undersea cables in the nineteenth century, various treaties, conventions, and international regulatory bodies have developed to deal with the unique challenges of integrating technical systems across borders in ways that facilitate the smooth operation of global communications.

One recurring issue in the international regulation of the telecommunications infrastructure is the degree of control over international regulatory bodies that powerful nations wield, particular the United States and Western nations. After all, the nation that exerts the greatest control over telecommunications can reap not only undue financial gain but also military advantage through abilities to intercept classified communications. Since the 1890s, different models of managing the telecommunications infrastructure have evolved, including unilateral, multilateral, and multistakeholder models.

In **unilateral** models of international telecommunications governance, a single nation is in control of the global communications infrastructure. This was the case with submarine cables in the late nineteenth and early twentieth century, which were controlled by a single, quasi-independent British company. Since that time, however, most international regulatory regimes have had some degree of **multilateral** control, where participant nations—even businesses and civil society representatives—have some degree of control over policy decisions.

The World Intellectual Property Organization (WIPO) provides an example of multilaterial control. WIPO includes representatives from 187 member states and is responsible for setting international policies regarding the protection of intellectual property around the world, as well as enforcing those protections. Because Western nations and multinational corporations headquartered there have long been some of the primary beneficiaries of WIPO policies, widespread skepticism exists among policymakers and politicians elsewhere about the fairness of WIPO policies. For instance, in 2013 Pirate Parties International, a global network of political parties dedicated to loosening intellectual property laws in digital media, applied for "observer" status at the WIPO, which would have allowed its representative to listen in on and discuss matters before the organization. However, because of objections from three nations, including the United States, the Pirate Parties International was one of only two civil society organizations to have its application rejected.[4]

Although the world's powerful nations may have less control in multilateral policy bodies than they do in unilateral ones, they tend nevertheless to wield an undue measure of influence. Another important multilateral organization that regulates the media industries is the International Telecommunications Union, a specialized United Nations agency that assigns spectrum space for satellites and develops international standards for **information and communication technologies**. Both the WIPO and the International Telecommunications Union incorporate representatives from the business world and civil society, but the representatives are not full voting members of these policy bodies.

Finally, the International Corporation for Assigned Names and Numbers (ICANN), which governs the structure of the global Internet and assigns the names and numbers to web domains that permit the global interconnection of computers, operates on a multilateral governance model, where governments, businesses, and civil society representatives all have representation on the governing board. Despite its elaborate governance structure, however, ICANN has not been free of complaints about Western—particularly American—influence. In 2014 a controversy arose over plans to hand over control of ICANN from the US Department of Commerce to an unspecified set of global Internet stakeholders when the Commerce Department's contract with ICANN expired in September 2015. Critics of ICANN policy claim that the United States has undue influence when it comes to nominating members of the ICANN board and therefore benefits unduly from its policies. Some critics even suggest that the multistakeholder structure masks the rather unilateral structure of ICANN, claiming that American companies, civil society, and regulators are overrepresented. As is the case of any aspect of international policymaking, these examples illustrate the complicated nature of creating policies for entities that easily transcend the national boundaries that typically delimit rule-making.

Self-Regulation

We close this discussion of who regulates with the concept of self-regulation, which is arguably the most substantive regulating mechanism for a commercial media industry with free-speech protection. The "regulations" that are most responsible for producing the media content we are familiar with emerge from **informal self-regulation** that leads industry workers to perceive certain types of content as more or less commercially viable. In addition to this self-regulation based on what media creators perceive as commercially viable (which many would probably not think of as a regulation), they also engage in **formal self-regulation** through the creation of self-imposed rules limiting or categorizing content. For example, there is not an external governmental body that requires films or video games to be rated or that requires record labels to note explicit lyrics. These are all practices of self-regulation that the industries developed and maintain themselves. For example, the Entertainment Software Association—the trade group for game developers—created the Entertainment Software Rating Board to assign content ratings to video and computer games and to maintain agreed-on standards regarding advertising.* The Motion Picture Association of America and its film ratings system function similarly. In both cases, these groups assign ratings rather than decree certain kinds of content as permissible or impermissible—as was the case from the 1930s to the 1960s in the film industry, when the so-called Hays Code provided strict—yet self-imposed—rules regarding what content could and couldn't be included in a film.

In many cases, media industries use formal self-regulation as a defensive move in order to head off actual government-imposed regulation, which almost always will be more stringent than what the media companies might enact on their own. One example of this can be found in the Family Hour regulation of television in the 1970s. In response to mounting cultural discussion about television content, the three networks agreed to broadcast only programs that might be suitable for the entire family during the first hour of primetime, 8:00 to 9:00 PM. There was no governing body set up to make sure that all the networks followed this agreement, and it gradually faded from practice after the threat of governmental regulation dissipated. Currently, many cable networks impose safe-harbor hours on themselves, choosing to air programming with adult

---

*This link to a story that discusses how the Entertainment Software Rating Board operates. Does this seem an adequate method for rating content? What are some of the strengths and limitations? http://www.npr.org/templates/story/story.php?storyId=123971771

content only after 10 PM in an effort to look like good citizens and avoid drawing legisla-tors' ire that might lead to government regulation. Fans of shows that originally air after 10:00 PM such as *The Daily Show* will sometimes see edited versions during daytime reruns and unedited version at night in response to Comedy Central's practice of airing content more appropriate for all ages before 10:00 PM.

All sorts of self-regulation were evident in the first decade of the twenty-first cen-tury in the US television industry as the networks attempted to figure out the boundar-ies of what the FCC felt was a finable offense. The immediate precipitating event was Janet Jackson's infamous "wardrobe malfunction" during the 2004 Super Bowl halftime show, when fellow pop star Justin Timberlake tore at her blouse, briefly exposing her breast. In the wake of this event, the Parents Television Council stepped up its pressure on networks and legislators to reign in indecency on television, and many networks toned down the sexual and violent content of series because they were uncertain what would be considered acceptable. A number of affiliates also chose not to air program-ming offered by their network. In one of the most profound cases, several ABC affiliates chose not to air the film *Saving Private Ryan* in 2004 (scheduled in honor of Veterans' Day) out of concern that the violence and explicit language might lead to fines from the FCC—despite the fact that the film had aired previously without penalty. In 2012 the Supreme Court voted unanimously that the FCC had overstepped its authority by levy-ing many of these fines for fleeting expletives and sexual content on live and scripted programming during the previous decade.

An interesting counterpoint to self-regulation in the broadcasting industries comes from the magazine industry. In this case, the industry changed its operating principles to avoid government regulation. In the late 1990s, a few states' attorneys general an-nounced they were seeking to ban magazine sweepstakes, a promotional practice whereby publishers seek to gain new subscribers through direct mailings that both pub-licize magazines and offer opportunities to win prizes. The attorneys general claimed the sweepstakes were deceptive because the mailings suggested purchases were neces-sary in order to win. The Magazine Publishers Association responded by setting its own new set of ethical guidelines, which included conspicuous "no purchase necessary" dis-claimers, in hopes of preventing an outright sweepstakes ban, although these changes made no real impact on the actual content of the magazines themselves.

In the cable industry, cable service providers responded to complaints from sub-scribers about having to buy large packages of cable channels that included content sub-scribers objected to. Though many subscribers remain frustrated with the large bundles of channels they must buy, many cable service providers did begin offering "family-friendly" tiers in response to these complaints, likely to ward off government interven-tion in their lucrative practice of selling cable channels only in these large bundles.

As some of these cases indicate, merely the threat of regulation can be enough to change media-industry content or practice, and self-regulation can be very real and significant. In another case, some media critics posited that one of the reasons that many of the networks accepted the increasingly stringent FCC policy on indecency in the mid-2000s was because they wanted the FCC to adopt more liberal ownership poli-cies. Of course it is impossible to know, but this points to the kinds of interconnections between structural conditions and industry practices that the Industrialization of Culture framework highlights.

WHAT IS REGULATED?

Content Regulations

Social panics—or widespread, often hysterical outcries related to fears about media content and their social and psychological effects—have existed since the beginnings of the media. Often, these panics raise concerns about the consequences of sexual and violent content and the effects this content might have on children. More recently, fears about how social media and mobile devices might replace human interaction and increase dangerous behaviors like texting while driving and cyberbullying have grown more acute. Social panics have developed around all types of media, from films (concern about juvenile delinquency in the 1950s), to music (explicit rap lyrics in the early 1990s), to video games (violence in first-person shooter games). Because of broadcasting's use of public airwaves, however, regulators have been able to impose more governmental regulations on broadcast content, while these concerns have more commonly been addressed in other industries through formal and informal self-regulation.

Content regulation by any body—government appointed or otherwise—in the United States is difficult because of the First Amendment guarantee of free speech. Most policies that attempt any prior censorship of the media—in other words, policies that prohibit or prevent speech—typically run afoul of the right to free speech, with a few significant exceptions. By rulings of the Supreme Court, content can be prevented from circulating—called **prior restraint**—if it is **obscene**, a type of speech that is not protected by the First Amendment. The Supreme Court provided the current working definition of obscenity in the 1973 case *Miller v. California*. This ruling emphasized the idea that different communities are likely to have varying definitions of obscenity—so what might be considered obscene is not the same everywhere. Obscene works are those "which, taken as a whole, appeal to the prurient interest in sex, which portray sexual conduct in a patently offensive way, and which, taken as a whole, do not have serious literary, artistic, political, or scientific value." As you can see, this definition isn't exceptionally clear, and because most media content is designed to circulate in many communities, most content created by the media industries steers well clear of the distinction of obscenity.

A second type of speech, that which is **indecent**, is also prohibited on the airwaves at certain times, but it is not subject to prior restraint. In a 1992 policy statement, the FCC defined indecency as "language or material that, in context, depicts or describes, in terms patently offensive as measured by contemporary community standards for the broadcast medium, sexual or excretory activities or organs"—a definition derived from the Supreme Court's finding in *FCC v. Pacifica Foundation* (1978). After extensive negotiation among the FCC, legislature, and the courts, the court of appeals upheld the FCC practice of establishing the hours of 10:00 PM to 6:00 AM as a **safe harbor** in which indecent content is allowed because broadcasters can reasonably assume children will not be in the audience. Although statements by recent FCC chairmen have led broadcasters to wonder, it is generally the case that broadcasters need not fear fines for airing content deemed indecent, so long as it airs during the safe-harbor time frame.

Despite the broad protections of the First Amendment, *there is considerable content regulation that develops as a part of a commercial system that is unrelated to regulatory mechanisms enforced by the government.* Commercial media determine their success by their profitability, and, consequently, commercial media industries are highly aware of general sentiment regarding the lines of acceptable content. Media makers limit themselves to content likely to be deemed acceptable because it will affect whether consumers are willing to purchase media directly (in the case of the film or music industries, for example) or companies are willing to place advertising messages within it. Particularly in the era of mass media, the need to draw the largest possible audience led media outlets to develop content as inoffensive to as many as possible. The television networks sought to create programs that could be watched by the whole family—from grandparents to the young children who were still likely to be in the audience during early-evening hours. Much of the **least objectionable programming** of earlier periods of television came less from any kind of governmental regulation than from more stringent social standards and from self-regulation based on commercial interest at the time.

Content standards have certainly loosened in the past few decades, and much of this can be traced to changes in the business of many of these industries, particularly the kinds of large economic changes that have swept the world economies. Consider television: as new cable channels and broadcast networks such as Fox, MTV, and ESPN began competing with the "Big Three" broadcast networks (ABC, CBS, NBC) for audiences, most achieved success by targeting narrow and specific audiences—such as teens and young adults in the case of Fox and MTV. These audiences had always watched television, but they were not specifically targeted by the Big Three, who had an economic mandate to simultaneously reach older adults as well. New networks and channels haven't tried to capture the broadest audience; instead, they've offered programming that might not be considered acceptable to all audiences (as those who might remember rules about what shows or channels parents wouldn't let them watch can recall).

Increasingly, risqué language and controversial stories uncommon in television's past have begun to appear more frequently. *Rather than a shift in regulation or even a change in nationwide cultural standards, adjustments in economic conditions and business practices account for much of this change.* The steady addition of many more narrowly targeted broadcast and cable channels created outlets for programming that attends to the more mature tastes of some audiences. In many cases, these new networks drew away the audience members who were most attractive to advertisers: the young and affluent. In order to compete to maintain these viewers, the Big Three then had to also broaden their definitions of acceptable content in order to stay competitive.

Even though we might think of content norms as regulated by official government sanctioned rules, in a commercial system it is arguably the case that the system of commerce also provides a stringent, and perhaps even dominant, form of content regulation—that informal self-regulation mentioned a few pages ago. Media producers are wary of including content that will not attract a profitable audience, and in the case of advertiser-financed media, they are also concerned about maintaining content standards that will be acceptable to advertisers. Every advertiser has a slightly different threshold of concern regarding the content it advertises in and its willingness to be associated with controversy. Some advertisers are highly risk-averse and back out of programming with even a whiff of controversy because they fear boycott from consumers or the tarnishing of their "family-friendly" brand (this, for example, has been the reputation of consumer health care products manufacturer Johnson & Johnson). Other advertisers might have a product less likely to be negatively affected by a boycott and be willing to accept this risk in exchange for the lower advertising rates they might receive as a result of boycotts by other advertisers. Film studios, for example, are rarely boycotted as a whole because of the advertising of a single film. Still others seek the audiences likely to consume media that garner controversy and find boundary-defying content particularly valuable—as is the case with condom ads and ads for hard liquor, which mainly air only cable channels targeting younger, but adult, audiences. As a result, this form of commerce-based self-regulation operates inconsistently.

Copyright

We often think of content regulations in terms of what the government or business conditions will or will not allow the media industries to create, and, as you've seen, the First Amendment tends to allow very few restrictions of this nature. A much more limiting type of content restriction that affects both the operation of the media industries and the behavior of media consumers are limits resulting from copyright laws.

Copyright law is crucial to the media industries because it ensures the ongoing economic value of their products. Copyright protects the creators of music, poetry, books, and all sorts of video creations from those who might access a copy and distribute this work as their own for profit. The need for and specificity of copyright law in some ways relates to those distinctive attributes of media we discussed in Chapter 2. The "public good" status of media makes them particularly susceptible to being stolen in a manner very different from private goods with a physical form. This susceptibility has only grown in recent years with the introduction of digital reproduction, which allows users to generate exact copies of original media files and then distribute that content digitally through **peer-to-peer networks** that allow consumers to broadly share media files. In these examples, changes in technological conditions and distribution practices have led to revised regulatory conditions for the media industries.

Many of our students enter our classes vaguely familiar with copyright laws as a result of stern warnings that they've received from their parents and universities about illegal downloading and piracy. We talk about the ways that digital distribution has complicated copyright law and led to some new thinking about intellectual property later in this section, but it is first important to understand that copyright is a very old legal concept, and, without it, it is likely the media industries would never have emerged as they have. Some scholars trace the origins of copyright to the advent of the printing press in the 1600s, and this concept has been part of legal thinking in the United States virtually since the founding of the country: the copyright clause was added to the US Constitution in 1787. Article I, Section 8, Clause 8 explains, "To promote the Progress of Science and useful Arts, by securing for limited Times to Authors and Inventors the exclusive Right to their respective Writings and Discoveries." Copyright law then protects "all works of authorship fixed in a tangible medium of expression" and gives to the author or owner of the copyright the "sole and exclusive right to reproduce the work in any form for any reason."[5] No one else may reproduce the work without prior consent, often given in the form of a license. Copyright thus prevents others from using or profiting from expressive or artistic creations.

Duration of copyright has been an issue of ongoing contention for regulators. Copyright law was revised in 1976 to generally allow for copyright to last for the life of the author plus 50 years or, in the case of corporate authorship, 75 years. In 1998, the Copyright Term Extension Act extended the copyright period to life of the author plus 70 years and for corporate authors to 120 years after creation or 95 years after publication, whichever endpoint is earlier. The relevance of copyright law to media industries is evident in the degree to which they lobbied heavily for the extension. Copyright law creates valuable markets in which media industries license their products to viewers, readers, or listeners. Without copyright protection, consumers would be free to use creative products in any way they desire. Or, of more concern to media industries, once copyright expires, media products fall into the **public domain**. This means that rights no longer need to be paid to the originator.

One important exception to copyright law is the **fair use** provision. Fair use allows for limited copying or use of a product that is protected by copyright as long as it is in accord with a few key provisions. The 1976 Copyright Act allows that "The fair use of a copyrighted work . . . for purposes such as criticism, comment, news reporting, teaching (including multiple copies for classroom use), scholarship or research is not an infringement of copyright."[6] Fair use is of great importance to your professors, who otherwise would have to license every clip shown in class and would prohibit class resources such as making readings available though electronic reserve systems.

There is also ongoing legislative debate about what counts as "personal use" for general (noneducational) media consumers, such as what kinds of personal uses consumers are entitled to after purchasing media. For example, when you buy a CD of music or pay to download a song, what rights do you have? A series of decisions growing out of the Audio Home Recording Act of 1992 and the Digital Millennium Copyright Act of 1998 have been enacted to set clear parameters on what consumers can do with the media they purchase and to authorize and require consumer electronics industries to create technological barriers to some actions. The recording industry was particularly keen to have these regulations enacted before consumer electronics companies introduced technologies that would allow digital recording, due to fear that consumers would be able to make "perfect" copies that they would then distribute illegally—an action often referred to as **piracy**. Similar regulatory actions have followed that allow for the DVD zone system (which enables film studios to maintain artificial scarcity around the globe in DVD release schedules), and other forms of **digital rights management** (**DRM**) that prevent copying purchased media files among devices or recording them to a physical medium.

Digital rights management can control your use of media in many different ways, such as allowing only a certain number of viewings, allowing digital files to work for certain periods of time, allowing only specified movement of files (loading to so many computers or players), and preventing printing or saving of files. Considerable debate and uncertainty about the stringency of DRM remains, as some argue that many aspects of DRM violate fair-use provisions. Much of the legal support for DRM can be found in the Digital Millennium Copyright Act of 1998. These provisions remain controversial; many have been subject to court rulings that have sometimes tightened, and at other times loosened, the act's original provisions.

As you may have guessed by the repeated use of the word "digital" in the last few paragraphs, the digital media are ushering in new challenges for the media industries in their efforts to maintain and enforce copyright protections—challenges that might force them to fundamentally redefine their operations. The ability to easily create "perfect" copies of media goods has heightened many of the concerns about piracy or illegal file sharing. To a considerable extent, it is the actions of a few—or even just the technological possibility of violating copyright—that has led to disabling personal use of media through DRM. Nevertheless, these threats remain very real for media industries, as widespread adoption of such behavior threatens to undermine their economic models.

Another challenging aspect of contemporary copyright policing results from the easy circulation of digital files over international boundaries. In many cases, international copyright is supported through a series of treaties, but adjudicating violations becomes much more challenging when dealing with different systems of law and varied national policies.

Chances are many of you wouldn't dream of selling "bootleg" copies of media (we hope), yet some of what might seem like basic media activities that you engage in daily may still violate copyright laws. Have you ever made a video and used a popular song in the background? Have you ever reproduced the lyrics of a poem or a song on a blog? These activities may also violate copyright unless you license the song or lyrics from the copyright holder (and in the case of poems and song lyrics, just a few lines are often held as violations).

Others who create media works may sample from licensed works or subtly alter an existing work in order to create a parody. To date, the Supreme Court has upheld the use of copyrighted works in parodies that add new perspective to the work, critique it, or encourage audiences to see it in a new way—although meeting these grounds is a fairly subjective judgment. Sampling, once a staple of hip-hop music, has diminished considerably in response to rising costs of licensing and more stringent interpretations of copyright law. In 2008 the average base cost of "clearing" a sample (establishing a legal agreement that allows the use of the sample and sets a payment for its use) was $10,000 and much higher in many cases. Samples must be cleared with both the owners of the master recording (typically the recording label) and the owner of the publishing rights (typically the songwriter). Legal action against unauthorized sampling has been much more expensive. In 2006 Bridgeport Music and Westbound Records won $4.2 million in damages because of unauthorized samples on Notorious B.I.G.'s *Ready to Die* album.[7]

Fear of lawsuits and high license fees have curbed the use of sampling by those within the commercial music industry, but sampling remains curiously central among alternative and underground DJs—even though they have no legal protection.

One notable case is a musician who performs under the name Girl Talk who has released a number of albums made up of mashups and sampling. To date, Girl Talk has never been sued despite the clear violation of copyright in his work. Such situations point to the complexity of media industry operation, as the major labels whose work he uses are certainly aware of his violations but allow him to continue. Chapter 8 begins with more on the issue of sampling and distribution.*

One response to the dangers and promises of the digital age—for both sharing and producing media—has been the **Creative Commons** movement. Those who establish a Creative Commons license for their work waive some of their rights in order to more easily allow others to share and build upon their work while still maintaining some of the rights of copyright. There are six different Creative Commons licenses. The most restrictive allows only redistribution with attribution; the least restrictive allows redistribution as well as changing and adjusting the work, even for commercial ends, as long as the original author is credited. Creative Commons founder Lawrence Lessig is a central thinker involved in exploring new models for the circulation of ideas and creative products, particularly on the Internet. Without a doubt, there remain many unresolved and unclear aspects of how copyright law will be enforced in the digital age and what rights users will maintain in their personal use of media.

Structural and Operational Regulations

As a media consumer, you probably have more familiarity with content regulations than with this second type of regulation, which we categorize as structural and operational regulations. These regulations are related to the business practices and functioning of media companies. Rules regarding who can own media companies and how many media entities an individual or company can own—either in a particular location or across the country—are prime illustrations of structural regulations. Regulations on ownership are quite extensive and varied in comparison with non-media industries; this increased attention to ownership mainly evolves from those factors we discussed in Chapter 1 that make media industries unlike others. We also include economic regulation of the media industries as a type of structural regulation. Such regulations include rate controls and policies that provide subsidies to the media industries. Structural regulations vary by industry and some industries, such as broadcasting, face much more extensive structural regulations than others. Table 4.2 offers a quick reference of different types of structural regulations and examples of each.

Ownership Regulations

Perhaps the most extensive form of regulation can be found in ownership regulations, some of which apply to specific industries and others that apply across industries. Some ownership regulations particularly target broadcasters; other media, however, also are

---

*This link to a documentary about Girl Talk, *Good Copy Bad Copy*, illustrates how this artist uses others' materials. Consider what value Girl Talk adds. Should this be allowed? http://www.youtube.com/watch?v=VlPkIS-uNMk

Table 4.2 Examples of Structural Regulation

TYPE	EXAMPLE	DESCRIPTION
Ownership	Local Radio Ownership	Limits the number of radio stations and services (AM/FM) an individual or entity can own in a single market. The maximum allowance for large markets with over 45 stations is 8 total, with no more than 5 in either AM or FM.
Economic	Franchise Fees	Fees paid by cable companies to local municipalities for rights of access. The 1984 Cable Act limited the maximum amount a municipality may collect to no more than 5 percent.
Licensing	Broadcast Station License	Establishes the conditions under which a TV or radio station can apply for a license, the guidelines it must abide by in operating the station, and the maximum term of the license between renewals (currently 8 years).
Monopoly and Antitrust	Comcast-NBC Merger	When Comcast set out to buy NBC in 2009, the deal was subject to review by the US Department of Justice and the Federal Communications Commission. The deal was finally approved in 2011 with several conditions imposed on Comcast. Comcast had to provide additional access to Spanish-level programming, expand local news coverage, offer Internet access to schools and libraries, and abdicate management responsibility in Hulu.

subject to regulations regarding ownership scale and concentration that distinguish media industries from the regulation of ownership common in other industries.

In the case of television, although we might associate a station in our home city with a network, it is likely that the network doesn't actually own that station. Most stations around the country were once stand-alone operations—"mom and pop" family businesses. Now, stations are typically owned by a **station group**—that is, an entity that owns stations affiliated with various networks located in cities around the country—or are network O&O stations. In the past, fairly significant limitations restricted the number of stations an individual entity could own nationwide. This number increased until the FCC shifted to the current "percent reach" standard. Now, instead of limiting the *number* of stations a single entity can own, the regulation specifies a *percentage* of the population that any station owner may reach, which is 39 percent as of this writing (although some exceptions were granted that allow a few companies to minimally exceed this limit as a result of mergers).

In the radio industry, the Telecommunications Act of 1996 lifted the limit on national ownership, and a massive consolidation of the industry quickly followed. Companies such as Clear Channel quickly amassed enormous station holdings, at one point owning more than 1,200 radio stations nationwide. This act also increased the possibilities for television-station ownership and set up a structure of regular review of rules with the possibility of continued loosening of the restrictions. The example of radio proved a cautionary tale, however, and efforts to continue to diminish the ownership limits of television have been met with protest and resulted in keeping close to the guidelines set out by the Telecomm Act. Ownership rules have also limited the number of stations (radio and television) that can be owned in a specific market.

The FCC has devoted much of its policymaking work since the Telecomm Act of 1996 to ownership—partially because the act requires review every few years. Why is ownership such a significant policy area? All industries face some ownership regulation—ultimately this is how we might categorize regulations against monopolies. More stringent regulations for media industries exist because of the undeniable social and cultural role of media and the perceived value of preserving a diversity of voices and particularly those of the local community. Ownership is a central site through which regulators can prevent the control of media outlets by too few entities and try to make them responsive to the communities in which they are located.

Another set of media ownership regulations deals with **cross-ownership**—or the ownership of companies in multiple media industries. Ownership of a newspaper and a broadcast station in the same market was prohibited until 2007 (now there are a complicated array of situations in which that is allowable), and cross-ownership of a cable system and a broadcast station in the same market was forbidden until 2003, yet limits on owning television and radio stations within the same market in cities of a certain size remain. These regulations have been in place because of the particularly local nature of media in the past and the value associated with local media. For example, if most of your news comes from the local radio station, television station, and newspaper, then it is desirable to prevent one company from dominating all of those outlets in order to maintain a diversity of voices—even if that media company also owns other media entities outside of the city. Ownership regulations, then, are typically structured to address the desire to maintain both a **diversity of voices** and **localism** in media industries.

Ownership remains one of the most contested sites of media regulation and policy. Many in the media industries desire continued deregulation to be free of the limits that prevent them from further expanding their businesses. From the perspective of the media industries, the advantage of expansion involves increasing the economies of scale of their businesses. For example, many stations desire to develop what are called **duopolies** (owning two stations in one city) so that many of the "backroom" costs can be consolidated—such as combining the sales forces of these stations and eliminating duplicate positions, since a single sales staffer can efficiently service two stations when making a sales call. Or perhaps in traveling around the country you've noticed radio stations that sound practically the same or television stations using identical graphics. This is because station groups combine as many of their needs as possible within one facility. For example, NBC has a production facility in Fort Worth, Texas, that produces many of the graphics and design features for all of the NBC O&O stations around the country.

Consolidating work such as graphic design and sales may not seem to threaten the diversity of voices in a community, but the efforts at cost-saving do not stop there. Clear Channel drew considerable criticism in 2003 when reports emerged that "voice-tracking" had become an increasingly common part of its operations. Voice-tracking involves using talent in another city; for example, a DJ based in San Francisco may voice the morning show in San Francisco but have an afternoon show in Dallas that is produced from San Francisco with no suggestion to the Dallas audience that the show is not produced locally.

In another disconcerting case that many media activists have pointed to as illustrative of the real dangers of lifting ownership limits, some stations operate with few or no live personnel, instead having their content piped in by satellite. This allowed for a dangerous situation in the town of Minot, North Dakota, in 2002.[8] A freight train carrying a dangerous substance—anhydrous ammonia—derailed, and a cloud of gas threatened the town. The city's emergency alert system failed, so police called the town radio stations—six of which were owned by Clear Channel. Police were unable to reach anyone at Clear Channel–owned KCJB, the designated emergency broadcaster, because the station did not keep anyone at the station, since the programming originated elsewhere.

A desire for cost savings and efforts to make news media more profitable have led to fewer jobs for journalists at local papers that instead rely heavily on news services such as the Associated Press. It was once the case that each of the television networks had news correspondents based around the world and large newspapers maintained their own reporters in Washington and other cities with important regular events. As media have consolidated, many of these jobs have been eliminated and just one reporter provides the same story for most of the country. Sometimes there may be valuable efficiencies here, but many of the local aspects of national and international stories get lost when a journalist is charged with writing a story as relevant to the residents of Albuquerque as of Ann Arbor.

Economic Regulations: Rate Control and Subsidies

Another way media industries are regulated is through rate control. In the United States, this typically has been applied in industries that are allowed to function as monopolies. Some media have argued that they are **natural monopolies**, monopolies that develop because it is so inefficient for there to be competition. The first such media monopoly was the telegraph. Connecting the country by wire required an enormous initial investment, and Western Union argued that it should be allowed to exist as a monopoly because it was so wasteful for a competitor to duplicate its effort in stringing wire. The outcome was for the government to allow Western Union to remain without competition as long as the government was granted more extensive regulatory powers. This same logic then followed with the telephone and cable television industries.

These days, we are probably most aware of rate regulation in cable television. As cable was deployed around the country, cable providers entered into contracts with cities and municipalities, called franchises. These agreements established a single provider of cable service for the community and allowed it access to use and dig up public property to create the physical cable system. To win these franchises, cable providers guaranteed a specific package of services—often the availability of a certain number of public access channels and some funding to support production for them based on its profits from local subscribers. These franchise agreements set up a monopoly for service in each community. The agreements are renegotiated periodically (roughly every 15 years), but they allow individual cable subscribers little recourse if rates rise precipitously or they receive poor service (other than dropping the service entirely). Cable rates nationwide rose so significantly in the 1980s (three times the rate of infla- tion in some cases) that Congress stepped in with reregulation of cable at the same time it took a deregulatory approach to other media. Once satellite television began compet- ing with cable in the mid-1990s and the Telecommunications Act of 1996 allowed phone companies to offer "cable" service as well, the market force of competition led to some- what greater accountability by the cable industry—at least until it became a largely monopoly provider of broadband service.

Certain kinds of taxes and requirements to fund various initiatives also function as a type of rate-related regulation. If you've ever taken the time to go through your phone or cable bill, you'll find a number of small fees that you pay each month for things such as the "universal service" fund and 911 fees, among others. In some cases, Congress has determined that access to certain media may be necessary for basic functioning in soci- ety. This is the case with the universal service fund, which was established to help sub- sidize the cost of basic phone service for those who cannot afford it. Additionally, access to emergency services, as provided by dialing 911, is thought to be a service fundamen- tal to the public good. Legislation requires its availability, and phone companies pass the costs of maintaining it to their customers.

These regulations do not always require fees; sometimes they have to do with man- dating certain services. For example, the cable industry is mandated to provide a basic service package (that it does not advertise) that provides truly basic service for $10 to $15 per month. This service, sometimes called "lifeline," typically includes no more than the local broadcast networks, public access channels, and the local public broad- casting station. In recent years, legislators have threatened to require cable systems to offer a greater array of packages for subscription, such as a "family tier" or even "à la carte" channels, meaning that subscribers could pick whichever channels they want and pay a fee per channel, rather than being forced to select from packages determined by cable providers.

Governments also offer provisions that aid the operation of media industries in the form of subsidies to various industries. For example, US corporate tax code allows cor- porations to deduct their spending on advertising from their profits to reduce their tax payment. In another case, many countries (not the United States) provide subsidies to their domestic film industries in order to help increase indigenous production and to help smaller national cinemas compete with the output of media capitals such as Holly- wood, Bombay, or Hong Kong. These subsidies often come in the form of tax breaks or outright grants. In the United States, various states and municipalities have been devel- oping similar programs in recent years in hopes of bringing productions to their regions that would spend considerably in the local economy.

Licenses and License Renewal

Licensing is a structural regulation that affects only broadcasters. The FCC grants li- censes. In the past, stations were required to file for renewal every five years, but recent deregulation has decreased that frequency to every eight years. Typically, renewal is the only time the FCC really checks to see if a station is making an acceptable effort toward serving its public interest obligations, and even this review is cursory. Citizens are invited to submit letters regarding the performance of the station, and if the FCC has received complaints since the last renewal or has levied fines against the broadcaster, these are also likely to be part of the renewal consideration.

All that said, it has been very uncommon for a station to lose its license; the FCC renews more than 98 percent of requests.[9] One of the rare and oft-cited times a license was revoked involved the television station WLBT in Jackson, Mississippi. Complaints against this station, which was accused of blatantly discriminating against blacks in the community—a group that comprised 45 percent of its audience—began in 1955, but the station's license was not canceled until 1969, when the FCC was ordered to do so by an appeals court.[10] The drawn-out hearings and legal decisions from this case are what led the FCC to recognize that citizens have legal standing in license renewal cases, rather than just considering whether there is signal interference or economic injury to another broadcaster, which had been the previous standards. Despite this, regular license renewal has not served as a significant form of regulating the behavior of stations so much as it has been a periodic bureaucratic exercise.

Recently, some activists concerned about media policy have attempted to use license renewal as an opportunity to hold broadcasters accountable. Organized efforts to contest the renewal of stations developed in 2006, with community advocates arguing that the stations had not served their public-interest obligations, particularly because they had afforded limited attention to local politics. To date, none of these efforts has resulted in the loss of a license; it may be the case, however, that the organized threat led stations to pay greater attention to serving the public good. Such a situation could be considered an example of self-regulation—illustrating how media industries often police themselves in order to avoid the incursion of governmental regulation.

Monopoly and Antitrust Restrictions

Monopoly and **antitrust regulations** prevent too much industry consolidation—and can be very significant to media industry operation, as our opening anecdote about the Paramount Decree illustrated. In the United States, the Department of Justice commonly handles these policies along with the FTC, which is also responsible for rules regarding truth in advertising and consumer complaints against companies. The nature of the media industries perhaps leads to more potentially monopolistic arrangements than others. For example, since 2000s, the government has considered, and made different decisions when posed with mergers that would create monopolies in the satellite television and satellite radio businesses. When these industries began, the FCC auctioned off a limited number of licenses for the necessary spectrum to operate these technologies, and in both cases two competitors outlasted the competition (television: DirecTV and EchoStar; radio: Sirius and XM). Also in both cases, after roughly a decade of competition, the companies proposed to merge. The television merger was turned down by the FCC in 2002.[11] The satellite companies argued that their merger would not really create a monopoly because satellite has cable as a competitor, and, in some places, telcos such as Verizon and AT&T would soon offer competing service as well. One of the most persuasive arguments against the satellite television merger, however, was what might have happened to many rural households that live far from major cities where cable or telco service is not available. These homes would face just one provider if a satellite monopoly were allowed.

In what seemed almost a case of déjà vu, the two satellite radio companies proposed a merger in 2007. The Department of Justice and the FCC both had to approve this merger, and they imposed some conditions before ultimately approving it. Significantly, the FCC required the merged companies to provide à la carte pricing so that consumers could purchase only stations of interest, that 4 percent of channels be reserved for pubic service or minority programming, and that the company allow any manufacturer to make sets capable of receiving the service.

As this edition went to press, a merger between DirecTV and AT&T was pending. The previous discussion illustrates the requirements that regulators often insist on when they allows mergers and acquistitions that are likely to decrease competition. In the case of media industries, regulators do not only worry about having enough competitors to allow for a competitive marketplace as they might in any industry, but maintaining a diversity of voices is also an explicit regulatory goal in media policy.

OTHER REGULATORY CONDITIONS

Regulations Governing Distribution

The question about whether to allow satellite monopolies highlights the increasing importance of regulating the distribution of media goods. The regulation of distribution involves rules about how media distributors use their technologies to help or hinder the messages that pass along their systems. This wasn't a big issue in the past because media service providers weren't really technologically capable of providing differential service. This is quickly emerging as a major policy concern as digital broadband networks become the central media infrastructure of society.

As we noted earlier in the chapter, the words most commonly associated with this area of media policy are **network** or **net neutrality**. Net neutrality is the principle that Internet service providers not discriminate among messages or users, that they pass along all messages at equal speeds, and that users be able to access all web pages regardless of their service provider. Concerns about establishing regulations ensuring net neutrality developed in response to suspicions that Internet service providers might try to be more profitable by selling premium speeds of delivery service and that some providers were not operating with neutrality by slowing peer-to-peer file sharing.

As we write, the broadband industry remains in its youth, and the history of other communication technologies has illustrated that these industries often evolve significantly from the industrial models that undergird their first years. In just a decade, we have witnessed a transition from a pay-per-minute model of dial-up access to the all-you-can use subscription model now common with broadband, and some providers have suggested a transition back to a use-based fee schedule. Though these are economic matters—which are more the provenance of the next chapter—we seek to point out the degree to which the Internet industry, such that there is one, lacks much certainty in these operating conditions. These issues were being contentionsly debated as we finished this edition and will continue to be an area of debate for media policy and regulation in coming years.

An Emerging Area: Broadband Policy

Just as regulators, citizens, and commercial interests struggled to develop the regulatory structure for broadcast technology in the first part of the twentieth century, the early twenty-first century requires the establishment of policies governing the broadband devices that will only continue to grow in importance. Although we are very familiar with broadband technologies, and would perhaps be lost without them, many countries have only limited governmental broadband policies (the United States lags particularly behind here). Many of the existing rules and ideas about how broadband services should be regulated are adapted from the precedents of broadcast and telephony policy. As we write in early 2015, the United States is beginning to embark on a coherent and systematic approach to broadband policy. The chances are good that much of this policy determination will remain ongoing as this book finds its way to readers.

Though there are far fewer rules, policies, and certainly limited judicial review of broadband regulation at this point, much of the history of broadcast policy may indeed provide a conceptual starting point for thinking about how broadband can and should be regulated. Imagine the likely policy difference if legislators determine the infrastructure of the Internet to be a public good in the same manner as the electromagnetic spectrum used for broadcasting. This would lead to a model of regulation very different than if they continue to leave most decisions about "regulating" broadband to the commercial marketplace. Or imagine how different broadband access and opportunities might look if legislators advance policies that make universal service a goal, in the same manner as was done in the case of telephony.

Prosocial Regulation

Content regulation can take on additional dimensions beyond those mentioned previously. In addition to *restricting* the kinds of content that the media industries produce, in some cases, regulations actively *encourage* the creation of particular kinds of content. Media scholars David Croteau and William Hoynes describe efforts to encourage the production of certain types of media as a **cultural interventionist** approach to media regulation;[12] such policies are most often found in the case of media with a public mandate. Cultural interventionist policies seek to encourage voices other than those of commercially motivated media and can take the form of content and structural regulations. Often in public media systems, the state is viewed as a legitimate intervener in cultural policy. Unlike the norm in a commercial system, in which the mantra is often "let the market decide," cultural interventionist policies encourage the production of media believed to have some sort of prosocial effect.

A historical example of this can be found in the early development of the British Broadcasting Coporation. Under the management of Lord John Reith as director-general, the British Broadcasting Coporation particularly developed programming believed to "uplift" the population—the sort of "high art" content that is often caricatured as the only content produced by a public system. In these early years of broadcasting, some argued that the medium could be used to bring art and cultural forms that had been available only to the upper classes to the mass population. Consequently, production budgets favored the broadcasting of operas and symphony performances and the staging of "great works" of theater in order to "advance" the tastes of mass culture.

Perhaps a more recognizable example of cultural interventionist policies can be found here in the United States: government support of the Children's Television Workshop and the production of shows such as *Sesame Street*. In addition to giving some financial support to programming designed to help children learn in an environment free of commercial messages, children's commercial television is also more highly regulated than other forms. For example, broadcasters are mandated to air a certain number of hours of children's programming per week, and specific regulations dictate how many commercial minutes can be included in that content.

Another regulation of content common outside of the United States, although not necessarily particular to public media systems, are regulations on the national origin of content. Such regulations—often described as production quotas—were created to help support the development of indigenous media content after years of heavy reliance on imports, particularly from the United States. The Audiovisual Without Frontiers directive, for instance, requires that European broadcasters air a majority of programming produced in the European Union. In addition, most countries, with the exception of the United States, have what are known as **co-production** treaties with other nations, which permit television programs and films created by an international production team to count as domestically produced content in both signatories' markets. In addition to import quotas and co-production treaties, many nations also provide subsidies to help fund domestic media production, a strategy that we take up in more detail in Chapter 10.

Technological Standards: The Case of the Digital Television Transition

Sometimes the government steps in with major regulations. We've discussed some aspects of the comprehensive Telecommunications Act of 1996 already, but perhaps the regulation most directly affecting many of our readers was to require a change in spectrum use by television broadcasters in mandating the shift from analog to digital television signal transmission. Since television's origins in the late 1940s, stations were licensed to use 6 megahertz (mhz) of spectrum, over which they broadcast an analog television signal. In the 1990s, as the legislature prepared a significant overhaul of some telecommunication policy, it reconsidered spectrum use and organization. Mobile telephone technologies were just becoming widely used, and industry forecasters identified a growing demand for spectrum by these technologies. The many reasons for the transition to digital television in the United States are too complicated to recount here—although the story provides an excellent case for exploring the intricacies of media industry operation.[13] Suffice it to say that for a variety of reasons (mostly related to lobbying by various industries), Congress decided to require all of the nation's television broadcasters to switch from transmitting an analog signal to transmitting a digital one.

The digital transition required considerable changes for both broadcasters and television viewers. Television stations had to purchase new equipment and transmitters—which cost billions of dollars—and to access these signals, viewers without cable or satellite service had to purchase sets with digital receivers. Despite this downside, the same digital signal required less spectrum, meaning that after the switchover, more room was available for new services, such as wireless broadband, expanding local television channels, and high-definition television. In theory, some benefits for the viewer included greater selection of channels and new features such as on-screen listings, interactivity, and audio description and subtitling for people with visual and audio impairments.

The digital transition may seem to be quite a big hassle, so the question you might have now is "why," and there are many reasons. At the time Congress was considering the legislation, the consumer electronics industry was poised to introduce **high-definition television**. Instead of the 525 scan lines of standard definition sets, high-definition sets can receive either 720 or 1,080 lines, creating a much crisper and superior image. The amount of data needed to transmit a high-definition signal (at least back in the mid-1990s), however, could not be compressed into the 6 mhz analog signal. Therefore, the perception was that in order to make high-definition television possible, it was necessary to switch to a digital signal that was capable of carrying more information. This transition was of great interest to the consumer electronics industry as an opportunity to sell more and higher priced sets. It was also the case that US standard definition was of poorer quality than the norms adopted in much of the rest of the world, so there was some technological logic behind this decision as well.

The stronger explanation of "why the transition" is probably the financial windfall Congress expected upon auctioning off the spectrum after broadcasters returned their analog space. Estimates placed profits in the range of $80 billion—which is also an important reminder of the value of what broadcasters are given to use for free (and justifies why we really should expect more from them).

The mandate to switch to digital transmission is an example of massive government regulatory involvement and should be regarded as fairly uncommon. Typically, such structuring regulations are established early in the life of a medium, and then they become too entrenched to alter. The United States is not alone in undergoing this transition. Countries as wide-ranging as Australia, Brazil, Kenya, Malaysia, and many others have transitioned from analog to digital or have plans to do so in place.

CONCLUSION

As in the cases of the mandates and other conditions discussed here, it isn't that specific regulations have clear or specific consequences for media industries. Rather, factors such as the nature of existing regulations; the current cultural, political, and economic environment; particular mandates, technologies, and economic norms; and the practices of individuals working in media industries channel the range of possibilities. In the examples we've noted throughout this chapter, it has often been the case that factors that comprise the broader cultural and economic contexts in which media operate are as significant in shaping what the media industries create as are regulations (or their absence). Concerns about government involvement led the networks to create the Family Hour and tamed the first hour of prime time, at least for a little while. Competition from

niche channels, fragmentation of the audience, and the erosion of family viewing necessitated that broadcasters loosen some of their content standards—suggesting that a shift
in the competitive environment can produce changes as substantial as a regulation. The
desire for greater deregulation of ownership caps can lead creators to self-regulate content to curry government favor.

QUESTIONS

1. Select a media good that you have consumed or interacted with today, thinking about
   it in terms of the three interconnected questions listed in this chapter. Can you identify who regulates the industry that created the good? What, exactly, is being regulated? Finally, think about a specific regulation in that industry. Can you explain the
   consequences it had on the good you have chosen?
2. As noted in this chapter's discussion of broadcasting, the FCC allows stations to use
   the publicly owned airwaves as long as they operate in the "public interest, convenience, and necessity." Do you think this is a fair deal, and, more important, do you
   think that broadcasters are currently holding up their end of the deal? What types of
   content and services do you think would fulfill that requirement?
3. We have discussed the importance of the ways in which industries formally *self-
   regulate*. Identify an instance of formal self-regulation in a particular industry, or
   think more thoroughly about one of the examples we provided. How did this self-
   regulation help secure the survival or profitability of the industry? How did it, in
   turn, affect the sort of media good that was produced—if at all? Can you make a
   case that it either limited or expanded the possible types of media goods available
   to us?

FURTHER READING

Books on issues of content regulation can be found about nearly every media industry.
See Eric Nuzum's *Parental Advisory: Music Censorship in America* (New York: Harper
Paperbacks, 2001); Stephen Tropiano's *Obscene, Indecent, Immoral and Offensive: 100+
Years of Censored, Banned, and Controversial Films* (New York: Limelight Editions,
2009); and Heather Hendershot's *Saturday Morning Censors: Television Regulation
Before the V-Chip* (Durham: Duke University Press, 1999). For more on the issues sur-
rounding intellectual property and copyright, see Kembrew McLeod's *Freedom of
Expression: Resistance and Repression in the Age of Intellectual Property* (Minneapolis:
University of Minnesota Press, 2007); Siva Vaidhyanathan, *Copyrights and Copywrongs:
The Rise of Intellectual Property and How it Threatens Creativity* (New York: New York
University Press, 2003); and Lawrence Lessig's *Free Culture: The Nature and Future of
Creativity* (New York: Penguin, 2005).

There are many much more detailed works on media policy and regulation. See
Susan Crawford, *Captive Audience: The Telecom Industry and Monopoly Power in the
New Gilded Age* (New Haven: Yale University Press, 2013); Patricia A. Aufderheide's
Communications Policy and the Public Interest: The Telecommunications Act of 1996

(New York: Guildford Press, 1999); Robert McChesney's *The Problem of the Media: U.S. Communication Politics in the Twenty-First Century* (New York: Monthly Review Press, 2004); Mara Einstein's *Media Diversity: Economics, Ownership, and the FCC* (New York: Routledge, 2004); and Des Freedman's *The Politics of Media Policy* (Cambridge: Polity, 2008). For a historical view, see William Boddy's *Fifties Television: The Industry and Its Critics* (Urbana: University of Illinois Press, 1990).

A detailed account of the forces behind the US digital transition can be found in Joel Brinkley's *Defining Vision: The Battle for the Future of Television* (San Diego: Harcourt Brace, 1997).

NOTES

1. Susan J. Douglas, *Inventing American Broadcasting 1899–1922* (Baltimore: Johns Hopkins University Press, 1987).
2. For a thorough overview and history of net neutrality in the United States, see http://www.fcc.gov/openinternet (accessed May 27, 2014).
3. These figures come from the Center for Responsive Politics web-based database on lobbying expenditures at www.opensecrets.org. https://www.opensecrets.org/lobby/top.php?showYear=2013&indexType=s
4. Mike Masnick, "Pirate Parties Blocked From WIPO After US & Other Countries Complained That They Don't Support WIPO Mission," *TechDirt*, September 25, 2013. http://www.techdirt.com/articles/20130925/12594024656/pirate-parties-blocked-wipo-after-us-other-countries-complained-that-they-dont-support-wipos-mission.shtml
5. Donald R. Pember, *Mass Media Law* (Boston: McGraw-Hill College, 1999), 459.
6. Ibid., 459, 469.
7. Matthew Newton, "Is Sampling Dying?" *Spin*, December 2008, 31–34.
8. Ben H. Bagdikian, *The New Media Monopoly* (Boston: Beacon Press, 2004), 1.
9. Sydney W. Head, Thomas D. Spann, and Michael A. McGregor, *Broadcasting in America: A Survey of Electronic Media*, 9th ed. (Boston: Allyn & Bacon, 2000).
10. Ibid.
11. Though talks of a merger reemerged five years later, after News Corp. purchased and again sold DirecTV.
12. David Croteau and William Hoynes, *The Business of Media: Corporate Media and the Public Interest*, 2nd ed. (Thousand Oaks, Calif.: Pine Forge Press, 2006).
13. Joel Brinkley, *Defining Vision: The Battle for the Future of Television* (San Diego: Harcourt Brace, 1997).

CHAPTER 5

—

Economic Conditions in Media Production

Key Takeaways:

Understand how the high sunk and first-copy costs lead to particular practices of media industries in the creation of media

Understand how the distinction of whether a media industry creates single or continuous goods leads to particular challenges in its financing

Understand the different financing norms for media funded independently versus those funded by studios/labels/publishers

Understand how the differences in how consumers pay for media can lead to the creation of different media content

I n the early 1800s, US newspapers were more comparable to contemporary magazines than the newspapers we are now familiar with, although even that isn't a great comparison. Many newspapers at that time were allied with political parties and published long treatises debating current issues, rather than the short, objective digests of the news of the day we are accustomed to now. Most Americans did not read the papers because of the high level of illiteracy and high cost of papers. Joseph Turow notes the costs and conditions of the time necessitated that publishers charge $6 to $10 per year, in advance, for a subscription to the paper—a rate that would be the equivalent of paying approximately $100 to $180 for an annual magazine subscription today.[1] As available technology changed, so too did the economic model supporting the newspaper industry, and with a new economic model, the content also changed radically.

In the early 1830s, entrepreneurs began imagining a newspaper that would circulate much more widely. To reach a broad audience, the paper would have to be more affordable—just a few pennies—and in order to entice readership, it would have to attract the interest of readers. Soon the political treatises were gone, replaced, as Turow describes, "with stories of crime and love, humor and human interest."[2] Here, the transition from a fairly expensive advance subscription as the means for financing the paper to a blend of advertising and direct payment from consumers led to a considerable shift in the very nature of the medium. In addition, as we explain in Chapter 6, the shift from rag-based to wood-pulp-based paper made newspapers far cheaper to produce and lighter, which reduced distribution costs and consequently helped drive down prices.

Much has been said in recent years about the "death" of the contemporary newspaper industry as the immediacy and ease of access provided by the Internet have led to changes in various aspects of production, how people read, and their willingness to pay for newspapers. As in the early 1800s, it is not the case that newspapers are dying, but rather that the economic norms of the industry are in a state of adjustment that is enabling a change in the content and cultural role of newspapers. The history of media industries is filled with many such stories because how media are financed and how audiences pay for their products can have significant implications for media content.

*   *   *

The second condition we consider encompasses how various economic matters lead media industries to function in particular ways. Like technological and regulatory conditions in the Industrialization of Culture framework, economic considerations that include who owns media, how media creation is funded, and how media are paid for produce a range of consequences. As with the other conditions and practices we study, it is difficult to speak in generalities when it comes to the impact of economic conditions on media goods and other dimensions of media industry operations because how media are financed contributes to wide-ranging variation in media content.

One significant distinction among media industries noted by media economist Robert Picard is between those that produce **single media goods**, media such as films, albums or tracks, games, and books that are each individual goods that are marketed based on the distinctive merits of each media product.[3] In contrast, **continuous media goods** are produced as a steady flow of regularly refreshed content—whether print, music, or video—but television, radio, newspapers, and magazines are primarily continuous media goods. Single media are most commonly purchased by individual transaction, whereas advertising has typically supported continuous media.[4] Table 5.1 illustrates the distinction in the characteristics between single good and continuous media good industries.

A close reader will note that we did not place television into either category. Before the 2000s, it was easier to think of television uniformly as a continuous media industry because it was difficult to experience television other than as a linear flow of programs

Table 5.1 Characteristics of Single and Continuous Media Goods

	SINGLE MEDIA GOODS	CONTINUOUS MEDIA GOODS
Types of Media	Films, Music, Video games, Books, Some emerging television	Newspaper, Magazine, Radio, Most television
Business Model	Transaction	Advertising; Subscription Advertising/Subscription;

available only at network specified times. With the arrival of DVRs, video on demand technologies, distribution of television seasons on DVD, and through digital download and streaming, certain types of television now take on characteristics of single media, though much of the traditional program day—talk shows, news, and other programs that produce a daily episode—still bear much in common with continuous media. The economics of television are crucial to understanding the many changes the industry is experiencing and why a range of new types of content have been produced in recent years.

In addition to the topics covered in this chapter, think back to the discussion in Chapter 2 about ownership structure, including conglomeration, consolidation, vertical integration, and horizontal integration. These broad economic issues are relevant here too. In this chapter, we explore the costs involved in making many media products and consider how the practices media producers use to finance these costs lead to particular consequences for the products they create. The second section of the chapter considers the various ways media products are commonly paid for and how this also affects the content of media.

To some degree, this chapter assumes that we are dealing with media industries that operate under a commercial mandate. This focus allows us to address the great majority of media industry operation; even nations with broadcasting systems dominated by a public mandate feature commercial media in sectors such as film, music, and publishing, and those with public broadcasting also tend to have a commercial broadcasting sector. It is also the case that the costs of media creation are similar regardless of mandate. Although this chapter cannot cover all of the ways that economic matters contribute to the production of media products in the particular situation of all mandates, it does offer a broad sketch of key considerations that might be applied to a variety of instances.

THE CREATIVE AND CULTURAL IMPLICATIONS OF COST STRUCTURES AND FINANCING MECHANISMS

When you think about financing media, the first thing that may come to mind is how you pay for the media you consume. This may be the most pressing concern for us as media consumers, but many significant financing and economic decisions take place well before media content reaches us. Some of the characteristics specific to media industries discussed in Chapter 2, such as high first-copy costs, require complicated strategies for financing products in the media industries that can have significant implications for what is created. Some media industries have extraordinarily high production costs (television and film), while in others, new technologies have made it increasingly possible for amateurs to produce high-quality media as well. New forms of distribution and digital media that we address in Chapter 9 are disrupting many of the traditional financing practices we discuss here. When trying to make sense of the implications of piracy or the availability of music, video, or print on devices such as tablets and mobile phones, it is important to consider how these practices challenge long-established business models.

There are countless different sites at which we can examine how matters of economics affect media industry operation and production. First, we explore the economics of making media and the costs and financing practices that producers negotiate. To do so, we must consider the many costs involved in making media, the typical financing structures used to fund media creation, the difference between independent and studio funding (or the equivalent), and the variations found in financing single versus continuous media goods. The second major section of the chapter then examines the audience as an economic entity and the different ways that audiences pay for media products.

Exploring the economics of media industries requires the introduction of many concepts and terms, but the key point of the chapter is to encourage you to think through how the various costs involved in media products and how the challenge of high sunk costs, unpredictable performance, and the different ways audiences pay for media goods leads these industries to particular production practices and to produce certain kinds of content.

The Costs of Making Media

What costs are involved in producing media? Certainly there are obvious costs, such as those related to **talent**—the cost of hiring performers (journalists, actors, musicians), securing the raw material for the media good (scripts, lyrics), and the basic costs of production (sound stage, cameras, news service, recording studio). These costs only scratch the surface, however. For at least the past half-century, one of the key characteristics of media industries has been the organization of the activities involved in making media products into highly specialized and distinct roles. A central consequence of this is that creating media products require vast staffs of people because their skill sets are not interchangeable. We really cannot stress enough how many workers play some role in the media products you encounter every day.

In order to try to make the broad array of costs more comprehensible, we distinguish between industries producing single and continuous media goods and classify costs into different categories. Industries making single goods have four categories of costs: development, production, marketing and distribution, and overhead. The costs of industries producing continuous goods are more generally either production or marketing and distribution. There are certainly many costs that don't fit any of these categories or that fit into more than one, but these categories provide a general framework. (Note that throughout the book, and especially in this chapter, we use the word "publishers" generally to encompass the roles of the primary industrial entity of single-goods industries; publishers include publishers of books and video games, labels in the case of music, and studios in the case of film.)

Development Costs

The first set of costs includes those sustained during planning a project, costs often distinguished as **development costs**. Development costs can encompass the costs of acquiring creative goods—for example, the fee a studio pays to secure a script, a book publisher pays for a manuscript, or a game developer sustains to develop a prototype to try to sell to a game publisher. Development costs are often risky expenditures, as they frequently involve monetary or time commitments that are never repaid because many media goods that begin "development" aren't ultimately created. In his research on the operation of the film industry, Edward Jay Epstein learned that only 1 out of 10 scripts that studios buy is ever developed into a film.[5] This is also the case in television, where development costs include scripts and also the production costs—over a million dollars each—for **pilot episodes** of shows that are never seen by more than a handful of executives. **Advance payments,** also referred to as "advances," are fees paid to creative talents to have them create a good. Sometimes the creator never delivers the work, and, historically, media industries have not litigated against creators to have these funds returned; so advances can be examples of development costs as well.

We highlight development costs as a specific category to draw attention to the risks and significant expenses of making media that are never directly recouped. For media that complete production, these development expenses become part of the costs of making that media. The cost of those never produced are borne by studios and labels and indirectly recouped through the overhead charges they make against projects that complete development, which we discuss later.

Production Costs

Costs multiply as production begins. **Production costs** include all those salaries and costs involved in the actual making of a media product. The salaries or fees of those who work on a single project (movie, show, game, album) consume a large percentage of production costs, as do the costs of the materials (costumes, sets, insurance) needed to produce it. In the case of film, Epstein notes that the start of production brings initial payments to talent agencies for the actors, directors, and other workers who must be paid in full as soon as the project begins. Another set of expenses, including the salaries of many of the technicians—as well as costs as tangential as catering—are incurred on a day-to-day basis throughout production. A wide range of independent vendors who provide computer graphics, digital effects, titles, and trailers must also be paid.[6] Additionally, work such as editing, sound synchronizing, mixing the various sound tracks, balancing the color, and cutting the negative are also part of making media goods. To consider production costs in another industry, we might look at the costs involved in recording an album. The cost of recording the sound tracks, mixing them, and preparing the master for reproduction typically can run to as much as $50,000.[7]

Again, media creating a continuous product are somewhat exceptional in that they maintain a steadier labor base, making production costs more similar to overhead costs. Indeed, there are still very high startup costs in a continuous industry, but the fact that there is some money coming in once a company begins production and that this income tends to be more predictable than that of single media goods make these costs a bit different for continuous media industries and more like any other industry.

Marketing and Distribution Costs

Marketing and distribution costs include the myriad costs of publicizing and making audiences aware of goods as well as costs such as having films printed and shipped to theaters or the cost of having CDs, newspapers, books, and magazines printed and shipped to stores. Before digital film became the norm, just making copies of a film to have enough prints to open in theaters across the county could cost $6 million.[8] Likewise, print industries incur marketing and distribution costs in printing newspapers and magazines, and the music industry has the costs of pressing CDs.

Media industries that sell their products through retailers face costs related to transporting their goods (albums, magazines, newspapers, games) to those retailers and sometimes added costs for desirable display. Significantly, some of these distribution costs have been diminished or eliminated as a result of new digital means of distribution that reduce the need to create and transport physical copies of media—such as when you purchase a download of a song instead of a CD, though digital distribution can add new costs and new types of distribution fees. We discuss the consequences of digital distribution on media industry economics in greater detail in Chapters 8 and 9.

Marketing and distribution also include the costs of promoting media, which often can be as considerable as the cost of making single media. Consider, for example, the expansive television advertisement buys common for big studio films that blanket the airwaves just before a film opens. In 2009 the studios reported average spending on advertising ranging from $30.4 million to $50 million per film for advertising, and those films intended to be international blockbusters require much more.[9] Warner Bros. was projected to spend $150 million marketing the 2013 international debut of *Man of Steel*.[10]

Further marketing and distribution costs might include those required to distribute the media product in additional markets—for example, the costs related to editing a film to prepare it for distribution on television or to produce and distribute DVD copies for rental or sale. Epstein reports that creating the DVD and adding features can cost $30,000 to $50,000 per film and require marketing costs of $4 to $5 per copy sold.[11]

Overhead Costs

What we term **overhead costs** include those required to maintain media institutions that manage and finance production, particularly of media that produce single products. These costs are not isolated to a particular product but are required to maintain the infrastructure used by film and television studios, record labels, and game and book publishers.* For many media in today's conglomerated industrial organization, these are the costs of the conglomerate or its subcomponents. For example, the Sony film studio employed 4,200 full-time employees in 2013, illustrating how a film or television studio maintains a staff of thousands year after year who work in varying capacities—including as executives, lawyers, bookkeepers, publicists, and clerical staff—who provide support for the different projects produced by the studio.[12] In addition to substantial salaries, overhead costs include the considerable real estate costs of studios and their back lots or office high-rises. Indeed, given the premium value of land in the greater Los Angeles area and in Manhattan, one of the biggest assets of the media conglomerates results from their land holdings and real estate.

---

*This article explores the many factors that film executives factor in when trying to determine whether a film will be successful. http://io9.com/5747305/how-much-money-does-a-movie-need-to-make-to-be-profitable

Another key category of overhead costs results from the materials needed to pay for the day-to-day expenses of labels, studios, and publishers, including everything from the computers and cubicles used by executives and studio employees to the cameras and technical equipment found on set. The significant expansion of overhead costs is a central consequence of how media production is organized today. Even though this organizational structure of large studios, labels, and publishers predominates in many media industries, it is not the only way media can be made. "Independent" media makers largely exist outside of this structure and may instead rent or subcontract many of the goods and services included in the overhead of conglomerates.

A key difference in the economic norms of single and continuous media goods are that publishers of single media goods set up each film, book, or album as a separate account, so that the production costs of a film are listed out and charged to that film, almost as if it was its own company. The studio then "charges" the production in different ways for the indirect fees related to being developed by the studio.

It is difficult to distinguish overhead for media industries that produce continuous products. The regularity of these industries—they produce the same product every day or every month—clearly differentiates them from industries producing single products. Though *Sports Illustrated* might have a budget for a particular issue, it doesn't set that issue up as its own economic entity. If it goes overbudget one month, it may compensate in a subsequent month. The regularity of continuous media allows most of their costs to be either general production or distribution and marketing costs.

How Are the Costs of Creating Media Funded?

If you remember back to some of the key economic characteristics of media industries explained in Chapter 2, you'll recall that media industries require considerable sunk costs or high first-copy costs. The development, production, and marketing and distribution costs illustrate this concept, as pretty much all of these expenses must be paid before a single dollar of revenue can be earned, although once the media product is created, producing additional copies has minimal cost. The fact that such considerable costs are incurred before producing any revenue requires that media industries pursue a range of funding mechanisms in order to finance these costs. The funding options vary, based on whether media being produced are single or continuous and the scale of investment needed. Continuous media industries sustain themselves with daily products and consistent sales, so they don't incur the massive promotion expenses for each new good that industries producing single goods do. Single good industries typically rely on the publisher (the studio, label, or game publisher) to finance new productions based on the profits earned from previous projects. An alternative, in a media space dominated by large corporations, is that of the **independent**. What it means to be independent varies by industry, but for the most part, independents either self-finance the creation of their products or solicit investors to pay for production.

Independent Funding of a Single Good

A case study about the making of the independent film *Winter's Bone* reveals much about the process of independent filmmaking. Collaborators Ann Rosellini and Debra

Granik came across the novel *Winter's Bone*, written by Daniel Woodrell and thought it would be a good film. A previous novel by Woodrell had been successfully adapted into a movie, further suggesting the potential of the literary property as a viable film. They "optioned" the manuscript "for a cost in the high-four to low-five figures," which means they bought the right to make a film and to prevent others from doing so for a period of time, for about $11,000.[13] Rosellini and Granik developed a screenplay and delivered it to producer Alix Madigan.

The three then went in search of funding and presented the script and a portfolio of photos of the Ozark Mountain area in which the film would be set to more than 25 potential financiers. A financier emerged who offered to fund half of the proposed $4 million budget and allow the filmmakers complete creative control. The creative team decided to cut the budget in half so that the one funder would be adequate. They crafted a standard equity deal in which the first money earned on the film (after expenses are paid in full) would go to completely reimburse the investor and pay him or her "an agreed-upon premium," commonly about 20 percent.[14] Any additional earnings were then split 50/50 between the investor and the filmmakers.

Thus one way to fund an independent media venture is by finding an investor, but this covers only the cost of making the media good—in this case, a film. Once a film produced independent of a studio is complete, the filmmakers then seek to secure a distribution deal so that audiences can see the film, hopefully paying to do so in a way that recoups the filmmakers' or investors' expense. Studios typically possess both production and distribution divisions, so both of these activities are performed "in house." For *Winter's Bone*, the first step was to show it at film festivals, which is where many distribution buyers gather. The filmmakers hired a publicist known to have strong relationships with key critics for a flat, standard fee for the duration of the Sundance Film Festival, which had accepted the film. They also hired a "producer's representative"—a job somewhat like an agent for the film—who would negotiate any distribution offers. Typically, producer's reps charge between 5 and 15 percent of the money earned in a distribution sale, but they only get paid if a sale is made.

The filmmakers received two offers from two buyers and selected the offer from Roadside Attractions, even though the other offer was higher. The filmmakers had the sense that Roadside had a genuine passion for the film, and the other bidder had been unwilling to meet with the *Winter's Bone* team during the festival. Roadside Attractions bought all North American rights (theatrical, VOD, and digital) for 15 years for a "low six-figure" payment (let's imagine $300,000) and also committed to spend $500,000 on prints and advertising. They also agreed to pay the filmmakers bonuses if and when the film achieved a string of box office achievements—in this case, if the film earned $2 million, $4 million, and $6 million. Though Roadside is not associated with a major studio, it would not be unusual for the distribution arm of a major studio to buy the distribution rights for an independent film.

Roadside arranged to play the film in 8 to 10 regional festivals to build buzz about it and then planned for an early summer release in theaters to counterprogram the blockbusters studios commonly release at this time. The film initially opened in New

York and Los Angeles, and Roadside planned to then roll it out to 25 cities over eight weeks. The press buzz was so significant, though, that they changed strategy and opened on 130 screens within two weeks of the New York and Los Angeles debut.

When the case study was written the following fall, the film was still doing well 16 weeks after it opened and had earned $6 million at the box office. Final reported box office proceeds for the film were $6.5 domestic and $7.3 million in international markets. In addition, the film is likely to have earned money from DVD sales and may have been sold for a license fee to be included in the offerings of a subscription content aggregator such as Netflix, as well as to cable channels in the United States and internationally.

The viability of creating media independently varies considerably by medium. A feature-length film is much more expensive to produce than a music album or news blog. Furthermore, different media industries have mechanisms for distribution that make independent distribution easier in some industries. Independent music distribution has been made exponentially easier in the digital era, as has basic "print" publishing. Blogs are really just self-published independent newspapers/magazines that eliminate the costs of printing and distribution by publishing online, and if there isn't a need to produce a profit from them, these are ventures that can exist without extensive funding. A key motivation for producing media independently is the ability to retain creative freedom. Also, it is frequently the case that independent projects emerge because no studio or label will take the risk of producing them.

The film industry has also long had mechanisms in place for the exhibition and distribution of independent films. Before the ease of burning films to DVDs or sharing digital files, film festivals provided the necessary showcase for films to find distributors, and film festivals remain important, despite the greater ease of reaching distributors with digital media. In contrast, the control of distribution in television by just a few broadcast networks during the network era prevented any kind of substantial independent television production from existing. There have been independent studios—or, those not associated with the major film studios—but even these "independents" were limited in creating for established networks and channels. It remains the "early days" for a lot of video that is created specifically for distribution over the Internet, but the aggregation of video created outside television studios on YouTube has offered a sense of what independent television distribution might look like. Although it is also the case that companies such Maker and other **multichannel networks** have quickly emerged and behave much like a traditional distributor.

In contrast to the independent route, most media are created by large conglomerates able to rely on past successes or other sectors of the company to finance the sunk costs. The profits a project eventually returns then go to finance subsequent projects. Next, we detail the process of funding video games and television in the United States to offer more specific case illustrations of corporate media funding strategies. Although the specific mechanisms vary somewhat in other industries, the general structures for taking on debt, earning outrageous profits from a few products, and using those profits to develop new products can be found in many media industries.

Financing a Single Media Good Through Publisher Funding

The creation of video games is largely controlled by a handful of game publishers; companies such as Electronic Arts, Nintendo, UbiSoft, Infogrames/Atari, and Take 2 are the video game industry's equivalent of film studios or recording labels.[15] Game publishers contract with game developers who are creative talent akin to directors, writers, or musicians in other industries. Game software development follows different models depending on whether a console manufacturer develops a game specifically for a platform (called first-party developers; e.g., Halo on Xbox) or whether the games are designed by third-party developers, or entities such as Electronic Arts that are completely independent from the console manufacturers.

Regardless of type of developer, the economics of gaming software is further complicated by the dominance of the game industry by three console manufacturers (Sony, Nintendo, and Microsoft) and the fact these hardware manufacturers use **closed hardware systems** that are **proprietary** and not interoperable. The closed-system hardware means that game developers must obtain licenses to produce games for each machine. The license fee, collected per game sold, is typically about 30 percent of the cost of the game. Thus the sale of games is extremely lucrative for the hardware developers and accounts for most of the revenue in their business model. As is the case for many technology-based media, the technology operates as a **loss leader**. Console companies try to price the system as affordably as possible to get the devices into the most homes and earn most of their profits licensing software. In some cases, platform manufacturers demand exclusivity so that a game will be available only for their platform.

Before the possibility of digital distribution, games were primarily sold by retailers independent from the publishers—large chains such as Wal-Mart and Best Buy. These retailers were estimated to gross about 30 percent on the full price of a game, which means these retailers earned roughly $20 from a $60 game (a high margin in comparison with many other industries). The possibility to distribute games digitally is changing the industry for both major publishers and independent developers and, as in other industries, enables self-publishing. Digital distribution has also helped create a healthy market for independent video game production as well, or games created outside of major publishers. Some independent games such as Jonathan Blow's *Braid* are made by just one or two people. Though independent games are also made by larger teams at independent game studios, digital distribution outside of relationships with major publishers has introduced significant changes to the way the industry operates and has contributed to the emergence of new game markets. In addition to allowing for more experimental play mechanics and storytelling techniques, independent games like *Gone Home* often provide more representation of those who are underrepresented in mainstream games, including women and lesbian, gay, bisexual, and transgender audiences. See Table 5.2 for a snapshot of how different entities in the video game industry make and spend money.

Other economic distinctions among games can be found as well. Notable differences exist between the console and PC game industries, and the increasing popularity of app-based games and mobile platforms is significantly disrupting old norms. Games playable on PCs have open, nonproprietary systems, which makes them cheaper to develop (and cheaper to consumers) but also leads to much more competition, as access to this market isn't regulated by platform companies that can control the number and type of games available for their systems. There are many more independent games developed for PCs than for proprietary consoles. Massively multiplayer online games require continuous support costs after development, typically monthly subscription fees. As digitization changes the operating norms of media industries, game companies are increasingly trying to expand monetization by allowing players to opt to pay additional fees for added capabilities and extras. We discuss the consequences of payment structures in the last section of the chapter, but, for now, note that although console and PC games have historically been monetized through a one-time purchase price, many other **business models**—such as pay per download, pay per play, advertising, and, with the rapidly expanding app market, in-game purchase—also can be found in some sectors of the game industry.

As is common in media industries, many development costs come early in the creation of gaming software. In the case of third-party development, the planning necessary to develop a proposal and design a prototype to shop to publishers typically costs about $1.5 million. To finance these expenses, developers seek funding from venture capital investors and other private sources in a manner that can be similar to the creation of an independent film. The cost of developing a console game can vary significantly; average costs may be in the $20 million range, but many tentpole games cost multiple hundreds of millions of dollars, especially those that require licensing of known sport or entertainment properties (Madden Football, Harry Potter). Third-party developers use their prototypes to secure a contract and advance funding from a publisher.

The advance funding, or receiving an "advance," is used to develop the games and is a funding structure also common to secure authors by book publishers and musicians by record labels. Profits for the game developer (author, musician) then are only achieved once a game goes to market and the publisher earns back the advance payment. The developer then earns a small percentage of subsequent sales. Many new developers (authors, musicians) are forced to sign over the intellectual property of the game to the publisher in order to obtain a contract and the initial financing needed to make the media product. The "publisher" is then at a contractual advantage; the developer is often contractually obligated to produce sequels for the publisher at the whim of the publisher and often cannot negotiate for better contract terms even if that property proves a big success. Developers with established track records and those who already possess the license for creative properties perceived as valuable have a stronger position for negotiating contract terms. In contrast, first-party developers face fewer initial hurdles, as the publisher has already determined that it needs a game of a specific genre targeted at a specified audience, eliminating many of the business-plan aspects that can be onerous for third-party developers.

Many of these features of financing creative goods can be found across publishing industries—simply replace the term "developer/publisher" with "director" or "producer/studio" for the film industry, "author/publisher" for the book industry, and "artist/label" for the recording industry. Similar variations on the dynamic of first-party versus

Table 5.2 Case of Financing a Single Media Good Through Publisher Funding

How do different entities in the video game industry make and spend money?

Publishers (Electronic Arts, Nintendo, UbiSoft):

- PAY salaried staff to develop games
- PAY independent game developers to develop games
- PAY console manufacturers license fee (30 percent)
- RECEIVE revenue from game sales (shared with console manufacturer and retailer)
- RECEIVE monthly subscription fees for massively multiplayer online game play; in-game purchase revenue; fees paid by advertisers for product placement

Console Manufacturers (Sony, Nintendo, Microsoft)

- PAY technology developers to design consoles
- PAY manufacturing and distribution costs of consoles
- RECEIVE license fees from game publishers for each game sold
- RECEIVE revenue from consoles sold (minimal)

third-party development also exist in different industries. In some ways, media industries producing continuous goods bear some likeness to the operation of first-party funding. A publisher does not need to be "sold" on the idea of creating these goods, rather, the publisher recognizes a need and then has the good created by an existing staff.

Financing a Continuous Medium

The dominant process for financing most US prime-time television programming is one that always seems to surprise students. The profits and costs of television aren't where many would expect, and some aspects of the business seem downright insane. Let's begin with a key practice: **deficit financing**. Deficit financing describes the dominant financing arrangement in US prime-time series television whereby production studios lose money in making series during the first few years, even if their show is a hit. This is how the process typically goes: A producer will pitch a show idea to a network, and if the network likes it, the network will give the producer some money to write a script. If the network likes the script, then it will give the producer money to shoot a "pilot"—typically the first episode of the series. A pilot is an expensive proposition; it requires building sets and developing a full cast, and most pilots (as many as 80 percent) are never developed into series and are typically never seen by anyone except the network executives (remember that practice of intentional overproduction).

If a network does like the pilot episode, and it has a good place for the show on its schedule, it will license the show. The license fee the network pays typically covers about 60 to 70 percent of production costs. By 2015 a typical drama might cost a studio around $3 million per episode to produce. The network license fee, which gives the network the right to air the episode a couple times (typically a first and rerun episode), would probably be around $1.95 million. It doesn't take strong math skills to recognize that the studio is going to lose money making this show—more than $1 million per episode, or about $13 million per year over the increasingly common 13-episode season of cable

Table 5.3   Case of Financing a Continuous Media Good

How do different entities in the newspaper industry make and spend money?

Publishers (*The New York Times* Co., Gannett, Tribune)

- PAY salaried and freelance writers and editors to develop and write a daily product
- PAY salaried advertising and sales workers to cultivate relationships with advertisers
- RECEIVE subscription fees from readers wanting guaranteed access/delivery (print and sometimes online)
- RECEIVE advertising fees from advertisers based on circulation/clicks

How do different entities in the television make and spend money?

Studios (Universal Media Studios, 21st Century Fox Television, ABC Studios, Warner Bros. Television)

- PAY top writers "overall deals" that function like a salary and guarantee the studio first right for each idea
- PAY freelance writers/other talent who are hired to work on particular series
- PAY all the production costs to make the show
- RECEIVE license fee from original licensor (typically 60 to 70 percent of production cost)
- RECEIVE fees when content sold to other licensors (international channels; broadcast syndication, cable channels; digital distribution)

Networks (NBC, CBS)/Cable Channels (FX, USA)/Broadband Aggregators (Netflix, Amazon)

- PAY studios a license fee for right to air a series for a specified period
- RECEIVE subscription/retransmission fees from service providers (subscribers for Amazon and Netflix)
- RECEIVE advertising fees from advertisers based on getting their message to a certain number of a certain type of viewer

---

dramas. See Table 5.3 for a summary of the major costs and revenue exchanges for both print and television.

This doesn't look like a very smart arrangement for the studio, which takes on the deficit not paid by the license (hence, deficit financing). But the studio still owns the show and can sell it elsewhere after the period of the initial license. After the studio makes enough episodes, the studio then sells the episodes again in **secondary markets** to entities such as local stations to air during the hours the network doesn't provide programming (also called **syndication**), to cable channels, to networks in other markets around the world, and by releasing DVDs and licensing rights to digital distributors such as Netflix. The studios earn the most considerable revenue from selling episodes to networks in other countries, and they are often able to do this nearer the beginning of the show's production.

Selling the show in all of these secondary markets gradually helps the studio recoup its deficit by supplying additional revenue, and some creative workers earn additional income—called residuals—based on these sales.[16] So, even though a brand-new show might be a huge hit, chances are good that the studio making it is losing money on its production, at least in the short term. See Table 5.4 for a general sketch of this process.

What we've presented here, though, is a best-case scenario. Most shows don't become hits. Most shows don't survive to make a second season of episodes; actually, most don't even make it through a first. So even though a studio might make millions,

Table 5.4   Primary and Secondary Markets for Television

STUDIOS	PRIMARY MARKETS	SECONDARY MARKETS
ABC Television Studios, Lionsgate TV, Sony Pictures Television	Broadcast networks (ABC, CBS) Cable channels (USA, FX, Showtime) Broadband aggregators (Netflix originals)	International channels, Cable channels (off-net), Broadcast stations, Broadband aggregators DVD or download sale
Produces and owns shows	Pays the majority of the original production cost for rights to the first run of the show	Studio sells rights to the show in a combination of secondary markets to recoup remaining production costs and earn profits

even billions, of dollars on a successful show (as was the case for shows such as *CSI* and *The Big Bang Theory*), far more frequently they never recover the deficit. Consequently, they rely on the profits from successful attempts—and in the past we are talking some pretty extraordinary profits—to cover the deficits of shows that fail.

This system of deficit financing leads to certain other industry practices and affects the creative content likely to be produced. First, because studios initially lose money, it effectively requires them to redistribute their shows in secondary markets. As a result, when they think about concepts for shows, producers think not only about what creative components might be likely to get their show on the network in the first place but also about what features might make their show likely to succeed in other markets. As the international marketplace becomes more and more important to profits, concern about themes and stories with international appeal leads producers away from some concepts and toward others. This system of finance also contributes to the similarity of so much entertainment fare. Shows similar to those that have succeeded in the past offer a sense of being a known commodity—even though they also often fail—and hits, likewise, can come in unexpected forms.

To give you a sense of how this works, the CBS series *How I Met Your Mother* was sold in various second-run markets in the fall of 2008. The cable channel Lifetime paid about $750,000 per episode (110 episodes were sold). In addition to this cash payment, Twentieth TV, the studio distributing the show, also received three 30-second commercials in each episode that it could then sell to national advertisers, and these were expected to be worth another $200,000 per episode over the four years of the deal.[17] In addition to the sale to Lifetime, Twentieth TV also negotiated deals with station groups owning local stations from which the series was expected to earn another $350 million.[18] Sales in these markets alone (as international sales are not included here) totaled nearly half a billion dollars. Additionally, Twentieth TV sold licensing rights to Amazon and Netflix to further expand earnings. The changing nature of television distribution, particularly the availability of "back catalog" or "library" content on services such as Netflix, or even video on demand provided by services such as Comcast, may decrease the value of these windows in time, but half-hour comedies that draw a broad audience, such as *The Big Bang Theory*, continue to be very profitable in these secondary markets. Warner Bros., the studio that produces *The Big Bang Theory*, began a $200 million deal with broadcast stations in 2011 and also had the potential to earn $2 million per episode in advertising. In addition, Warner Bros. sold the show to cable channel TBS for $1.5 million per episode, and the series earned strong DVD revenue—roughly $30 million per season. As of 2014, the series had yet to be licensed to Hulu, Amazon, or Netflix, likely in order to help ensure the value of the purchases made by TBS and the stations, but was certain to produce even more revenue as it moved through these additional windows.

There are other ways to finance continuous media. A model that has been common in the public mandate sector of the British television industry is called the **cost plus** system. In this case, a producer brings an idea to a network, and, if the network wants to develop the idea, the network pays the cost of production plus a fee or profit to the producer, perhaps 10 percent. The cost plus system greatly reduces the risk for the studio producing the show, as it does not take on deficit expenses and is guaranteed a certain amount of profit. In this arrangement, however, the studio effectively sells the show to the network, so any value to come from selling the show in another market would benefit the network rather than the studio. In exchange for the reduction of risk, then, the studio gives up the opportunity for exceptional reward.

Although this need to distribute television shows through multiple markets has long been a part of the television industry, increasingly the film industry is also becoming defined by revenue from other markets. At the close of the studio system in 1947, the film studios earned more than 95 percent of their revenues from theatrical exhibition, but now the studios routinely lose money on the theatrical release.[19] By 2003, the studios earned five times as much from home video as from theaters and were increasingly reliant on licensing their films for all manner of home viewing.[20]

In the early 2000s, Epstein found that 85 percent of studio revenues came from viewing movies on DVD or television or from other licensed adaptations such as games.[21] By 2005, studio reliance on the home entertainment market suffered a setback as DVD sales began to decline dropping to as much as 20 percent below a peak of $22 billion in 2004.[22] The growth of the digital market altered the home entertainment market in a number of ways, including through growing piracy, but also because consumers became less interested in purchasing movies for ownership and more focused on accessing movies online through subscription services such as Netflix or through digital rental or purchase via iTunes and Amazon. By 2013, the sale of physical discs had fallen to 64 percent of the home entertainment market compared to 96 percent in 2004.[23]

Though the digital market became an increasingly important part of the home entertainment market, this area grew at a slower pace than the decline in physical disc sales, which concerned the studios. To counteract this decline, Hollywood became increasingly reliant on the international box office and placed greater emphasis on digital sales and experimenting with release dates. Movies considered box-office failures in the United States consequently could double and even triple the box-office revenue in overseas markets. One example is *Gulliver's Travels*, which netted $42 million dollars in the US box office but earned $150 million in the international box office—primarily because of strong interest from Russian and South Korean movie-goers.[24] Nevertheless, despite the gains in the international market, the home entertainment market and other ancillary markets remain a very viable and lucrative revenue source for Hollywood films.

Likewise, the economic norms of the music industry might not be what you expect, and these too have undergone considerable adjustment as a result of the ways digital distribution has disrupted previous industry norms. Most of the money earned by artists comes through touring and the merchandise they sell, rather than from music sales. Others supplement income earned through performing with songwriting income.

The involvement of large corporations that are capable of taking on the considerable debt of production costs must be understood to have profound effects on the creation of media content. These consequences aren't simple to define or uniform, but they lead strongly to certain tendencies. Many of the norms tilt the playing field in favor of the conglomerates, and, in many cases, it is difficult to work in media without working with the conglomerates. Because creative workers need the publisher to create and distribute their projects, most have very little leverage in negotiating contracts unless a bidding war develops among multiple studios, publishers, or labels.

Most creators work on a freelance basis and enter into contracts that may provide a share of net profits; yet in the film industry, the norm of **Hollywood accounting** prevents that from ever amounting to much, if anything. Hollywood accounting is the casual term used to describe a manner of accounting for the costs of production—mainly through overhead charges and nonspecific fees for things like "distribution"—done within the conglomerate that reduces the net profits of a media good to a loss, thereby allowing the studio to avoid payment of royalties or percentages of net profits. The studios closely guard the details of their budgets, and detailed accounting is often only available in legal documents in cases of payment disputes. To be sure, studios and conglomerates do take a considerable risk in financing media products, but they are also handsomely rewarded in the case of success. The conglomerate control of media industries has also contributed significantly to the level of unionization in the industry, as the unions serve as a key mechanism to help workers negotiate for a fair share.

Another key theme throughout this section is the question of who owns intellectual property rights. Giving up the rights to something not yet made might not seem significant, but in nearly all media industries creative workers must give up creative control and the right to the future creative status of their project in order to access the financing and distribution networks needed to create the good. Many cautionary tales exist of writers, musicians, and filmmakers who have found their creative goods locked up by media industries. Aspiring creatives have little choice but to enter into these agreements because giving up the rights to one's work is a standard condition of entering into dealings with media industries, and mostly only established star talent has been able to self-release and promote goods outside the industries. The documentary *Artifact* (2012) traces the struggles the band Thirty Seconds to Mars (headed by actor Jared Leto) experienced trying to leave a label following a royalty dispute.

THE ECONOMICS OF AUDIENCES: WAYS OF PAYING FOR MEDIA PRODUCTS

The audience, or consumer, is a crucial component of the economics of media industries, and the first thing to understand is that there are two versions of the audience. The first audience is the **"real" audience**—the actual people who show up for a film, subscribe to a newspaper, or buy a new album or song. The problem with the real audience is that it doesn't enter into the equation until after the product has been created and all those costs have been "sunk." Though real audiences can be more meaningful in some of the financing structures discussed later, for the most part, the more important version of the audience is the **"constructed" audience**. Importantly, we use this distinction of the constructed audience to help conceptualize how ideas of "the audience" work in media industries; people who work in these industries do not make this distinction.

The constructed audience is the audience—its characteristics, likes, and dislikes—imagined by creators and those throughout the industry while making media. Though this audience may be, as Angela McRobbie describes it, a "useful fiction," the constructed audience is often based on knowledge about how real audiences have behaved in the past but mostly as perceptions and extrapolations.[25] The constructed audience is important because it is the entity held in mind when hundreds of daily decisions are made in the process of making a media product: Will "the audience" think the end of the movie too depressing? Is this an issue "readers" care about? Will "fans" think that song goes on too long? In all these cases, it is not an actual audience, reader, or fan but the constructed audience—decision-makers' perceptions of how they think the audience will answer—that will render the final verdict. In seeking to design media products that will be attractive to an audience, creators develop constructions of the audience in their minds whom they seek to serve. The constructed audience consequently drives the creation of media products.

The financial underpinnings of how media content is made and paid for affect it in many different ways. We explored the differences in commercial and noncommercial mandates, while noting that there are many variations in the practices of commercial media that affect the content of media produced under this mandate and how it is produced. This is because different structures for commercial media lead to different business strategies. The primary options for funding commercial media are through advertising or various forms of direct payment, although, as we will see, there is also a range of ways of using each of these payment methods that can affect the strategies media industries use in making the content.

Characteristics of Advertiser-Supported Media

We often perceive advertiser-supported media to be "free," but it is important to remember that old adage you may have heard in an economics class: there is no such thing as a free lunch. Indeed, even if we don't pay a particular fee for advertiser-supported media such as broadcast television, we do pay for it—at least the people who buy the products that advertise in the shows do, because the costs of advertising are added to the cost of the goods. Setting that aside for now, advertiser funding sets up certain conditions that affect how media industries operate. Advertiser support is the common economic model of continuous media industries. Though many media also require some subscription payment, those media that blend advertiser and audience payment typically rely most heavily on the advertiser support.

Most important, introducing advertisers is what makes many media **dual product markets**. This is because there are effectively two things ("dual products") being sold. The main commodity is the audience: a radio station is selling an audience of listeners to an advertiser. Most listeners, however, never consider this, and it seems the station is also "selling" a schedule of programming to them. Too often, we focus on the part of this equation that is likely most of interest—what songs the station is offering and whether we like them. Instead, it is important to remember that the programming is just the bait the stations use to draw us together so that we hear the content of real importance (in an economic sense at least), which is the advertising message. We don't mean to suggest that it is not also important to examine the content of advertiser-supported media. Even as stations and networks gather us to sell us to advertisers, the content they offer still does significant cultural work, but we are focusing on economic matters here.

Because the advertisers, rather than the audience, are paying networks and radio stations, the advertisers gain a significant role in the creative process. In the early days of radio and television, the company doing the advertising was often responsible for developing programming—or it was the responsibility of the advertising agency that the advertiser hired. The agency would then bring the programming to the network, and the network had little involvement in developing the programming at all. This was the case as long as **single sponsorship** was the norm. In the case of single sponsorship, there is typically only one advertiser—or sponsor—associated with a program, and that sponsor pays all of the costs of production, as well as fees to the network and the advertising agency. The lower production costs of radio made this system more feasible for that medium. However, the costs of video production—as well as a variety of other industrial factors—made sponsorship less practical for television. In addition to television production being too costly for most single advertisers to finance on a weekly basis, the networks desired to take greater control of their schedules and programming as audiences moved from radio to television.

If you were an advertiser, think about how your expectations and concerns might differ if you sponsored a program, in comparison with just paying for one of a handful of advertisements in the show. If you were sponsoring, chances are that a huge percentage of your advertising budget would go to financing just one weekly show. Having so much of your advertising budget concentrated in one place and having your product so closely associated with that program—for example, the name of your product would likely be part of the title of the show, as in the *Texaco Star Theater*—would probably lead you to be very concerned with every aspect of the content of the program. Everything about the show would reflect on your product, and you might want to use the show to try to create some type of association between how viewers regard the show and how they regard your product. Unlike the advertising we are accustomed to now, when single sponsorship dominated, many companies sought to use advertising to advance **company voice** rather than to focus on the attributes of the product. Sponsorship, and the amount of control over content that came with it, was particularly ideal for this advertising strategy.

As television developed, however, single sponsorship faded as the dominant advertising strategy. What is often called **magazine-format advertising**, because magazines had long featured advertisements from multiple companies, soon became the norm on television. Instead of paying the production costs of an entire program, advertisers purchased 30-second spots in the manner we are accustomed to now. Competition from television led to radio's transition from radio programs to the music and talk formats familiar today. These formats also lent themselves to an array of advertisers.

For the television industry, this switch in strategy had a number of consequences. This practice allowed the networks greater control as they became responsible for developing programming and deciding how to schedule it. Advertisers now had their budgets spread across spots in multiple shows, which decreased their association with any one show. Advertising could attend more to selling attributes of the product because it became unnecessary to integrate the good into the program in some way, as viewers quickly came to understand the commercials as separate from the content of the shows.

Given this history, perhaps it is somewhat surprising to witness the increasing prevalence of older strategies such as **product placement** and **branded entertainment** in the past decade. In the case of television, the addition of this commercial strategy—while maintaining traditional commercial pods as well—has developed as a response to the new technological abilities of viewers that enable them to skip commercial pods and to the type of content that has proven successful on broadband distributors such as YouTube. Placement brings yet other concerns and issues for media industries. Many in the advertising industry believe that product placement must be "organic"—that it must seem natural or fit well—if it is to succeed. This, then, leads certain types of content to be more likely to receive product placement advertising dollars, which, in the long term, might curtail other types of programming from being created. Product placement works much better in "reality" programming than scripted programming, and some fear for the future of scripted programming if it isn't able to make use of this additional financial stream.

Advertisers still worry about the content surrounding their commercials, but they offer less direct, day-to-day influence over the process than was once the case. Advertiser influence is now more indirect and often a matter of the perceptions creators have of what advertisers desire. Similar to the constructed audience, creative executives often have a "constructed advertiser" in mind. Advertisers do see the shows that their commercial will air in before they are broadcast (or, rather, the advertising agency responsible for buying the spot typically manages this work), but it is rare for them to withdraw an advertisement. If they do, it is typically not because of major ideological conflicts with the show but because of concern about correlations viewers might draw. For example, a car company might pull an advertisement set to air in the midst of a storyline about a grizzly car crash on a hospital show. It is not that the company wants to keep stories about car crashes from being told; it is just that they don't want to promote their brand in the midst of that story and risk viewers associating their product with the crash.

Advertisers' perceptions of their market also can make it difficult for some content to find sponsors. Gloria Steinem wrote of the challenges *Ms. Magazine* faced finding advertisers in the 1970s. As a feminist publication, its creators wanted to avoid the types of ads common in women's magazines that sent the message that women needed lots of beauty products just to feel good about themselves. When the editors tried to replace diet and beauty products with goods from other sectors, they found several industries, such as the automotive and electronics industries, didn't think targeting women was important because they didn't realize women's significant role in buying these goods. *Ms. Magazine* ultimately became funded by subscription alone because it couldn't find enough advertisers to match its message.

Despite the rarity of direct advertiser influence, the perception of what advertisers might and might not like certainly governs much of the thinking of media creators throughout the creation process. Media workers have internalized many of the concerns various advertisers have had in the past, and they are likely to steer content in certain directions even if they aren't given specific directions. The experience of "getting notes" from advertisers and managers also influences creative staffs. Jimmy Draper uses the term **discerning savvy** to describe how writers learn the preferences of their editors and come to propose stories based on how well they think the editor will like the story even when the editor never gives any specific guidance.[26] Though every creator may react to these situations differently, over the course of working in the industry, writers and producers quickly learn what types of content superiors and advertisers prefer and what types of stories will require fights and negotiation. Many different personal and professional factors then contribute to their agency in pushing for particular content and their willingness to engage in those negotiations. Even if the influence of advertisers isn't direct—as in the case of an advertiser refusing to run its commercial in a particular show or magazine—the indirect influence on what creative workers perceive as possible is very real and powerful.

In selecting and developing content that will be supported by advertisers, media creators must negotiate a fine balance with both viewers and advertisers. Creators must try to figure out what content will attract audiences as well as be acceptable to advertisers. Given the unpredictability of audiences when it comes to their tastes for cultural products ("nobody knows"), this is no small feat. All of the things we've discussed for advertising-only industries are true for those that rely on both advertising and direct payment, but they are made more complex by the need to entice audiences as well as advertisers to spend on their goods. Before turning to media with dual revenue streams, the next subsection discusses media that primarily rely on some form of audience payment, which is characteristic of most media producing single goods.

Characteristics of Media Not Supported by Advertising

Audiences or consumers pay for media that are not advertiser supported, typically either through **subscription** or **direct pay,** which is also sometimes called **transaction payment**. In this case, the viewer, reader, or listener is the only source of revenue for the media outlet. Premium television channels such as HBO and Showtime operate with a subscription model, as does streaming service Netflix and some music streaming services such as Pandora, in which consumers buy access to package of goods. Even a few specialized print media (*Ms. Magazine* and *Consumer Reports*, for example) are funded without advertisers.

The film, music, and book industries and most of the gaming industry rely on direct payment for specific goods. In some ways, the tasks of these media are easier, since they don't have the extra layer of advertisers in their process, though they must achieve a higher level of interest with consumers and create products desired enough that potential audience members are willing to pay to access them. This also means that we might expect them to operate in much different ways than advertiser-supported media.

Direct Pay

Many media that produce single goods rely on direct payment from audiences for their revenue. The direct payment of film admissions, movie rentals, and music sales— whether you purchase a CD or pay for a download from iTunes—are similar. In all of these cases, media industries need to convince their audiences that their products are worth paying for. And unlike in the case of subscription payment, these industries have to marshal audience interest for each and every product, which leads to marketing costs that often rival the costs required to produce the goods. Certainly the fact that audiences develop some attributes—for example, that the movie-going audience tends to be young—leads these industries to emphasize particular types of content.

Subscription

The consequences of subscription payment vary by media industry. Most everyone has encountered subscription in the form of a communication service such as a mobile phone plan or a subscription for Internet, cable, or satellite service. In the case of subscriptions for content, it is important to begin by thinking about how it is different to buy access to a package of goods—as through a Netflix subscription—instead of purchasing particular goods and, likewise, how it is different to sell a package of goods instead of particular ones.

Relying solely on subscription payments allows channels such as HBO and Showtime to operate much differently than channels that are advertiser supported or rely on a blend of advertiser and subscription funding. Most people assume the biggest differences have to do with the greater content freedom that comes from not having advertisers who might worry about offending part of the audience and because advertiser-supported industries such as broadcasting are regulated differently. Though these factors are important, the more significant consequence comes from the way that focusing on keeping viewers happy enough to maintain a monthly subscription allows subscription-funded media to worry less about the ratings of each and every program or every issue.*

---

*This article takes a close look at the economics of subscription outlet HBO and the varied ways it earns revenue. How does HBO's business model explain its early and aggressive move into streaming access though HBO Go? Why would HBO want to have its own platform, as opposed to licensing content to Netflix? http://www.economist.com/node/21526314

Premium television channels don't care how many or which shows on their channel you watch. All that really matters is that you find enough of value to maintain that monthly subscription fee. This allows them to approach programming much differently than an advertiser-supported channel. In some ways, the most viable strategy is to maintain just a little programming that meets the needs of vastly different audience groups, particularly program content those audiences can't get anywhere else. HBO provided a good example of this strategy in the early 2000s. Chances are that the channel's sports programming, such as boxing and *Inside the NFL*, reached a different audience than might have tuned in for *Sex and the City*. What HBO hoped, however, was that the young, single women who loved *Sex and the City* would want to watch that show so badly, and maybe a movie every now and then, that they would maintain their subscriptions, while young men would want to be able to see the big boxing matches badly enough that they too would maintain their subscriptions, even if they watched little else on the channel. (Of course, men also watched *Sex and the City*—a fine example of the broad generalizations characteristic of the constructed audience.) In contrast, the advertiser-supported network has to gather a big audience to sell to advertisers throughout every day. Just having a few specific programs isn't enough for them to succeed.

The question of how an industry is financed is of crucial importance to the way it develops content. When *The Sopranos* appeared on HBO in the late 1990s, it led many to reassess the storytelling potential of television. Certainly, some aspects of *The Sopranos*—its exceptional violence, use of profanity, and incorporation of sexual content—would be impossible for broadcasters because of their different regulatory conditions. Much of the storytelling sophistication, however, such as concentrating on a morally ambiguous hero and the use of actors who did not conform to conventional looks, were aspects that could work in other forms of television. The FX cable channel in particular quickly made a name for itself by developing shows such as *The Shield*, *Rescue Me*, and *Sons of Anarchy* that reproduced various aspects of *The Sopranos* template. The past decade of US television has indicated just how different media industry operations can be when financed in part or whole by viewers/readers/listeners rather than just by advertisers.

In the case of the few magazines funded solely through subscription, this financing is meant as an indicator of independence and of a particular editorial mission. For example, the reputation of *Consumer Reports* largely depends on consumers knowing the magazine's editorial staff operates independently of the products that they review and that there is no chance of bias toward an advertiser. Sometimes the reason for relying on subscribers is more vague. *Cooks Illustrated* magazine does do some of the product reviews typical of *Consumer Reports*, but, for the most part, it is just a cooking magazine absent advertising.

Emerging Payment Models

The growing ubiquity of smartphones and tablet computers has created opportunities for media companies to explore newer forms of payment as well, specifically in-app purchases and **freemium** content. In-app purchases are, of course, merely a form of direct pay, but the nature of gaming and digital distribution make it possible to continue to seek payment from the same consumer with minor improvements or incentives. For instance, many gaming apps offer premium content or greater player functionality if the consumer pays a small price.

A particular form of payment that digital media and devices have ushered in is known as "freemium" content, in which some content or basic functionality is available for free but added functionality requires payment.* The highly successful Madden NFL Football game, for example, adopted a freemium model when it released Madden 25 to smartphones and devices, celebrating the game's twenty-fifth anniversary. What had been a pricey download was now available for free; however, in order to acquire better packages of players and more types of competitions, players needed to pay small fees. Sometimes, players can earn freemium packages through extensive playing, which is valuable to game makers who have advertising embedded in their games.

Although freemium content is primarily restricted to gaming, we can also see similar practices in online music sales, where potential consumers can listen to a portion of a song or an album before paying to download the whole thing. Likewise, when Amazon released its new TV series *Transparent* in the fall of 2014, it made the pilot episode available for free in order to try to induce consumers to sign up for its "prime" service to see the entire season. Although these examples from beyond the world of gaming might just as well be considered as free samples, as opposed to the distinction between basic and premium content in the gaming industry, all of this free content takes advantage of media devices and the ease with which consumers can purchase additional content in order to entice us into paying for media.

Characteristics of Media With Dual Revenue Streams

To complicate economic conditions in commercial media industries further, many media rely on some blend of advertiser support and subscription or direct payment by the media user. This is the case of most print media, basic cable television, some satellite radio, Hulu Plus, and some YouTube channels.[27] These media are often discussed as having **dual revenue streams**, as they receive funding from both advertisers and viewers/readers.

Dual revenue streams enable these industries to operate in ways that have particular consequences for their creative content. These media must be more attentive to their audiences than free media, because they require the viewer or reader to pay some amount for their product. In other words, there is a cost for use that is not the case for fully advertiser-supported media, but most media with a dual revenue stream depend most heavily on advertisers. For instance, advertising generally accounts for 50 to 60 percent of a magazine's revenue, although that figure may be closer to 80 percent depending on the magazine type, with the rest of the revenue coming from subscriptions and newsstand sales. Consequently, keeping advertisers happy remains as essential for dual revenue as it is for media supported by advertising alone.

---

*This YouTube video features Chris Anderson explaining Free! What other ideas can you think of for how media companies can earn revenue if they give content away in the manner Anderson suggests? https://www.youtube.com/watch?v=RZkeCIW75CU

The reconfiguration of business models required in response to digitization is changing these norms. In a significant shift that illustrates just how substantially the newspaper industry has changed, in 2013 *The New York Times* earned more revenue through subscription than advertising, a shift that coincided with the erection of a pay wall for extensive online access.

Like media supported only through advertising, those operating with a dual revenue stream have significant pressure for their content to appeal to a sizable audience. The dual revenue media need subscribers to derive enough value that they keep paying their subscriptions or making direct payments, but they also want to keep that vast audience base, because that is part of what they are selling to advertisers. Losing a subscriber hurts in two ways, then: one fewer subscription fee paid to the media company and one fewer audience member to sell to advertisers. This explains why you sometimes might receive offers for magazines discounted so considerably that you wonder how they can make any money off of your subscription (they don't). In this case, the title is probably seeking to increase its advertising rates by showing growth in its subscription base.

The dual streams also explain some of the differential pricing evident in some media industries. For example, *Wired* magazine editor Chris Anderson notes that readers might face three different price points in accessing magazine content.[28] Readers can find articles free online, although typically with less design and fewer photographs; they can buy an issue for $4.95 on the newsstand; or they can subscribe and receive a year's worth of issues for as little as $10. The economics of each is a bit different, as you might guess. The Internet reader provides only advertising revenue—which Anderson notes amounts to between $5 and $20 per thousand views, or between one and four cents per person. Many publications make the same content available online as is in the print edition. This allows the magazine to amortizing the cost of creating the content over the entire audience (print and online), which means it can cost the magazine less than a cent to make that content available online.

The revenue from the newsstand version is split with the retailer (retailers typically receive a bit less than half). The magazine typically earns $1 or $2 of profit after the printing and distribution costs are factored in. More than half the copies of most magazines printed for retail, however, don't sell. These are returned and pulped, cutting into the profits of those that do sell. Anderson explains that most magazines lose money on newsstand sales but that newsstand sales provide a good promotional strategy for obtaining new subscribers, and they do earn advertising revenues on the copies that sell.

Finally, the actual cost of printing and mailing 12 issues of a magazine is about $15 (and more like $30 if you include the costs of acquiring subscribers). Yet magazines routinely charge less, which provides some direct revenue while the advertising makes up the difference. Interestingly, Anderson notes that most magazines earn enough from advertising that they could be made available for free. Even a minimal $10 charge is psychologically important, however, because it suggests that the reader values the magazine (unlike, say, junk mail), which makes advertisers willing to pay as much as five times more in advertising rates for that reader.

As this magazine example illustrates, the combination of revenue streams offers some flexibility in how dual revenue media target audiences. Notably, despite the dual revenue, in most cases the more lucrative funding stream comes from advertisers. Thus when seeking to understand dual revenue media, it is important keep in mind all of the factors addressed in the advertiser-supported and direct-pay sections as well.

EMERGING BUSINESS STRATEGIES
FOR MEDIA INDUSTRIES

It seems certain at this point that how advertising supports media industries in the future will look quite different than it has in the past. What is far less certain is what that new norm will look like. Advocates of the future of digital media industries have argued these industries have a competitive advantage over older advertising norms as a result of their ability to more precisely connect advertisers not just with people but with people who are actually interested in the products of specific advertisers.

By 2015, Google's AdWords was the most successful of these ventures, earning an estimated $30 billion in 2013. AdWords features flexible pricing based on a bidding system for key search terms determined by the advertiser. But Google's algorithms set rates based on more than just ability to pay top dollar, which prevents the companies with the largest advertising budgets from crowding out smaller operations. Google also factors in a "quality score" based on the relevance of what the retailer offers to the specific search, which helps to ensure a relevant search experience that helps keep searchers using Google.

For example, if you search "lizard-skin sandals," the top returns in Google "ads related to lizard skin sandals" are for Sandals Resorts and Zelli, an Italian shoe retailer, while online shoe retailer Zappos is the highest result in the right-side bar of ads. Sandals Resorts likely bid a lot to be the top return anytime someone searches "sandals," even though it is irrelevant to this search. In addition to the amount it bid for these terms, Zelli likely rose to the top because of the specificity of the link, which means it has a high quality score in the Google algorithm. The link takes you to a page with eight pairs of lizard skin shoes. The Zappos link, in contrast, just takes you to its sandals page, where Zappos offers 6,840 pairs of sandals but none made from lizard skin. In 2014 AdWords accounted for 70 percent of Google's revenues, a lower percentage than was once the case. Google has developed more revenue streams, but AdWords remains the lifeblood of the company, and its revenue allows Google to offer many of its other products and services for free and to participate in significant research and development endeavors. *

AdWords illustrates a change from past dominant advertising strategies built on blanketing vast audiences with an advertising message and instead allows much greater precision in messaging. In fact, the most revolutionary aspect of AdWords is that advertisers only pay when potential customers actually click through to their pages—a radical departure from media advertising where a dog food advertiser pays for all those

---

*This video provides a helpful explanation of AdWords. What are the key differences in the advertising arrangement offered by AdWords and traditional models found in newspaper and television advertising? https://www.youtube.com/watch?v=TgyFEutUGnw

who hear or see a message, even those who don't own dogs, as well as those who have dogs but have no intention of changing food brands.

Another notable refinement of advertising strategies in the digital media environment comes from companies seeking to better leverage what they know about media users. A key example of this is Facebook's efforts to monetize its "Like" button. When a Facebook member acknowledges that he or she "Likes" something, Facebook is able to target that person's friends as a potentially like-minded community. In other words, if your Facebook friend acknowledges that they "like" Levi's jeans, Facebook may then sell you to Levi's as a potential consumer. The behavior of friends proves a far more precise way of identifying shared interests or buying habits than the much more blunt demographic sorters such as gender, age, and income level that have supported media advertising until now. The ability of Facebook, or another company that it sells its data to, to combine knowledge about social media participants' lives and the goods and services they like, and to then serve that specialized audience to advertisers, offers a giant step toward the precision in advertising messaging advertisers have long sought.*

It is too soon to know how this might change media industries and their products. Though opportunities for targeting exist, the difficulty of obtaining accurate data about advertising views and the potentially endless supply of online ads have prevented advertisers from moving aggressively into these advertising spaces outside of search. The disruption of established advertising norms will continue for years as the industry sorts out the ways in which online media advertising is like and different from the advertising practices they've long engaged in, as well as the ways new distribution technologies enable direct pay and subscription for some products and consumers. Among many challenges are the revision of standard pricing practices—digital distributors can charge much more per person because of their precision (typically measured as cost per thousand), and this may enable media drawing smaller audiences to achieve significant advertiser support. Also, strategies for reach (number of people who see an ad) and frequency (how often an ad is seen) may need reevaluating in the digital advertising world. Some companies may still find paying lower rates for less precise targeting preferable to the higher rates of precision targeting. And, of course, nothing is stopping enterprising workers in legacy media from trying experiments with their own advertising methods as well. Many emerging routes of digital distribution of legacy media allow the same possibilities to know more about who watches ads to allow these industries access to more specific ad sales as well.

CONCLUSION

As this chapter illustrates, economic conditions can influence the operation of media industries in many different ways. The methods used to finance production and the range of mechanisms through which audiences pay for media all combine to push

---

*Within this podcast, there is an informative story about how Facebook monetizes the "Like" button. Again, how is this different from traditional advertising? How does it differ from AdWords? (The story plays from 43:15-48:00) http://www.marketplace.org/topics/tech/marketers-you

content in various directions. As the Industrialization of Culture framework points out, these economic considerations combine with a set of possibilities made feasible by regulations and, as we discuss in the next chapter, the technology of the day.

Though we have tried to address the broad range of factors that contribute to media economics, we've only scratched the surface and emphasized media industries with established histories. The business models of all media industries are in the midst of considerable change—some more than others—as a result of the many ways that digitization is reconfiguring the costs of production and distribution, as well as how and how much audiences pay for media and their increased ability to avoid advertising.

The business model of every media industry established before digital distribution is in some sort of crisis as we write. Such moments provide exceptional opportunities to radically reconfigure businesses; but in the midst of that change there is also considerable uncertainty. We imagine this chapter might look very different if we revise it 10 years from now. We've emphasized the known and tried-and-true components of media economics throughout the chapter, though we by no means forecast these as likely to dominate the future.

Nevertheless, as a conceptual framework, it remains helpful to begin by thinking about how a media organization can finance the creation of its products and how it will then recoup those costs as new uses and forms of media develop. We offer the reminder to be wary of the Underpants Gnomes discussed in Chapter 1. Some of the new media that currently have the most "buzz" lack that middle step of earning profit, and many are earning them in entirely new ways, for example, by selling their vast data. Although they seem dizzyingly cool to users, revenue models have proven frustratingly difficult to incorporate in many cases, at least to an extent that captures the level of audience interest and engagement characteristic of the service. The Internet makes a great many things possible, but, in commercial media industries, those things must also have a profit model to recoup costs if they are to be sustained.

New experiments appear constantly, and some experiments of five years ago have become norms. The dual product market of advertiser support allowed for some "free" media in the past, but digital distribution reconfigures the economics of many industries so that there may now be ways for media industries to profit even if allowing free distribution of their content.[29] One strategy involves subscriptions for premium access to content— or the freemium strategy we discussed. In this model, media companies give away access to some features—perhaps the ability to stream, to play certain levels of games, or to read recent newspaper or magazine coverage—but they also charge audiences to download songs, access additional game levels, or search and access archived stories.

Shifting the profit center of media industries is another strategy. At this point, this is best seen in the music industry, where musicians have given away access to their music or experimented with pricing as in the oft-cited case of Radiohead's 2007 *In Rainbows* release, in which the band allowed fans to select how much to pay for the album. Bands and artists receive most of their earnings from touring and merchandise, so, for them, the purpose of album and song releases is expanding the base of potential concert-goers. In this case, the free—or reduced price—content works as a way to promote the more lucrative concert experience.

Certainly, this type of loss leader or cross-subsidy economics was in use throughout the media industries even before the digital era. Game companies have discounted the cost of game hardware and made up the costs in the charges for game licenses, and mobile phone providers often discount phones considerably in exchange for a service commitment. **Crowdfunding** has appeared as another possibility, particularly for artists with a devoted fan base, as evident in the 2013 Kickstarter campaigns for the *Veronica Mars* movie and for Zach Braff's *Garden State* sequel *Wish I Were Here*. Some of these strategies may be more applicable to some media industries than others, and the degree of experiment evident is largely correlated with the level of crisis the industry is experiencing. Nonetheless, such experiments may offer the foundation of economic conditions in the future.

QUESTIONS

1. Select media content that you purchased or experienced this week and list all of the expenses involved in its creation that you can think of in the four categories (overhead, development, production, and marketing and distribution). Which categories seem the most and least excessive and why?

2. Say an up-and-coming actress friend of yours just came to you seeking advice on her latest movie contract. She has just secured the lead in a mid-budget studio movie. Expectations for the movie are high, and it is predicted to do well at the box office. The producers offered her the choice of making the standard actors' guild minimum rate, which would amount to $200,000 for her work and the potential of also receiving 7 percent of the net profits, or earning a flat fee of $250,000 for her role in the movie with no profit participation. What advice would you give her and why?

3. You have a fairly unique idea for a new console game; however, the concept and graphics required to execute the game flawlessly will require a significant amount of financing and an extended development process. Given these constraints, would you rather pursue the development on your own or seek to work for a major publisher or console maker? Why did you select either option? What are the influences, if any, from the various forms of production on the final product? How would a game produced by a first-party developer differ from that produced through an independent producer or by a third-party developer? Are there any specific advantages/disadvantages to either production context that you can think of?

4. If you were a journalist, how might the content of the articles you develop differ if you were guaranteed a weekly paycheck versus if you had to sell a magazine on an idea in order to be paid? Or, from a different vantage point, why might a studio or magazine prefer to keep workers on a freelance-only basis? What consequences would this likely have for the creative products they make?

5. Imagine that you are a television producer. How might selling a show in deficit financing lead you to behave differently than in the cost plus system? What type of show would you think is likelier to succeed in one versus the other? Or, how might you develop the same show differently in each system? Thinking through these questions

should give you some sense of how the method of financing a show contributes to determining the creative forms likely to circulate in a culture.

6. Think about the media you subscribe to. What do you expect from them to maintain your subscription? Also, think about the nature of your experience with other media you pay for. Many of our students buy much of the music they listen to through single-song transactions on iTunes. How does your media use differ when you buy a "subscription" allowing access to any song you want as long as you pay a monthly fee? How might subscription services be profitable for media industries beyond the licensing fee paid by the service?

7. Can you imagine how films might be different if they were advertiser supported? How about the music industry?

FURTHER READING

More detailed accounts from an economics perspective can be found in Richard E. Caves, *Switching Channels: Organization and Change in TV Broadcasting* (Cambridge: Harvard University Press, 2005); Gillian Doyle, *Understanding Media Economics*, 2nd ed. (London: SAGE, 2013); Robert G. Picard, *The Economics and Financing of Media Companies*, 2nd ed. (New York: Fordham University Press, 2011), and *Creative Industries: Contracts between Art and Commerce* (Cambridge: Harvard University Press, 2002); and Colin Hoskins, Stuart M. McFadden, and Adam Finn, *Media Economics: Applying Economics to New and Traditional Media* (Thousand Oaks, Calif.: SAGE, 2004). For matters of media economics with attention to culture, see Bernard Miege, *The Capitalization of Cultural Production* (New York: International General, 1989) and David Hesmondhalgh, *The Cultural Industries*, 3rd ed. (London: SAGE, 2012).

Various accounts of concerns related to ownership structure and conglomeration can be found in Ben H. Bagdikian, *The New Media Monopoly* (Boston: Beacon Press, 2004); Benjamin M. Compaine and Douglas Gomery, *Who Owns the Media? Competition and Concentration in the Mass Media Industry*, 3rd ed. (Mahwah, N.J.: Lawrence Erlbaum Associates, 2000); and almost anything by Robert McChesney. An interesting contrast can be found in the cases explored in Michael Curtin's "Feminine Desire in the Age of Satellite Television," *Journal of Communication* 49 (1999): 55–70, and Christopher Anderson's "Creating the Twenty-First Century Television Network: NBC in the Age of Media Conglomeration," in *NBC: America's Network*, edited by Michele Hilmes (Berkeley: University of California Press, 2007), 275–290.

Also see the Further Reading section at the end of Chapter 2 for sources that deal with the particular operations of various industries.

NOTES

1. Joseph Turow, *Media Today* (New York: Routledge, 2008), 301.
2. Ibid., 305.
3. Robert G. Picard, *The Economics and Financing of Media Companies*, 2nd ed. (New York: Fordham University Press, 2011), 27.

4. These distinctions are adapted from Miege's tripartite distinctions of publishing, written press, and flow industries. Bernard Miege, *The Capitalization of Cultural Production* (New York: International General, 1989).

5. Edward Jay Epstein, *The Big Picture: Money and Power in Hollywood* (New York: Random House, 2005), 117.

6. Among industry workers, these costs are often defined as post-production because they take place after shooting, but we are working with a broader definition of production.

7. Turow, *Media Today*, 400.

8. Epstein, *Big Picture*, 117.

9. Larry Gerbrandt, "Does Movie Marketing Matter?" *The Hollywood Reporter*, June 10, 2010. http://www.hollywoodreporter.com/news/does-movie-marketing-matter-24514 (accessed February 13, 2015).

10. Kevin Jagernauth, "Does *Man of Steel* Need to Make $1 Billion to Be A Success?" *IndieWIRE*, June 7, 2013. http://blogs.indiewire.com/theplaylist/does-man-of-steel-need-to-make-1-billion-to-be-a-success-20130607 (accessed February 13, 2015).

11. Epstein, *Big Picture*, 118.

12. http://www.g2mi.com/company_description.php?id=1751&name=Sony-Pictures-Entertainment-(SPE)-Inc

13. "Toolkit Case Study: How Indie Hit *Winter's Bone* Came to Be," *IndieWIRE*, November 4, 2010. http://www.indiewire.com/article/toolkit_case_study_winters_bone (accessed February 5, 2014).

14. Ibid; John Lyons Murphy, "Independent Film Finance: A Primer—Part Two—Private Equity," December 12, 2012. http://socialstorytellers.aboutfacemedia .com/11136/independent-film-finance-a-primer-part-two-private-equity (accessed February 13, 2015).

15. Information found in Aphra Kerr's *The Business and Culture of Digital Games: Gamework/Gameplay* (Los Angeles: SAGE, 2006) was crucial to the development of this section.

16. This PDF summarizes the complicated union and guild agreements regarding residuals in various markets: www.jhandel.com/s/Residuals-chart-v-33.pdf

17. John Dempsey, "Lifetime Nabs Mother Cable Rights," Variety.com, September 23, 2008, http://www.variety.com/article/VR1117992752.html?categoryid=1238&cs=1 (accessed September 28, 2008).

18. John Dempsey, "Twentieth Hits Mother Lode," Variety.com, September 14, 2008, http://www.variety.com/article/VR1117992173.html?categoryid=1238&cs=1 (accessed September 16, 2008).

19. Epstein, *Big Picture*, 5, 16.

20. Ibid., 19.

21. Ibid., 355.

22. Lauren A. Schuker, "Plot Change: Foreign Forces Transform Hollywood Films," *The Wall Street Journal*, August 2, 2010. http://online.wsj.com/news/articles/SB1000142 4052748704913304575371394036766312 (accessed February 13, 2015).

23. "Home Entertainment Market Grows Modestly for Second Straight Year as Disc-Sale Declines Remain Moderate," IHS Pressroom, January 16, 2014. http://press.ihs.com/press-release/design-supply-chain/home-entertainment-market-grows-modestly-second-straight-year-disc (accessed February 13, 2015).

24. http://www.economist.com/node/18178291 (accessed February 15, 2015).

25. Angela McRobbie, *British Fashion Design: Rag Trade or Image Industry?* (London: Routledge, 1998), 152.

26. Jimmy Draper "Theorizing Creative Agency through 'Discerned Savvy': A Tool for the Critical Study of Media Industries," *Media, Culture & Society* 36, no. 8 (2014), 1118–1133.

27. Not to risk confusion, but it is arguably the case that by 2010 in the United States, broadcast television also had dual revenue streams because of the "retransmission consent" fees that broadcasters came to demand from cable and satellite systems.

28. Chris Anderson, *Free: The Future of a Radical Price* (New York: Hyperion, 2009), 57–59.

29. Anderson, *Free*, 57–59.

CHAPTER 6

—

Technological Conditions of the Media Industries

Key Takeaways:

Appreciate the value of the circuit of cultural production for developing understandings of media technologies and how to apply it to contemporary technologies

Understand the complex intersection of technology with regulatory and economic conditions and be able to identify examples of those intersections

Understand how and why media industries prevent technological innovation

---

The nonprofit organization One Laptop per Child aims to give free, durable laptops run on manual power that can be connected to the Internet to the poorest children in the world. By 2012, the organization had delivered nearly 2.5 million such laptops to children in developing nations. The initiative is an effort to help disadvantaged children overcome the limitations of poor local schools by allowing them to connect to the vast educational resources of the Internet and make available its tools to those lacking educational opportunities. Underlying this mission is the assumption that technology alone—absent any institutional or cultural support—can interest children in learning and improve their educational development. Becoming better-educated world citizens is not the ultimate goal, according to the Nicholas Negroponte, a professor at MIT and the driving force behind One Laptop per Child. Rather, the goal is to eliminate poverty. Negroponte hopes that, by using technology to help individuals, communities, and entire nations leapfrog from preindustrial to postindustrial societies, young people in developing nations will not only be able to compete for jobs with their more privileged counterparts in the developed nations but will also be able to become successful local entrepreneurs able to lift their communities out of poverty as they themselves acquire more wealth.

The science fiction writer William Gibson has much different visions of technology. In his version, large conglomerates dominate the near future, creating social and psychological alienation and using intense surveillance, all made possible by unchecked technological growth. His visions have had a strong impact on Hollywood films about the future, including such blockbusters as *Avatar*, the *Matrix* and *Terminator* series, and

Minority Report. One of Gibson's short stories, "Johnny Mnemonic," is a good illustration of these themes, and it was made into a movie that is something of a precursor to *The Matrix.* "Johnny Mnemonic" follows a futuristic "courier" who carries information stored in his cybernetic brain. After receiving some highly sensitive and deadly information, Mnemonic struggles to remove the data in order to escape an assassin and prevent an overload of information from "crashing" his brain. His search leads him into The Sprawl, a huge, postindustrial, poverty-stricken area where criminals, drug addicts, and mutants live "off the grid" in a nightmarish underworld that is almost completely isolated from the high-tech cities where Mnemonic has lived his life. More recent movies that reflect societal concerns about how technology is reshaping culture include *Source Code* (2011) and *Elysium* (2013).

Negroponte's faith in the power of technology to create positive change in the world, almost regardless of the forces that stand in the way of that change, is something that we would characterize as **technological utopianism**, an idea that dates back as far as the Enlightenment in Western societies and that sees technological innovation as bringing about an idyllic human society on Earth. While this kind of excitement about new technology may feel very modern to us, it has, in fact, attended every new media technology since the nineteenth century. Likewise, **technological dystopianism**, like that of Gibson, may make for good reading and raise important questions about our technological future, but such visions also intentionally tend toward hyperbole in order to make their point and evoke a response from the reader or viewer.

In contrast to these two extremes, we view media technologies and technological change as one of three powerful conditions that—in conjunction with economic conditions and regulatory conditions—shape the media industries, the goods they produce, and the societies in which they are consumed. Though technology is powerful, it is also powerfully shaped by the other conditions, as well as the various practices to which those technologies are put and the cultures into which they are introduced. In other words, the ultimate impact of any media technology on media industries depends on a range of factors that come from both within and beyond the technology itself.

In this chapter, we explore the technological conditions within which media industries operate. Our aim is not to provide a thorough overview of current technologies or initiatives of technology companies but rather to address some of the larger questions about the relationships between technological conditions—particularly innovation—and the media industries, as well as to account for the historical conditions that have shaped the media industries to date. Since this chapter concludes the discussion of "Conditions," we also attend extensively to the interplay among regulation, economics, and technology. We discuss in greater detail the role of digitization as a current force of technological change in Chapter 9.

To some of you, drawing lessons about media technology from technologies more than 50 or even more than 100 years old might seem odd, given the popular impression that we live in a thoroughly different technological environment than we did even 20 years ago. And, in many ways, it can be argued that technology is a particularly significant condition of media industry operation in this time of growing digital and mobile uses of media. If we are to truly understand how technological conditions are influencing contemporary media industries, however, we must realize that recent changes have not occurred in a vacuum. Instead, the details of those changes have a lot to do with how prior technological conditions had already shaped the industries. For instance, the ways in which cable television, Internet news, and political blogs have undermined the idea of journalistic objectivity in today's world can only be understood against the backdrop of how the earlier technology of telegraphy helped usher in the era of objectivity in journalism in the first place, as newswire services tried hard to market their products nationwide to newspapers with quite distinct—and blatant—political sensibilities.

Technological conditions may seem to operate independently of the other conditions we discuss in the book, but they intersect extensively with the regulatory and economic conditions of the media industries. The television networks of the 1960s, for instance, wielded great economic and political power due to regulatory conditions that minimized competition from cable television. The *technology* of the time would have permitted the development of cable channels much earlier than was the case, but *regulatory* conditions, specifically the ban against cable channels originating their own programming, prevented these developments. Beginning in the early 1970s, however, the Federal Communications Commission began loosening restrictions on cable, which ushered in the beginnings of the television landscape with which we are familiar today.

Technological changes, then, can be both helped and hindered by economic and regulatory conditions. In addition—at the level of practices—media production, distribution, and aggregation processes can have profound influences on technological conditions and, of course, vice versa. As we mentioned in Chapter 4's discussion of regulation, radio broadcasting was initially an extension of the telegraph and was used not for entertainment or news but instead as a way to carry messages, much like a telephone. In fact, early radio developers promoted it as a "telephone booth of the airwaves," or a way to send personal messages to one another without wires, not unlike contemporary mobile phones.[1] In an effort to sell radio sets, some entrepreneurs began sending signals over the airwaves that carried music that anyone with a set could access. This use of the technology came to be known as "broadcasting," a term taken from farming that refers to the practice of throwing seed widely when planting, or "casting" the seed "broadly." The creation of public messages for multiple listeners, rather than private messages for a single listener, squeezed out the earlier use of the technology to the point where almost no one today thinks of radio as a private communication medium. Today, we can imagine a time when the now ubiquitous devices we carry in our pockets and call "phones" come to be called something else because using them as devices for talking to another person becomes less important than their other functionalities.*

---

*These links to NPR stories provide a helpful context for thinking about the role of technology in changes in music formats and for the application of the vocabulary of the chapter. The first story discusses the rise and fall of the CD as a technology. Although the clip mainly deals with the economic decisions of the record industry concerning the CD between 1982 and 2000, think about which technological features of the CD also simultaneously contributed to its rise and fall. http://www.npr.org/player/v2/mediaPlayer.html?action=1&t=1&islist=false&id=134391895&m=134400569 The second story discusses the development of the MP3 format and reasons for its popularity. Considering the stories together, what best explains the success of the MP3? http://www.npr.org/player/v2/mediaPlayer.html?action=1&t=1&islist=false&id=134598010&m=134604923

THEORIES OF TECHNOLOGICAL CHANGE

The example of early radio carries two important lessons for thinking about the relationship between technology and media industries. First, the uses of new technologies are difficult to predict, even when powerful economic and regulatory forces try to shape them in particular ways. Second, technologies have inherent **technological affordances** that make certain uses more or less possible. For instance, at the advent of radio, the US Navy tried to harness the technology for secure communication about fleet maneuvers, but, despite its best efforts, the Navy could not prevent the signals from spreading across a wide geographic area where enemies might intercept them. So the very property of radio that made *broadcasting* possible initially was seen by those who desired it to be a **point-to-point** medium as a limitation.

The idea that technologies have particular affordances and abilities may seem an obvious one, but a good deal of debate has arisen about the degree to which those potentialities are "determinant" of their uses within the media industries, a theoretical perspective often referred to as **technological determinism**. In the One Laptop per Child initiative, technology is understood as dictating its own uses: it is the technologies, not the institutions that deploy them or the children who use them, that create learning. Technological determinism attributes strong, nearly omnipotent, powers to the technologies that surround us. In fact, both the technological utopian and technological dystopian perspectives discussed previously are versions of technological determinism, though one strain of thought evaluates technology positively, while the other evaluates it negatively.

A similarly weak version of the impact of technology on society also exists, known as **cultural determinism**, which argues that the cultural uses of a technology determine how that technology develops and the influences it has on industry and society. At its root, cultural determinism sees technology as an inert force shaped by other, far more powerful forces in a manner that disregards the meaningful role played by technology, including the engineers who design it and the corporations that manufacture and market it, as well as of other industrial and regulatory conditions.

Consider the example of television, which had been conceptualized as a technological possibility as early as the 1840s but did not develop as a widespread communications technology until a century later. Though it is true that the earliest forms of television had images that were far inferior to those of the 1940s, it is also the case that no one could envision a useful purpose for the medium; the best application they could imagine was something akin to a fax machine. It wasn't until the development of nationwide advertising, the success of radio broadcasting, and the migration of middle-class families from the cities to the suburbs that companies and government came to see television as a potentially useful medium of information and entertainment, after which investment in the technology began in earnest. Moreover, these uses demanded a certain degree of visual and audio fidelity, as well as requirements of size and design of the physical set in order to fit into the home and routines of daily life.

As we've already said, we think any type of single determinism—whether technological, cultural, economic, or regulatory—goes too far. We believe that technologies do, in fact, have affordances that influence their uses but also that powerful interests have a good deal of capacity to shape how technologies are used. In rare instances, the technologies may thwart the desires of these powerful interests, as was the case of the Navy's desires for early radio, but much more frequently, those in power are intimately involved with developing the new technology, heartily embrace the changes it brings, and largely get the technology to work the way they want it to.

Still, it's almost inevitable that no technology will work exactly as predicted and many technologies that affect media industries are created without the interests of media industries in mind, so new technologies do change the media industries in some unexpected ways. The television and film industries, for instance, pushed hard to integrate computer technology into editing and distribution beginning in the 1980s. New digital editing techniques saved time and money and increased the visual sophistication of television and film, while the development of DVD technology drove the widespread adoption of home DVD players and sparked sales and rentals of movies and television programs. The industry, however, did not anticipate how much easier **piracy** would become as a result of digitization. Suddenly, any number of people with access to the final edit of a film or television show could make a digital copy of comparable quality to the original and sell it. So a technological innovation that powerful media interests pushed for simultaneously produced unintended negative consequences for them.

Importantly, change—whether within the culture or in terms of the operation of media industries—is always gradual. Even quick adoption of a new technology often takes 5 to 10 years before it reaches half the population. Media theorist Raymond Williams established the helpful distinctions of "emergent," "dominant," and "residual" as classifications of technological change. Many of the trends and behaviors most attended to in press coverage of media industries—such as receiving all your "television" over the Internet or doing most of your watching on a mobile screen—remain "emergent" in 2015. Emergent trends and uses are important to media industry decision-makers, but they cannot know whether emergent uses will become dominant or how quickly they might become so. Entire sectors of financial analysts exist to try to understand adoption patterns and to forecast future technology use to help companies and investors strategize.

Another important factor for media industries is that those industries we have traditionally considered central because they make media *content* are often not the same as the ones that make media *technologies*. The consumer electronics industry produces many of the technologies crucial to the media industries; however, their concern isn't managing intellectual property and monetizing content but rather creating "must-have" devices. Consequently, though it might seem that the media and consumer electronic industries are closely related, they often are at cross-purposes and are known to have very different cultures. This point is explored at the end of the chapter in relation to the fight between content creators and consumer electronics companies over technologies that allow viewers to skip commercials in television content.

All technologies, then, have inherent potentialities that are sometimes only partly understood by the people and organizations involved in developing and deploying them. Typically, these technologies have minimal impact on the media industries, but in some instances, those changes can be profound and unanticipated. This is one of the reasons that large media firms tend *not* to be innovators of media technology; they prefer to leave this unpredictable and risky segment of the business to smaller upstarts. At the same time, and as we explore more thoroughly in Chapter 9, once these startup media businesses do begin to turn a profit, they are often bought by large corporations. Examples of this include the purchase of Whatsapp and Instagram by Facebook. Both were startup endeavors (like Facebook was once) that developed significant users. Rather than develop a competing service, Facebook purchased the app companies to add their functionality to the Facebook universe.

The Circuit of Cultural Production

One model for understanding the complexity of the role of technologies in cultures and of technological change in a way that includes these many contextual factors is the circuit of cultural production depicted in Figure 6.1. This model identifies five "cultural processes" that affect cultural goods: identity, representation, production, consumption, and regulation. In their book *Doing Cultural Studies: The Story of the Sony Walkman*, Paul du Gay and colleagues explore the introduction and early years of the Walkman, tracing how these five processes interacted as 1980s societies first encountered personal, portable music. Though the Walkman may seem an "old" technology, the bit of historical distance is helpful to see how it changed the way people in society used and thought about music over time. It may seem a small development now, but the availability of portable and personal music mirrors many of the technological capabilities offered by contemporary technologies.

Du Gay et al. argue that to study a technology "culturally" "one should at least explore how it is represented, what social identities are associated with it, how it is produced and consumed, and what mechanisms regulate its distribution and use."[2] A key

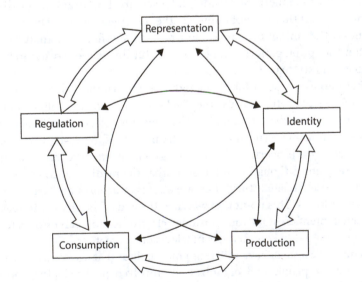

Figure 6.1 Circuit of Culture

aspect of this model is its emphasis on the interconnectedness of the various processes. It counters theories of technological determinism and instead offers a way to understand how culture intersects with technological capability to influence how we come to use and understand media technologies and how subsequent media technologies are created. Although the circuit of culture model is intended for application beyond media technologies, the case of the Walkman reveals how helpful it is for understanding the complicated cultural processes involved in the creation and dissemination of media technologies. All of the same questions and points of analysis apply easily to newer media technologies such as the latest generation of mobile devices, DVRs, tablets, and, obviously, iPods.

The cultural processes du Gay et al. consider include *representation*, or the attributes and characteristics that the company making the technology tries to associate with it. Illustrations of this can be found in how the company advertises and markets the technology, as well as the statements about the product it offers in press releases. Corporations predict certain uses of technologies, and when they first introduce a technology they often have to try to convince consumers that they need such a device or must explain how it is valuable.

Consider the representation strategy Apple used when it first introduced the iPhone in 2007. The first ads "taught" consumers how they would use the phones, emphasizing that it was "3 devices in 1"—a phone, a way to access the Internet, and an iPod. Apple has used a similar strategy in advertisements for subsequent versions of the phone that introduce new capabilities that don't already exist in the market. One print advertisement "explained" how to use a touch screen when this capability emerged (see http://www.intomobile.com/wp-content/uploads/2007/07/070712_iphone_print_ad.jpg).

Representation is similar to a second process, *identity*, which includes the attributes, characteristics, and purposes that come to be associated with technology regardless of the manufacturer's intention. Sometimes identity and representation are closely related, but often efforts to "brand" a technology fail and devices come to take on unintended meanings. Consider the early 2000s advertising campaign by Apple that posed two actors (Justin Long and John Hodgeman) as the human embodiments of "Mac" and "PC." In these ads, Apple reinforced its *representation* as a "cool," young, flexible, and reliable computing technology and played up the *identity* of many PCs as prone to error, stodgy, and difficult to use (see http://www.geckotales.com/mac-pc-commercial.jpg).

Production considers how processes of production, systems of organization, aspects such as how a technology is manufactured and where (Canada versus China), and what type of company owns it all contribute to cultural use of the technology. In the case of the Sony Walkman, the corporate culture of Sony and the fact that it was a Japanese company—during a time when the United States was feeling threatened by Japanese productivity and innovation—were both significant to perceptions and attitudes about the product. Today, US industry and consumers harbor much greater concern about the "threat" and consequences of Chinese manufacturing. Concerns about labor practices involved in the making of iPhones and tablets led to extensive investigation of subcontractors such as FoxConn used by Apple in 2011. Apple is also regarded as masterful at supply chain management, another production feature that has been credited with

Apple's innovative technologies and ability to meet consumer demand.* It is sometimes more challenging to find information about a technology's production in general interest publications, but searching business and manufacturing trade publications often yield rich insight about this component.

A fourth cultural process of *consumption* incorporates how consumers use the technology, examining questions such as who uses it and how they use it. Often, audiences discover unintended uses or place greater priority on attributes that the manufacturer thought were secondary. This leads to adjustments in manufacturing (production) and marketing (representation), illustrating the dynamism and interrelation the two-way arrows of the circuit of culture indicate. For example, the early generations of iPhones featured only a camera lens on the backside of the phone. As the phenomenon of taking selfies emerged and grew more common, Apple engineers designed a phone with a front-facing camera as well so that people could see what their self-photo would look like while taking it, illustrating how consumer use can affect production.

The final cultural process is *regulation*, which includes include both regulations enforced by governments and **formal and informal self-regulations** such as manufacturing norms agreed on within the industry or norms of use adopted by those using the technology. For a technology such as the iPhone, many technical regulations govern how signals are sent and received. These regulations are enforced by government bodies that we are likely never aware of. Also, lawmakers began creating official regulations banning texting and talking on mobile devices while driving, thereby regulating how consumers could use their phones.

Countless informal regulations also take time to develop when a new technology comes into use. We once had to include a line in our syllabus requesting that students silence their phones in class, but now we can assume this as a norm of behavior. Other informal regulations rely on social norms that are constantly being renegotiated—what we might consider phone and texting etiquette. Think about how you communicate and how your messages vary depending on whether you are corresponding with a friend versus an employer. That sense that your behavior should change reveals informal self-regulations are in place.

TECHNOLOGY AND OTHER CONDITIONS

As the Sony Walkman and iPhone examples make clear, changes in technological conditions have implications throughout the media industries and even in society at large. Returning to the Industrialization of Culture framework, we often find that technological changes have a strong impact on economic conditions, because they can alter power relationships among different players in the industry, as well as bring in new

---

*See the Pulitzer Prize–winning work *The New York Times* did investigating iPhone manufacturing and globalization. The reporting uncovers that many factors beyond wage have contributed to China's emergence as a manufacturing center. What are they? Should we see the iPhone as a globally produced product? Why or why not? In what ways does the manufacturing of the iPhone contribute to its "identity" in terms of the Circuit of Cultural Production? www.pulitzer.org/files/2013/.../01ieconomy1-22.pdf

competitors and ways of doing business that threaten to undermine established interests. As the Circuit of Cultural Production also makes clear, the condition of regulation
is also an important component in understanding the impact of technology on culture.
Technological changes can lead to changes in industry structure, which can affect regulatory practices and prevalent business models. This section provides some examples
of the connections between technological, regulatory, and economic conditions.

Technology and Industry Structure

One recurring theme in the history of the media industries is the idea that certain industries lend themselves to **natural monopolies**. This regulatory idea posits that some
industries can only operate efficiently and profitably if they are controlled by a single
monopoly organization. The need for a monopolistic industry structure is typically seen
as a result of a combination of technological and economic conditions, at least in the
media industries. For decades, regulators treated **common carriers**—or telecommunications network operators that do not originate media content, such as the telephone
industry—as natural monopolies.

The quintessential example here was AT&T's decades-long monopoly over the telephone industry, though this concept remains central in contemporary debates about
regulatory policy for broadband service. In the early years of telephony, AT&T con-
vinced the federal government of the social importance of nationwide telephone connections, arguing successfully that even the remotest parts of the country should have
telephone service. The problem with providing service to remote areas, however, was
that it was prohibitively expensive because of the amount of wire and infrastructure
required to reach rural homes and low population density of these areas (economic
conditions combined with the technological condition of telephony as a wire-based
communication technology). In large cities, telephone providers could charge pennies
per phone call because of the thousands of calls being placed daily, but in small cities,
each phone call would have had to cost perhaps hundreds of dollars in order to pay for
the installation and maintenance of the system! What AT&T proposed was to over-
charge users in urban areas in order to **cross-subsidize** undercharging users in rural
areas. Such a strategy could work, however, only if AT&T faced no competition in urban
areas; otherwise, competitors would charge lower prices in lucrative areas without the
need to cross-subsidize rural markets. Regulators agreed with this argument and
granted AT&T a monopoly that lasted from 1913 to 1984.

Following AT&T, the technology of cable television was the next to try to be considered a natural monopoly. Cable was regulated differently because it provided content—the
channels and programming—instead of just providing a connection for two people to talk
to each other. Cable service developed based on the creation of city-specific franchises, or
long-term agreements between a cable service provider and a municipality, to be that city's
cable service. Given the disruption of ripping up city streets to run cable, it seemed appropriate to select one company to provide service and create the infrastructure.

Many of these issues remain with us today as regulators try to figure out proper
policy for broadband. A key debate has been whether to regard broadband as a common
carrier, which would prevent broadband services from discriminating against any form

of content. New policy offered by the **Federal Communications Commission** (FCC) in 2015 in relation to **net neutrality** did just this, although the judicial challenge of these policies had just begun when we completed this edition of the book.

Regulatory conditions, then, work together with media and communications technologies to create industry structures. Another way to think of this is that technology may make a whole range of communicative practices possible, but the regulation of technology sets parameters on those possibilities and enables a certain industry structure that becomes the "playing field" for media industries. In the AT&T case, the high costs of installing a phone system and the desirability of nationwide telephone connections resulted in a monopolistic industry structure.

Regulatory and technological conditions are powerful forces of industry structure. Consider another example of how regulation can override technological capability: In the television industry of the 1950s, the FCC, made decisions that created the oligopoly structure of three broadcast networks that lasted until Fox Broadcasting successfully began in 1986. A series of FCC decisions about how to organize the broadcast spectrum led regulation to be a stronger determiner of how broadcasting would work than the technological affordances of broadcasting. The FCC decided to allow only two VHF stations in each market, which led the incumbent radio broadcasters of CBS and NBC to dominate the first 30 years of television. In most places, ABC, a network started later, operated on UHF, a signal type that many television sets could not even receive. Eventually, the FCC required all manufacturers to make sets capable of receiving both types of signals. Shortly after, cable systems developed and began including broadcaster's signals. Delivery over cable made the distinction between VHF and UHF irrelevant. The three-network oligopoly—which was dominated by just two networks for half that time—was as much a product of regulation as of technology.

Regulation forms an important component of both the AT&T and the network television examples because both of these industries were highly regulated at the time their industry structures were created. Other media industries are far less regulated, and, as a result, other conditions have much more influence on industry structure. Technological conditions alter regulatory conditions as well; it is a two-way street. In fact, in each of the previous examples, it was the introduction of new technological conditions that prompted changes in government regulations. These issues certainly remain relevant today. For example, some sectors of the print media industry are concerned that Google will hold a monopoly on digital access to published books as a result of its Google Books endeavor. Also, some of the problems of the digital divide are emerging because of a lack of regulation comparable to that which made AT&T subsidize rural telephony. In many cases, contemporary telecommunications providers introduce new and fast services in the most affluent communities. Rural areas, especially, have suffered from the lack of access to high-speed Internet because there are no regulations requiring its development.

Technology and Prevalent Business Models
Technology also affects economic conditions other than industry structure, particularly **business models**, or whether and how businesses plan to offset the costs of making

media with revenues from it. In two examples from the print industries—changes in newspaper printing in the late nineteenth century and technological changes in industries that have come to compete with magazines in the early twenty-first century—we see how technology can create or undermine the economic viability of an entire commercial medium.

For much of the nineteenth century, newspapers in the United States served as organs of political parties. They tended to have quite small circulations, due to the costs of publishing and distribution. Newspapers were printed on rags, which were expensive, heavy, and thus costly to send via mail. As a result, newspaper publishers printed only a small number of copies and generally didn't send them very far around the country. Beginning in the 1870s, however, due to increased costs and scarcity of rags, most newspapers had begun using wood pulp for newspaper, a relatively new technology that caused newspaper prices to plummet. By 1882, almost every newspaper in the country had begun to use wood pulp for paper. Wood-pulp paper, moreover, was lighter than rag-based paper and cost less to distribute. In the wake of this technological change, the newspaper industry took off. Between 1870 and 1880, as the newspaper industry faced significant changes in economic conditions that we detailed at the beginning of Chapter 5, more newspapers were published than had been published in the previous century, and average newspaper circulation increased 240 percent between 1860 and 1880.[3]

Along with increased competition and circulation due to cheaper prices, newspapers began to change from political to commercial enterprises, in large part due to the fact that they could now serve as vehicles for national advertising. **Penny presses**, as these newspapers came to be called, not only began to reach a truly national readership but were also read by a wider cross-section of the population, most notably the working-class immigrants who formed the backbone of the growing national consumer society of the time. Following the advent of printing newspapers on wood-pulp paper, it became much more common for advertisers, rather than political parties, to fund newspaper publishing. In a very direct way, then, the technological development of wood pulp as a base for paper led to the development of the commercial newspaper industry. These changes also deeply influenced the target audience for newspapers, the costs of newspapers, and the content and social role of newspapers.

Fast-forwarding 130-some years, we may be witnessing the transformation of another commercial print medium, the magazine, due to the development of the Internet. Of course, the magazine industry has survived more than a few predictions of its death, perhaps most notably the introduction of television, which undermined general-circulation magazines and destroyed some of the best-known and most influential magazines at the time. More recently, however, even longstanding, carefully tailored magazines have begun failing, and at an alarming rate.

When television was introduced in the 1950s, the biggest magazines in the country were titles such as *Life* and *Look* that were aimed at a general mass audience and reported on news and human-interest stories with high-quality, glossy pictures. Broadcast television promised to deliver even more powerful visuals, as well as similar news and human-interest stories, all for "free," since no subscription was required.

The magazine industry responded by focusing on certain segments of the audience, or **niches**, and creating content tailored specifically for those niches (we detail this process more thoroughly in Chapter 9.) In other words, decades before the television industry, and even prior to the radio industry, the magazine industry changed from a mass to a niche industry—to such an extent that few of us can probably even imagine magazines as a mass-appeal medium.

Beginning in the 1980s, a technological innovation known as desktop publishing rapidly changed the economic conditions of the magazine industry. Desktop publishing utilized computers and automation to make the publishing process simpler, more efficient, and cheaper. As a result, competition in the magazine industry exploded, as hundreds of new competitors flooded the market. The number of consumer magazines grew nearly 500 percent between 1981 and 2000, from 1,192 to 5,649. Since 2000, however, the number of new magazine launches has dropped, and the number of failures has risen. Since 2008, such long-running magazines as *Gourmet*, *Teen*, *PC Magazine*, *Home*, and many more have ceased publication.[4]

The main culprit, most industry observers agree, has been the emergence of Internet publications that don't require nearly the production infrastructure of print-based magazines. Also, much as television channels rivaled magazines in the 1950s, niche cable channels can provide the kind of tailored media experience that magazines do but with more immediate access and more engaging visuals and stories. The Internet, meanwhile, offers content equivalent to magazines that is often cheap or free, is more readily accessible, and often has even greater niche specificity than any other media. Like most established media industries, the magazine industry was slow to develop an online presence. When magazine websites did begin appearing, they tended to carry the same content as the print edition, delayed by a few days or weeks. More recently, some magazines have developed Internet-only content and editions in order to lure online subscribers. Like the newspaper industry, the print magazine industry continues to struggle to find a way to monetize their product in an environment in which many readers just want to read and share certain articles rather than pay for the "bundle" of articles in an issue. Still, the eventual success of these adaptations and whether online advertising can replace traditional economic models remains uncertain.[5]

The most successful adaptations to the present technological and economic conditions of the magazine industry seem to be those publications that form a central part of a successful, multimedia brand.[6] An early, pre-Internet version of this strategy can be seen in the success of *Martha Stewart Living* from the 1990s and early 2000s—so this strategy isn't exclusive to digital media. The magazine drew readers from Martha Stewart's television series and talk-show appearances while also sending interested readers back to the television series. Both the television series and the magazine also drove consumers to the stores to buy a wide range of Martha Stewart–branded household goods. More recently, we see an even more ambitious example of this trend with the launch of the Oprah Winfrey Network (OWN). The network expands from Oprah's magazine, *O*, which was established by leveraging Winfrey's personality, first built through her television program, *The Oprah Winfrey Show*.

The key point of this section is to make clear how technological, economic, and regulatory conditions are quite intimately interwoven. Most commonly, the development of new technologies that alter established conditions serves the economic interests of the most powerful media corporations, even though the technologies may lead to altered economic conditions. Similarly, regulatory changes typically serve the same interests, even though technological changes may lead to changed regulatory conditions. As we examine much more closely in Chapter 9, however, there are times when technological conditions change somewhat more unexpectedly, and entrenched media corporations and established production and distribution practices are consequently challenged. Although media industry players constantly encourage and prepare for technological changes, once unleashed, those changes can prove unpredictable.

TECHNOLOGICAL CONDITIONS AND MEDIA INDUSTRY PRACTICES

In the previous examples, we illustrated how technological conditions intersect with other conditions to affect the goods media industries produce. Though we haven't yet examined practices in detail, technologies can also affect media industries by enabling changes in creative, distribution, and aggregation practices. This may seem like an obvious point to some. Without technology, we wouldn't even have a media industry to speak of, at least not in the way we define the industry. The points to keep in mind, however, are (a) technology doesn't change media content, but it does open up opportunities for new content norms that certain entrepreneurs pursue, and (b) these new content norms are also shaped by—but *not determined* by—economic and regulatory conditions as well as technological ones.

We primarily focus on the impact of technology on production practices in this section, even though technology affects distribution practices equally as profoundly; we address the impact of technology on distribution extensively in Chapters 8 and 9. The previous example about changes in the magazine industry and how technological developments have undermined prevalent business models is also a story of technology altering distribution practices. Specifically, we saw how the distribution of print media has changed from practices largely built around the physical distribution of newspapers and magazines to ones built around the electronic distribution of individual stories.

The technique of sampling in music production offers a good example of how technological changes lead to changes in production practices and media content. Sampling is the strategy of finding prerecorded music from a variety of different sources and combining it into a new song or musical piece. Although sampling began during the analog era, it really became established as a dominant feature, particularly of rap music, in the late 1980s and early 1990s with the introduction of digital sampling technologies. It suddenly became quite simple and relatively cheap to take music from numerous sources, and the sounds that came to dominate rap and dance music were closer to collage than the harmonies that one finds in rock music, R&B, and soul.

The composition of the primary creative roles in contemporary music changed as a result of sampling technology as well. Using sampling, DJs, at first working with vinyl albums and tape machines, could create music without other band members, basically functioning as a one-person band. Though sampled music has come to include singers and other performers, the centerpiece of sample-based music remains the DJ, rather than a lead singer.

The story of sampled music would not be complete, however, without also commenting on how regulatory conditions changed as a result of rap music production practices and how these newer regulations likewise changed music and production practices. The era of collage that sampling ushered in quickly caught the attention of the courts and regulators, because most samples were used without the consent of—or payment to—the original artist. Although short samples of prerecorded music, especially ones that are unrecognizable, had been permitted under copyright law prior to the 2000s, since that time the courts have held that *any* use of prerecorded music without the permission of the copyright holder is illegal. Moreover, since using samples requires the payment of **royalties** to the copyright holder, the kinds of complex, sampled soundscapes that characterized rap music of the 1990s have all but disappeared due to costs— as we discuss in the copyright section of Chapter 4. One of our colleagues, for instance, working on a documentary about sampling and rap music, discovered that if he were to use all of the sampled songs he wanted to in his hour-long video, the costs would have topped $1 million. And yet despite this, artists such as Girl Talk persist in creating music entirely from samples without legal challenge.

The example of sampling offers a complex portrait of the relationships among technological conditions, regulatory conditions, production practices, and the media we ultimately consume. We want to emphasize again the importance of regulatory conditions in shaping the relationship between production practices and technological conditions to remind you that it is not technology alone that influences media production and content. Technological changes in one media industry can influence production practices in other industries, particularly in today's world of convergence and conglomeration in which producers in one industry are constantly aware of developments elsewhere.

When the production practices and content characteristics of a new medium influence an older medium, we call this process **remediation**. When the newspaper *USA Today* began publishing in 1982, it distinguished itself primarily through its use of arresting, full-color graphics in an effort to emulate the kinds of visuals we see on television news. In fact, the newspaper was even sold in specialized vending machines that were designed to look like TV sets. In another case, television itself has been influenced by the production practices of newer media, especially computer games. One prominent change has taken place in televised sports, particularly professional NFL football, which has come to use camera work similar to that in computerized NFL games. This includes cameras suspended from zip wires over the head of the quarterback or at eye level behind the field-goal kicker. Not only do these newer shots look more like computer games than earlier television sports production practices; they also require quite different skills in operating cameras and editing the game's live feed. In both of these cases, the jobs of camera operators and editors have become more complex due to efforts to mimic computer games.

The key takeaway that we've tried to underscore through many examples is that technology works in concert with the conditions, practices, and mandates explored throughout this book to shape the media environment within which we live. In examining any technological innovation, we need to look at how that technology developed and interacted with these other phenomena in order to understand how that innovation changed the media industries, including their economic and regulatory conditions; prevalent production, distribution, and aggregation practices; and the content that they produce. This approach necessarily prevents us from making arguments about how technology itself has changed media or culture, because such questions only make sense in specific historical and social situations.

INDUSTRIAL RESTRAINTS ON TECHNOLOGICAL INNOVATION

We end this chapter with a brief overview of the ways in which media organizations, especially for-profit media organizations, stand in the way of technological progress. We do this because we often find that our students have little trouble with the idea that governmental entities restrain innovation through regulation, but few believe that normally functioning competitive markets can also hold back progress. Entrenched media companies and their interests have very good reasons to thwart technological advances; these arise from the companies' recognition that changes in technological conditions lead to changes in economic conditions. Technological changes can undermine successful business models and bring in new competitors. As a result, corporations will go a long way to try to prevent change from happening, whether we are talking about technological change, social change, political change, or other types of change.

We offer two brief examples of this tendency—one from history, one much more recent—that demonstrate the ways in which corporate interests impede technological progress. Again, let us reiterate our main point at the outset: because of their investment in maintaining prevalent economic conditions, entrenched media companies frequently thwart changes in technological conditions, sometimes by influencing regulatory conditions, at other times by purchasing technologies to keep them out of the market.

The first example comes from 1930s radio, when the powerful Radio Corporation of America (RCA) successfully quashed the development of FM radio, despite the technological capacity for FM to deliver a higher quality signal than AM radio, the dominant broadcasting standard at the time. Edwin Howard Armstrong, one of the pioneers of early radio, developed FM broadcasting technology in 1935. FM was a superior technology to AM because of the fidelity of its signal. Most of you likely know that commercial music stations typically broadcast on FM because it has less noise and interference than AM radio.

Armstrong assumed that RCA would be interested in his FM technology simply because it was better, but RCA rejected his technology for several reasons. First, RCA had a lucrative radio-set sales business. These sets tuned in only AM stations, and RCA did not relish the idea of reengineering its sets to support radio stations that would compete against its own network affiliates. RCA could have supported FM radio and made obsolete all of its previous sets, requiring tens of millions of Americans to buy new sets, but the company's attention at the time was focused on efforts to develop television. It used profits from radio-set sales to fund its research and development of television and had little interest in risking those profits with redesigned sets.[7]

RCA did more than rebuff Armstrong, however. The company actively lobbied the FCC to kill FM as a viable business. By the time RCA realized the potential competition posed by FM, Armstrong had already assembled a nationwide network of FM stations, and manufacturers—including powerful manufacturers like GE—had begun selling sets with FM capability. By 1940, FM stations existed in every major city in the United States, and NBC—owned by RCA—had even begun experimental FM broadcasts. That same year, however, the FCC relocated the FM radio band in the electromagnetic spectrum, effectively making every FM radio station and every FM radio obsolete. For example, say you had previously been listening to your favorite FM radio station on 99.4 FM, and suddenly it had to relocate to 299.4 FM—but your radio didn't even go above 107.9! Every FM station had to completely redesign its broadcasting equipment, and every consumer—many of whom had only recently purchased a new FM-compatible set—had to buy another new one. Needless to say, the FCC's decisions effectively killed FM radio for the time. Most historians think that the FCC was merely doing the bidding of the most powerful radio company in the nation, RCA.[8]

Large corporations do not need regulators to quash technological innovation, and even companies that specialize in innovative technology often work to curb their inventions in order to please their larger corporate partners. DVR technology like TiVo is a good case in point. TiVo's predecessor and early competitor, ReplayTV, allowed users the ability to skip commercials while recording and to share programming with other DVRs. The company was bankrupted by lawsuits before broadband Internet services became widespread, but you can imagine how broadband-enabled DVRs that could share programming among each other would be assumed to undermine the business models of just about every television network currently in existence. The major media content producers came after ReplayTV aggressively for including these features, winning numerous lawsuits against it, and those features were eventually removed.

When TiVo came along, its executives wanted to avoid the fate of ReplayTV, and the company began courting investments and guidance from established media corporations so that the technology would not damage the prevalent revenue models of established companies.[9] As a consequence, the ability to record programs without commercials or share them with friends and family had to wait until technologies such as YouTube and BitTorrent had disrupted the industry status quo so significantly that it was no longer feasible to continue this fight. Who knows what other innovative DVR functions have been squelched because they were seen as too much of a threat to powerful business interests?

The lawsuits brought by established players—RCA in the case of FM and television content creators in the case of ReplayTV—often kill entrepreneurial technologies by costing them millions of dollars in legal fees and casting enough uncertainty about their survival to make it impossible to secure venture capital funding. In some cases, established players will simply acquire startups with "threatening" technology so that they can control how that technology is deployed and do so in a less disruptive way. The possibility also exists for an established player to purchase a disruptive technology simply to keep it out of the market.

CONCLUSION

In all of the examples we have encountered in this chapter, technological conditions have not developed independently but rather in conjunction with economic and regulatory conditions. These changes in conditions have led to changes in production, distribution, and aggregation practices. At the same time, changes in practices initiated by technological innovations have sometimes "filtered up" to change regulatory and economic conditions. An example here is the MP3, a digital file format developed by computer science engineers wholly outside of the music and recording industries. But this technology of music file caught on among users and contributed to radically reconfiguring the economic norms of the recording industry.

One of the many ironies of the media industries is that they both depend on and fear changes in technological conditions. They depend on them because technological changes drive demand for both media hardware and software. Recently, the movie industry has begun betting on 3D technology to lure viewers into the theaters. The hope here is that such a spectacular technology will be worth the extra driving and additional cost of seeing a 3D movie in the theater. But, so far, 3D has mainly caught on in international markets, and its future seems uncertain in the United States. In addition, the introduction of new audio formats—the transition from vinyl albums to cassettes to CDs to MP3—has been lucrative for the recording industry because listeners tend to repurchase favorite "back catalog" material in the new format. Technological innovation is often commercially appealing and is built into the very fabric of the media industries.

But established media corporations also work hard to resist forms of technological change that have unclear or likely negative implications for their profits. They resist with lawsuits, acquisition of upstart companies, and lobbying the federal government to develop restrictive regulatory conditions. Of course the reason for this somewhat schizophrenic approach to technological change is that powerful companies want to develop only those technologies that they see as increasing their revenues while hobbling those that seem like a threat. The wild cards in this equation are the technology itself, the technological affordances of the technology, and how people come to use it, which can rarely be predicted. Despite their best efforts to promote only technologies that serve their interests, large corporations never know how technologies are going to be taken up or how they are going to alter the prevalent conditions and practices of their industry until those technologies have been unleashed. In sum, while technologies are certainly bound up with the other conditions we examine in this book, technology also operates as a condition in its own right.

QUESTIONS

1. Recall discussions that you had or that you heard in the media or among family about the Internet as you grew up. What concerns or hopes were expressed? Was it discussed in a way that you would characterize more as technological utopian or technological dystopian? Can you identify ways in which ideas about technological determinism and cultural determinism factored into the fears of, and hopes for, the Internet?

2. Consider our claim that media industries both depend on and fear changes in technological conditions for a variety of reasons. Select a specific technological development and try to imagine the reasons why a media industry would have both welcomed *and* resisted that change. What was at stake in the technological development? What could have happened that might have made the industry nervous? Did the technology end up changing the production and/or reception of particular media goods?

3. As discussed in this chapter, the magazine industry has had a difficult time figuring out how to adapt to the Internet. What are some aspects unique to the magazine industry that have made this adaptation to the Internet particularly difficult or that may affect the magazine industry more than other industries? What advantages and disadvantages are involved in a magazine being part of a multimedia brand, such as *ESPN Magazine*? Can you think of a strategy that might help magazines adapt to the Internet?

FURTHER READING

More on other models for understanding media can be found in Paul du Gay et al., *Doing Cultural Studies: The Story of the Sony Walkman* (London: SAGE, 1997); Julie D'Acci, "Cultural Studies, Television Studies, and the Crisis in the Humanities," in *Television After TV: Essays on a Medium in Transition*, edited by Lynn Spigel and Jan Olsson (Durham: Duke University Press, 2004), 418–446; and Richard Johnson, "What Is Cultural Studies Anyway?" *Social Text* 16 (1986–1987), 38–80.

More reading on history of technological innovation and the development of contemporary technological and regulatory conditions can be found in Harmeet Sawhney, "Information Superhighway: Metaphors as Midwives," *Media, Culture & Society* 18 (1996), 291–314; Ithiel de Sola Pool's *Technologies of Freedom* (Cambridge, Mass.: Belknap Press, 1983); Robert Britt Horwitz's *The Irony of Regulatory Reform: The Deregulation of American Telecommunications* (Oxford and New York: Oxford University Press, 1989); Ken Burns' *Empire of the Air: The Men Who Made Radio* (Washington, D.C.: Florentine Films and WETA Television, 1991. Original broadcast date: January 29, 1992); Leslie Cauley, *End of the Line: The Rise and Fall of AT&T* (New York: Free Press, 2005); and Tim Wu, *The Master Switch: The Rise and Fall of Information Empires* (New York: Vintage, 2011), 217–219.

NOTES

1. Harmeet Sawhney, "Information Superhighway: Metaphors as Midwives," *Media, Culture & Society*, 18 (1996), 291–314.
2. Paul du Gay et al., *Doing Cultural Studies: The Story of the Sony Walkman* (London: SAGE, 1997), 3.
3. Ithiel de Sola Pool, *Technologies of Freedom* (Cambridge, Mass: Belknap Press, 1983); David C. Smith, "Wood Pulp and Newspapers, 1867–1900," *The Business History Review* 38 (1964), 328–345.
4. Samir Husni and Emily Main, "Life After Death in the Magazine Industry," *Publishing Research Quarterly* 18, no. 2 (2002), 3–11; Advertising Age, "A Guide to Magazines That Have Ceased Publication," December 15, 2009. http://adage.com/mediaworks/article?article_id=132779 (accessed August 31, 2010).
5. Lisa M. Guidone, "The Magazine at the Millennium: Integrating the Internet," *Publishing Research Quarterly* 16 (2000), 14–33; Husni and Main, "Life after Death."
6. Ibid.
7. Robert Britt Horwitz, *The Irony of Regulatory Reform: The Deregulation of American Telecommunications* (Oxford and New York: Oxford University Press, 1989); Ken Burns, *Empire of the Air: The Men Who Made Radio* (Washington, D.C.: Florentine Films and WETA Television, 1991) (Original broadcast date: January 29, 1992).
8. Horwitz, *The Irony of Regulatory Reform*.
9. Matt Carlson, "Tapping into TiVo: Digital Video Recorders and the Transition from Schedules to Surveillance in Television," *New Media & Society* 8 (2006), 97–115.

CHAPTER 7

—

Creative Practices and Media Work

Key Takeaways:

Understand how the media industries distinguish between creative and noncreative work

Explain what forms of personal agency creative people are able to exert within the media industries

Explain how various commercial and organizational realities constrain *and* allow for creative expression

Explain how digitization is changing the nature of creative work in profound ways

The early years of the US film industry are often described as the years of the **studio system**. Prior to the 1948 Paramount Decree, the studios maintained a production arrangement characterized much more like an assembly-line process than it is today. From the early 1920s through the early 1950s, the studios controlled creative production by keeping all film production personnel—actors, directors, writers, and much other talent—under long-term (typically seven-year) contracts that controlled every aspect of working in film. The studio heads would select what films would be made; assign a producer, director, and actors to make the film; and then reassign them to new projects when that film was completed. Stars could be rented out to other studios, although the studio holding the star's contract would receive the salary difference. The studios even controlled all aspects of publicity and stars' public images.

In this system, the creative workers had very little control over of any aspect of their work. They were guaranteed a salary, although Edward Jay Epstein notes that they were paid comparatively little relative to box office revenue at the time.[1] This system allowed the studios to control many of the most substantial production costs.

The contemporary film industry works much differently. A **star system**, in which a few established actors and directors are seen as indispensable to creating a hit movie, has, arguably, replaced the studio system. Some of these individuals are compensated beyond reason, and they wield considerable power in selecting the projects in which to be involved and which are ultimately produced. The breakup of the studio system also expanded the role of the agent in the film industry. Agents are responsible for negotiating deals between studios and "talent," and, in many cases, they construct packages of actors, directors, and creative properties (scripts) together in the best interest of the agency.

The transition from the studio to the star system illustrates an immense change in the practice of making movies that required adjustments ranging from the financing of films to what types of films can be and are made in Hollywood. As Epstein notes, "The collapse of the studio system also radically changed the social landscape of the community."[2] The center of wealth shifted from the studio heads to select stars, directors, writers, and musicians. The result, he notes, has been increased studio attention to factors other than simple financial profit to include a desire to produce some works that have high artistic merit or valuable social commentary.

The anecdote of the transition from a studio system to a star system in Hollywood shows how the operating conditions of the industry also influence the workaday worlds of the people employed in the industry. From who has decision-making authority to how workers think of themselves and the day-to-day autonomy and job satisfaction they experience, the economic, technological, and regulatory conditions that characterize a media industry have a profound impact on the exercise of creative work in the modern world.

* * *

Despite the importance of mandates and operating conditions, these aspects of the media industry alone do not ultimately determine the products that they create. The final layer of the Industrialization of Culture framework involves a wide variety of what we term **practices**. At the level of practices, we begin to attend to particular roles of individual workers in media industries and the day-to-day routines in which they participate. There are far more practices than we can possibly address in just a few chapters, so we group a wide variety of practices into this chapter and the next. This chapter focuses on some of the practices involved in the actual making of media products while the next chapter addresses the practices required to get the media product to the audience—also known as the processes of distribution and aggregation.

Although much of the book to this point has focused on what might seem like massive and unalterable structures of industrial operation, in the end, the actual functioning of the media industries happens in day-to-day decisions made by individual people. The final layer of our framework, then, addresses the people who work in the media industries in various roles. Even though one person may seem insignificant when thinking about a vast, multinational media corporation, we need to realize that these workers often take a great deal of pride and meaning from their work and that most of them exercise a certain amount of **agency**. The promise of being able to bring one's creative visions to life remains a big draw that compels people to pursue media industry work.

Joseph Turow calls many of the activities we call "practices" "power roles," and his power-role framework remains a valuable tool for understanding how media systems operate. We intend our Industrialization of Culture framework as an update that streamlines some of the activities he notes, incorporates others, and addresses the different types of power that operate in the various levels of industry operation. In this context, power is related to having an extensive amount of what we defined as **circum-scribed agency** in Chapter 1: the ability of groups or individuals to shape their environments. In the context of the current chapter, then, power refers to the agency of creative workers to shape media content.

This is also a good time to think of alternative ways work in creative industries can be organized. David Hesmondhalgh reminds us that the precursors of the contemporary media industries began with creative work being supported through a patronage system.[3] In a patronage system, the creative worker plied his trade at the will of the patron, though the artist likely received some level of economic security in exchange.

Next, an organization allowing for a "market professional" emerged. The market professional was an intermediary who existed between the artist and those who might purchase the art; the modern-day art gallery owner might be the easiest example. In this organization, artists share the profits from their goods in order to be free of the duties of marketing and selling their wares. The artist gains both greater creative freedom and financial insecurity in comparison with the patronage model.

The media industries we consider here are characteristic of a "complex, professional era" in which the creation of media content requires extensive teams of workers, all with specialized skill sets. Though the patronage and market professional models may seem historic relics, they provide valuable points of comparison, and we may even consider whether some of the opportunities of digital technologies may make them newly relevant.

In this chapter and the next, we explain many of the practices that are part of the daily operation of the media industries. These practices occur because people perform them—people who have their own opinions and perspectives on the world and who make many decisions every day that have meaningful implications for media content. In the next few pages, we explain some of the many jobs that are crucial to the operation of various media industries, and we offer some examples of how individuals' decisions or perceptions—what we call their agency—affect media production. We also look at the various forms of creativity that are available in the media industries and how changes in the industry may be affecting the **creative autonomy** of media workers—particularly the economic and technological changes that **digitization** is causing for creative workers. Throughout this chapter, it might be helpful for you to "role-play," and once you understand the type of activities that are part of a particular role, imagine the decisions you would make and the consequences they might have.

CREATIVE VISIONS: APPROACHES TO MAKING MEDIA

Nancy is a television writer. Television writing is typically done "by committee," meaning a show's writers brainstorm ideas for episodes together and take turns developing those ideas into scripts. Nancy began her career "on staff," which means she was a member of a television series' writing team. The show's executive producer supervises the team, approves the writers' ideas, and sometimes does some of the writing as well. After working many years, rising through the writers' room hierarchy, Nancy became the executive producer of her own show. Nancy created the show—she came up with the idea and pitched it to various networks before finding one that was willing to develop and schedule it.

Nancy is one of those creators whom economist Richard Caves is talking about when he refers to someone pursuing **art for art's sake** as a particular characteristic of the media industries; at least, she is at this point in her career. Nancy has very particular ideas for her show—a specific story she wants to tell that she hopes will make the audience think about the issues she cares about. She has worked in television long enough to have established herself, and she has saved some money, which leads her to be less concerned with making this show a huge hit and more focused on telling her story precisely the way she wants.

Nancy didn't have much control over what she wrote during the many years she worked on another executive producer's writing staff. She was often the only woman in the writers' room, so she was given the task of writing the female characters who were the victims in crime stories. She often didn't have the power to determine who was the victim or why because she was a staff writer on someone else's show. Sometimes she could subtly slip ideas that were important to her into stories—perhaps writing a female character who was more empowered—but the executive producer and the network always vetted her ideas and scripts, and the executive producer often completely rewrote scripts if it wasn't exactly what he or she envisioned. This might sound frustrating, but at that point in her career, Nancy knew that it was more important to "pay her dues" and establish a successful track record.

Now, as executive producer, she still has to contend with network executives who may want her to tell a different story than she intends, but she also can argue and negotiate with them. The network executives often suggest changes to Nancy's stories that they think will make the show more successful or expand its audience. Even though Nancy's show is mainly about two women who are in their 40s, the network that licenses the show keeps pushing Nancy to include more stories about the teenage daughter of one of the women as a strategy for drawing in younger viewers.

Nancy has many responsibilities as executive producer. She is mainly concerned with the content of the show, so she spends much of her time talking with the writers and approving their story suggestions or sending them in other directions. She also keeps track of daily production, watching what is shot every day and meeting with other creative staff—such as directors and actors—about upcoming scenes. The studio also employs executive producers who attend more to matters of budget and production logistics to free up Nancy to focus on the creative aspects of the show that interest her. Although these executive producers may not directly influence what stories the show tells, they indirectly influence the creative product through their decisions about how to allocate the budget.

Aaron is also an executive producer. He too has worked in the television industry for a long time, but his focus is different from Nancy's. Aaron is more of a businessman. When he has an idea for a show, it is typically because it has a lot of elements that he thinks will make it a successful show. Aaron is less concerned with telling a particular story and more focused on developing shows that will make him a lot of money. Aaron also argues with the network from time to time. Unlike Nancy, though, he typically argues with the network in cases in which he feels the network idea is likely to decrease the audience his show could reach. He is less committed to the specific stories his writers tell and doesn't have the same aspirations for his shows to be the kind of stories that stay with people and lead them to think about ideas. Aaron spends less time with his writers than Nancy does, and, as executive producer, he focuses more on budget issues. Aaron also serves as the executive producer of another show, so he spends much of his time attending to issues on that show and working on developing new shows to sell to the networks.

These paragraphs describe two very different approaches to one job in one media industry. Nancy and Aaron may exist on opposite ends of a continuum, as both Nancy's "art for art's sake" approach and Aaron's profit-driven focus are deliberately extreme to illustrate a point. Most creators exist somewhere in between Nancy and Aaron in terms of their desire to attempt to communicate particular ideas through media and their awareness of the conventions perceived to lead to profitability. At some point in his career, Aaron too may have placed greater emphasis on creating a "great" piece of television, just as Nancy recognized the need to create a successful reputation as she started out in her career in order to make having her own show a possibility one day.

The cases of Nancy and Aaron—and every incarnation in between—suggest the wide variation in approaches among what we might describe as the central "creative" personnel of a commercial media product. There is slight variation in the roles of the central creative figure in each media industry, and some industries allow creative tasks to be shared by many different workers. In film, the key creative worker is the director; in the music industry it can be the artist, the producer, the songwriter, or the record label, depending on the particular project. In the magazine industry, a range of editors typically works with a mix of staff and freelance writers to ensure each issue's articles reflect the magazine's overall "voice," although the editor-in-chief ultimately decides what appears in print.

We are not suggesting that the only important creative role in media industries is that of the creative worker who has final authority. Media productions require an incomprehensibly vast range of creative attention to all sorts of things the audience may not specifically notice but that contribute to the final creative product. Whether they are set designers, those who select costumes, or music mixers, these individuals affect the production of creative products in countless ways. The executive producer, director, or editor-in-chief may have the final say or veto power, but they are typically not responsible for originating the hundreds of ideas and decisions that they accept and that contribute to the substance of the product.

Here we focus on just one creative task—that of creation, an activity that remains relatively common regardless of media. The **creator** is typically the person who holds the guiding creative vision. As you can see in the previous examples, that power isn't absolute—creators often negotiate their power with the networks, studios, or editors that enable them to distribute their message—and we explore that more in the next section. Creators also cannot divorce their creative tasks from the financial pressures that are part of media production. Creators make myriad negotiations between their visions and the economics of their projects. These concerns might lead an executive like

Nancy to revise a script so that a scene takes place on a studio stage, which is far cheaper than shooting on location and perhaps represents a small negotiation in comparison with entirely eliminating what she feels is an important storyline. Budget and financial concerns also influence how Aaron does his job, although differently. Aaron might not develop a potentially controversial show simply because it is not as likely to succeed or not as likely to sell in international markets.

The different cases of Nancy and Aaron also illustrate the variation in the priorities that might govern someone working in the creative fields and the array of approaches to how creators build and develop creative products. It is frankly difficult to compare Nancy and Aaron because their approaches to their jobs and what is important to them differ so significantly. A key lesson here is the impossibility of making general statements about how the creative personnel in media industries behave. It is crucial not to assume that all creative workers function the same way and have the same power. Let's say that, over his career, Aaron has produced many successful shows that have earned a lot of money for him, the studio, and various networks. This history of success is likely to afford Aaron more control, and a studio or network may be more likely to leave him and his creative teams alone because of that track record, whereas they are more likely to micromanage a newcomer without a proven record.

Creators are also real people, often with spouses, families, and financial responsibilities that likewise might affect the creative risks they are willing take at different times. Nancy and Aaron are creative workers who are fairly far up on the food chain. Creative decisions are also available to those with much narrower and circumscribed roles, although they may be much more limited.

CREATIVE ROLES ABOVE AND BELOW THE LINE

Despite their difference, both Aaron and Nancy are creators of television content, and the work they perform is considered "creative" work. Hollywood has historically distinguished between creative work and what is considered noncreative, or "craft," work. Although this distinction is somewhat arbitrary and hard to draw, the idea that some media jobs are creative while others are not is a widespread idea in our culture. Most of us, for instance, would agree that the director of photography for a film, who is responsible for designing the lighting, camera framing, and camerawork for a film, is a creative worker, while the gaffer, who implements the lighting design and manages the lighting crew, is not generally considered a creative worker.

Creative workers in Hollywood are known as **above-the-line** workers, while non-creatives are **below-the-line** workers. These terms themselves come from Hollywood accounting forms in the early twentieth century, when an actual line was drawn to calculate a film's budgets for above-the-line workers, which were fixed costs, and below-the-line workers, which were variable. That is, regardless of how many scenes a film encompasses, the cost of hiring the director is fixed; however, the cost for the crew to construct sets varies depending on the number of sets needed.

The concept of above- and below-the-line workers is useful to be aware of because of its prevalence, especially in the television and film industries. Nevertheless, all media industries—from newspapers to gaming—involve jobs that most of us would categorize as creative and jobs that we would not, though many jobs that might not seem creative at their core still have creative dimensions.

Creative responsibility and agency are complexly related in media industries. David Hesmondhalgh and Sarah Baker begin their study of contemporary media industry work with the observation that creative work has many attributes that individuals might regard as desirable or "good work"—it is independent, self-directed, and capable of producing feelings of self-worth and accomplishment.[4] In addition, creative work involves working and reworking the symbolic resources of a given culture to produce expressive goods.

Obviously, this definition of creative work is quite broad, a point that Vicki Mayer takes up in her study of media workers who are frequently considered noncreative, below-the-line workers.[5] She makes a forceful argument for expanding our notion of what constitutes media "production" to include a range of trade workers, production assistants, manufacturing workers, and even regulators, all of whom contribute to the creation of media goods in various ways. Too often, the media industries use the distinction between above- and below-the-line jobs to justify extreme inequalities of pay, security, and autonomy among workers, all of whom collectively contribute to the creation of media. Likewise, this cultivates the myth of the author—a sense of individual creative authority that may persist in book writing and painting but is difficult to sustain in the complex, professional era of contemporary media.[6]

Mayer's point is that the distinction between above-the-line and below-the-line workers is quite blurry and that we risk buying into a self-serving industry distinction if we insist too much on distinguishing between jobs that are creative and those that are not. Digitization and the rise of self-generated and amateur media production have further contributed to the blurring of this line and, in some cases, have allowed media organizations to exploit and degrade creative work more than in the recent past, a topic we take up later in the chapter.

INDUSTRY EXECUTIVES: ENABLING AND LIMITING CREATIVITY

In addition to the distinction between above-the-line creative workers and below-the-line technical workers, distinctions are often made between creative workers whose central job is the creation of media content and the executives and managers in media industries that oversee that creative process. Unlike in previous eras of cultural production, in which individual creators could develop novels, paintings, or sculptures on their own, the contemporary media industries require many workers doing specialized tasks. Stop and count the number of people included in the credits of a movie sometime or those listed in the masthead of a magazine or the liner notes of a CD. One thing that has always amazed us when we've visited a television production is the number of people it requires—and this is only one stage of the process. Managing all of these people and coordinating and funding these massive undertakings requires a good deal of skill and creativity as well—the skills we associate with media industry executives.

"Industry executive" is an imprecise and general term, yet we feel it is meaningful for signaling the many workers who play necessary roles in providing institutional support for the development and circulation of media products. Many creators often don't view these workers as enabling them at all but as people obstructing their creative vision. It is reasonable to view these executives as gatekeepers, since they perform tasks such as selecting which projects are developed and make suggestions to the creators about changes to their product. Although executive input is typically described as detrimental to the creative process, it is important to acknowledge that there are also executives with strong artistic instincts who make creatively valuable suggestions as well. Nevertheless, as a help, hindrance, or something in between, they do play a significant role in shaping media content. In this section, we look at the various ways in which industry executives influence the creative processes of the media industries.

Some job titles that we'd include in the role of industry executive are "development and programming executives" at television studios, "record executives" in the music industry, "co-chair and/or CEO" at film studios and video game publishers, and "managing editors" of magazines and newspapers. These roles are primarily "business" roles, meaning that the people working in these positions often have advanced business degrees such as an MBA, but their day-to-day duties involve a fair amount of creative work as well. Unlike the creators we discussed previously—who are often driven at least on some level by a particular creative impulse or vision that they seek to communicate—industry executives primarily are charged with maintaining the financial interests of their employer. Although many do want their projects to tell a good story or to intervene in the culture in meaningful ways, industry executives are evaluated on their ability to bring in projects that ultimately yield profits for their studio, label, organization, or publication. The work of the industry executive involves many tricky negotiations because of the peculiarity of media industries and the difficulties of predicting the commercial success of cultural forms that we've already explained.

One way that industry executives influence creativity is to interpret audience desires by trying to keep their fingers on the pulse of cultural sentiment in such a way as to produce the "right" content at the right time. This description may be less relevant for executives working in news organizations, who might pay less attention to cultural sentiment than to major political and economic developments, but it is very relevant for print executives who assign feature articles that are more closely tied to cultural developments and perceived reader interests. Executives have to be immersed in their medium and hyperaware of new trends as soon as they happen while remaining conscious of whether established trends are in danger of passing from fashion.

As we discuss in Chapter 2, one of the most common strategies for identifying new successes is to reproduce something that was successful in the past—such as using established stars, engaging a known formula, or creating a new version of an existing hit (such as spin-offs in television, sequels in book publishing and film, or different incarnations of a popular magazine brand, such as *Teen Vogue* and *Men's Vogue*, that target varying demographics). The industry executive also must be sensitive to when repetition won't work. Successful creative forms often go through cycles. In the 1990s, the Seattle musical style known as "grunge," featuring heavily distorted guitar licks and disaffected lyrics, started to gain international popularity through the work of groups such as Nirvana, Stone Temple Pilots, and Pearl Jam. After a period of wild popularity, however, grunge acts largely disappeared from the billboard charts by the end of the decade, although bands continued to perform and put out music. In the early 2000s, however, a number of grunge bands reunited, put out new albums, and began to tour as the genre experienced another rise in popularity.

All of the media industries experience similar cycles in which a new trend becomes successful, the trend is replicated many times, the audience tires of the trend, and a new trend replaces the old one, following the same pattern of replication and burnout. Industry executives balance their knowledge of the new concepts or acts that come across their desks daily with a sense of what audiences are responding to and awareness of the recent and past history of successes and failures.

Industry executives are responsible for winnowing the thousands of new possible ideas they encounter to a handful, knowing full well that maybe only one or two of that handful has a chance to really become a success. Once they've selected the projects to be produced, executives continue to be involved in developing media products—although often one group of industry executives is responsible for the acquisition of ideas, and they then pass the role of development of the projects to another set of executives. Industry executives who work with creators once their projects are under contract balance knowledge of what has worked in the past and what might turn off segments of the audience or advertisers with the vision the creator puts forth.

Another key role of an industry executive that limits creative freedom is to offer input, often geared at making a project more commercially successful. For example, creators of television shows typically have to run their ideas by the network's current programming executive before they are developed into a script and again after the episode is shot. The industry executive then gives the creator notes that he or she may or may not be forced to incorporate. The magazine industry is similar: an editor-in-chief must justify the content of the magazine to executives at the publishing company, who may suggest that certain types of content be emphasized or downplayed in order to more effectively appeal to a particular readership. If the executives decide the magazine is not living up to its potential in terms of circulation or advertising revenue, they may even replace the editor-in-chief with someone who will bring a completely different editorial vision to the publication. These examples illustrate the significant creative role available to industry executives and how they are held accountable for that vision.

In addition to those executives overseeing production, other executives, such as those in **standards and practices** departments in the television industry, also evaluate creative products and provide assessments before they are finalized. Standards and practices is the office charged with maintaining network policies about content and making sure that the show being prepared for the network will not result in any kind of legal action—such as indecent content or defamation of an individual or corporation.

Standards and practices executives typically rely on a more stringent set of norms than legally is required, and here too there is a fair amount of space for the individual executive to interpret standards. For example, the documentary *Anatomy of Homicide*, about the making of an episode of the series *Homicide: Life on the Streets*, depicts a writer's experience negotiating his script with the network's standards executive. The writer explains to the documentary team that he had included more potentially offensive language than he desired because he knew he'd have to take some out. When the standards executive objected to the language, the writer was able to leave in much of what he wanted as long as he took out other words. This process of negotiation illustrates more of the creative work done by industry executives, as it makes clear how standards executives play a role in crafting scripts.

Commercial Influences: Audience Research

Industry executives don't rely *only* on their perceptions of cultural trends when acquiring and managing new media content; every commercial media industry today also employs researchers charged with various methods of audience research and testing to help executives make informed decisions about audience sentiment. Audience- and consumer-measurement services test how well media products might perform, are performing, and have performed at various stages of the production and distribution process, although what is measured, why, and how does vary considerably.

You may be most familiar with the television audience measurement company Nielsen Media Research, as the name "Nielsen" has slipped into the popular awareness more than those of most measurement companies. Perhaps you were once a member of a "Nielsen family," those selected to be part of the nationwide sample of viewers from which the viewing of all audiences is extrapolated. One of the biggest surprises to our students is often the size of the Nielsen sample. Until fairly recently, Nielsen used a national sample of 1,200 households to base viewing figures for, at the time, a nation of nearly 100 million homes. The expanding number of channel offerings and viewer adoption of technologies such as VCRs, DVRs, video on demand, and Internet streaming have made measuring television viewing more complicated. Nielsen consequently has had to develop new panels to measure different aspects of television use and has expanded its nationwide sample to 37,000 homes covering some 100,000 people.

Nielsen now uses a number of mostly technology-based methods for counting viewers; in some cases, however, it still uses some fairly low-tech methods. The beginning of audience measurement, which dates to radio in the pre-television age, was little more than announcers imploring listeners to send in a postcard with their names and maybe some limited information about themselves. A next stage involved telephone polling, in which audience measurement services would call a sample of homes and inquire about what they were watching or listening to at that moment, or perhaps the night before. Companies, including Nielsen, also made use of diaries—small notebooks that would be sent to a sample of viewers who were then asked to fill them in by writing down everything they watched over a two-week period and then to return them by mail.

A substantial advance began in the late 1950s and has arguably just recently become fully functional. In 1959 Nielsen began implementing a device called an "Instantaneous Audimeter," a mechanical device that recorded what channel the television set was tuned to on a minute-by-minute basis. At first, viewers had to send these meters back, and their tabulations would be figured with some delay, but by 1971 Nielsen had introduced its "Storage Instantaneous Audimeter," which could be connected to the set and would relay tuning information nightly to a data-processing center over a telephone line. The next big development arrived in 1987, when Nielsen introduced the People Meter, a technology that expanded the ability of audimeters by adding a mechanism to report who was in the viewing audience. While audimeters only reported what channel the set was tuned to, the People Meter added another crucial layer of information by requiring viewers to indicate who in the family was viewing with the click of a remote. The most recent development in this history began in the early 2000s as Nielsen began introducing Local People Meters in the largest cities in the country in order to provide overnight data about local television stations, instead of using the less reliable diary method for local markets.

We develop these paragraphs on Nielsen's evolving methods with such depth because how audiences are measured is crucial to understanding the meaning of the data that are produced. For example, until 2007 Nielsen measured only "family" viewing in the home, leaving out millions of other viewers, including college students. When the company did finally introduce college viewing panels, it tracked only the viewing habits of students who had come from Nielsen homes. Still, even with this small sample, ratings for some shows and channels increased dramatically, including *South Park*, *Family Guy*, and the Adult Swim programming block on the Cartoon Network. Certainly, those who rely on audience data recognize that a fair amount of inaccuracy in measurement methods persists. What does not exist, however, is any systematic way to account for these inaccuracies.

In the radio industry, Nielsen Audio (formerly Arbitron) is the primary measurement company, though at one time Nielsen and Arbitron competed in both television and radio measurement. The technologies that have gradually taken over television audience measurement have been much slower to come to radio. In much of the nation, radio audience levels are still measured by a sample of listeners who are asked to complete a week-long diary of their radio listening. Nielsen Audio rolled out a technological advance called the Portable People Meter in 2012 and currently measures radio listening with the device in larger US cities. The device is worn like a beeper by people in the sample and can record information about any radio or television signal that the person comes in contact with through inaudible codes embedded in the broadcast.

The challenges of audience measurement—and the information that is particularly desirable—change as we move into those industries that sell a more precisely measurable good such as a CD, magazine, movie ticket, or even digital download. Yet key differences exist among industries selling these goods as well, particularly depending on whether the media product is supported either entirely or partially through advertising, because audience size and composition are crucial factors in determining the cost of advertising.

In the magazine industry, companies pay organizations such as the Audit Bureau of Circulation and Business Publications Audit of Circulation to regularly inspect their shipments and certify that the number of issues a company claims to circulate is indeed true. As in the case of television, however, magazine advertisers not only are interested in how many people subscribe but also want to know something about those subscribers. Sometimes magazine companies compile this information themselves, but more often they contract such reader surveys to a media research firm.

The recording industry uses a couple of services to keep track of the performance of its industry. Since 1991, Nielsen's SoundScan system has automatically recorded music sales at participating retail outlets in order to compile a weekly list of top sellers. (Incidentally, SoundScan is not the data used by the Recording Industry Association of America in its certification system. So, for instance, if you hear that the association has declared a CD "platinum," the certification doesn't indicate that 1 million copies have actually been sold but rather that 1 million copies have been shipped to retailers.) The industry seeks information about frequency of radio play as an indicator of popularity and contracts with various firms that monitor radio stations electronically in order to develop a count of the most played songs.

Similarly, the film industry collects its basic performance data from box-office reports that come out at the end of each weekend, but they also employ audience measurement services from companies, such as the National Research Group, which survey audience awareness of and interest in upcoming films. In the case of the recording and film industries, data about audience behavior are used primarily for informing the industry about the performance of their acts and to develop release and marketing strategies, because these industries derive most of their revenues from consumer purchases rather than from advertiser sponsorship.

While different sectors of the media industries engage in varying degrees of audience research after a media good is released, all of them conduct research prior to and during the development of products. This type of research falls under the general category of **market research**, which includes a wider range of practices as well. Nielsen and Arbitron are big players in this type of market research, although countless other firms also subcontract them and conduct original market research for various clients. All of these researchers take media products at various stages of completion and elicit responses from members of targeted demographic groups in an effort to integrate audience preferences more fully into the final product, thereby increasing sales. As you might imagine, the creative people in the industry are often wary of these efforts to influence their creative expression. Undoubtedly, this type of market research is one of the clearest examples of how commercial interests can alter a society's cultural life.

Market research firms typically handle an array of clients, including advertisers and manufacturers, as well as media companies. Using surveys, focus groups, and specialized techniques designed for specific products, market research firms specialize in gathering the responses of a small group of research subjects, who represent the intended demographic for the client, and use those responses to test the popularity of the products and make adjustments before they go into production. For products with an ongoing life cycle, such as television series and magazines, follow-up market research is often done as well. For films and recorded music, however, once a movie or album is released, follow-up research with the intent of changing the product is impossible.

Market research makes much more widespread use of focus groups and other non-quantitative forms of audience analysis than does post-release audience and performance research, because there is time for the qualitative impressions of potential audiences to feed back into the production process. In recent years, Las Vegas has become a hotbed of market research, especially for the media industries. The popularity of Las Vegas as a travel destination for people from all walks of life gives the city ready and quick access to just about any demographic group. Market research for media products includes having audiences watch or listen to a brief media clip and fill out a survey; having them watch a television show or film in a special theater that allows them to give feedback on how much they like or dislike the program in real time; tracking subjects' eye movements as they watch a commercial; and discussing elements of content such as characters, plots, singers, and genres in small focus groups. In addition, market researchers often use cable television, the US mail, and the Internet to deliver movies and television shows to potential consumers and test their responses.

We know very little about how market research activities feed back into the production, selection, promotion, and performance of media goods. In 1983 Todd Gitlin reported that, when it comes to decisions about whether to green-light particular television series, market research was mainly used to verify executives' gut feelings; if a show that they liked performed poorly in testing, however, they rarely cancelled the project.[7] While anecdotal evidence suggests that market research now has more influence in decision-making than it did 25 or 30 years ago, we are not aware of any recent research that examines this question in depth. However, one thing is certain: the technological changes of the past two decades, combined with growing pressure to shave costs and squeeze profits in the media industries, have led to a marked increase in the volume and variety of market research conducted before the release of media products.

Indeed, audience research of all types has exploded in volume and variety since the introduction of digital distribution technologies that allow companies to track, log, and correlate everything we do when connected to a digital network. Undoubtedly, this explosion of information has had an impact on the business of media and the content media industries produce. For example, the video delivery service Netflix has touted the data it collects about what subscribers view, how quickly they view, and what they re-view as data helpful in its decision to create original programming. However, few systemic, published studies of this phenomenon exist. To be sure, media industry executives have a lot more data about consumers than they have ever before had, but how and how well they use this data remains a mystery.

Commercial Influences: Industry Norms, Organizational Cultures, and Circumscribed Agency

The activities of industry executives are not only curtailed by the profit motive of commercial media; their activities are also circumscribed by various practices and conventions that are part of how their industry operates. For example, television has long been defined by its daily schedule, which is an entirely arbitrary construction that limits the number of shows available, their length, and how many new episodes are created each year. Similarly, films operate with conventions such as the notion of "opening" on Friday nights, featuring "blockbusters" during summer months, and lasting between 90 and 180 minutes. The music industry long relied on the norm of collecting a group of songs for simultaneous release (the album) that has been challenged because of the creation of new forms of distribution that make single-song transaction efficient. The point here is that industry executives face a structured range of options and opportunities that have meaningful implications for the nature of the creative products that they are involved in developing.

In addition to working within a system of prescribed norms that limit some of the possibilities for media products, industry executives also work within organizational cultures that reproduce particular ways of thinking about aspects of the creative process and tendencies for success and failure. While "indoctrination" may be too strong a word, there are certain "common sense" ideas and perceived "best practices" that a worker in any industry encounters. We call these beliefs **industry lore**. Industry lore is not necessarily true—quite often it is not. Rather, industry lore describes myths regarding what audiences like or don't like and explains how these beliefs become entrenched and seemingly unalterable.

One example of industry lore that long governed the television industry was the perception that white audiences wouldn't watch a comedy about a middle-class, professional, married, African American family. Certainly, many creators suggested shows with black casts, and industry executives would say something like, "Oh, you can't do that. It will never succeed, because white people won't watch." Then, eventually, an industry executive decided to take a risk and test the industry lore. In this case, NBC programming executive Brandon Tartikoff challenged it with the production of *The Cosby Show* in the mid-1980s. The show, a conventional family situation comedy about a professional-class, African American family, went on to spend five years as the most watched television show in the United States.

The record industry of the 1950s provides an example of how prevailing industry lore can shape a variety of industrial structures and practices. At the time, the key to making hit records lay in getting songs played in heavy rotation on popular radio stations, and individual disc jockeys determined the playlist. Industry lore about disc jockeys held that they were highly individualistic, egotistical, and hedonistic. So record executives turned to independent contractors who plied disc jockeys with money, drugs, and sex, as opposed to trying more conventional methods of industry promotion, such as sales pitches and large conventions.[8]

Ultimately, these practices led to the payola scandals of the 1950s that are chronicled more fully in Chapter 8. The question that might naturally arise is, "Were these efforts necessary and successful?" The answer is hard to know: most likely, some disc jockeys responded better to the hedonistic approach, while others would have responded better to the more conventional approach, and a large number of them probably would have responded similarly to both approaches. Nevertheless, the point is that industry lore about what disc jockeys were like influenced the amount of money spent on persuading them, the use of outside contractors to approach them, and the particular perks that they were offered.

We could list numerous examples of the ways that unexamined industry lore hampers creative freedom and profits across the media industries. Here are a couple more: in the British magazine industry, the failure of several publications targeted toward men in the late 1950s through the 1960s led to the widespread belief that "men don't buy magazines." Although executives eventually realized they were wrong and began to conceive of men as a desirable audience in the 1980s, that notion limited both the quantity and quality of magazines targeted to men for decades.

In another case, many owners of art house theaters did not consider black audiences a primary target for art films and believed that the largely white art film audience wasn't interested in stories about African Americans. These beliefs led the theaters to decline films about black characters to such an extent that, in 2012, when Ava Duvernay became the first black woman to win best director at the Sundance Film Festival for her film *Middle of Nowhere*, she had to arrange alternative distribution to get her film to the public.

As these examples illustrate, industry lore can have significant consequences for enabling certain kinds of content and viewers while disabling others. Here we see the ideological implications of media industry practices and the real power in the circulation of culture that industry executives can exercise. Consequently, it is wise to be suspicious when industry executives claim "it would be bad for business" when justifying creative decisions. It may just be the case that no one has challenged the industry lore, as it is often the case that things once thought impossible are now considered good for business.

The making of industry lore is a complicated process—and it frequently originates from a kernel of truth or something that was true at one point in time. Industry executives are bombarded with often-contradictory information about their products and industry, from detailed statistical focus groups and box-offices reports to anecdotes filtered through friends and colleagues. They form perceptions based on this stew of information and often what they know "from their gut." Those with more agency pass these perceptions on to those below them and those they mentor, and the industry lore remains in place.

The unpredictability of the media industries ties back here as well. Often a product that challenges industry lore may be developed and fail, but it is difficult to know precisely why it failed. It is still the case that many network executives rely on the industry lore that a drama with a predominately nonwhite cast won't succeed (at least by broadcast network standards of success). When shows have challenged this presumption and not succeeded, it has been attributed to the color of the cast, rather than the possibilities that it was not promoted well, had a poor place on the schedule, or was not a well-produced, -written, or -acted show, regardless of the color of the actors' skin.

Just as in the case of the difference between Aaron and Nancy as creators, there are many different versions of industry executives. Some executives are like Jim, who is a real lover of film, grew up watching all the films he could get his hands on, and majored in film in college before attending business school. As a studio executive, he wants his studio to have the reputation for making important and significant films, and he's sympathetic to the creative visions of the creators he manages. He often goes to bat for his filmmakers with the studio heads above him, arguing for increases in budgets or changes in promotional strategy that he believes are necessary for the film to succeed and achieve its potential. At the end of the day, however, Jim's job performance is measured by evaluating the economic achievements of his division, and sometimes he has to rein in a creator who is going over budget or force a director to edit a film into a more manageable length.

In contrast, there are also executives like Jessica, who never really thought much about films or creative forms but who was placed in an executive position at a studio after performing well in another division of the studio's conglomerate that was not involved in the media industry. Jessica has a very different approach than Jim. She is very budget oriented. When other executives or creators want to expand the budget on products, she typically wants some sort of proof of how this added investment will make the film more profitable. She is less concerned with making "important" or highly acclaimed films and instead emphasizes commercial hits.

Again Jim, who might be described as "creative champion," and Jessica, the "bean counter," are extremes and perhaps caricatures of media industry executives. They, however, also illustrate the variability in the approaches of industry executives and the impossibility of understanding the influence they have on media content in a singular or consistent way. As with creators, different executives approach their jobs in very different ways, and a single executive may tend to his or her job in different ways at different points in his or her career. This may be related to the need to establish a track record of successes in order to gain more responsibility; the managerial style, system of reward, and general culture of the company in which the executive works; or the degree to which executives (and their families) are dependent on that salary for their livelihood.

Many see the devotion to creating profits at the core of a commercial media industry as a constraint that reduces creativity—and there are many times this is likely the case—but budget limitations can also force solutions and deviations from convention that have creatively productive outcomes. For example, the FX channel sought to create a "broadcast-quality" show with *The Shield*, but because it aired on a cable channel—with smaller audiences and, therefore, smaller revenue possibilities—it had to find a way to produce the show on a significantly smaller budget. The production staff experimented with using handheld cameras and natural light that didn't require the extensive set-up time required by traditional cameras and production strategies in order to reduce the number of days required to shoot each episode. The result was a jerky, rough visual style that was uncommon on most television shows but suited the unconventional storyline of the show, which explored the ethically dubious doings of a police unit that wasn't made up of conventional "good" guys. In this case, the reality of budget limitations forced creative innovation.

Another aspect to consider when assessing the influence of executives on content is that the path to profits is often unclear, and there is more than one way to increase profitability. An executive like Jessica may consistently try to reduce budget costs, but other executives understand that sometimes going over budget can be the key to both creative excellence and profitability for the studio. What makes being an executive in media industries so challenging is the uncertainty about when returns on those increased expenditures are likely to be realized. Although these kinds of uncertainties exist in all industries, as we've noted in many previous chapters, the unpredictable nature of cultural products and their generally high initial costs make them especially risky. Because success is so difficult to predict, there are often a variety of paths that might lead there.

Also, although we might have a romantic notion that a creator with a vision should be left alone and that any suggestion from an industry executive should be seen as inherently likely to compromise that creative vision, leaving creators to their own devices isn't always a good thing. Sometimes creators and their products benefit from the perspectives and ideas offered by executives. One way that you can judge this tension for yourself is by comparing the version of films released by studios and the "director's cut" typically available as an extra on DVD.

The key ideas to take from this section include the significant creative work performed by those not primarily defined as creative workers in media industries and the many different ways these executives can affect media content. Executives work within routines, expectations, and environments that allow them agency that is not unfettered. As we term it, their agency is circumscribed but meaningful nevertheless. The actions of media workers are structured by parameters such as the need to produce profitable content, but they may perform that task in a variety of ways.

Industry executives can be crucial to the success, failure, or mere existence of various media products. In his book *Desperate Networks*, Bill Carter tells the story of the creation of the reality television series *Survivor*, which ultimately became one of the defining successes of US reality television.[9] The show's creator, Mark Burnett, shopped the series to multiple networks, multiple times, without any executive expressing much interest. Finally, a junior development executive at CBS became intrigued with the series and worked as its champion through the ranks of the CBS development department. The persistence of this one industry executive enabled the existence of this show that became a phenomenal hit, and there are many similar stories across the media industries.

CREATIVITY IN AN ERA OF CHANGE

As with so much else in the media industries, creative work is currently in flux due to digitization, which has expanded markets for media content while also permitting the industries tighter control over the practices of creative workers and audiences. What it means to be a creative worker in the media industries today is radically different than it was even in the first decade of the twenty-first century. Some of the changes have allowed creative people more control over their craft, while others have resulted in less creative control and a decline in workplace satisfaction for creative workers.

For example, in his recent book examining how digital production and distribution are changing the recording industry, Tim Anderson presents cases of musicians such as Jonathan Coulton and Amanda Palmer who have experimented with emerging distribution and financing strategies.[10] Coulton has cultivated much richer relationships with fans through social media and distributed music through a website for which he creates a wide range of content, while Palmer was able to fund a new album through a Kickstarter campaign that raised $1.2 million. This funding allowed Palmer to retain full ownership of her master recordings and song publishing rights. Both artists acknowledge the new labor of cultivating fan relationships so directly often requires that they spend hours a day on the computer instead of with their instruments.

This type of connection between artist and fan in which no intermediary—no studio, label, and its layers of executives—is required to produce and distribute material led Kevin Kelly to imagine the new economic model of "1,000 True Fans."[11] Building from Chris Anderson's thought experiments about how digital distribution makes possible greater monetization of non-Blockbuster content, Kelly thinks about how many true fans—those that engage deeply with an artist, support endeavors such as Kickstarter, and so on—would be required to allow an artist to make a living. Subsequent analysis has suggested the number is likely quite a bit higher than 1,000, but what are thought experiments now might someday allow substantially different operations within media industries.

The examples of Coulton and Palmer provide clear evidence of how new markets and peer-to-peer file sharing created by digitization have increased the opportunities for creative people to break into the industry, gather a fan base, and stay true to their creative visions independent of executive influence. Similar kinds of opportunities have opened up for artists targetting ethnic minority and lesbian, gay, bisexual, and transgender audiences as well, who are now able to reach niche audiences with more culturally relevant media content and finance their projects through direct-pay or **crowdfunding** websites like Kickstarter. Frequently, their success in this space provides proof of the fallacy of industry lore and in some cases has then led to expanded opportunities in the legacy media industries. These endeavors allow the creation of media that often pushes beyond what media industries have produced. Its existence can be important for cultural and artistic reasons even if it does not prove commercially successful.

Creativity and Labor Practices in Digital Media Industries

At the same time, digitization has changed the very nature of creative work, blurring the line between work and leisure hours, increasing work hours while decreasing job security, and requiring creative workers to perform more and more tasks that used to be left to executives. Some observers believe that, all in all, digitization and the changes it has enabled have degraded job satisfaction for creative workers across all industries. Ultimately, while we agree with these critiques, we think it's probably most accurate to understand that losses and gains in creative work due to digitization go hand in hand.

For example, consider Phil, an animation editor for William's Street production house in Atlanta, a major supplier of programming for the Cartoon Network's Adult Swim adult animation block. His job involves taking storyboards, voice tracks, and images and creating a rough cut of an entire episode of a series, which is then finalized by an outside company. Most of his work involves computers: he receives voice and image files electronically, edits them together on his Macintosh computer, and sometimes even submits his final edits electronically.

Although he has worked in his current position for several years and considers himself well compensated, Phil also faces long stretches of time when he goes without work and without pay. He loves the laid-back atmosphere of his workplace, the flexible hours, and seeing his name in lights—or, more accurately, dots—on the television screen. He also, however, endures occasional long nights and early mornings during "crunch time," an arrangement that becomes more and more difficult to accommodate after getting married and starting a family.

While Phil works squarely within what we have defined as a media industry—specifically, the cable television industry—he is also undoubtedly a computer software expert. In many ways his work is not all that different from someone who specializes in database management or statistical analysis software—jobs characterized by regular hours, salary, and stability. But his working conditions—casual work environment, flexible hours, high pay with unpredictable periods of unemployment, and long hours during crunch time—are remarkably similar to conditions in both the gaming and software development industries.*

Phil's example tells us a great deal about the changed work environment for creative people in the media industries today. Although guilds and unions once held great sway in most of the media industries, guaranteeing wages and enabling steady employment for many above- and below-the-line workers, today's creative workers are much more likely to do project-based work. That is, they are hired on for a single project—say, developing a game or writing scripts for a television series—and when that project is done (or the season is over), they are let go. Among people who study labor practices, this piecemeal type of work arrangement is known as **casualization**.

Several factors have contributed to the casualization of the labor force in the media industries but perhaps none more than the **outsourcing** of media work. We discuss outsourcing in greater detail in Chapter 10. For the moment, it's only important to know that, much as has happened in many other industries, outsourcing jobs to workers in other parts of the world, many of whom are willing to work for much less than unionized workers in the United States, has led to job losses, wage declines, and the dissolution of collective bargaining. One study estimated that more than $3 billion in television and film production funding—along with the jobs that that sum would have paid for—were sent abroad by Hollywood between 2004 and 2011.[12] Outsourcing has, in turn, been made possible by digitization: high-speed broadband connections, computer-enabled production- and post-production, and a variety of teleconferencing options all allow creative work to be done in multiple locations around the world, while domestic producers and executives retain centralized control.

So digitization provides both the technical capacities *and* the economic incentives behind the casualization of the media workforce and outsourcing. The growing precariousness of media work, in turn, explains two other features of current labor conditions in the media industries: **crunch time** and increasing work hours. Crunch time involves working 60 or more hours per week in the weeks leading up to the release of a new game, movie, or television show. Originally developed in the software industry due to the unpredictability and complexities of programming, crunch time has become a ubiquitous practice across the new media industries. In some instances crunch time still exists

---

*This article explores the emergence of a job crisis in Los Angeles. What factors does the article discuss that are particular to media industry work? http://www.thewrap.com/tv/article/struggling-tv-industry-maybe-its-your-state-31999

This article discusses the labor issues that have emerged in the video effects (VFX) industry. What has caused the compromised working conditions VFX workers face? http://www.carseywolf.ucsb.edu/mip/article/things-know-about-labor-conditions-vfx-industry

because of the unpredictability of production practices, but just as often employers make workers put in such long hours simply because employees know how precarious their jobs are. While crunch time involves excessively long work hours over a short duration of time, telecommuting allows for an overall increase in work hours every week. Telecommuters often discover that, even though their work schedules are more flexible, always being "connected" also means always being at work.

Media scholar Mark Deuze refers to the increasingly blurry distinction between work life and leisure as "liquid life"—a term he borrows from the social theorist Zygmunt Baumann, who defines liquid life as "a precarious life, lived under conditions of constant uncertainty."[13] That constant uncertainty for media workers of when the next project will come along or whether they've saved enough to live on between projects leads workers to feel like they always to need be working. Although the state of "always working" can be found across numerous professions today, Deuze argues that media work has in many ways become the template for this kind of liquid life, which other professions follow.

One main reason that many media professionals feel the need to work so much is because they now do several jobs at once: as in the stories of Jonathan Coulton and Amanda Palmer, creative workers today not only have to ply their crafts; they also need to work as financiers, accountants, and self-promoters. David Hesmondhalgh and Sarah Baker conducted interviews with dozens of media professionals across several different industries and found that, across the board, they report spending much more of their time on the business end of the commercial media and much less time on creative work. For Hesmondhalgh and Baker, this shift in how creative workers spend their time signals a degradation in the quality of the work, making media work less satisfying than it used to be.

Although observers of media work today may disagree about how to evaluate the changes that many jobs are going through, most agree that workers have both more freedom and more responsibility than in the predigital era. No longer do creative people need to work for a single company and follow the creative decisions of superiors, as they did during the studio era of film production. The ability to have some degree of creative control over one's projects and one's career has expanded to included types of workers who did not have such autonomy in the past. However, this autonomy comes at the price of less stability, less predictability, and longer hours.

CONCLUSION

Although we've only been able to scratch the surface of the many ways individuals, organizations, and their conventional practices contribute to the creation of media products in significant ways, we hope that the cases we have noted illustrate the importance of considering production work at this level. Indeed, there may be hundreds of other cases we could have mentioned: one consequence of allowing for the agency of individuals at this level is that attempting to explain the operation of media industries begins to get very messy. The Industrialization of Culture framework allows for this "mess"—and, as we hope the examples throughout this chapter illustrate, even the workers responsible for day-to-day decisions play an important role in media industry operation.

Acknowledging the meaningful work that occurs at this level makes it nearly impossible to make generalizations about media industry operation. There are two ways of thinking about this: on one hand, if we allow for all of this individual influence, it becomes quite stunning that so much media production ends up being so similar. This similarity indicates how powerful industrial aspects such as routines, industry lore, and norms of practice may well be. On the other hand, this type of framework also provides a way to understand those uncommon—but nevertheless important—cases in which these industries produce something that is notably and meaningfully different.

QUESTIONS

1. Imagine you are in a position to make creative decisions on your favorite television show. What specific changes would you make? Would you take the show in a more "art for art's sake" direction or perhaps aim for greater commercial appeal? Why? How might taking such an approach change the nature of the program? What are some of the compromises involved in picking one approach over the other?

2. Imagine you are a music-industry executive who must decide which song will be the first single from a CD. To help make up your mind, you hire a team of researchers to provide feedback from potential consumers. What sorts of audience testing will you request, and what information do you think will help you make a final decision? Will you choose the single based strictly on the researchers' report, or will you base your decision on other criteria as well?

3. Think through your recent media consumption and identify any goods you think may have been produced for art's sake and any content that may have been produced for commercial reasons only. What characteristics of those goods help support your assessment?

4. Can you think of some common industry lore that is prevalent among each of the various media industries? What impact does that have on the type of content that is produced? What advantages, if any, might there be to industry lore?

FURTHER READING

Many books include assessment of production in the making of cultural goods. Several of these are noted in the further readings for Chapter 2. Some others include Mark Deuze's *Media Work* (Digital Media and Society Series; Cambridge: Polity, 2007); Sean Nixon's *Advertising Cultures: Gender, Commerce, Creativity* (Thousand Oaks, Calif.: SAGE, 2003); Ben Crewe's *Representing Men: Cultural Production and Producers in the Men's Magazine Market* (Oxford: Berg, 2003); Julie D'Acci's *Defining Women: Television and the Case of* Cagney and Lacey (Chapel Hill: University of North Carolina Press, 2004); Serra Tinic's *On Location: Canada's Television Industry in a Global Market* (Toronto: University of Toronto Press, 2005); Laura Grindstaff's *The Money Shot: Trash, Class, and the Making of TV Talk Shows* (Chicago: University of Chicago Press, 2002); and Michael Chanan's *Repeated Takes: A Short History of Recording and Its Effects* (London and New York: Verso, 1995).

NOTES

1. Edward Jay Epstein, *The Big Picture: Money and Power in Hollywood* (New York: Random House, 2006), 8.
2. Ibid., 257.
3. David Hesmondhalgh, *The Cultural Industries*, 2n ed. (London: SAGE, 2007), 53–54 for a much more in-depth consideration of these eras.
4. David Hesmondhalgh and Sarah Baker, *Creative Labor: Media Work in Three Cultural Industries* (New York: Routledge, 2011).
5. Vicki Mayer, *Below the Line: Producers and Production Studies in the New Television Economy* (Durham: Duke University Press, 2011).
6. Hesmondhalgh, *Cultural Industries*, 55.
7. Todd Gitlin, *Inside Prime Time* (New York: Random House, 1983).
8. Michael Chanan, *Repeated Takes: A Short History of Recording and Its Effects* (London and New York: Verso, 1995) 113.
9. Bill Carter, *Desperate Networks* (New York: Doubleday, 2006).
10. Tim J. Anderson, *Popular Music in a Digital Music Economy: Problems and Practices for an Emerging Service Industry* (New York: Routledge, 2014), 168–175.
11. Kevin Kelly, "1,000 True Fans." *The Technium*, June 15, 2008, http://kk.org/thetechnium/2008/03/1000-true-fans/ (accessed September 24, 2014).
12. http://filmworks.filmla.com/filming-facts/
13. Mark Deuze, *Media Work* (Cambridge: Polity Press, 2007).

CHAPTER 8

—

Media Distribution and Aggregation Practices

```
┌─────────────────────────────────────────────────────────────┐
│                        Key Takeaways:                        │
│  Understand the differences between media distribution and   │
│  aggregation and what activities both encompass              │
│  Identify factors that lead to different distribution and    │
│  aggregation practices                                       │
│  Understand how distribution and aggregation groom audience  │
│  tastes and shape media consumption                          │
│  Understand the practice of windowing, different factors     │
│  that affect its use, and how and why digitization is        │
│  changing its practice                                       │
└─────────────────────────────────────────────────────────────┘
```

In early 2004, the music producer and artist Danger Mouse (aka Brian Joseph Burton) released a collection of songs that came to be known as *The Grey Album*. Mixing lyrics from Jay-Z's *The Black Album* and hundreds of samples from the Beatles 1968 album *The Beatles*, known popularly as *The White Album*, *The Grey Album* was released to a handful of online music stores. These files were quickly removed when the EMI Group, which holds the copyright to *The White Album*, complained that Danger Mouse had infringed upon its rights. In response, hundreds of Internet websites, organized and encouraged by the activist group Downhill Battle, hosted illegal copies of *The Grey Album* for 24 hours in order to signal their opposition to the corporate interests that dominate the music industry and the ways in which it has responded to sampling as an art form and the Internet as a platform for distribution. More than 100,000 copies of the album were reportedly downloaded during that 24-hour period, now known as "Grey Tuesday" among copyright activists.[1]

The example of Grey Tuesday offers a wide range of lessons for scholars and consumers of popular media. What catches our eye in this story is the way in which new forms of distribution are shaped by existing regulatory and economic conditions at the same time that they also threaten to alter those very conditions. The new form of distribution is, of course, digital distribution over the Internet, which eliminates the need to ship physical copies of media goods to exhibitors (movie theaters) and retailers (stores that sell physical media such as DVDs, CDs, print) and also, in theory, eliminates the need for exhibitors and retailers. Nowadays, anyone with a broadband Internet connection can download and listen to, read, play, or watch most any media they want, without the inconvenience of having to go to a music store or a movie theater. Additionally, with the necessary technical savvy and enough time, a lot of us can find just about anything we want somewhere online for free.

It's obvious, then, how digital distribution over the Internet threatens to undermine long-standing economic conditions in which massive corporations with deep pockets cover the costs of production, promotion, and distribution and make their money by controlling the avenues of distribution and accessing media. Danger Mouse bypassed all of these existing conditions to release an album that became both a popular and a critical success. EMI tried, but largely failed, to stop distribution of *The Grey Album*, demonstrating how existing regulatory conditions also worked against digital Internet distribution but ultimately could not stop it. As one Harvard law professor noted at the time:

> As a matter of pure legal doctrine, the Grey Tuesday protest is breaking the law, end of story. But copyright law was written with a particular form of industry in mind. The flourishing of information technology gives amateurs and home-recording artists powerful tools to build and share . . . valuable art drawn from pieces of popular cultures. There's no place to plug such an important cultural sea change into the current legal regime.[2]

In other words, the development of Internet distribution requires, in this observer's opinion, changes in the regulatory conditions that govern media copyright.

In this example, changed distribution practices hold the potential to alter longstanding economic and regulatory conditions, but most of the time the practices covered in this chapter—namely, distribution and aggregation—have less profound implications. Nevertheless, these processes influence not only the content of the media we consume but also where and when we consume them and consequently the kinds of social purposes that media serve.

* * *

DISTINGUISHING DISTRIBUTION
AND AGGREGATION PRACTICES

Once a media good is created, someone needs to distribute, promote, and sell it in order for the good to find an audience and, with any luck, begin to pay back the various stakeholders who invested in its production. We might graphically represent the structure of the distribution and aggregation industries as follows:

Producer → **Distributor** → **Aggregator** → **Consumer**

We refer to these activities collectively as "Distribution and Aggregation" in the Industrialization of Culture framework, though this title can be a little misleading.

While some media, particularly film and television, are usually "exhibited" for audiences, others, such as music, print, and video games, are most commonly purchased through retailers. "Exhibition" has long been the term used to describe the business of actually making content available to audiences; however, changes to the media industries over the past decade have led us to use the term "aggregator" or the activity of "aggregation" to more precisely describe this role across media industries. Note that throughout this chapter we pay attention to both similarities and differences among media that are exhibited and those that are retailed. In many industries in which digital downloading and streaming have decreased reliance on physical media forms, companies best understood as aggregators—such as iTunes and Amazon—have emerged to replace the previous retail model. Likewise, Hulu, Netflix, and similar services around the globe have come to challenge the dominance of television exhibition by networks and channels.

At the outset, we want to emphasize the fact that both exhibitors and retailers respond to a combination of corporate promotions and consumer preferences in deciding what media goods to carry and how to sell them to consumers. Because these ways of getting media to consumers have been around for a long time, we know much more about how they operate than we do about digital aggregators and how their operations may differ from legacy exhibitors and retailers. Aggregators are the primary sites in a commercial media system in which the industry tries to groom the public's tastes and in which the public's tastes influence the industry through consumer purchases and ratings. For both practical and legal reasons, different companies often handle distribution and aggregation of particular media, and they are treated as distinct sectors of the media industry. In addition, both distribution and aggregation involve a wide range of related activities.

Distributors are basically middlemen; they buy from producers and sell to aggregators, and they have little actual contact with consumers. In fact, many casual media consumers have never even heard of some of the largest media distribution companies. For instance, many of us know the television series *Mad Men* (2007–2015) and are aware that it was broadcast on the AMC cable network in the United States. Few, however, are probably aware of the fact the series is distributed by Lionsgate Television in the United States and abroad. The array of middlemen involved in selling media rights can become dizzying, especially when we begin to talk about worldwide rights that are sold across multiple media platforms. Some producers, for instance, use not only different distributors in different parts of the world but also a different distributor for television, for Internet, and for DVD rights because these newer distribution outlets change so quickly and earn such small revenues that few distributors have the resources or personnel to specialize in all of them.

Distribution includes both the physical—or technological—transfer of media content to an aggregator *and* promotional activities that distributors engage in to convince aggregators to stock or show specific media. The way that television programs were distributed in the United States in the 1940s and 1950s offers a good example of the physical transfer of media content. In these early years, independent distributors traveled the country trying to convince each local station to purchase their programming. Stations that agreed would receive their copies of each episode a few days prior to its broadcast date and send it along to another station via mail after the episode aired. These practices may seem far removed from the creation or enjoyment of media, but they did have an impact on both: this "bicycling" of telefilms effectively isolated the program producers from the preferences of local stations or their viewers, increasing the creator's autonomy but perhaps decreasing the relevance of the programming for the actual viewers.

In many media industries, including music, film, and television, the large corporations that produce media also retain their own distribution divisions. These divisions specialize in distributing their parent company's media goods, but they also provide upfront funding for other independent producers in return for distribution rights. In other words, these major distributors function at times as banks, lending money in return for distribution rights and a share of the profits.

Why do major distributors carry their competitors' products? First, because some of these independent productions can become incredibly popular and lucrative, and the major distributors want to get in on a cut of the revenue. For their part, independent producers often prefer to work with major distributors because they have the clout to push productions into wide circulation. Michael Moore's documentary, *Capitalism: A Love Story*, for instance, was produced independently but distributed by Paramount Pictures in the UK and France. Distributors also use independent productions to round out their **libraries**. Larger libraries generally help increase sales, because they can provide one-stop shopping for buyers. Distributors often also sell goods in a bundle—sometimes called an "output deal"—and additional titles help increase the value of the bundles. Bundles often contain a mix of highly desired and less desired products.

Independent distributors serve some of the same functions as major distributors, but they generally carry far fewer media properties and sell to smaller aggregators. Sometimes, independent distributors provide upfront funding to producers, but by and large, they approach producers *after* the media good has been created and try to convince producers to let them distribute it. Like their larger counterparts, independent distributors also seek the largest possible libraries, which offer a diverse range of programming from numerous different producers. For example, Rockstar Games, which both produces and distributes (or, in the parlance of the video game industry, "develops" and "publishes") the *Grand Theft Auto* video game series, also distributes titles for other game developers, perhaps most notably the Bungie game *Halo*, which Rockstar distributed prior to Bungie's acquisition by Microsoft.[3]

Both major and independent distributors often pull out all the stops to convince aggregators to carry their products, from offering bulk discounts, helping with consumer advertising and promotion, giving free trips and trinkets, and guaranteeing **make-goods** that ensure aggregators will receive some kind remuneration if media goods underperform in sales revenues or audience ratings.

A distributor's promotional efforts not only work to convince aggregators to buy a distributor's products but also build relationships of trust that help both kinds of companies survive the uncertainties of media markets. Imagine, for instance, that you are a program director for your college radio station, a role that requires you to decide which songs to play throughout the day. Obviously, you would want a mix of popular contemporary songs, well-loved classics, and probably a good dose of new music. But how do you decide which of the thousands upon thousands of "new" songs to play? Certainly, you could listen to all of the new songs and make your own judgment, and this might be a good method for a nonprofit station. But in a commercial enterprise, you would want some guarantees that your tastes are not idiosyncratic. One place where program directors seek those guarantees is from trusted distributors and promoters that have good track records when it comes to distributing hit music. That is, over years of grooming their relationships with program directors, music distributors have been able to build trusted relationships that simplify the program director's job and make it seem less uncertain to program new songs with hit potential.

In our framework, program directors would be classified as aggregators. **Aggregation** refers to a range of activities that bring together media content and consumers. Entities that engage in these activities include television channels, YouTube, iTunes, Netflix, movie theaters, and even the brick-and-mortar music, book, and video game stores that remain. Aggregators select among the wide range of content and then make it available to consumers.

One of the most important activities that all of these different aggregators engage in is *selection*. Aggregators cannot carry all possible media content, so they narrow down the consumer's options to a manageable range of choice. That is, for practical reasons like the size of a store, newsstand, or movie theater, or the limited number of broadcast hours in the day, it is physically impossible—not to mention prohibitively expensive—for most aggregators to carry every single media good. Indeed, online retail outlets give us access to a seemingly endless variety of media choices. Even these stores also try to guide our selections by narrowing our range of choices. Amazon, for instance, provides us suggestions about which books to buy when we log on, based on the company's analysis of our previous purchases. Likewise, the display page for each book includes links to other books that have been bought along with the book. These too are forms of selection that the aggregator employs to channel the consumer toward certain products—perhaps because the retailer has a financial stake in these products or because the retailer seeks to ensure customer satisfaction with the experience. It is important to remember that the aggregator's task of selection serves two functions: first, it makes the job of selling media more predictable and therefore more profitable; and second, it helps consumers make appropriate choices in an increasingly crowded media marketplace.

Regardless of whether you think that aggregators' efforts to control our media choices are occasionally appropriate and helpful, it is certainly the case that they employ such efforts. Many of these practices are a response to the "nobody knows" feature of media commodities that we discussed in Chapter 2: if companies cannot predict what media content will be popular and which will be difficult to sell, they can at least limit the range of options we have to choose from.

There are various distinctions in the nature of aggregation across media industries. Aggregators of single media goods, as well as those of the print industries, still often acquire physical products to sell. The exception is in film during its initial theatrical release, where aggregators acquire the **rights** to aggregate content for audiences, rather than the physical products themselves. Usually, these rights specify how long the aggregator can offer the good, or what the **rights period** is, and what media channels (i.e., theater, on-demand, Internet, etc.) the aggregator can release the content through. The aggregator may choose to pay a higher price to receive exclusive rights to the content for a period of time. For example, Netflix paid a hefty license fee to be the exclusive Internet source for *Mad Men* (preventing others from also licensing it).

There are a variety of economic models used in aggregation. Here we highlight two—one old and one new and contested. The "wholesale model" has been common for some time and persists today. In this model, a publisher sets a recommended retail price (say $25 for the latest from a best-selling author). The publisher then sells the book to a retailer at a wholesale price that is typically 50 percent of the recommended retail price ($12.50), and the retailer is free to charge whatever it likes. It might use it as a loss leader and sell it at wholesale or even less in hopes that it drives people into the store and they buy more undiscounted material while there. Amazon did precisely this at the beginning of the e-book industry. The service priced all e-books at $9.99, even if the wholesale price was higher. The common pricing led many publishers to worry consumers would come to think of $9.99 as a standard e-book price, much as the $.99 or $1.29 iTunes song fee, even though some books (like textbooks) might require a higher fee. But Amazon was trying to drive people to purchase and experiment with their Kindle technology, which made the losses part of a broader business strategy.

In contrast to the wholesale model, Apple introduced the "agency model" in its online distribution. It was found guilty of price fixing for pushing this model in the e-book market in an effort to wrest market share from Amazon, though this also describes its model for iTunes transactions and that use of the model has not drawn litigation. In the case of the agency model, the publisher sets a retail price for an e-book, let's imagine $15 in this case. Apple's deal with the publisher requires Apple to sell the book at the publisher's retail price and guarantees Apple 30 percent of that sale. Apple got into trouble because its agreement contained a "Most Favored Nation" clause. Such clauses prevent the publisher from giving another retailer an advantage by requiring that the publisher cannot set a wholesale price lower than the one paid by Apple, which eliminated Amazon's ability to price at $9.99 and enabled Apple's iBookstore to always have the lowest price.

The point of explaining the difference in the wholesale and agency models is to illustrate the various financial deals between distributors and retailers, which might help you understand some of the variations in pricing you have experienced. As we noted in Chapter 5, how goods are paid for affects what goods are created, and differences in pricing models can affect the media goods we consume. It is also the case that this highly dynamic period in which online retailers have emerged and nonphysical media forms compete with physical copies make all these issues especially complicated.

The close business and even personal relationships that develop between distributors and aggregators demonstrate how difficult it is to draw clear lines between these two kinds of industry practices. In some media industries, this distinction is merely an analytic one that can help us understand the behaviors and consequences of certain kinds of commercial media operation, while in others there are clear distinctions in duties. In the case of subscription media that are shipped or streamed directly to consumers—such as newspapers, magazines, and even films via services such as Netflix—distribution and aggregation practices are fairly mechanical.

As this last example suggests, the present age of digital media delivery has begun to undermine the traditional distribution and aggregation practices in some industries, as users connect more directly to content producers. Eliminating the costs of distribution can allow creators a greater share of profits, though in some industries it is simply the case that old distribution and aggregation industries are being replaced by newer ones. For example, iTunes has become a key aggregator for the music industry and earns about 40 percent of the price you pay for each download. This money helps cover the costs of maintaining servers, tallying rights information, and organizing millions of tracks. The relationship between consumers and content providers, it would seem, has changed quite a bit since the days of bicycling telefilms, as have distribution and aggregation practices in bringing media to audiences.

DISTRIBUTION AND AGGREGATION INDUSTRY ROLES

We can distinguish a variety of different roles that distributors and aggregators play in the process of bringing finished media content to consumers. These are listed in Table 8.1. Of course, not all roles appear in all industries; as we suggested earlier, some of the roles are quite mechanical in certain industries. For instance, in magazine distribution, which is dominated by two national companies, Anderson Merchandisers and Alliance Entertainment, the rights-acquisition role is fairly uncomplicated, because major publishers have only two real choices.[4] By contrast, in international film distribution, the rights-acquisition role with regard to art films is quite complex and highly personalized. Art film distributors spend considerable time and expense cultivating relationships with art film directors in the hopes that, when they complete a project, they will turn to a trusted colleague to ensure that the film finds appropriate venues abroad.

Sometimes, all of these roles can be found within a single distribution or aggregation company. These are usually the largest companies in a respective industry. The Hollywood "majors," for instance, tend to both produce and distribute their own television shows and films. Similarly, the major labels in the music industry—Universal Music Group, Sony Music Entertainment, Warner Music Group, and EMI—also produce and distribute recorded music. On the other hand, smaller companies tend to divide these roles across several different companies.

The Roles of Distributors

In order to get a clearer picture of how these various distribution and aggregation roles play out and interact with one another in daily practice, it may be helpful to take a

Table 8.1 Distribution and Aggregation Roles

DISTRIBUTION	AGGREGATION
Rights acquisition (from producer)	Rights acquisition (from distributor)
Sales (to aggregators, redistributors)	Sales/aggregation/transmission (to the public)
Promotion (to aggregators, other distributors, public)	Promotion (to the public)

couple of concrete examples of real people who work in distribution and aggregation. The first example is someone we'll call Mario, who used to run one of the largest independent television distribution companies in the world, handling worldwide rights to programming produced by other companies, especially well-known, independent producers who had created several popular network series. The company flourished during the days of the **Financial Interest and Syndication Rules**, which prevented the networks from producing the programming they aired. After the repeal of Fin-Syn in the early 1990s, the company foundered but managed to stay afloat, thanks in no small part to the close relationships that Mario had built with a wide network of television producers. In the late 1990s, the company scored international distribution rights to a popular and critically acclaimed series starring a major pop star that had been produced by a Hollywood studio and broadcast on its television network. The studio could have easily sold the program abroad on its own but chose instead to license the program to Mario. The studio believed that, despite the show's success in the United States, it was not likely to be picked up by large, general entertainment networks abroad because it featured a nonwhite family. Because Mario had much better connections with buyers at cable channels and satellite broadcasters abroad, the studio decided that he could sell it more effectively than they could.

Why would any producer, especially a major producer with its own worldwide distribution wing, not distribute its own program? The answer is the same for large and small producers: because their efforts are focused on production, they cannot do an adequate job of distribution in a complex, far-flung, and constantly changing environment like international television. Of course, the studio could also have turned to its own international distribution wing, but these executives are focused primarily on high-end programming and large, general entertainment broadcasters, particularly in Europe.

The program that Mario handled, by contrast, was not a network blockbuster and appealed mostly to small, startup satellite and cable channels that targeted a particular segment of the viewing audience, rather than the broad audiences that large broadcasters typically seek. As it happened, Mario not only had good relationships with producers that prompted them to turn to him with such programming but also had good intelligence about potential buyers abroad, as well as good relationships with many of those buyers. In other words, a combination of market conditions, business strategies, and professional relationships worked together to allow Mario to distribute this particular program.

Still, Mario had to work hard to sell the series. He attended several international television trade fairs. He traveled the world making in-office courtesy calls to potential buyers, actively trying to interest them in this and other series. He sent out slick fliers, videotapes with clips from the series, and information about ratings data to dozens of other potential buyers. In other words, Mario took on not only the roles of acquiring and selling rights to this television program but also the role of promoting it to potential aggregators.

Three important general lessons about the distribution of media content can be drawn from Mario's example. First, the predictability of the distribution market influences how complex the process is in a given industry. When the number and stability of buyers is fairly consistent, distribution is either handled in-house or by established companies that have fairly straightforward relationships with content producers and aggregators. For example, a film such as *Elysium*, which was produced and distributed—both domestically and internationally—by Sony films. Many, many films and television programs are handled this way.

To take another example from the television industry, the domestic American distribution market is dominated by the major Hollywood studios and a few large distributors, as well as television stations run by large ownership groups. These ownership groups include the national networks, CBS, ABC, NBC, and Fox, which focus on stations primarily in the top 20 markets in the country, and independent groups like Sinclair, Nexstar, and Raycom, which own dozens of channels in the top 100 markets in the country. The process of buying and selling rights to television programs in the domestic market, then, consists of fairly straightforward business meetings involving well-known buyers and sellers with few chances for new entrants or surprises. In this way, domestic television distribution is not dissimilar to magazine distribution, while international television syndication is quite a different animal due to quite different market conditions.

A second lesson we can draw from Mario's example is that the more volatile distribution markets are, the more likely it is that distribution will be handled by a complex web of distributors and redistributors. Mario was primarily a distributor, but he also acquired the rights to distribute a handful of programs from another company, then resold those rights to other distributors, making him a "redistributor" as well. Many other people in international television work primarily as redistributors, acquiring rights to programming from another distributor and selling the rights to other distributors or broadcasters. This was also the case in the recorded music industry in the early 1960s, before the major record labels developed their own distribution divisions, when local or regional distribution companies would get albums from both major and independent labels and resell them to record stores or other distributors.

Finally, we can see from Mario's example that in volatile and complex rights markets, distributors spend a great deal of time and expense grooming relationships with buyers and other distributors, as well as promoting their companies and their programming to other industry insiders. While most of us are quite aware of how heavily media content is promoted to the general public, we may be surprised that distributors sometimes have to promote their products just as intensely to others within the industry.

In predictable distribution markets, the types and range of media content available to consumers tend to be decided by the companies involved in distribution and aggregation. In other words, the media consumer's choice basically boils down to taking or leaving what established media producers, distributors, and aggregators offer us. The classic example here is commercial broadcast television, a system in which viewers had a restricted number of programs to choose from at any given moment—in most places in the United States, five or fewer channels.

In more volatile markets, by contrast, consumer demand has a far greater role in deciding what media we view, read, listen to, or play, because small, independent distributors and redistributors will find ways to meet unfulfilled demands. Online news aggregators offer a good example of this tendency; these are applications that persistently scan a set number of online news outlines for new stories and deliver links to these stories in a common location, such as one's computer desktop or blog. Hundreds of different news aggregators are available online, and all of them can be customized to aggregate only the kinds of websites and news articles the reader selects. For instance, the reader can choose to receive only sports news, only international news, only business news, and so forth.

The Roles of Aggregators

Now let us turn to an example taken from the day-to-day life of an aggregator, whom we'll call Larry. Until 2008, Larry owned and operated a newsstand in Pasadena, California, which had been in his family since the 1950s. Centrally located in the old town, his newsstand was a city institution for many years, selling perhaps more magazines and newspapers than any other in the area. Despite the large number of titles and customers at the stand, however, Larry insists that the newsstand was as much a community-gathering place as a place of business. Some customers would stop by for hours on weekends to discuss politics and entertainment news. Because of its location in Southern California, not far from the Hollywood foothills, Larry's newsstand featured entertainment industry and gossip magazines more prominently than newsstands in other cities in the Midwest or East might have. In addition, the interest in entertainment news provided Larry with corporate clients that bought magazines in bulk to distribute to their employees, as well as conventional foot traffic.

Despite his stand's long-standing success, Larry was forced to close his doors in 2008 due to two main factors: first, the decline in sales that resulted from changed city ordinances that prohibited nearby street parking; and second, the fact that his distributor began to favor a nearby newsstand over his. Several other factors helped contribute as well, particularly the bad economy, which depressed overall magazine and newspaper sales, as well as the explosion of online content, which cut heavily into newsstand sales. Newsstands that continue to operate in Southern California report similar kinds of stresses on their businesses, and one operator even says that she has begun trying to sell titles at car windows when drivers are stuck in nearby traffic.[5]

The fate of Larry's newsstand in Pasadena may seem an isolated case, but it does, in fact, demonstrate the many roles that media aggregators play. First, Larry must acquire content from newspaper and magazine distributors. When he had trouble fulfilling this role because the distributor began to privilege Larry's competitor, his business foundered.

Second, we see how Larry's role as an aggregator involves more than taking media goods and placing them before an audience; in fact, he actively selected which titles to carry and how to display them based on his perceptions of his consumer's interests. This practice of anticipating which media consumers will want is known as the **surrogate consumer** role: aggregators act as our surrogates with distributors and make deliberate selections based on what the aggregator believes the consumers will want. Put another way, aggregators *push* certain content on consumers, rather than letting us *pull* what we want from all available content. In fact, as we explore in more detail in the following section, aggregators, distributors, and others all play this surrogate consumer role to some extent. Most of us recognize and accept these surrogates, as long as we believe that they are acting in good faith. Problems can occur when distributors give aggregators incentives to favor some goods over others.

Larry's role as a surrogate consumer was part of his overall effort to promote particular magazines and newspapers to consumers, in particular by selecting which titles to carry and arranging them within his stand. The story of the newsstand employee who tried to sell to drivers stuck in traffic is also a part of this effort at promotion, and it demonstrates too how all promotion involves selection: after all, she can carry only a tiny fraction of all the titles the newsstand sells. All of these efforts at selection are attempts to shape consumer demand as much as they are reflections of that demand.

Together, the roles that distributors and aggregators play in bringing completed media goods to consumers demonstrate a high degree of selection and shaping of consumer demand. As with much we've discussed throughout this book, these practices reflect the efforts to decrease the high risks inherent in the media industries, particularly the "nobody knows" principle. By having experts who deal more directly with audiences, there is a higher likelihood for media products to "find" their audience. Media companies cannot predict the popularity of their products, but they can at least try to limit access and shape demand.

DISTRIBUTION AND AGGREGATION STRATEGIES

In their various roles, distributors and aggregators engage in a wide range of practices designed to shape both media content and consumer behavior in order to maximize profits and minimize loss. We identified some of these previously, such as using promotional techniques to influence which media goods we consume; in this section we detail the range of these practices more fully.

Distribution and aggregation are risky undertakings, and they can be richly rewarded. In the television programming industry, for instance, distributors typically take about 25 percent of the profits "off the top," which means that they get a percentage of **gross sales**, or total sales revenues before overhead and other costs of production are subtracted out. In the late 1980s and early 1990s, *The Cosby Show*, for example, earned more than $4 billion in domestic syndication markets, which probably earned its distributor, Viacom, roughly $1 billion. At the same time, distributors sometimes have to make substantial investments in media products (sunk costs) in order to secure distribution rights from the producer before they know how popular those products are going to be. Increasingly, distributors are participating in funding the initial production of content in order to secure distribution rights once it is complete.

For aggregators, making the wrong acquisition choices can advantage competitors and also mean that valuable space in the retail outlet, theater, or program schedule might be taken up by unpopular media content. The commercial organizations that handle the distribution and aggregation of media products have developed several business strategies to try to deal with these financial risks and rewards.

One strategy—**overstocking**—that both distributors and aggregators engage in is akin to the **intentional overproduction** that characterizes the media production business. One of the ways that commercial media organizations deal with high production costs and uncertain sales is by creating a large number of products, with the understanding that only a handful will become successful. Distributors help guarantee overproduction because they subsidize production and pay producers for rights to much more product than they can ever hope to sell. They overstock media products for the same reasons that producers overproduce: in the absence of reliable predictors of what might appeal to aggregators and consumers, distributors carry as wide a range as possible in order to increase the possibility that some of their properties will hit big.*

In addition, having a large number of titles helps increase the overall value of a distributor's library, as we explained earlier. Distributors combine the practice of overstocking with **differential promotion** of the material they acquire. Differential promotion refers to the strategy of showering praise, attention, and money on only a small fraction of the products they acquire, specifically, those songs, artists, films, and television series that they believe have the greatest potential to become hits. These products benefit from large promotional budgets and strong-arm promotional efforts designed to cajole aggregators, retailers, and even critics to give those products privileged treatment.

By contrast, distributors largely abandon goods that they see as potentially unsuccessful, releasing them to the public with little fanfare or promotional support. The sequel to the critically acclaimed Afghan war biopic, *Jarhead*, *Jarhead 2: Fields of Fire* (2014), for example, bypassed theaters and pay-per-view television channels and was released directly to DVD because its distributor, Universal Pictures, thought it unlikely to attract many viewers in other outlets. Several films every year are released in this manner.

Differential promotion is one of the most obvious ways in which distribution works to determine what media content is popular in the United States and abroad: by making a lot of noise about one media product, a distributor can help create positive "buzz" about it. At the same time, the clamor can drown out excitement over unendorsed products.

Aggregators also engage in differential promotion, except that their lopsided promotional efforts focus primarily on consumers. This differential promotion includes advertising certain goods more prominently in local media outlets; coupons, rebates, and differential pricing—such as the common practice of charging more for 3D movies than for 2D—and the strategic placement of goods, whether placement in stores and newsstands or on a television schedule or in certain types of theaters. In fact, a main aim of a distributor's promotions is not simply to get aggregators to carry its products but also to encourage aggregators to feature them prominently as well. Some distributors even offer ready-made consumer promotions for the media they sell, such as recording plugs for a buyer's radio station made by well-known musicians.

---

*This article explores the particular strategies used in the marketing of the first *Hunger Games* book. What steps did the publisher take in distributing and promoting the book to encourage the likelihood it would be a blockbuster hit? http://www.salon.com/2012/03/18/the_making_of_a_blockbuster/

All of these efforts to promote media products to one another and consumers can require a good deal of money, favors, and even graft within the distribution and aggregation industries. The federal government has even shown occasional interest in the methods that distributors employ to get aggregators to treat their goods favorably. In one of the most notorious examples, known popularly as **payola** scams, music distributors in the 1950s and 1960s gave cash, drugs, and prostitutes to popular DJs in order to get them to play their songs and rave about them on air. More recently, in 2007, four of the largest radio broadcasting companies—Clear Channel Communications Inc., CBS Radio, Entercom Communications Corp., and Citadel Broadcasting Corp—were fined $12.5 million by the Federal Communications Commission for accepting money and gifts in exchange for promoting songs distributed by several major and independent record labels.[6]

Windowing: A Changing Strategy of Media Distribution

One of the most unusual aspects of media commodities and the industries that support them is the practice of **windowing**, which refers to releasing new products on a staggered schedule, differentiated by medium or territory. For instance, non-blockbuster films are sometimes released through "platform release," which means the distributor releases the film to a very small number of theaters (usually fewer than 200) and spends little on promotion. If the movie generates sufficient buzz among moviegoers and critics, the film is then promoted and released more widely. In the music industry, individual songs are often released to stores and radio stations before an entire album is. Although windowing is not common in the gaming industry because of the reliance on retailers rather than distributors, some video games do have staggered release dates in different parts of the world. *Grand Theft Auto 5*, for instance, was released in September 2013, in the United States but not in Japan until a month later.

Windowing serves two basic economic functions: first, it is an effort to build excitement, word of mouth, or buzz about new media products in order to drive people to consume them. When it comes to platforming movies, for instance, one of the purposes is to build up positive press coverage of a film in larger cities, which might bring in audiences around the country. Platforming also reduces the risk in cases where media fail to perform. For example, if a film does not open strongly on early screens, then its distribution may be limited or it may be removed from theatrical release and sent directly to home video.

Second, windowing ensures that distributors can squeeze the maximum amount of profit possible out of media products. The major determinant of when to release a good in a particular window is the price that the consumer will pay. For instance, movies start out at theaters, where each audience member pays in excess of $10 per person. Next, they can be found on pay-per-view, where groups of audience members can watch the movies, probably for less than $10. Similarly, the movie may move to a second-run theater, where tickets cost much less than $10. Finally, a very popular movie at the end of its distribution windows may show up on a local television station on a Sunday afternoon; the audience pays nothing to watch it, and the local television station probably pays very little to air it.

Table 8.2 Typical Windowing Order for Blockbuster Movies

First-Run Theaters

Hotel Pay-Per-View; Airlines

DVD

Video on Demand and Pay-Per-View

Subscription Cable/Broadband (HBO, Showtime, Netflix)

Second-Run Theaters

National Television Network or Basic Cable Networks

Local Television Stations

We can distinguish between **upstream windows,** or distribution channels that occur earlier in time, and **downstream windows,** or those that occur later. Table 8.2 provides a list of the typical order of distribution windows for a blockbuster film, where the upstream windows are at the top of the table and downstream windows are at the bottom.

A broad variety of factors influence decisions about how exactly to order distribution windows and when to release content into a downstream window. Increasingly, windowing is a complex practice that is tailored to each individual good. The most important factors that influence the order and timing of windowing are (a) per capita revenues in each window, (b) differences in potential audience size in each window, (c) the degree to which audiences will consume the programming in downstream (later) windows, (d) the loss of interest among viewers following a product's initial release, and (e) how vulnerable the distribution channel is to illegal copying or piracy.[7] In addition, for media products with large promotional budgets, such as blockbuster films, distributors want to take advantage of the buzz and increased audience awareness that advertising creates before it fades by moving through later windows more quickly.*

Windowing always involves a trade-off between holding content in upstream windows, where it generates higher per-viewer revenues, and releasing it into a downstream window, where the audience is quite likely to be larger but the total payment may be lower. Distributors want, for example, to wait until every person who is willing to pay $10 to watch a movie in the theaters has gone to see a film before releasing it to pay-per-view, where an entire family can watch it for $8. If a distributor releases into the downstream window too quickly, consumers who might have paid full price may wait and pay the lower price. Wait too long, however, and consumers who might have paid the lower price in the downstream window may lose interest and move on. This is what we mean when we say that windowing is an effort to wring maximum profits out of media content: it is a very careful calculation to try to get us to spend the maximum amount of money we are willing to spend by giving us multiple times to spend that money, in decreasing quantities.

---

*The audio story from National Public Radio looks at the evolution in windowing strategies by major film studios. How did the emergence of Netflix force studios to adjust their windowing practices? http://www.npr.org/templates/story/story.php?storyId=126115011

Outside of the film and television industries, windowing is a less common practice because fewer venues for accessing other forms of media content exist. Windowing doesn't work well for news because immediacy is a particularly important characteristic of this content. The book publishing industry has long released paperback books after hardcover versions, which illustrates a print industry version of this practice. Like windowing in film and television, the book industry is also shifting more toward simultaneous releases across platforms.

For some kinds of media content, the channel of distribution matters little to audiences and end users. It generally doesn't matter, for instance, whether we receive a new hit song via CD, an online store, or a peer-to-peer sharing network, or whether we watch a recent film at home on HBO, pay-per-view, or DVD, except if we are sensitive to the various prices required or in cases where, as avid fans, consuming the media early matters a great deal. For other kinds of media, however, the channel of distribution matters very much. Consider action and fantasy films: you've probably heard friends insist on watching certain kinds of spectacular films in the theater in order to fully experience all the graphics and special effects. Perhaps you are one of these people who likes to watch spectacular films in the theater, whereas you don't much care whether you watch, say, a romantic comedy at home.

Such distinctions in viewer behavior go to our third point stated previously—that the organization and duration of windows depends on how likely viewers are to consume programming in a downstream window. Note, however, that these norms can change. For example, depending on one's setup, it's possible today to almost recreate the theater experience at home with BluRay DVDs and HDTVs increasing the number of people willing to consume spectacular films in a downstream window and, likely, shortening the theatrical window for such films. To put this in the language of the Industrialization of Culture framework, here we see how changing technological structures alter distribution and aggregation practices.

The fourth point—that windows are determined by the degree to which the channel of distribution is vulnerable to piracy—is perhaps most obvious in the trepidation with which music, film, and television distributors approached Internet distribution for a number of years. Due to the ease and high quality of digital reproductions (see Chapter 9 for clarification), digital release windows are extremely vulnerable to illegal copying and unauthorized redistribution. Because windowing basically builds walls between different types of distribution platforms and audiences, distribution mechanisms like the Internet that tear down those walls are particularly troubling for media industries. As media industries have gained experience with digital distribution, they've also found that eliminating windows and allowing day and date release decreases piracy.

Some in the industry question whether digitization and Internet distribution have forever undermined the idea of windowing and foresee windowing slowly eroding as a business strategy. Increasingly, movies are being released to DVD and on-demand channels on the same day as theaters, and there is speculation about the possibility of pre-releasing certain films to on-demand channels *before* their theatrical releases, charging consumers perhaps $100 or $150 for the privilege of being the first to see, for instance, the final installment of the *Harry Potter* movie series. In fact, some powerful people in the media industries, such as Steve Jobs, the founder of Apple, argued in favor of such developments.

The industry term for this unbundling of media goods from their legacy distribution platforms is **disaggregation**. In a disaggregated media environment, consumers would be able to access any media good through any device or distribution channel they choose—though at a price; this is a strategy that essentially eliminates windowing. Powerful media corporations fear disaggregation because control over which distribution platforms carry which goods at which times is central to their current business models and there is no way to know whether alternate models would be as profitable. These corporations are fighting to maintain the practice of windowing, for example, by encouraging technological advancements that make digital copies more secure, developing their own distribution sites where protected content is available, and trying to devise business models that give people access—though require them to pay—for downloaded content. It remains to be seen, however, whether the days of the release window are numbered.

CONCLUSION

As the vital link between producers and consumers of media, distribution and aggregation are important and powerful practices but ones that most of us have never really considered in much depth. Far from being mechanical or simplistic processes, distribution and aggregation typically involve a good deal of business acumen and creativity to successfully manage. Whether we are at the local theater, at home watching TV, at the Best Buy browsing computer games, or on iTunes buying music, both the media content we encounter and our watching/listening choices are shaped by media distributors and aggregators. These cultural gatekeepers are not all-powerful masterminds manipulating culture and society, but neither are the processes of production and consumption wholly absent of their influence.

Clearly, distribution and aggregation practices show us that the commercial media industries do not merely give the public the media content they want. Rather, to varying degrees, these practices influence where and when we consume media, how much we pay for it, and what kinds of content we are allowed to choose from in the first place. In other words, distribution and aggregation groom our tastes and shape the programming we enjoy.

The important social question that distribution and aggregation practices raise is: To what degree are the media we consume and our own personal tastes shaped by large media companies that primarily aim to fatten their bottom lines? In general, we see a trend *away* from straightforward efforts to control our behaviors due to changes in technological conditions of distribution that have turned distribution and aggregation into practices centered more around the pull of consumer desires than the push of corporate control. Today, the emphasis of the commercial media industries centers more on surveilling, aggregating, and predicting our media preferences than on limiting our choices, as was once the case, though industry practices continue to evolve.

QUESTIONS

1. Say you are a distributor responsible for selling the television series *How I Met Your Mother.* Gross profits for selling the series amount to $200 million, of which $100 million is **net** profits, or the amount of profit left after deducting production, distribution, and promotional costs. Assuming you have a conventional contract with the producer, what are your company's total distribution profits? Explain why. (Answer below).

2. Imagine you have created a new media product and plan to release it on a staggered schedule taking into account the four factors that influence windowing. How would you window it, by medium and territory, to best maximize the audience demand and size? What upstream and downstream windows exist for this type of product? Depending on the particular product you have created, is windowing a useful practice? Why or why not?

3. Consider the work of countless surrogate consumers who "guide" you through your media choices. In what ways are they helping you make selections? In what ways are they limiting what you can consume? How has digital distribution changed the influence of surrogate consumers?

4. Think about the implications of a disaggregated media environment. Which traditional distribution platform would you most like to see unbundled and why? What might be the economic consequences of the disaggregation for that particular industry and for consumers? It may be helpful to think about the unbundling that has already occurred through online stores such as iTunes and Amazon that allow people to buy songs à la carte instead of demanding that they purchase an entire CD. How has this changed the way you buy music, and what have been the consequences for the music industry?

- Question 1 Answer: $50 million. A "conventional" distribution contract is 25 percent of gross.

FURTHER READING

Other than research on movie theaters, the study of media distribution and aggregation is less well developed than the other conditions and practices we explore in this volume. On film aggregation, see Edward Jay Epstein's *The Big Picture: Money and Power in Hollywood* (New York: Random House, 2005), and Barbara Wilinsky's *Sure Seaters: The Emergence of Art House Cinema* (Commerce and Mass Culture Series; Minneapolis: University of Minnesota Press, 2001). Also, Ina Rae Hark's edited anthology *Exhibition, The Film Reader* (In Focus, Routledge Film Readers; London: Routledge, 2002) offers a good collection on the scholarship in film studies on exhibition.

General overviews of distribution and aggregation in the commercial media industries can be found in Paul J. Hirsch's "Processing Fads and Fashions: An Organization-Set Analysis of Cultural Industry Systems," *American Journal of Sociology* 77, no. 4 (1972), 639–659, and Joseph Turow's *Media Systems in Society: Understanding Industries, Strategies, and Power* (New York: Longman, 1997).

Timothy Havens' *Global Television Marketplace* (London: BFI Press, 2006); Toby Miller et al.'s, *Global Hollywood 2* (London: BFI Publishing, 2005); and Paul Torre's "Block Booking Migrates to Television: The Rise and Fall of the International Output Deal," *Television and New Media,* 10, no. 6 (2009), 501–520, all address aspects of the international distribution and exhibition of American films and television.

NOTES

1. Matthew Rimmer, *Digital Copyright and the Consumer Revolution: Hands Off My iPod* (Northampton, Mass.: Edward Elgar, 2007), 130.
2. Bill Werde, "Defiant Downloads Rise From Underground," *The New York Times,* February 25, 2004, http://www.nytimes.com/2004/02/25/arts/music/25REMI.html?pagewanted=1 (accessed February 24, 2010).
3. Business Wire, "Take-Two Interactive Software's Rockstar Games Announces Oni for the Playstation 2," March 16, 2000, http://www.factiva.com (accessed February 3, 2010).
4. Ed Christman, "Magazine Distributors Clash With Publishers," *Billboard,* February 5, 2009, http://www.billboard.biz/bbbiz/content_display/industry/e3id42 5eb6001d58ee75185dcf0bcceee17 (accessed January 26, 2010).
5. Sharon Knolle, "Death of L.A. Newsstands," *L.A. Weekly,* May 27, 2009, http://www .laweekly.com/2009-05-28/news/death-of-l-a-newsstands (accessed February 2, 2010).
6. John Dunba, "FCC Unveils Settlement with Radio Firms," *USA Today,* April 13, 2007, http://www.usatoday.com/money/economy/2007-04-13-2144814802_x.htm (accessed February 3, 2010).
7. Adapted from Bruce M. Owen and Steven S. Wildman, *Video Economics* (Cambridge, Mass.: Harvard University Press, 1992).

CHAPTER 9

—

Digitization

Key Takeaways:

Understand how digitization changed the business operations and revenue models of legacy media industries

Describe how media industries developed in the digital era are different from legacy media industries

Recognize evolving regulatory and economic conditions that affect digital media industries

The modern recording industry can trace its origins to the late 1890s. In those pre-record player, pre-radio days, people who desired musical entertainment at home purchased wind-up music boxes and player pianos. Over the past century, many fundamental aspects of the recording industry remained the same, although the delivery technology by which favorite songs and artists reached eager listeners evolved from music boxes, to sheet music, to records, tapes, and finally to compact discs. The most recent evolution of that history—the availability of digital music files—has introduced far greater consequences to the operation of the recording industry.

Compact discs provided the first digital format for music, but this delivery technology largely continued the norms of industry operation because it still required the transfer of music to a physical form—the CD—that record labels manufactured and then distributed to stores around the world. The digital music file, and online retailers such as iTunes, substantially disrupted these norms of distribution in the recording industry. Economic models had to be reassessed as substantial manufacturing, distribution, and shelving costs were eliminated as listeners embraced the ability to purchase individual tracks instead of complete "albums," which had dominated music distribution since the advent of vinyl LPs in 1948. Divorcing the sale of recorded music from a physical form (a technological condition) also made it much more difficult for the recording industry to manage the circulation of music, and the relatively small size of digital audio files made illegal sharing over the Internet rampant (a regulatory condition with economic consequences). The sale of physical forms of music still remains substantial. In 2014, the Recording Industry Association of America reported that permanent digital downloading accounted for 41 percent of total music shipments (not counting illegal downloading), streaming music accounted for 27 percent of shipments, and 28 percent of shipments came from distribution of physical products (primarily CDs).[1] However, the shift in pricing of digital and physical albums—now $10 compared with the $18 for CDs common before digital downloading—and the rise of the single over the album as the preferred unit of purchase has significantly affected the economic norms of the recording industry.

*   *   *

A development that may be the single most revolutionary event in every media industry has occurred in your lifetime. By the time you were old enough to use media on your own, this revolution had already swept in, so it is likely that you don't even recall what it was like to use media before this monumental shift. Perhaps older siblings or your parents have told you tales of the challenging nature of the "bad old days" of media use before current conveniences and capabilities. We are speaking, of course, of the wide-ranging consequences wrought upon media industries by **digitization**.

Despite the fact that the digital revolution can be traced back to the 1970s and beyond, digitization is still in its infancy when it comes to its impact on **legacy media industries**—those industries established before digitization. Nevertheless, the digital era is certainly upon us, and we've already noted many examples of the changes it is bringing to media industry operations throughout the book. While all media industries have experienced some adjustments in their established operations, few have figured out what the new norms of their industries will be. A wide variety of experiments can be found across media industries as they struggle to innovate and respond to the new ways audiences—enabled by this massive change in technological conditions—seek to access, engage, and share products. The capacity of digital networks continue to expand, which suggests that it is likely that all of the disruption to established media operations by digitization have not even been realized.

UNDERSTANDING DIGITIZATION

What is digitization? Or, more precisely, what distinguishes digital media? **Digitization** refers to a technical process or a technical specification describing the way media are recorded, transmitted, and accessed; digital media are those media that translate the content of media—images, sounds, printed words—into digital code, a language of ones and zeroes. This digital language has many advantages: it uses space efficiently, maintains quality, and operates as a common language that allows different types of machines to speak to one another. Media goods shared digitally are far more malleable, and the transition of becoming accustomed to digital files that can be changed may lead us to regard media differently. It is difficult to overstate the ways in which digitization is changing media. Digitization has (and continues to have) enormous consequences; it has created new media industries and irreversibly altered the operations of legacy media.

Although this elaboration may be decreasingly relevant, allow us to say a few words about analog media in order to make the distinction of digital clearer. Media using an **analog** method of recording store signals in a manner that represents the message using an "analog," or direct facsimile, of the original. To explain the concept, Joseph Dominick, Barry Sherman, and Fritz Messere encourage us to "Think of the grooves in a phonographic record. As the needle travels through the grooves, it vibrates in a pattern similar to the vibrations made by the guitar string or vocal cords it represents."[2] In the case of analog tape media, this "analogy" of the original is created through a process of magnetizing the tape in patterns that represent the audio or visual signal. Film works because chemical changes in photographic film are altered by light exposure so that a representation of the image in front of the camera appears on the film. In all of these cases, accessing analog media—whether tape or film—requires a machine that can decode the analog language, such as a record needle, the heads of a tape player that read the magnetic coatings, or a film projector.

There are strengths and weaknesses to both analog and digital recording. In terms of media industry operation, analog had considerable limitations. For one, because analog recording requires transfer to a physical medium, analog media take up considerable space, which requires extensive storage space for producers and shelf space for retailers. The physical form also limits potential users by making portability cumbersome. Early videotape, for instance, required nearly 20 miles of tape to record a single hour of programming and required large vaults for storing originals. Or imagine how little music you could conveniently carry with you when you had to carry CDs compared with the volume of music you carry in a digital player (though CDs were already a digital improvement on vinyl recordings, which you couldn't carry with you at all!). From an industrial perspective, the bulkiness of the analog media added costs related to the production of physical commodities, transportation, and storage.

Degradation of quality is another limitation of analog media, although this is significant in different ways to media users than to media industries. A common practice among media studies teachers in the analog era was to share videotapes, as it was easy for us to copy one another's tapes to gain access to recordings not available for commercial purchase (and in an era before YouTube provided a rich repository). The quality of the recording, however, was always notably less than the original. By comparison, digital copies remain pristine and do not lose quality when copied. This limitation of analog media was actually quite valuable to the media industries because it made it comparatively more difficult to make, illegally sell, or otherwise circulate pirated copies.

For those of us who knew the analog age, though, probably the main advantage of digital media that we appreciate each and every day is the interconnection among our technologies that digital recording allows. As we noted, digital code operates as a common language across many machines that could not speak to each other in the analog age. The common digital language allows digital television recorders, computers, and audiorecording devices to all speak to each other, while digital media also enable the distribution of information over the Internet, allowing for quick and "perfect" transmission of a media product without physical transportation.

Convergence is often the word used to describe the new connections among media enabled by digitization. Convergence can be seen first in terms of technical language but increasingly in terms of media products and the media industries themselves. Convergence can refer to many different aspects of media industries, and it is a term used with varying specificity. Sometimes convergence refers to the coming together of cultural or technological forms, such as the convergence of television and the Internet as technologies that distribute video. Other times convergence is used in place of "conglomeration" to reference the coming together of once discrete media industries or corporations. Finally, convergence can indicate the merging of communication systems—as in the instance of cable providers offering Internet and phone services. Media scholar Henry Jenkins, a leading thinker in this area, deliberately reminds us that *convergence is more than a technological process.* He argues that convergence also "represents a cultural shift as consumers are encouraged to seek out new information and make connections among dispersed media content."[3] This insight is important for media industries because it suggests that particular strategies—such as those that enable personalized experiences with media—have increased value in the age of digital media.

Another important insight from Jenkins regarding convergence is the difference between *delivery technologies,* such as tapes, CDs, or MP3 files that facilitate the distribution of media content, and *media texts,* such as recorded sound, printed words, or visual images. By making a distinction between delivery technologies and actual media texts, Jenkins gives us language that helps us avoid **technological determinism** and stops us from dwelling on silly assertions—such as the notion that the introduction of new media will "kill off" existing media. As we've seen countless times now, radio did not kill the newspaper, television did not kill radio or cinema, and so on. Rather, in each case—and as we see now—new delivery technologies can make existing delivery technologies obsolete or require reconfiguration, but the media themselves—messages based in sound, print, or visual images—persist.

The existing media industries often must make substantial adjustments in their norms and operations to respond to new delivery systems—as was the case for radio after the introduction of television. As more and more homes purchased televisions, established radio shows transferred to the new medium (radio was much like television today, distributed over a national network with an evening schedule of comedies and dramas). Certainly, few who had the choice to listen to *and* watch their favorite stories would want to settle for audio alone. The arrival of television did bring the network era of radio to an end. The networking of content dissolved and was replaced by an emphasis on locally operated stations featuring music or talk. The radio industry rebuilt itself on affordances that distinguish it from television, particularly that people can listen while doing something else (with emphasis on creating portable radios and introducing radio into cars), and as a more locally specific form in comparison to television's national focus. More than half a century after its predicted death, radio lives on.

You can likely think of countless examples of the convenience that sharing a common digital language provides. One that springs quickly to our minds is that it would have been much more tedious if we had been writing this book together a mere 15 years ago. In a digital age, we can quickly trade drafts back and forth over the

Internet—editing and reviewing each other's work effectively in real time. In the era before digital distribution (at least assuming the existence of computers), one of us would have to finish a draft, print it out, and mail it to the other. Digitization produces consequences for many aspects of media industry operation, but its enhancement of the ability to separate a media product from its physical form and transport it to any location in the world via wired or wireless means in seconds—building on the revolution of telegraphy, telephony, and broadcasting before it—may be the most substantial change that we've realized to this point.

The implications of digitization are much more far-reaching than those we consider here. We particularly focus our discussion on the consequences of digitization for the operation of media industries, but digitization also adjusts commercial practices in many industries—even the operation of governments. The rise and eventual fall of the Silk Road website, popularly known as the "eBay" of illegal drugs, was due to digitization, including: the use of digital money, known as Bitcoins, to buy and sell drugs and the use of digital surveillance techniques by the FBI to bring down the drug ring. Obviously, we can't address all of the ways that digitization has changed business practices around the world and enabled new ones; instead, we skip developments such as Silk Road and focus instead—as we have throughout this book—on industries that deliver entertainment and information *content*, rather than those that have a connection to the digital world but otherwise operate in wholly different markets.

In addition, we approach this chapter more from the perspective of media *industries* than the standpoint of the individual user/consumer, although we do address the experiences of users in the final pages of the chapter. We concentrate on how digitization challenges norms of operation established for the analog era, but we are a bit more tentative in some of our assertions and claims about new media industries. One of our goals in creating the Industrialization of Culture framework is to provide a relevant tool in just these instances, as a way to guide you through the salient aspects of future developments in emergent industries or to help you understand the differences in a single industry before and after the introduction of digital technologies.

The remainder of this chapter attempts to cover the breadth of digital change by subdividing into areas of production, distribution, and consumer use. Although this provides a convenient way of introducing some order to a vast topic, we must be clear that the significant consequences of digitization result because of the intersections among these areas. In other words, the shifts in production introduced by digitization are sizable alone, but, in combination with digital distribution, these effects increase exponentially.

DIGITIZATION AND SHIFTS IN PRODUCTION

The transition from analog recording and distribution of media to digital techniques has had considerable consequences for the production norms of media industries. Many of these changes have been gradual and experienced by various industries on different timelines. It is difficult to address all of the potential adjustments wrought by digitization on any single industry—let alone all of them—as, in many cases, digital technologies have substantially reconfigured even the most mundane and particular of operations, such as revolutionizing special-effects work in video media or radically changing the workforce needed to publish a newspaper. Instead, we focus more on broad practices that are likely relevant to many media industries.

One overriding influence of the digitization of media production has been the shift to finding intellectual property that media industries can repurpose and profit from across multiple media **platforms**. As Henry Jenkins, Sam Ford, and Joshua Green have noted, content developers of all types are increasingly seeking out media projects that can "spread" across multiple media, especially through social media.[4] Even people who design health campaigns realize that, in order to have the greatest impact on people's health-related behaviors, it's necessary to ensure that messages get picked up and spread across multiple media channels. The spreading of media often combines the mediated interpersonal communication networks of social media with the intellectual property created by legacy media industries.

We can begin to glimpse further similarities in the impact of digitization on media production if we organize media industries in terms of whether they are primarily print, audio, or audiovisual media because the associated technological differences and requirements of these media provide various lessons and indicate different levels of integration of digital development. For example, the technological tools required by print are minimal compared with video, and the size of the digital file means that print has had easy digital distribution for some time, while this is a fairly new development for video: Netflix, for instance, only introduced its stand-alone video streaming service in 2010. The amount of data required to stream video still can make it difficult to consume on devices connected to mobile networks and expensive for those with data caps. Audio, meanwhile, falls somewhere in between print and audiovisual in both necessary technology and file size.

Consequently, at the moment we write, newspapers and magazines are facing different trials than the music and video industries and are at a different stage in working through new capabilities and challenges. The struggles the recording industry experienced with file sharing and adjusted distribution models during the early part of this century were not a concern for video-based media until later the following decade, but now the film and television industries face these challenges as well. It is difficult to know at this still-early moment in the digital revolution whether all media will follow a similar path or if there will be significant long-term differences in the adjustments wrought by digitization for these media.

Print

A combination of production and distribution adjustments have affected print industries in particular ways. For many consumers, the nature of their use of print media has changed because digital technologies enable instantaneous update, revision, and delivery of content, although online access to print media does not neatly replace use of the original print source. Consider the situation of most local papers. In terms of pre-Internet competition with other media, one of the biggest limitations was the paper's tendency to get "scooped," since it could deliver information only once a day, while radio and television could offer live news or newscasts updated at intervals throughout the day. An Internet version of that newspaper allows it to break stories and share information throughout the day and for it to be available whenever a reader wants an update.

A key challenge print media have faced in adapting to new digital capabilities has been figuring out the relationship between their online and print-edition content and what economic strategy to use during a period with considerable uncertainty. Many of us expect to pay for physical versions of print media, including the newspapers that arrive at our door in the morning or the magazines we receive in the mail or purchase at kiosks. As the Internet has enabled print media to have online versions, however, many of us have come to expect to click on links or search and read stories for no cost at all. Although the online version does not have the expenses of the physical paper medium and its distribution, there are still considerable costs involved in its creation. Many print media titles have struggled to develop a profitable Internet strategy as it has grown increasingly necessary to make content available in this form. Advertisers have not moved advertising budgets into the online space adequately to support new costs or to fully compensate for the decreasing subscriber base of the physical form, while readers balk at paying for digital subscriptions if equivalent content is available free elsewhere. As an indication of change, in 2013, the subscription fees for *The New York Times* produced more revenue than the paper's advertising—a profound shift for a newspaper's business model.

In previous moments of delivery technology transition, established media initially used their legacy business to help fund the emerging form. For example, CBS was able to fund its early years in television from the ongoing revenues of its still successful radio network. However, the disruption of digital technologies to existing business models and practices eroded the legacy practices of the print and music industries before they established viable alternatives. Print media have lost both subscribers and the significant revenues of classified advertisements, as seemingly comparable content that does not require subscription and functionally superior alternatives such as Craigslist emerged online. The television and film industries have had more time to develop strategies and to learn from other industries' mistakes, but it remains to be seen if they will do so.

The competitive arena of print media is also changing because of competition from print media that don't have a physical version—and it remains difficult to evaluate the impact of these journalistic outlets. Some online papers are connected with print-edition newspapers, others are all that remain of former papers, and yet others are entities that have only existed online. In many cases, Internet-based journalistic outlets and blogs are breaking news faster or drawing more readers than the online version of long-established print media.

It is important to realize that the number of readers isn't the only relevant way of measuring how blogs and other variations of new journalism produce important consequences for the media industries. We now witness frequent examples of news being broken on sometimes obscure online sites; the news is then picked up and covered extensively by legacy media. In late 2013, for example, the blog Gawker broke a story that Toronto mayor Rob Ford had been videotaped smoking crack cocaine. The news spread like wildfire in legacy print outlets and created a major political crisis for the mayor. Such developments indicate the importance of considering the many ways the easy production of print media in the digital era can affect media industry operation.

While some observers are optimistic about the possibility for a greater diversity of voices in journalism in an era when "anyone can be a publisher," we need more time to assess what really is happening as a result. The truth is that very few of these new publishers break through to a large readership. Certainly, recent history gives us numerous examples of **citizen journalists** who played substantial roles in scooping mainstream news outlets. Perhaps the most famous cases involve the numerous "Twitterati" in the Middle East who documented, popularized, and spurred on the various protest movements and insurrections known as the Arab Spring. In many instances, the blog posts, Facebook posts, and tweets of these citizen journalists were the primary source for Western news media.

Determining new business models and understanding what features are most important to audiences are long and complicated processes. Though much of the legacy print business was severely affected by the transition to online distribution, the decreasing advertising dollars available, and diminished subscriber support, by 2014 signs of a new equilibrium had begun to emerge. The industry came to realize that people won't pay specifically for breaking news, because that type of content is so readily available. Print sources—whether online or physical—that provide a different value proposition, such as informed investigative reporting, proprietary data or analysis, and even just distinctive, well-crafted journalistic perspectives, have found audiences will pay to access such content. It remains too soon to know how more recent experiments will turn out, but the print industry now shows signs of norms that can be successful in an era of digital media.[5]

Despite triumphal stories about the democratic power of digital media, we should also remember the tendency toward **technological utopianism** when it comes to popular discussion of new technologies. It is worth exploring, for instance, how expanded popularity of an amateur media outlet requires it to evolve and whether it takes on characteristics of legacy media in that process. In other words, as amateur productions increase in scale to the point that they become more than vanity projects, it is important to assess whether they maintain industrial aspects that differentiate them from conventional media industries. For example, when the news and commentary blog the *Huffington Post* launched in May 2005, it was largely run out of the home of its founder, Arianna Huffington (granted, it was a mansion), and its operations likely differed considerably from established media entities. A little over a year after its launch, it had secured $5 million in venture funding to expand its staff, and it raised $15 million by November 2008 as it moved into local news and investigative journalism, seeking to be the "Internet newspaper." Such funding and success, though, may have also led it to operate more like the legacy media industries it once contrasted. When the site was acquired by AOL in 2011, many observers worried that the *Huffington Post* would come to function just like other mainstream news sites.[6]

Audio

Digitization also has had significant implications for the recording industry as a result of changes in both production and distribution. Joseph Turow explains that considerable fragmentation in production has occurred partly because digital technologies have made professional digital recording technology more accessible.[7] He notes that studio rates—the cost for time in the recording studio—which typically ran as much as $50,000 for an album, have been cut in half in recent years because of the greater competition spurred by affordable, professional-quality equipment.[8] Some emerging artists can even create decent-quality recordings in basement studios for as little as a few thousand dollars.

These decreases in the costs of professional or near-professional recordings have significant implications for those who are trying to break into the recording industry. Paired with the possibilities that the digital distribution of music enables, entirely new routes into the recording industry are being created, even if, at this point, those routes still seem to lead to the established recording studios for many artists who ultimately achieve "success." The availability of decent, affordable digital audio production technologies (paired with do-it-yourself distribution as available through personal websites and aggregators such as Bandcamp) have revolutionized the common methods for finding new artists. In the past few years, it has become increasingly common for record label executives to find new artists by trolling artists' websites to hear samples of their work instead of searching out new acts in bars, coffeehouses, and small venues. Artists such as Lorde, Ingrid Michaelson, Lily Allen, and the Arctic Monkeys have broken onto the national and even international scene after signing with labels that found them online, although stories about artists breaking into the top of the charts without a label seem to be myths at this point.

Some have wondered about what value labels add in an era of digital distribution. As in many media industries, legacy media continue to be powerful tools of promotion, but it is worth considering whether that promotion work continues to be worth the high costs artists pay in revenue sharing (the label gets most) and in giving up intellectual property rights. The labels have done crucial legal work in terms of licensing rights to emerging streaming and downloading services, which is new work that might be cumbersome for artists. However, notable cases have emerged in which labels severely underpaid artists' royalties, thus calling into question whether labels are even adding value through this task.

The 2014 Grammy success of Macklemore drew attention to the new relationships artists are developing with labels. The band released their *The Heist* album "independently" on their own label, Macklemore LLC, but they did hire the Alternative Distribution Alliance, which is an independent arm of Warner Music Group, to help with distribution and radio play. This model allowed the band to retain all the rights to their music and retain full creative control. They paid the Alternative Distribution Alliance a flat monthly fee for help promoting the album, which is credited with helping them sell 1.2 million copies of the album and 5 million singles.

Digitization also threatens one of the staple formats of modern popular music, the album. The UK newspaper *The Guardian* reports that, in raw numbers, album sales declined more than 60 percent between 2002 and 2012. The main drivers of this decline were sales of individual tracks on digital music services like iTunes and the popularity of music streaming apps, such as Spotify, which offer subscribers customized playlists streamed to their computers and mobile devices. Both of these shifts in distribution have led the industry and artists to focus more on creating individual songs, rather than coherent albums. Of course, the album itself was a product of industrial conditions in the music industry of the 1940s, not the brainchild of creative artists. The erosion of the album as a dominant form has been difficult for record labels because CDs were exceptionally lucrative. Artists, on the other hand, may find the ability to release single songs allows greater creative opportunities.

Video

Think about the visual difference in the films and television shows that dominate industry production now in comparison with those of the 1980s and before. Digital technologies account for many of the differences—particularly the wide range of what were once most certainly considered "special effects" that are now increasingly commonplace.* The development of high-quality digital recording technologies that could be merged with digital editing effectively created entirely new universes for visual storytelling, all with much better quality and at a fraction of the cost of older effects efforts. Or consider the refinement in video game images. The latest versions of games are stunningly realistic and appear far removed from predecessors such as Pong or Pac-Man, as evident in Photo 9.1. Digital technologies shape advances in gaming production as well.

In fact, television scholar John Caldwell argues that the development of various digital technologies as well as a changing competitive environment (or economic conditions in our terms) were responsible for fundamental shifts in the aesthetics of television.[9] He coined the term "televisuality" to describe the new attention to aesthetic style that became increasingly de rigueur for television shows beginning in the 1980s. Much of this style—everything from the sophisticated graphics and crawls that now commonly fill our screens to television shows that approximate the production values of studio films—owes its existence to a digital technology. More recent television storytelling has expanded these early moves of the 1980s. Shows such as *The Walking Dead*, *Game of Thrones*, and many others rely heavily on worlds created on computers instead of in front of the camera.

This is most certainly true in cinema as well. Consider that the film *Lord of the Rings* (2001) used computer animation for more than 1,000 separate shots, a total of 70 percent of the film.[10] Such films combine "digital composting," which blends computer generation with live actors using "motion capture" technology to create complicated visual imagery (also used in television and video games). This shift has had significant implications for the type of labor involved in filmmaking and the budgets of contemporary films. For example, George Lucas's original 1977 *Star Wars* lists

---

*This Vimeo video demonstrates the VFX work on *Boardwalk Empire*. How would the reliance on animation change the nature of television production? http://vimeo.com/34678075

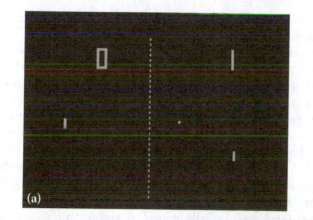

Photo 9.1A, 9.1B Refinement of digital imagery in video games—an image from *Pong* versus *Grand Theft Auto V.*

143 graphic technicians in the credits while his 2003 *Attack of the Clones* prequel required 572.[11]

As in the cases of both digital print and audio technologies, new capabilities have reached the amateur video producer that allow for the creation of what was near-professional grade video just a decade ago at costs affordable to the amateur market.* Digital video shooting and editing is increasingly a basic form of expression familiar to many of our students, and it is hard to believe that, little over a decade ago, college

---

*This radio story explores how the increasing use of DSLR cameras for videography is upending the traditional video production business. What other effects do you imagine the affordability of high-quality cameras might have on the film and television industries? http://www.npr.org/blogs/pictureshow/2011/06/22/137349372/say-cheese-or-wait-maybe-action-hm-is-that-fancy-camera-for-you

editing classes involved the cutting and splicing of tape. Basic computer software packages routinely include applications that allow casual users to create audio/visual products that rival those of professionals in a previous era.

The availability of digital production technologies has also led to less specialization in some sectors of media production or, more precisely, the expectation that workers possess a wider range of skills. Students seeking journalism careers are increasingly advised that the greatest opportunities exist for those with the skills to be "one man (or woman) bands"—capable of shooting video, editing their material, providing the talent, and composing both video and print forms of their stories. New production technologies have emerged that even allow studio talent to "switch" their own shows—meaning the same person talking on air is deciding which camera angle is being used and switching between the cameras through a set of controls. Such changes have led to cutbacks and reallocation of staffing, especially in local television stations.

Another effect of digitization on the jobs available in media industries is expansion in global outsourcing, a development that we look at more closely in the next chapter. Outsourcing alters both the production practices and economic conditions of the industry. A case in point is contemporary animation. Animation is a time-consuming and labor-intensive process that requires the creation of thousands of images, backgrounds, and objects. Consequently, a good deal of this heavy lifting is subcontracted to foreign countries where workers earn significantly less than in the United States, particularly India. Outsourcing is made possible by two recent developments related to digitization: first, the spread of cheap computers and computer storage, which makes it feasible for companies in the countries to create the massive digital audiovisual files that animation requires; and second, the development of high-speed digital networks that allow those large files to be transferred back and forth between the originating and outsourcing nations. These developments enable the production houses to retain close supervision of the production process, including making decisions and corrections along the way, even while the physical production occurs thousands of miles away.[12]

Because of developments like the global outsourcing of animation, we are perhaps more skeptical than those who forecast an amateur revolution and overthrow of legacy media industries as a result of access to production tools. A digital media environment allows the possibility for new entrants and competitors because the tools of production are accessible to a previously incomprehensible degree, but success on par with established media institutions remains unlikely despite buzz about these possibilities and the multiplicity of contenders.[*] It is nevertheless important to acknowledge the growing coexistence of amateur media content and the significant role digital production and distribution capabilities have had in enabling these developments. Although amateur production may not overthrow the established media industries, it does provide new routes into industry work that may begin to change the makeup of the industry. At the least, the work of amateurs may challenge industry workers to imagine their work in new ways.

---

[*]This promotional video explains the all-digital production of the television show Leverage. How do you think the changes the producers note affect production budgets and labor on a show? www.electricentertainment.com/news/leverage-digital-workflow/

DIGITIZATION AND SHIFTS IN AGGREGATION AND DISTRIBUTION

As we saw in Chapter 8, aggregation and distribution encompass the activities and processes involved in transporting the completed media product from its site of production to the audiences who seek to consume it. In the case of many media industries, this traditionally involved transferring—often to paper, vinyl, tape, or disk—the contents of the media product and then physically transporting it to a store. Once at the store, the product would sit on a shelf until someone came to purchase it. Digital technologies introduce many tools for eliminating various inefficiencies in this process.

Digital technologies eliminate the need to transfer the product into a physical form, as well as the need for a "bricks-and-mortar" store for displaying and transacting sales. Much of the waste of the analog era developed from the uncertainty surrounding the likely success of a product relative to the efficiency of creating many physical copies at a single moment in time. For example, a record label or book publisher would want to "run" a number of copies all at once without knowing what sales might be like. Often, they guessed wrong (remember the problem of "nobody knows" explained in Chapter 2) and were left with thousands of copies. In another case, consider the film industry's need to make thousands of copies of a film for it to open in theaters nationwide on the same day—a practice used to maximize its promotional strategy. In 2003, the average cost of making prints for a studio film was $4.2 million. The per-film cost for distribution on digital discs is 1/20th of this, and these costs will be further diminished as the industry continues to transition to transmitting films to theaters without a physical form.[13]

Digital technologies introduce two solutions for the gamble on how many copies to produce that was characteristic of analog media: (a) they eliminate the need for physical copies, and (b) they enable the efficient production of limited, small runs. The music industry provides the best illustration of the first solution. Digital technologies have enabled those who so desire to have music collections without any physical copy. Listeners can create vast libraries of music simply through downloading music from online retailers. This is similarly the case of print industries in which readers can call up stories of interest and read them in their entirety without printing a single piece of paper.

In the case of some media—music, magazines, and newspapers—consumers have willingly forgone the physical version of media products in exchange for the convenience and quick and ready access provided digitally. Other industries have not yet seen that willingness to trade delivery technologies; one of these is the book industry. Although digital book sales grew as e-readers such as the Kindle came to market, sales of physical books remain strong and even have grown in some sectors of the industry. Digital media, however, also provide media industries with strategies that aid the distribution of physical media; both the music and book industries have particularly benefited from the limited, more flexible production runs digitization enables. Because of the convenient storage of digital information and the purity of new copies, these industries can now "print" to order.

It is hard to say which is the more significant change—the elimination of the creation of physical media products or the adjustments in these industries that result from not needing a physical place to aggregate and sell them. Chris Anderson, the former *Wired* magazine editor who proposed the term **long tail** to describe the shift in distribution practices related to online media, has done most of the thinking on this second aspect.[14] The long tail describes the slope of the curve when graphing **Pareto's principle**—also known as the "80/20 rule": that in most industries, 80 percent of the profits are made from 20 percent of the products. (See Figure 9.1.) In the case of media industries, this illustrates the value media industries can find outside of the blockbuster hits that have dominated industry operation in other eras. The peak of the slope illustrates the very few products purchased by vast mass audiences. At the other end of the slope is the long tail, or the many products that are purchased by only a few. Although few purchase any one of these products, the many titles, albums, and so on purchased by a few add up.

Anderson argues that digital distribution significantly shifts economic strategies of media industries away from blockbusters and toward niche products. He draws on various data that suggest that the legacy experience of mass culture resulted from the inefficiencies of delivering niche products that digital distribution now makes possible. Digital distribution enables savings that come from not having to maintain brick-and-mortar stores and not having to manufacture physical copies of products. He also notes that having efficient ways to search for products is crucial to the success of digital distribution. Amazon's automated book suggestions and the search and suggestions of music available at iTunes are good examples of sophisticated digital search capability.

Anderson's theory of the long tail for media industry products continues to be tested as new media industries mature and legacy media adjust their practices. In many cases, it remains too early to commit concrete new practices to print, as it is still unclear how these industries will continue to evolve. Anderson recently augmented his argument about digital distribution by posing a new economic model—that of giving away content for free—as the future of media industries (as mentioned in the conclusion of Chapter 5).[15] He imagines how many of the direct-pay media industries might reconstruct

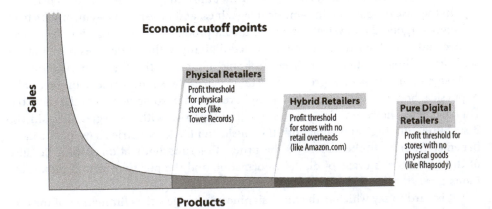

Figure 9.1 Slope of Available Goods from Different Types of Media Retailers (from *The Long Tail*).

their economic practices to be more profitable by giving away content or enabling certain services while deriving greater economic value from others; for example, it might be more profitable for theaters to eliminate the cost of admission to films and make money from concessions (although the theater owners already rely on this to a considerable degree) or for pop stars to give away their music (as they do in China) and profit instead from public appearance fees or endorsements.

At the core of his argument is the assertion that "information wants to be free." Anderson's solution, then, is to give it away in cases where there is no **marginal cost**— as is the case when products are distributed digitally—but to charge for physical copies in the cases users want them or by converting users from a basic free version to a premium paid version. In this strategy, users can do certain things for free but must pay a fee to engage with the full array of capabilities—typically through a subscription.[16] For example, the video content on Hulu is free (or supported by advertisers), but one must upgrade and pay a subscription to accesses the greater array of content of Hulu Plus— although still with commercials. In fact, this **freemium** pricing is emerging as a dominant revenue model for mobile gaming apps, as the example of Madden NFL 25 in Chapter 5 explains. For Anderson, then, digitization reduces the marginal cost of media distribution to such a degree that offering "free" content might become a viable business model.

This leads to one of the key challenges that media industries face as a result of digital distribution—namely, **piracy** or other means of circumventing the established economic model by illegally sharing or circulating media in violation of **copyright**. Again, those core attributes of the products that media industries create—such as their "public" nature and the way that one person's "use" does not "use up" the product—make this particularly challenging. All of the advantages of digital distribution in terms of convenience for users have amplified the problems associated with maintaining copyright and legal circulation of these products.

In many cases, the established media industries have sought to maintain the same terms of payment and use that supported them in the analog era. While generally willing to create routes of digital distribution for paying customers, they are eager to make sure that allowing such distribution does not destroy their existing business models. As discussed in Chapter 6, established players are almost always slower to adapt to new technological conditions for this reason. A closer examination of the opportunities and dangers that digital distribution poses to newspapers offers a good case study.

Digital Distribution in the Newspaper Industry

Similar to the entertainment examples noted earlier, mobile devices like tablets, Kindles, and smartphones offer new forms of digital distribution that hold the promise of restoring some of the readership to traditional news outlets. Although both blogs and mobile news content are produced and distributed digitally, consumers are generally more willing to pay for content on their mobile devices than on more traditional computers. In 2014, the Reuters Institute for the Study of Journalism found that owners of smartphones and tablets were both more likely to pay for newspaper subscriptions than those without these devices, with tablet owners nearly twice as likely to pay.[17] Digital subscriptions such

Top 25 Newspaper Daily Digital Editions
By Rank (September 2012)

	DIGITAL REPLICA	DIGITAL NONREPLICA	TOTAL DIGITAL
New York Times	13,089	883,263	896,352
Wall Street Journal	-	794,594	794,594
New York Post	28,659	149,454	178,113
Denver Post	44,116	132,330	176,446
Los Angeles Times	23,992	127,585	151,577
New York Daily News	29,072	117,533	146,605
Newark Star-Ledger	15,892	111,538	127,430
Newsday (N.Y.)	-	114,620	114,620
Los Angeles Investors Business Daily	46,075	51,696	97,771
Houston Chronicle	69,595	21,736	91,331
USA Today	69,006	17,301	86,307
Detroit Free Press	82,863	1,941	84,804
Cleveland Plain Dealer	10,106	63,524	73,630
Chicago Sun-Times	20,207	50,725	70,932
St. Paul Pioneer Press	55,788	11,372	67,160
Minneapolis Star Tribune	47,222	18,580	65,802
Dallas Morning News	64,788	-	64,788
San Francisco Chronicle	27,931	28,119	56,050
Boston Globe	9,028	40,404	49,432
Salt Lake City Deseret News	14,882	32,829	47,711
San Jose Mercury News	35,061	8,257	43,318
Philadelphia Inquirer	25,572	17,652	43,224
Detroit News	39,992	347	40,339
Riverside Press-Enterprise	30,351	9,506	39,857
Milwaukee Journal Sentinel	38,499	-	38,499

Source: Alliance of Audited Media

Note: The Dallas Morning News and The Milwaukee Journal Sentinel chose not to report nonreplica digital

PEW RESEARCH CENTER

2013 STATE OF THE NEWS MEDIA

Figure 9.2 Top 25 Newspaper Daily Digital Editions.

as those available via devices or the web offer newspapers the same kinds of dual-revenue streams that traditional print offered: advertising and subscriptions. Unfortunately for news providers, the dollars advertisers have been willing to pay to advertise in online content represents only a small fraction of what they had paid in physical media, and this sector of online advertising is much smaller than achieved by search and social media.

The saving grace for the news industry, however, may lie in subscription revenues for both digital and specifically mobile access. Many traditional print sources have begun to place their content behind pay-walls, while permitting "metered" access to nonsubscribers, which allows them to read a certain number of articles per week or per month for free. The *Washington Post*, for instance, allows free access to 10 articles per month; more frequent readers must buy a digital subscription.[18] The growth in mobile device use encourages digital access and digital subscriptions, which has allowed some news organizations to stabilize and even grow in recent years. Even at smaller newspapers around the country, business models have begun to change from a heavy reliance on advertising dollars to a greater reliance on subscription revenues. Still, the future of print media remains uncertain in a digital age. One of the largest challenges that all print media face is how and when to take their money and energies out of print and redirect them toward digital content.

Figure 9.2 shows the popularity of digital editions of major US newspapers. It compares the readership of "digital replica" and "digital nonreplica" versions of 25 daily newspapers. A replica version presents the same editorial, photo, and advertising as the print version of a newspaper and is often delivered by PDF and is therefore "pushed" by the news outlet. Nonreplica versions feature original content not in the print version, reporter and commentator blogs, more interactive features such as links to related content, embedded video, comments, and other multimedia features. These versions are designed for the digital audience and also contain different advertising. Though a strong preference for digital nonreplica versions is clear from this data, these versions require a lot of additional effort on the part of newsrooms—essentially the creation of two different formats—which must be financed through a combination of subscriptions revenues and advertising.

Understanding the dilemmas of digital distribution is complicated, as the issue involves a nexus of economic and regulatory conditions. Moreover, the debate is multisided, and a lot of uncertainty exists regarding the consequences of both new and old ways of operating. As pictured in Figure 9.3 and summarized in Table 9.1, in one corner

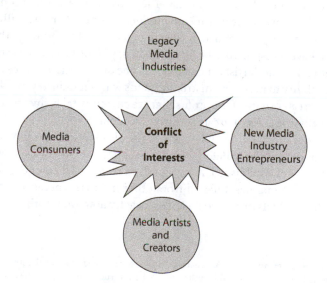

Figure 9.3 Dynamics of Digital Distribution.

Table 9.1 Dynamics of Digital Distribution

Legacy Media Industries

   Desire to expand revenue streams through making content more available through distribution now technologically possible

   Fear losing established revenue streams and levels

New Media Industry Entrepreneurs

   Seek to enter media creation and distribution without regard to maintaining structures developed for analog and physical media

Media Consumers

   Desire greater accessibility, convenience, and ease of use (contrary to legacy media's established practices)

   Financially maxed out by simultaneously paying legacy media and for new opportunities enabled by digital distribution

Media Artists and Creators

   Desire a greater share of profits now that distribution costs are reduced

   Recognize digital environment creates opportunities for more direct relationships with fans and more creative freedom

are many of the legacy media industries (particularly the recording industry) that have detailed economic models and practices built on predigital distribution norms. These industries would happily expand their profitability by adding revenue from digital distribution, as long as they can replace each dollar they lose from the sale of physical products in the digital market. In another corner we have new media industry entrepreneurs who seek to use tools of digital production and distribution to remake these industries by taking advantage of new technological possibilities and eliminating inefficiencies built up in the legacy media. The consumer of media products is in yet another corner. Some want cheaper media products, while others are willing to pay but want greater accessibility, convenience, or ease of use. Finally (although there are likely others yet), we have a disjuncture between "industry" (entities such as studios, record labels, and networks) and "artists or creators," as one of the consequences of digitization is an increased ability to make and distribute goods without industry middlemen.* Some creators want a greater share of the profits that are currently taken by the industry, while others seek an environment of greater creative freedom.

The properties of digital media—such as the elimination of a physical product—require new economic and regulatory conditions, and, in many cases, these new conditions have not yet been established. A key question remains whether digitization affects media industries in a manner different from other industries because of the particular properties of the products produced and, if so, exactly how. Many other industries could

---

*This article discusses comedian Louie C.K.'s success distributing a comedy special directly to his fans. How did "digitization" create this opportunity? Why might others be less successful despite the affordances of digital distribution? http://variety.com/2011/tv/news/louis-ck-direct-distribution-nets-200000-in-four-days-9742/

not get by without a physical version of the product they exchange, so it is reasonable to understand these developments as fairly specific to media industries.

DIGITIZATION AND CHANGES IN USE

If we consider the consequences of digitization from the perspective of legacy media industries, we see how challenging these developments have been and continue to be. The spread of digitization happened despite the efforts by established media industries to maintain traditional practices and behaviors. In this case, new capabilities were largely introduced by the computing and consumer electronics industries, which had less of a stake in preserving the ways of the past. The revolution we're observing couldn't have been imposed by these industries alone, however. The adoption of the new technologies by users—and their continued desire for greater convenience, choice, and control in media use—also played an important role. Any effort to imagine how the media industries of the future will operate must consider the capabilities audiences most desire and how the economics of the industries will then change if those capabilities are made possible.

We turn now to some of the ways in which users of media products experience digitization, the outcomes of digitization on our daily engagement with media, and the social and cultural consequences of media that take advantage of the opportunities digitization allows. As this section indicates, the road of new media is already littered with companies that had great ideas but failed to connect with the desires of media users—or failed to connect at the right time. Although the Industrialization of Culture framework does not particularly highlight the role of media users or consumers in any particular level, we have tried to acknowledge the influence that they nevertheless provide. To some degree, the emerging patterns of use, behavior, and media engagement that audiences support provide key conditions for assessing the consequences that digitization has forced upon legacy media and under which digital media entities are surviving and thriving as a result. Digital technologies also provide valuable mechanisms through which the media industries can connect with audiences and obtain greater and more immediate feedback about their products. So, even though we've tried to focus our attention throughout this chapter on the consequences of digitization for media industries, it is fair to say that shifts in media use by consumers are playing a key role in adjustments of industry operation as well.

Digitization allows many changes in the use of media products. As we already noted, the affordability and quality of digital technologies better enables those who traditionally only consumed media products to produce and circulate them as well—even if not on the scale of the conventional media industries. Although digitization arguably produces many other consequences, perhaps its greatest outcomes can be loosely categorized as expanded choice of media, the fragmentation of the mass audience, and increased convenience in accessing media.

Emerging shifts in digital media may provide one of the best illustrations of the many multidirectional influences that shape the creation of media products. The technological capabilities provided by digital media make some things possible, but users take up these abilities based more on their needs and desires than on what particular corporate interests might have desired from an economic perspective or than what was permissible via established regulatory structures. The very different nature of media industries today and the products increasingly available cannot be traced through simple, causal developments but can be explained only as the result of a confluence of shifts in technology, economic models, regulatory mechanisms, and consumer activity.

Choice

A consequence of digital recording, production, and distribution in the media industries has been an exponential increase in choice among available media products. Consider the music industry. Once bound to the choices available in brick-and-mortar distributors, listeners have ready access to many more recordings far down the long tail with great ease. On the production side, the affordability of "garage band" recording software enables amateurs to record their music and easily make it accessible (although this doesn't guarantee that anyone will actually listen to it).

Or consider the expansion in choice that digital technologies have enabled in cable television. The possible compression of television signals through digital transmission has allowed cable service providers to offer many more channels than analog transmission allowed, as well as services such as on-demand content. The expanded choice in cable (a newer part of a legacy medium) has led to changes in broadcasting as well. Broadcasters have adjusted their content and pushed boundaries in form, style, and attitude in response to being forced to compete with cable and its specificity in targeting tastes. Although still largely economically unsustainable, digital distribution has offered print readers far greater choices and access to articles in more discrete forms. As people interested in all things television, we now enjoy the opportunity to read the columns of critics who write for papers around the country. We also have a much easier time finding articles of interest as a result of digital digests that link to a wide range of print sources, even as the print industry faces the many challenges chronicled here.

Of course the added number of choices across media platforms has also complicated the process of selecting what to read, watch, listen to, or play. With so many options available on a service such as Netflix, how can consumers ever hope to find the right film or television show to fit their leisure time? Of course, the answer is that Netflix and digital distributors of all kinds use **recommendation algorithms** to monitor our tastes and those with similar tastes to suggest content that we are likely to find appealing.

The use of algorithms to recommend content has raised a slew of broad social and cultural issues regarding privacy and the creative autonomy of workers. Privacy advocates worry about how much information digital media and algorithms collect about us, the security of data storage, and how closely commercial industries and government agencies collaborate to monitor our individual tastes, opinions, and activities. In late 2013, for instance, the *Washington Post* broke a story about the National Security Agency's "Co-Traveler" program, which monitors the location of every mobile phone in the world with global positioning satellites to determine who might be meeting with whom in what locations, in order to assess whether any illegal activities are being planned.[19] Meanwhile, some observers have questioned the extent to which creative workers in the media industries are capable of producing their own, independent visions in an algorithmic era when companies such as Netflix supposedly know everything about audience members' tastes and preferences. Are creative workers merely forced to reproduce what the audience already wants, some wonder?

Fragmentation

A key consequence of the greater range of media content in the digital era is the **fragmentation** of media consumption. In thinking about media and culture at a very broad level, the most unprecedented aspect of the change in media use today results from the steady erosion of various mass media industries without their replacement by other mass media—a change produced, as discussed in the introduction, by the proliferation of media outlets enabled by the affordances of digital distribution. Digitization works very much in tandem with the processes of **mass customization** to make targeting narrow and specific audience segments, or niches, a central strategy of media industries that long profited by producing goods designed to be acceptable to broad and heterogeneous audiences. Shifts in media industries to targeting narrower audience groups have happened previously—recall the transition in the focus of magazines in the mid twentieth century. The recent trend away from mass toward niche media is different from these past transitions, however, as no new "mass" medium is emerging.

Some of the earliest thinking on this issue can be found in Joseph Turow's book *Breaking Up America*, which considers this trend relative to the magazine and advertising industries.[20] Turow explains the value advertisers find from the more narrow targets of niche media and asserts that this trend will continue as a result. He warns of the creation of the "electronic equivalent of gated communities" rising up as a norm, as large media companies "separate audiences into different worlds."[21] Writing in the late 1990s, Turow forecast much of what we see across media industries today— what he describes as a shift in US media in the balance among **society-making media** and **segment-making media**. Society-making media are "those that have the potential to get different cross-sections of the population talking to each other"—broadcast television in the network era may have been the quintessential example—whereas segment-making media are those that "encourage small slices of society to talk to themselves."[22]

Many of the ideas that media scholars have developed about the significance and power of media grew out of the norms of society-making media. Consider for example the change in the nature of television news. In 1980, 52.1 million viewers tuned in to one of the broadcast networks' three evening newscasts. By 2012, that number had fallen by more than half to 22.1 million.[23] It isn't fair to say that in the intervening 32 years people have become half as informed. A range of segment-making news forms now exist—everything from those network newscasts that are watched by much smaller audiences to the news with a conservative spin offered by the Fox News cable channel to the not-quite-the-news (but pretty serious enterprise of media criticism nevertheless) offered up by *The Daily Show* or *Last Week Tonight with John Oliver*.

This doesn't even take into account the array of news perspectives offered by radio, newspaper, or online venues, which allow even greater segmentation.*

The concern raised by Turow is similar to the possibility that technology scholar Nicholas Negroponte wrote about when he imagined, in 1995, a newspaper of the future called *The Daily Me*, which would be customized to individual interests. Today, dozens of news aggregating and personalization websites and mobile apps exist, including one called DailyMe.[24] "Individualized news" has elicited both considerable excitement and concern. On one hand, the prospect of news or other media that is personally relevant is attractive to those who seek to reduce the time spent searching for material of interest. On the other hand, such targeting reduces the likelihood of using media to broaden our horizons beyond established interests and the ability of news services to function as agenda-setters that tell audiences what is important. The implications of being exposed only to things we have liked before can also affect our entertainment experience; we may be less likely to expand our taste horizons if we rely exclusively on what genius lists and recommendation engines presume of our preferences.

This fragmentation of audiences has considerable consequences for both the operation of media industries and the role of media as a force in culture and society. In terms of media industries, the reality that audiences have spread across so many media outlets has changed the nature of many media businesses. Media industries utilize different strategies in this era in which a broadcast television show is "successful" if it reaches 15 percent of those watching television as opposed to the 40 percent needed in the network era.

One particular consequence is that media industries create content to reach subgroups of populations instead of the mass audience. Research on the rise of female-centered television dramas beginning in the late 1990s offered one such lesson. Throughout television history, there had been few successful drama series centering on a female character until the mid-1990s—a point by which significant fragmentation of audiences had occurred. This fragmentation made targeting a more narrow population (such as women) a viable competitive technique in a way that was different from the competitive practices in an earlier era, when male members of the audience were perceived as the program decision-makers during prime time.

Fragmentation changes the strategies of media industries and, as a result, also requires reassessing the role of media in society. In some ways, a fragmented media system would suggest that any single piece of media would be less powerful because it is less widely shared. On the other hand, potentially positive society-making functions may also be lost. Perhaps it might be difficult to imagine the negative consequences of fragmentation—especially when we experience more personally relevant media as a gain. As a society we've become increasingly accustomed to operating inside our fairly individualized gated informational and entertainment communities, and those of us privileged enough to attend or work for universities probably have more media targeted toward us than is the case for many others. We've noticed moments of surprising

---

*This audio story considers the erosion of a common American popular culture. Can you think of ways digital media help promote common culture? http://www.npr.org/2011/01/24/133182903/cultural-common-ground-getting-harder-to-come-by

disjuncture when we are jolted out of our familiar media community to see what is "normal" in other media and are reminded that our worldview is just one of many. While this is purely an anecdote, the consequences of fragmentation of media remain key concerns over which coming generations of media scholars will struggle.

The widespread adoption of social networking applications for sharing media content may reinforce the insular tendencies of digitization, even as it may increase the range of uses that people find for media in their lives. Increasingly, social media websites and applications such as Facebook and Twitter permit individual members to share links, files, and comments related to media products with familiar and like-minded people. Social media also can simultaneously reinforce conventional uses of media, as when groups of people live-tweet an episode of a favorite show. Wanting to be part of a social media conversation returns us to the conventions of the broadcast era when everyone watched television programs at the same time. Social media adds to the fragmentation of the audience, even as they may bring those fragments closer together and make them more engaged and discriminating consumers of media content.

Convenience

Another contribution of digital technologies can be categorized as convenience. Indeed there is nothing inherently convenient about digitization—rather, media users experience the efficiency of digital recording and transmission as an advance in the convenient use of technologies. Whether in the portability of vast quantities of music, the efficient storage of DVRs and DVDs, or the quick and ready access to searchable print media online, digital media makes media use more convenient.

Another component of digitization is the way it allows content to be removed from its previous source to allow greater audience control. Whether people are downloading a radio show or segment as a podcast, recording a television show to a DVR, reading a newspaper online or on a portable device, or buying a film on DVD, some media industries are embracing the ways digitization can enable consumers to use media products in increasingly varied ways. These changes then feed back into the operation of media industries—in how they seek to profit, in their practices for creating media products, in their presumptions of the constructed audience—to yield adjustments in operations.

The growth of streaming film and television content provides a good example of how the convenience and choice that come from digitization can rework the operations of legacy media in multiple ways. Film distributors, for instance, are looking into releasing some films through streaming services *before* they release them in theaters—for a premium price, of course. So you might pay, say $100 or more to stream a movie a week or two before it opens in theaters. Though this may seem like a high price, it might be spread across a group of friends wanting to watch together or even be cheaper than paying for a babysitter in addition to movie tickets and snacks.

Streamed content also is being used to test new content. This has been the case with musical artists for years now, many of whom release singles and videos directly to streaming services and social media sites in the hopes of getting picked up by a major label. Amazon has done something similar with television series, producing pilots for series like *Alpha House* starring John Goodman and *Bosch*. The company decided to develop these series for entire season runs after the pilots proved popular with subscribers to the Amazon Prime video streaming service.

COMING CHANGE

The consequences of digitization have been reconfiguring the operation of the media industries for more than two decades now, yet it remains impossible to know how much industrial practices will continue to be adjusted as a result. Looking forward from the vantage point of 2016, we would expect to see four further consequences in coming years: greater fragmentation, cheaper production costs, the development of business models based on different approaches to distribution windows, and increasing surveillance of users to counter problems of fragmentation.

Our forecast of greater fragmentation is based more on the user experience than the situation of particular industries. For example, in coming years we probably won't see many more television channels (at least in the manner that we are currently accustomed to thinking of channels) or additional newspapers or magazines built around print editions. However, there is a good likelihood for the development of more on-demand television offerings, which will likely be organized in something more akin to a folder (in the manner that you are used to sorting things on your computer) than as the channels we have known. Netflix's ventures into original programming, in which entire seasons of a new series are released at once, rather than parceled out once a week for months like in cable and broadcast television, is a good example of this trend. The consequences of

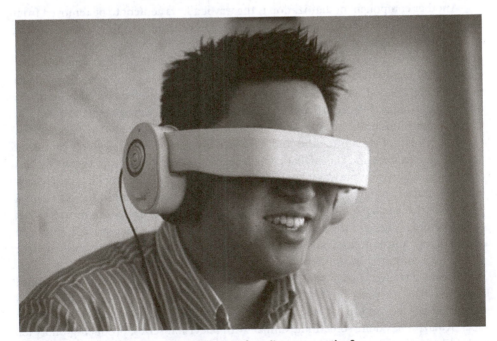

Photo 9.2 The Glyph by Avegant: the future of media consumption?

digitization will similarly continue to reconfigure print industries as fewer industries maintain hardcopy print productions, but the possibilities of online distribution may actually further fragment audiences if these industries can find a viable business model.

Certainly, across media industries the basic costs of production will continue to fall as compression technologies improve and allow more memory and functionality in computers and mobile devices. We may never really appreciate these as gains, however, as the potential cost reductions may quickly be offset by continued expansion in the quality and sophistication of digital imagery and sound that lead us to continue to desire newer and more advanced versions of technology. Although it may be difficult to imagine how video games could get any more lifelike or the production quality of film or television could be significantly augmented, there remain largely unexplored realms of virtual reality, 3D, and ultra 4K high definition that may become increasingly commonplace, rather than remaining purely science fiction.

We would also expect that the media industries will develop a better sense of viable business models that will come to dominate their operation in a digital era in the very near term. The global economic crisis beginning in 2008 certainly began pressuring these industries to reevaluate many of their experiments with new distribution and financial models as advertising dollars became increasingly difficult to access, especially without provable results. Like contemporary industry workers, we are not sure what business model or models might ultimately work, as we remain very much in a period of innovation and experimentation despite the pressures of the larger economic environment.

One thing we would expect is that pricing will become more variable, based on spatial rather than temporal dimensions. What we mean by this is that the old mechanisms for creating artificial scarcity such as tiering the release of films through different distribution windows that release content at different times will become increasingly obsolete as what the industry terms "day and date" release (availability in all places at the same time or nearly same time) becomes more common. The US media industries also historically have released content domestically and then waited a period of weeks or months before releasing it in international markets. These windows too are becoming narrower as concerns about piracy lead to near simultaneous international debuts.

As distribution windows continue to evolve and stabilize, business models and major players will stabilize as well. We can see this in the streaming video industry, which was virtually nonexistent in 2010 when we finished the first edition of this textbook. In 2015, Netflix had 57.4 million subscribers worldwide and was available in 50 countries. US estimates reported more than 30 percent of all Internet traffic comes from streaming content through Netflix. The media landscape of the future, then, will be filled with new names as well as old ones, but the "wild west" days of digital distribution, where illegal sharing was rampant and small startups dominated, are already coming to an end.

Finally, we would expect surveillance to become an increasingly common social issue and potentially a strategy by which media industries attempt to build their digital era business models. One of the advantages of digital distribution of media from an industry perspective is that it often provides expanded opportunities for the distributors to know things about their audiences. For example, digital cable boxes can report data about precisely what channel you watch when, when you channel surf, how long you stay on a channel, and when you begin turning again, which is of great value to those trying to design media products. Also, online distribution of video features much greater ability to report how and when the content is watched and even information about the viewer that may be gathered by "cookies," as well as information about your viewing habits or search history. All of this information is exceptionally valuable to distributors who seek to sell audiences to advertisers, and it may well be the case that advertisers are willing to pay as much for 10 viewers if they have detailed information about them as they would have paid for 100 or even 1,000 relatively unknown viewers in another era. While the expanded mechanisms for audience surveillance are of great value to the media industries, users may raise legitimate concerns about this new access to their lives and seek greater privacy controls. Or viewers may decide that relinquishing personal data and an expectation of privacy is a worthwhile exchange for continued "free" access to various media products and services.

CONCLUSION

This chapter has assumed the ready availability of the Internet and a host of other digital technologies that are increasingly taken for granted by some populations as though they are as common as running water and fresh air. Even though their use may be common in our daily lives, it is important to remember that the revolution in media production, distribution, and use being wrought by digitization is not a uniform experience around the globe. Indeed, one of the new interesting measures of global comparison is the rate of Internet availability and the sophistication of the digital technologies deployed. The United States has long perceived of itself as a leader of technological development, but with 18 percent of homes lacking access to the Internet and comparatively slow and overpriced access for those who do, it increasingly lags behind because of its lack of comprehensive national policy and willingness to leave development, innovation, and implementation in the hands of commercial interests.

Some argue that digitization and all that it presents provide a challenge to top-down models of industry operation that long have organized the industries that we have discussed here. While we would acknowledge that digitization is driving innovation and challenging these older models of media industry operation, we would also first note that those top-down models were overly determinist even before digitization—a problem we've attempted to assuage with the Industrialization of Culture framework. We would also note that it is probably too early to assert that digitization will lead to a fundamental reordering of power in the media industry in the long term, despite its ample consequences for industry operation. Following the argument of Harvard Business School professor Debora L. Spar, we think it is important to acknowledge that we have witnessed only the beginning stages of the influence of digital technologies on the media industries.[25] Spar draws parallels between the current moment and the revolution the Internet seems to be delivering with similar moments in the introduction of other media technologies. The situation borne out over and over is that after initial periods of innovation, commercialization, and creative anarchy, rules are imposed that significantly contain the revolutionary potential that once seemed inherent.

Different structural conditions—those matters of technology, regulation, and economics that we discussed at length earlier—are playing an important role in establishing norms and possibilities for media industry operation and media use in the digital era. The scope of change that digitization makes possible for media industries is stunning. Although seemingly just a matter of technology on the surface, digitization affects all aspects of making, distributing, using, and financing media as well. Significant adjustments in media-industry norms have already occurred, and yet the reordering of norms remains far from complete.

QUESTIONS

1. How have digital technologies introduced more convenience in your media consumption habits? How does that compare to the media consumption habits of your parents when they were your age? The chapter suggests that the rise of digital media has introduced more choice for consumers. Based on your consumption habits, do you agree with this finding; why or why not? What are some of the negatives of having so much more choice?

2. Beyond the issues discussed in this chapter, what do you think are some other consequences of digitization for the media industry that most interest you? What are some of the benefits for that media industry? Overall, do you think digitization is a welcome change for this industry or not?

3. As noted in this chapter, the Internet has created problems for print media. Why do you think people have come to believe information distributed online should be free—and do you think this can (or should) be changed? Can you think of a new business model for newspapers and magazines that might allow them to benefit from this development? Might an iTunes for newspapers or a Netflix for magazines be helpful? What are some of the benefits and problems that might be associated with such models?

4. Consider the source you use most frequently for news. Is it a society-making or segment-making form of media? If it is the former, how does it define society? If it is the latter, how would you characterize the segment it caters to? Think specifically about the type of news it presents, and how it presents it, to back up your claims. Then consider the same questions in relation to entertainment media you consume.

5. Think of a media good you have in both physical and digital form, such as a song you own on CD and as an MP3 file. Why do you have it in more than one format? Which do you use more often and why? What are the pros and cons to each delivery technology? Are there some types of media that you want only in physical format or only in digital format? Why?

6. Think about Chris Anderson's idea that direct-pay media might want to consider giving away content and generating revenue through other forums, such as pop stars making money from performances rather than music. What are the advantages and disadvantages to this approach? Consider different ways this idea could be implemented across various media industries—what could be given away and what could be used to generate profit? Might it work easier for some industries than others? Is there media that can't be free and why?

FURTHER READING

Many recent publications explore the "new" media being created digitally, although attention to their nascent industries is rare and the very newness of their topics makes it difficult to know which books will serve as classic references. Nevertheless, Nicholas Negroponte's *Being Digital* (New York: Vintage Books, 1995); Henry Jenkins' *Convergence Culture: Where Old and New Media Collide* (New York: New York University Press, 2006); and Jay David Bolter and Richard Grusin's *Remediation: Understanding New Media* (Boston: MIT Press, 2000) deal with issues related to digitization broadly.

There are also several newer works attempting to make sense of media in a digital world. Much of this work is preliminary but provoking. See Chris Anderson's *The Long Tail: Why the Future of Business is Selling Less of More*, rev. ed. (New York: Hyperion, 2008) and *Free: The Past and Future of a Radical Price* (New York: Hyperion, 2009).

For more on how contemporary media companies exploit the possibilities for surveillance as a way to increase profits and the social implications of these processes, see Mark Andrejevic's *Infoglut: How Too Much Information Is Changing the Way We Think and Know* (New York: Routledge, 2013). For debates about the effects of recommendation algorithms on creative practices, see Andrew Leonard, "How Netflix Is Turning Viewers into Puppets," *Salon*, February 1, 2013, http://www.salon.com/2013/02/01/how_netflix_is_turning_viewers_into_puppets/ (accessed February 27, 2014), and Timothy Havens, "Media Programming in an Era of Big Data," *Media Industries Journal* 1, no. 2 (2014).

For comprehensive and up-to-date analyses of news media in a digital world, visit www.stateofthemedia.org, which is maintained by the Pew Research Center's Project for Excellence in Journalism. For current updates, analyses, and contemplations on the film, media, and gaming industries, the University of California-Santa Barbara's Media Industries Project (http://www.carseywolf.ucsb.edu/mip) is an excellent resource.

For discussions of consolidation of ownership and the blurring of media types due to digital production and distribution, see Henry Jenkins, Sam Ford, and Joshua Green, *Spreadable Media: Creating Value and Meaning in a Networked Culture* (New York: New York University Press, 2013), and Derek Johnson, *Media Franchising: Creative License and Collaboration in the Culture Industries* (New York: New York University Press, 2013).

NOTES

1. Recording Industry Association of America, 2014 News and Notes on 2014 Mid-Year RIAA Shipment and Revenue Statistics, http://riaa.com/media/1806D32F-B3DD-19D3-70A4-4C31C0217836.pdf (accessed February 15, 2015).
2. Joseph R. Dominick, Barry L. Sherman, and Fritz Messere, *Broadcasting, Cable, the Internet, and Beyond: An Introduction to Modern Electronic Media*, 4th ed. (Boston: McGraw Hill, 2000), 48.
3. Henry Jenkins, *Convergence Culture: Where Old and New Media Collide* (New York: New York University Press, 2006), 3.

4. Henry Jenkins, Sam Ford, and Joshua Green. *Spreadable Media: Creating Value and Meaning in a Networked Culture* (New York: New York University Press, 2013).

5. Jane Sasseen, Kenny Olmstead, and Amy Mitchel, "Digital: As Mobile Grows Rapidly, the Pressures on News Intensify," http://stateofthemedia.org/2013/digital-as-mobile-grows-rapidly-the-pressures-on-news-intensify/ (accessed February 24, 2014); Rick Edmonds, Emily Guskin, Amy Mitchell, and Mark Jurkowitz, "Newspapers: Stabilizing, But Still Threatened," http://stateofthemedia.org/2013/newspapers-stabilizing-but-still-threatened/ (accessed February 24, 2014).

6. Ian King, "Business Big Shot: Arianna Huffington, Online Entrepreneur," (London) *Times Online*, November 21, 2008, http://business.timesonline.co.uk/tol/business/movers_and_shakers/article5201252.ece (accessed April 9, 2009).

7. Joseph Turow, *Media Today* (New York: Routledge, 2008), 391.

8. Ibid., 400–401.

9. John Caldwell, *Televisuality: Style, Crisis, and Authority in American Television* (New Brunswick: Rutgers University Press, 1995).

10. Edward Jay Epstein, *The Big Picture: Money and Power in Hollywood* (New York: Random House, 2006), 22.

11. Ibid., 165.

12. Ted Tschang and Andrea Goldstein, "Production and Political Economy in the Animation Industry: Why Insourcing and Outsourcing Occur," paper presented at Industrial Dynamics, Innovation and Development Conference, Elsinore, Denmark, 2004.

13. Epstein, *The Big Picture*, 348; Richard Verrier, "Paramount Stops Releasing Major Movies on Film," *Los Angeles Times*, January 18, 2014, http://articles.latimes.com/2014/jan/18/entertainment/la-et-ct-paramount-end-to-film-20140118

14. Chris Anderson, *The Long Tail: Why the Future of Business is Selling Less of More*, rev. ed. (New York: Hyperion, 2008). In addition to the original long tail article in *Wired* and the 2006 book of the same name, Anderson maintains current examples of the concept on his webpage: http://www.thelongtail.com/

15. Chris Anderson, *Free: The Past and Future of a Radical Price* (New York: Hyperion, 2009).

16. Chris Kohler, "SXSW: Wired Editor Chris Anderson's *Free* Will Be Free," *Wired .com*, March 17, 2009, http://blog.wired.com/underwire/2009/03/anderson-kawasa .html (accessed April 2, 2009).

17. Reuters Institute for the Study of Journalism, "Digital News Report 2014," http://www.digitalnewsreport.org/survey/2014/paying-for-digital-news-2014/ (accessed February 16, 2015).

18. Richard Perez-Pena, "The *Times* to Charge for Frequent Access to Its Web Site," January 20, 2010, http://www.nytimes.com/2010/01/21/business/media/21times.html (accessed February 24, 2010).

19. Barton Gellman and Ashkan Soltani, "NSA Tracking Cellphone Locations Worldwide, Snowden Documents Show," *Washington Post* [online], December 4, 2013, http://www.washingtonpost.com/world/national-security/nsa-tracking-cellphone-locations-worldwide-snowden-documents-show/2013/12/04/5492873a-5cf2-11e3-bc56-c6ca94801fac_story.html (accessed February 26, 2014).

20. Joseph Turow, *Breaking Up America: Advertisers and the New Media World* (Chicago: University of Chicago Press, 1997).
21. Ibid., 2.
22. Ibid., 3.
23. Emily Guskin, Mark Jurkowitz, and Amy Mitchell, "Network: By the Numbers," StateoftheMedia.org, http://stateofthemedia.org/2013/network-news-a-year-of-change-and-challenge-at-nbc/network-by-the-numbers/ (accessed February 27, 2014).
24. Nicholas Negroponte, *Being Digital* (New York: Vintage Books, 1995).
25. Debra L. Spar, *Ruling the Waves: Cycles of Discovery, Chaos, and Wealth from the Compass to the Internet* (New York: Harcourt, 2001).

CHAPTER 10

Media Globalization

Key Takeaways:

Understand why US-based media industries traditionally have dominated the field of global media

Describe the commercial opportunities that prompt the globalization of the media industries

Identify the cultural and political barriers to media globalization, as well as strategies for overcoming those barriers

Understand the social issues that media globalization raises

In 2009, Nintendo released the European and American versions of *Lux-Pain*, a graphic-novel-based video game for its handheld DS platform, in which the main character, Atsuki, seeks to save the inhabitants of Kisaragi City from a mysterious force known only as Silent. Hailed as innovative for its creative use of the DS's touch screen, its impressive anime-inspired graphics, and its carefully evolving storyline that features eight different possible endings, *Lux-Pain* has also become a textbook example of how *not* to **localize** video games, due to its awkward translation, egregious spelling errors, and ambigous, surreal locations that many Western players found unnerving.

Lux-Pain provides a quintessential example of how globalization has changed the media we consume, as well as the promises and perils that globalization poses for media industries. The game's developer, Killaware, is a Japanese-based gaming company with a multinational staff of 10 developers. Though based in Japan, the company targets teenage and young adult gamers in East Asia, Europe, and North America, specifically aiming at both young men and young women. As such, its developers try to draw on global cultural trends, including anime, which are popular with this transnational target market, rather than on trends that are specific to an individual national market. Killaware, then, is not a Japanese company with international operations, and *Lux-Pain* is not a Japanese cultural export; instead, both the company and the game are inherently global in nature.

Still, despite its global characteristics, *Lux-Pain* and its developer had to navigate the remaining complexities of global cultural difference, the most obvious of which is language differences. That is, in order to exploit its global markets and ride the wave of global trends, the company needed to overcome the vast differences that separate its targeted consumers in East Asia, Europe, and North America. **Localization** is the term that most people in the media industries use to describe this process of unmooring media texts from their immediate cultural surroundings and securing them in another locale. Localization includes language translation, as well as the translation of settings, such as Kisaragi City, narrative techniques, characters, allusions, and more. The commercial and popular success of a global text like *Lux-Pain* depends crucially on how well developers achieve this localization.

Lux-Pain, then, is a perfect example of how the structures of the global media industries have run ahead of the content strategies necessary to make global media a reality. Slowly, the industry has developed a range of strategies to try to deal with the persistence of global cultural differences, especially how those differences make the popularity of texts even more unpredictable than in national contexts. Put another way, globalization increases the **nobody knows** principle of the media industries. Ironically, the very strategies that the industry uses to deal with uncertainty—such as deliberately designing goods to be accessible to a global audience—can also sink a potentially popular text when they are poorly executed, as was the case with *Lux-Pain.*

In this chapter, we examine the economic opportunities that globalization offers and the history of how those opportunities developed. We also look at the kinds of barriers that media industries face in their efforts to globalize and the adaptive strategies they have used to try to overcome those boundaries. Finally, we address some of the social and political questions that the globalization of the media industries has raised.

* * *

Along with digitization, globalization is one of the dynamics presently reshaping every media industry at every level of the Industrialization of Culture framework. For instance, as we noted in Chapter 1, the growth of global markets for media commodities has exploded since the 1980s due to the introduction of new distribution technologies. These developments have required the creation of a single, international entity that can enforce **intellectual property rights**, the World Intellectual Property Organization, which is a change in regulatory conditions that affects every media industry. At the level of industry practices, creators of film, television, games, and popular music all need to take into consideration international audiences and local adaptations when producing content.

The *Lux-Pain* example may lead you to conclude that globalization, as a dynamic of change, is already well established in the media industries. Though this is true in certain sectors of the industry, such as video games and blockbuster films that tend to earn more revenues from international markets than domestic ones, other sectors such as newspapers and television are still predominantly domestic in character, at least in the United States. As we explore in this chapter, however, various aspects of these media industry sectors are increasingly global in terms of the workers they employ, the content they produce, and the markets where they sell that content. Of course, one of the main drivers of globalization today is the shift to digital media detailed in the last chapter.

Given the inherently global nature of the Internet—that anyone anywhere can connect to a website anywhere else in real time—the forms and practices of globalization that we discuss here may change profoundly as digitization continues to change the media industries.

THE HISTORY OF MEDIA GLOBALIZATION
AND AMERICAN DOMINANCE

Globalization refers to a variety of complex and sometimes contradictory social and economic developments that have been taking place for centuries. Even in ancient times, several civilations sought to conquer distant lands and integrate them into vast empires that spanned continents. These empires coordinated markets and laborers over vast expanses of territory, not unlike contemporary media empires do. Over the centuries of human history since these first empires, countless empires have risen and fallen. What is unique about the present stage of **media globalization** is the capacity of worldwide communications infrastructures to send messages anywhere in the world almost instantaneously. This capacity for instantaneous communication makes the coordination of media production, distribution, and aggregation much more efficient.

The contemporary form of media globalization aims to spread as widely as possible the considerable risks and rewards of commercial media. That means the global media companies try to hire the cheapest workers they can anywhere in the world through **outsourcing**; they seek to sell their products to as wide a global audience as possible; and they try to generate production funding from as wide a range of international corporations, governments, and nongovernmental organizations as possible. Global communication makes all of this possible: it allows industry executives and creative workers to communicate with their counterparts abroad about the production, funding, buying, and selling of media texts.

Globalization has been a strategy of the American media industries at least since the early decades of the twentieth century, although it has progressed at different speeds in different industries. The film industry was the earliest entrant into international markets, with Hollywood films dominating most of the developed world's film theatres by the time World War I ended. Hollywood earned $26 million from international box office revenues in 1926, the first year that the Motion Picture Association reported foreign sales data. In 2013, the major Hollywood studios earned $35.9 billion from foreign box office receipts and only $10.9 billion in the United States and Canada. Since the 1970s, foreign box office sales have outpaced domestic sales, with the ratio of foreign to domestic increasing year on year.[1]

One main reason American media industries have dominated the world's media industries in some sectors is because they have long operated under a commercial mandate. Commercial media industries have a strong incentive to take advantage of the cost savings and revenues available from global markets, while industries with noncommercial mandates are primarily incented to serve the stakeholders—typically citizens—for whom they are aimed. Today, media industries around the world frequently follow a commercial mandate, but American industries often still enjoy what's known in economics as

first-mover advantage. First-mover-advantage refers to the fact that the first company (or industry sector) to move into a specific market often remains the main player in that market for years to come. Some observers think that first-mover advantage comes from better intelligence about the markets and technological innovations that the first-mover possesses. It also results from first movers possessing better brand identification than subsequent competitors. In film and television, Hollywood tends to maintain such an advantage over competitors.

A second reason for the relative global dominance of some US media industries in global markets is the size and affluence of the global English-speaking market. With the possible exceptions of video games and popular music, most media are rooted in a specific language, and the process of dubbing, subtitling, and translating tend to diminish the appeal of media content in a foreign language. Moreover, the costs and time requirements associated with translation often work to diminish the potential profits for a media product in a foreign-language market. Consequently, media industries tend to export to and import from linguistically similar countries. Because English-speakers control a greater proportion of the world's gross domestic product than any other language group, media industries producing in English have a ready population of well-off audiences available.

Social concerns about American media globalization, in particular the spread of commercialism and the disappearance of cultural diversity worldwide, are taken up later. For now, we only want to note that there have been very particular historical circumstances that led the United States to dominate worldwide trade in the film and television industries. Many observers today believe that this dominance is in decline—that the current global media landscape is characterized not by one center of production and distribution but rather by multiple centers of regional dominance, or **media capitals,** in a range of nations including China, Japan, India, Mexico, Brazil, Egypt, the US and the UK.

DRIVERS OF MEDIA GLOBALIZATION

Globalization takes advantage of both **economies of scale** and the **long tail** of media commodities that we discussed in Chapters 2 and 9, respectively. Economies of scale monetize the large audience global reach makes available, take advantage of cost savings by using the cheapest labor available, and eliminate redundancy among operations in multiple locales, allowing these companies to undercut their smaller rivals. Globally integrated media conglomerates are also able to gather and share market intelligence from around the world. Simultaneously, the long tail of media commodities allows corporations to continue to profit from content for years to come in market after market; for instance, every major Hollywood studio today sells rights to broadcast or remake television series from the 1970s, and even earlier.

Commercial media organizations have long recognized the economic advantages of globalization, but only in recent years have the economic benefits been so great for most industries that they have actively sought to develop business and content strategies designed to exploit global markets. Any explanation of why globalization has become such an important dynamic must begin with changes in the media industries. We have already covered a number of these changes, including the slow demise of the mass audience and the decentralization of channels of distribution, which have led all sectors of the media industries to focus on leveraging popular texts across multiple media and multiple territories. However, the specific opportunities that globalization offers differ from industry to industry.

Film

As already mentioned, the film industry has been internationalizing for more than a century. One of the driving forces for globalization is the fact that the major Hollywood studios own numerous movie theaters abroad and can therefore profit directly from international box office sales. The kinds of high-priced blockbuster films that contemporary Hollywood tends to produce can't easily earn back their production budgets through domestic sales alone; they need international box office sales in order to turn a profit. Moreover, as DVD sales of films have decreased in recent years due to piracy and legitimate streaming services, foreign revenues have become even more important. With only the exception of perhaps the gaming industry, the US film industry has learned to take advantage of global markets through worldwide promotion of new films, global merchandising, and the simultaneous (or near simultaneous) release of films in most markets.

Television

Television has been a global medium since its inception in the early 1950s as well, with both finished programming and programming ideas circulating among many nations. The current market in television developed in the 1990s with the introduction of cable and satellite channels in much of the world and the expansion of commercial television alongside the legacy public service broadcasters across Europe and Asia. The increase in program services led to an explosion in the number of programming hours needing filled in most countries around the world. Buying international programming was an easy and cheap way to fill this sudden explosion in schedule time, though most channels began to replace imports with domestic programming as soon as they were economically able to do so.

Numerous transnational satellite channels that target audiences in multiple territories also now exist, and several popular cable channels have international counterparts, including several international versions of the Disney Channel, Discovery, and BBC. At the level of particular programs, television **formats** that can be remade in multiple countries with local talent have flooded the global markets since the late 1990s. These formats—including shows such as *Big Brother* and *Dancing with the Stars*—are the quintessential global cultural form; they are designed to be popular in specific locations but flexible enough in their design that they can be remade in almost any other culture.

Gaming

Unlike other media forms, video games were never national products, although specific games themselves sometimes target national audiences. Instead, many of the earliest games were developed by Japanese companies with the intention of targeting consumers in the United States, Europe, and Asia. Today, many of these same game developers—Sega, Nintendo, Sony—remain major players. As the anecdote that began this chapter discussed, many contemporary games are designed by multinational teams with the intention of reaching a multinational market. Much as with Hollywood films, the largest game titles are usually released on or about the same date in most major markets around the world in an effort to take advantage of worldwide promotion and merchandising tie-ins.

Music

Arguably, music has been an international phenomenon since long before the modern music industry developed. Songs, techniques, and musical performers have traveled the world longer than any form of media. Today, the music industry tries to leverage the transnational appeal of music by actively grooming talent and marketing it for the world music scene. Acts tour far and wide in support of their newest albums, and music executives scour the globe in search of the newest musical trends. More than other industries, the development of digital distribution over the Internet enabled the creation of worldwide fan communities due to the ease with which music files could be shared. One consequence of the globalization of the music industry has been worldwide consolidation. The BBC reports that 90 percent of global music sales revenues go to one of the "Big Five" music companies: EMI Records, Sony, Vivendi Universal, AOL Time Warner, and BMG. Although numerous smaller labels do exist, they are typically owned by one or more of the large conglomerates.[2]

Magazines

The magazine industry has successfully developed numerous global brands centered around particular lifestyles, including *Cosmopolitan*, *Marie Claire*, and *FHM*. Newsmagazines, by contrast, tend to be popular primarily within only their own linguistic region, although feature magazines, such as the French magazine *L'Historie*, a glossy, wide-circulation magazine dedicated to new developments in the field of history, are sometimes sold into multiple linguistic markets. International magazines are typically a patchwork of both global and local content, with some stories translated directly from the original language and some articles written specifically for the local market. Typically, these internationally consumed magazines are owned by one of a small handful of magazine publishers, such as Time Warner, CondeNast, Advance Publications, Hearst Corporation, or Meredith Corporation. However, much as with newspapers (discussed next), magazine reading largely remains concentrated primarily on national or regional titles.

Newspapers

The readership of newspapers is usually limited to their immediate linguistic region, whether that region is a single nation or several nations. Nationally well-known papers such as *The Times* of London and the *Chicago Tribune* have online versions that can attract readers from around the world with appropriate English skills. However, the print editions of newspapers rarely cross national boundaries. Local newspapers, of course, seldom attract readers or generate any revenues from abroad. But this doesn't mean that the industry is untouched by globalization. Several local newspapers, particularly those that publish "hyper-local" content on their websites, including local sports scores, reports of school board meetings, and so on, outsource the writing of reports to English-speaking writers abroad. The foreign writers earn substantially less than American writers. The local newspaper still sends a "reporter" to collect facts for articles, but those raw facts are then submitted to the foreign journalist, who writes the story. For instance, for a period of time in 2012, a company known as Journatic provided content that was written by both local and foreign journalists to the online edition of the *Chicago Tribune*.

Advertising

For nearly all of the media industries, the global spread of advertising agencies has been a major catalyst for globalization. These agencies facilitate globalization in several ways. First, they design advertising, find appropriate media outlets, and buy ad time around the world for products with a global reach. Second, advertising agencies identify particular population segments around the world and help develop media outlets and cultural products that encourage a sense of global community among them. Finally, the international expansion of advertising agencies has required the development of global communications infrastructures, such as broadband Internet, which has spurred other forms of media globalization. In this way, even those segments of the media industries that are not advertiser supported may now take advantage of communications networks that were subsidized in whole or in part by advertising agencies and their clients.

Worldwide, hundreds, perhaps thousands, of advertising agencies have international operations, but the most dominant global agencies that carry the most prominent, most lucrative, and most powerful advertising campaigns are generally owned by one of three major holding agencies that together accounted for over $50 billion in revenues in 2014. These agencies are WPP Group ($18.9 billion), Omnicom Group ($15.3 billion), and Publicis Groupe ($9.6 billion).[3] Together, these agencies generate slightly more than half of their revenues from US-based operations and the remainder from abroad.

Global advertising agencies work hand in hand with global corporations, global media conglomerates, and global telecommunications companies to cultivate and exploit markets for media culture around the world. For instance, the advertising agency Arnold, which is owned by the sixth-largest global ad agency, Havas, developed a promotional campaign for McDonald's franchises in the Pacific Rim that offered Justice League dolls with meal purchases in New Zealand, Australia, Singapore, and elsewhere to help promote the Warner Bros. movie *Justice League: The New Frontier*. The movie, in turn, was based on comic book characters owned by DC Comics, a subsidiary of Warner Bros. This is an example of a global, multicorporation attempt at **synergy**, with its core commodities centered around media texts.

BARRIERS TO MEDIA GLOBALIZATION

Despite the great opportunities that global markets present, and the grand plans of some media executives to exploit those markets, social, cultural, and political differences among nations and regions of the world often make the global exploitation of intellectual property difficult, if not impossible. As the *Lux-Pain* example demonstrates, the production, distribution, and aggregation of global media texts face a variety of hurdles that domestic texts generally do not. Among the more obvious and difficult hurdles are language and cultural differences among potential consumers. Related barriers involve national and international regulations that block or reroute global cultural flows in various ways. In response to these challenges, media companies with global aspirations have developed a variety of business practices—including emphasizing universal elements in their content, co-producing content, localizing, branding, and making direct investment in foreign markets—all in an effort to give imported content privileged access to potential consumers.

Cultural Barriers

The degree to which cultural differences serve as hurdles to media globalization differs among types and genres of media. Local news is probably the least transferable of all media content, while instrumental music is probably the most transferable. All other types and genres of media content fall somewhere in between these extremes, and different media content has led to varying levels of globalization and different adaptive strategies across industries and genres.

Some industries, such as Hollywood films and popular music, have arguably been globalized for more than a century. Others, such as the magazine industry, have a handful of global brands, such as *Maxim* and *Cosmopolitan,* that carry international and local content, along with a much larger number of domestic titles in most countries. The main distinction between media content that can and cannot travel well abroad is the degree to which that content relies on language to communicate. In movies, for instance, action films that tell their stories largely through visuals and expensive special effects tend to travel well across cultural barriers, while romantic comedies that rely heavily on verbal humor tend to have difficulty reaching audiences beyond their immediate language markets. The exception to this rule seems to be popular music, which can often overcome language barriers because listeners are more interested in the music tracks. Still, history is littered with examples of songs being reformatted from one language to another in order to increase their popularity.* The German popular music industry in the 1950s and 1960s, for instance, relied heavily on translated versions of popular American hits, rewritten and sung by German bands, such as Werner Overheidht's version of Elvis Presley's "Heartbreak Hotel," titled "Hotel zur Einsamheit" or "Hotel for Loneliness."[4]

---

*Consider the examples in this radio story about the Burmese adaptation of popular music with the video examples in the second link. Which strategy—changing the lyrics or translating the song—do you think best allows localization of a media good? http://www.npr.org/2011/12/01/143014871/shakira-and-collective-souls-hits-with-a-burmese-twist; https://www.youtube.com/watch?v=a_YSydDh3Vo

Language differences are, of course, one of the most difficult challenges for any media product to overcome in global markets. On the other hand, language differences do not coincide perfectly with national boundaries, so language can actually help encourage international media trade when mulitple countries speak the same language. Perhaps the best example of this phenomenon is media trade in Latin America. Despite residing in many different countries, many of the continent's people speak Spanish, which has led to well established and long-standing trade in all types of media. Generally speaking, however, language differences make trade difficult, and entire industries have grown up around the world to translate media from one language to another.

While the example of language differences among nations may be obvious, other kinds of cultural differences can be equally as difficult to overcome, and language is no guarantee of cultural similarity. For instance, the extended song-and-dance routines in Hindi films, popularly known as "Bollywood," are off-putting for many non-Indian Americans, while they are the main lure for the audiences in other parts of the world who have made Bollywood the world's second-largest film industry. These cultural differences boil down to differences in expectations that movie-goers have of how a film's story will unfold, as well as expectations about film genres, namely, the expectation among viewers raised on Hollywood films in which only musicals involve singing and dancing. Cultural differences such as these can either weave together or keep apart audiences in different nations or language groups. Most of these differences and similarities have deep historical roots that have evolved over time.

Culture, then, "channels" worldwide flows of media in particular directions. Observers use the term **geocultural markets** to refer to these transnational media markets that are based on culture rather than national boundaries. Unlike national boundaries, however, one cannot easily draw a map of the world that shows where cultural boundaries begin and end. The identification of cultural similarities and differences is more of an act of imagination and interpretation than cartography. For one thing, culture works at many different levels, so that different societies may share some cultural elements but not others. Depending on which of these cultural elements specific media content activates, those texts may or may not find willing audiences abroad. For instance, the predominantly Islamic members of the Commonwealth of Independent States, which have long-standing historical, political, and folk culture ties with non-Islamic members, import media heavily from Turkey, Iran, and Saudi Arabia because of shared religious cultures. In addition, media flows can call attention to cultural similarities that otherwise might go unexplored, such as the shared sensibilities, gender politics, and economic challenges in Latin America and Eastern Europe that the popularity of Latin American telenovelas in Eastern Europe calls attention to.[5]

Technological and Regulatory Barriers

Communications infrastructures and government regulations often pose additional challenges for media corporations with global aspirations. Communication infrastructures helped propel the wave of television globalization in the 1980s, as nations around the globe added cable and satellite television channels. Yet, cable, satellite, and Internet delivery platforms remain quite unevenly developed around the globe, frustrating attempts by large corporations to access the world's audiences. National-level regulations also helped pave the way for the globalization of television, as country after country opened its broadcasting market to commercial competition, especially in Europe. At the same time, many countries have retained quotas on percentages of foreign content on television channels, especially content of American origin. These content quotas date back to the early days of the film industry, when a number of European nations established them to protect their domestic film industries from Hollywood dominance after World War I. Today, many foreign governments employ such quotas, along with co-production funding that helps defray production costs, and limit direct foreign investment in media production, distribution, and aggregation.

For its part, the US government has worked hard to help American media conglomerates expand abroad. Throughout the decades—but especially beginning in the 1990s—the US government represented Hollywood's interests in bilateral negotiations with other nations, securing the studios the right to purchase movie theaters and multiplexes abroad, as well as protection of intellectual property rights, among other concessions. Ironically, many of the protectionist measures that nations currently use to try to protect their domestic media industries were common in the United States during the development of the American film and broadcasting industries. Obviously, national governments in many parts of the world believe that domestic media industries are central to their interests. The decision to base industries on different mandates emerges from different perceptions of how media industries serve state interests. Some might desire public mandates to ensure the media industries cultivate an informed citizenry, while those prioritizing commercial mandates see them as contributing to economic growth. Most countries desire both ends, and many present-day nation-states work hard to protect and improve the state of their media industries on the world stage. For instance, since the late 1990s, the People's Republic of China, has protected its film industry from competition by limiting film imports as well as subsidizing its own industry's efforts to create films that are distributed outside of China.

The United States and the West in general have been quite successful in their efforts to promote their media industries worldwide through regulatory innovations. As we already discussed, the United States in the 1980s and 1990s succeeded in convincing several countries to privatize their media environments by cutting subsidies to publicly funded media outlets, which forced them to compete against commercial ones.

But the more important regulatory condition—from the perspective of Hollywood—has been the development of global intellectual property regimes that favor the interests of powerful nations and industries. As we discussed in relation to copyright in Chapter 4, intellectual property is an old idea whose purpose is to guarantee that people who come up with ideas can't have them stolen by someone else; in its purest form, it's a legal guarantee that authors, inventors, researchers, and others get to keep the right to determine how their intellectual efforts are released to the general public and who profits from them. Most observers believe that, without intellectual property rights guaranteeing that someone can profit from their ideas, the best and brightest people might not enter fields as diverse as media, computer programming, and crop research—or, basically, any form of intellectual or creative work—which would stag-nate innovation.

So, in its origins at least, intellectual property is designed to be a cultural and social virtue. In today's world, international intellectual property rights, including those of media content, are generally held by commercial entities, and the creative forces behind them have little control over how media are shared with the general public. Instead, intellectual property rights generally serve the interests of commercial companies trying to maximize profits.

As Hollywood has become more and more reliant on global revenues, it has likewise sought to crack down on illegal **piracy**, or the buying and selling of illegally produced copies of television shows, films, computer games, software, music, and so forth. Holly-wood's claims about how much money it loses worldwide due to piracy are probably overinflated, because a large number of people who buy pirated copies of media prod-ucts in less affluent nations probably couldn't afford to purchase them at standard prices. For this reason, a number of people think that piracy is a relatively minor problem for global media conglomerates. Rather it is the small media operations that operate on a shoestring budget and for whom every sale is crucial that suffer most from piracy. In addition, some countries, most notably the People's Republic of China, have been reluc-tant to crack down on piracy because such **parallel economies** employ a large number of people. In short, the legitimate economy of some countries might suffer if the parallel economies built on illegal piracy were shut down.

OVERCOMING BARRIERS TO GLOBALIZATION

While globalization may conjure up images of people everywhere drinking Cokes, eating at McDonald's, listening to Beyonce, and watching *The Simpsons*, in reality, a host of barriers stand in the way of media corporations that want to make money from countries outside their own—even the largest, richest, most seasoned media conglomer-ates. Century upon century of cultural development, as well as national regulations, differences in infrastructure development, and international regulations, all stand be-tween content producers and audiences abroad. Of course, the media industries have also had decades of experience in developing ways to overcome these barriers.

Although the barriers we have discussed shape potential media flows in obvious and subtle ways, the priorities of media conglomerates, advertisers, and other powerful actors often clash with those cultural differences. In the early 1990s, media baron Rupert Murdoch developed a pan-Asian satellite service called Star that was designed to reach affluent, English-speaking viewers across Asia with programming from the United States, Europe, and Australia. Murdoch, however, quickly ran up against the incredible cultural diversity of the Asian Pacific-Rim region, as well as different time zones, com-munications infrastructures, and national political climates, all of which conspired to scuttle his plans for a worldwide satellite service. Undeterred, Murdoch decided to split his satellite service into different feeds serving different parts of Asia; partnered with local television producers, managers, and channels; and worked to bring his operations more in line with the technological and political realities on the ground in countries where he was most active.[6]

Rupert Murdoch's difficulties with Star TV in Asia point to both the complexities of global media operations and the persistence of large media conglomerates with aspirations to expand around the world. Although the lesson in Murdoch's case was that media conglomerates have to work with the grain of political, technological, and cultural realities in order to be successful, it is also the case that large media conglomerates have a sometimes powerful influence on audience tastes, including worldwide audience tastes. Perhaps the best example of this power comes from Hollywood films. For more than a century, Hollywood has spent lavishly on costuming, set design, special effects, and stars in an effort to develop and sustain a signature Hollywood "style" of moviemaking. Although this style has changed through the decades, it still retains widespread recognition around the world and tends to set the technical standards against which movies everywhere are measured. That is, even audiences in small countries with weak economies critique their domestic film industries for lacking the technical standards of Hollywood, despite the reality that those standards are prohibitively expensive. Global media operations, then, do not simply reflect the cultural diversity of the globe, nor do they impose their own cultural order on the globe; rather, they simultaneously *reflect and impose* global cultural patterns.

Global Promotions and Buzz

Worldwide distribution windows are increasingly being synchronized so that media audiences everywhere can consume the same texts at the same time. This strategy of simultaneous worldwide release is particularly evident in the film, gaming, and magazine industries and less so in popular music. In the television industry, simultaneous release is becoming more prevalent, but it is stymied by concerns about piracy and the lack of coordination among distributors and companies that aggregate content for consumers.

Simultaneous release permits distributors and aggregators to generate worldwide "buzz" about new releases, as potential consumers read blogs, watch television, read entertainment magazines, and talk with friends and fans abroad about the newest films and video games. The hope among industry insiders is that all of the talk and excitement that simultaneous release generates will get consumers everywhere more excited about the movie or game than they otherwise would be. Because promotions are centrally controlled and planned, they can also be cheaper to produce than if different promotional campaigns are developed in each market. Moreover, tie-ins such as toys and action figures can also be shipped and stocked at the same time all over the world, again cutting down potential costs. Finally, and perhaps most important, simultaneous global release can cut down on illegal copying, because most media piracy attempts to take advantage of lags in release times to sell pirated copies in a market before its official release.

With regard to globally distributed magazines, simultaneous release helps generate sales by promoting and reporting on prestigious global events. For instance, local versions of global fashion magazines that cover fashion week in Paris need to be released soon after the event, before potentially interested readers find the reports elsewhere. We could make similar observations about online content, newspaper reports, and television programs built around these kinds of seasonal, global cultural events. To take another example, news reports about the winner of the Cannes Film Festival are transmitted almost simultaneously around the world as soon as the announcement is made. Of course, digitization has helped make possible the simultaneous, worldwide distribution of news and entertainment media; at the same time, it has also created demand for immediate access that often drives consumers to turn to digital piracy as a way to obtain the latest content.

The synchronized release of certain kinds of media content adds to the perception that we are living in an increasingly globalized world, one in which tastes and trends transcend national boundaries. Of course, it's important to remember that these seemingly global phenomena fit the needs of the industries first and foremost: they help fight piracy, they cut promotional and advertising costs, they streamline promotional campaigns like action figure giveaways, and they generate higher sales in early windows than would staggered-release windows. Simultaneous release, then, is a clear example of a successful attempt by large media conglomerates to use their reach and their muscle to increase the popularity and sales of their products. The creation of buzz surrounding the newest releases is one strategy for trying to overcome cultural differences among media consumers worldwide, and one that avoids, rather than confronts, the problems associated with cultural difference. Other strategies seek much more actively to work with, rather than against, cultural realities.

International Co-Production

One of the most successful formulas for balancing cultural realities with the desire to exploit international markets has been international **co-production**, which refers to a business arrangement in which production staff and creative workers from more than one country work together on a project with the aim of distributing the final product in each participant's home market and, perhaps, beyond. Part of the rationale behind co-production is that, by drawing on creative talent from different global locations, the final product will be more culturally relevant in those places. Co-production has been particularly prominent in film and television and less common in popular music or print industries. Likewise, gaming has only recently begun to develop its own international co-production models, but this is primarily a way for smaller producers with different core competencies to work together to bypass the large game publishers, rather than a strategy to break into different international markets.[7]

In television, public service broadcasters in Europe, North America, and the Pacific Rim were among the first and most active proponents of international co-production, dating back to the early 1980s when many of them began to face competition from domestic commercial competitors. Co-production became a way for such broadcasters to defray costs and maintain production by working together with similar institutions in different countries. It also permitted producers from foreign nations to get around domestic import quotas, as most co-production treaties specified the percentage of domestic and foreign workers necessary for a co-production to "count" as domestic. In theory, co-production provides an opportunity for a multinational group of creative people to work together to create programming that transcends national differences. In practice, at least in the early years of this strategy, partners had difficulty imagining what kinds of television programs could overcome those differences, and they tended to rely heavily on stories derived from classic works of fiction or historical events that affected the world as a whole, or at least each country in the target market. The problem with these strategies was that they often led to such watered-down programming that few audience members found them interesting enough to watch. In Europe, this led observers to coin the derisive term "Euro-pudding" to describe the seemingly simplistic and unappetizing mixture of cultures and creative forces.

As the years have passed, however, co-producers have gotten better at identifying good partners and projects, and extensive work with one another has led to a degree of cross-cultural understanding among producers that results in more culturally relevant programs for viewers. In particular, Canadian companies and the public service broadcaster the Canadian Broadcasting Corporation (CBC), have become significant players on the international co-production market. Canadian commercial players are appealing to foreign co-production teams because of their close proximity to the US market and the track record of success that the Canadians have in getting programs picked up in the United States, which remains the largest and most lucrative national television market. Producers from around the world who hope to have their programming aired in the United States often seek out Canadian co-production partners for these reasons.[8]

Meanwhile, co-productions between the CBC and other broadcasters with public mandates, especially in Europe, are a way for these broadcasters to maintain their distinctive television storytelling techniques in an increasingly globalized and commercialized media environment. Let us be clear about this: public service broadcasting everywhere has been under assault for the past three decades because it is inherently national, not international, and it is publicly rather than commercially funded. Although commercial broadcasters and their proponents have long insisted that public service broadcasters do not offer much that is distinct in their programming and that they should be limited to only those types of television that commercial outlets cannot produce, Canadian media scholar Serra Tinic has demonstrated how very different public service broadcasting stories are from their commercial counterparts, even when they tackle the same topical material. Using the example of two made-for-television movies based on the global sex trade involving Eastern European women, Tinic shows how a commercial Canadian–United States co-production blames the entirety of the sex trade on a single individual, namely a Russian mob boss, while a co-production by the CBC and the UK public-service broadcaster Channel 4 on the same topic ultimately blames global capitalism, American business, and the United Nations for the trade. The comparison of these two television films nicely delineates the different reasons behind—and consequences of—commercial and noncommercial international co-productions.[9] Even in the realm of global media, it seems as though the mandate of a media outlet influences the kind of content we are likely to receive.

Dubbing and Subtitling

The translation—or language transfer—industries make it possible to watch films and television and read magazines from other language cultures. These industries have a long history of translating works into many different languages, along with well-developed industry structures and main players in most countries. At first glance, the process of dubbing or subtitling may seem simple and mechanical—and, indeed, the common way of referring to these processes within the American television industries as "language transfer" encourages such a mechanical view of the process. As anyone who has ever tried to translate a poem or a piece of short fiction can tell you, however, translation is as much an art as a skill. In fact, subtitling and dubbing have a significant impact on the success or failure of imported media culture.

As with almost everything we've studied thus far in the commercial media industries, the degree of attention and care that dubbing and subtitling receive depends on how important the commercial success of the particular program is for the company that pays for dubbing. According to one often-told anecdote, during the 1980s Pepsi began marketing its soda drinks in China, but the market was not yet a large consumer of Pepsi, and so it made little sense to spend heavily on developing new marketing campaigns or even translating the American campaign. Consequently, the company translated its slogan "Come Alive With the Pepsi Generation" as "Pepsi Brings Your Ancestors Back From the Grave."[10] How this alleged mistranslation may have affected sales is uncertain, but the case clearly demonstrates the importance of good translation.

Beginning in the 1990s, as cable television was introduced across Europe and Latin America and US cable channels began expanding into those regions, good translations became more important, as well as more costly, for the distributors. Rather than handle translations in-house and in the exporting country, major television distributors began to outsource those activities to local firms that employed people with a better grasp of the local language, as well as better writing skills. Unlike in our conventional view of outsourcing, however, it actually proved more expensive for distributors to ship these jobs abroad. One prominent, early example of this process was the dubbing of the animated series *Duckman* (1994–1997), an irreverent and profane cartoon that was the precursor to *Beavis and Butthead* and *South Park* and was also one of the first hits on USA Network. Turner Broadcasting, the owner and distributor of Cartoon Network, had recently launched a channel in Mexico and was trying to build that channel's reputation around the series. Turner hired a local firm that subsequently brought in a group of writers and comics not only to translate the words of the script but also to rewrite the script for local references, tastes, and sense of humor. The subsequent popularity of the series in Mexico led other distributors quickly to follow suit.

As we saw in Chapter 8, the trade in media products takes place between two distinct entities—distributors, or sellers, and aggregators, or buyers. Even when these two entities are owned by the same conglomerate the seller and the buyer must still agree on who will pay for the dubbing. This is no small issue, either, as top-of-the-line dubbing can cost as much as one-third of a distributors' profits. Typically, in larger language communities in which distributors expect lucrative sales, the distributors will cover most or all of the dubbing costs. This is because distributors expect to sell into multiple markets that speak the same language and to sell the dubbed version to several buyers in each market. In smaller linguistic markets, especially those countries that do not pay high license fees for media imports, the buyers will shoulder a larger burden of translation costs. Today, most Spanish-language translation for US products comes from firms in Miami, allowing companies to draw on local voice actors from numerous Latin American nations and keep a pulse on both US and Latin American cultural and linguistic trends.

Translation costs also differ within countries and firms, depending on the type and quality of the translation. Subtitling is generally quite a bit cheaper and quicker than dubbing, because it does not require a studio to hire multiple voice actors and it's technologically simpler. Dubbing, meanwhile, not only tends to be more carefully translated but also requires multiple actors to come into the studio to voice different characters. Often, at least in European countries, prominent local theater and film actors take on dubbing projects during the off-season. For instance, a well-known local actor might voice Clint Eastwood in all imported Clint Eastwood films; if that actor happened to be unavailable, the process would have to wait until he had time. This not only adds to the expense of dubbing but also leads to the common practice of certain dubbing actors being associated with certain Hollywood stars—although the demands of the industry are altering this practice.

In most markets nowadays, new Hollywood films tend to be subtitled in the theaters, because the timing of release **windows** among distributors does not leave enough time for translation studios to dub them. This tends to be the case even in countries in which audiences prefer dubbing to subtitling due to conventional, historical practice. That is, particularly in Europe, different nationalities and language cultures tend to have a preference for *either* subtitling *or* dubbing; this preference developed over the twentieth century and depended upon a variety of cultural factors. In Denmark, for instance, dubbing is generally viewed as something done for children's programming; adults, most Danes feel, can read subtitles. By contrast, in Hungary, where the language is radically different from English and other Germanic languages, both adults and children tend to prefer dubbing. These cultural differences in translation preferences, however, are being erased by the needs of the Hollywood studios to have precise control over blockbuster release dates.

In television, historical preferences for dubbing or subtitling still tend to prevail because release dates are not as carefully timed as they are for theatrical releases. In dubbing countries, a range of qualities and prices tend to be available, including "cable-quality," "broadcast-quality," and "theatrical-quality" dubbing, as well as subtitling. The quality of the dubbing is determined by expectations of how popular the import will be among viewers. Unsurprisingly, these expectations are often self-fulfilling: the more one spends on dubbing, the better the quality and the more likely audiences will watch.

The translation industries are currently undergoing significant change, in part due to the increasing coordination of release windows for both television and film but also due to technological changes. One of the biggest problems with dubbing has always been the mismatch between image and soundtrack, something that has led to endless mockery of Chinese "Kung Fu" movies among American audiences. Digitization, however, promises to reduce, even eliminate, this dissonance, because it can allow for the subtle manipulation of both audio and video tracks to match each other's timing more precisely. In addition, high-end dubbers often try hard to write translated scripts in a way that reduces the difference in lip and mouth movements between the original and the translated languages. Together, these innovations seek to reduce and perhaps, one day, even eliminate the traces of translation that today are so obvious in dubbed media texts.

Localization

Dubbing and subtitling are specific examples of localization, as are rewriting and rerecording popular songs in the local language with local pop stars. Unlike co-production, which is generally limited to the film and television industries, media industries of all types make use of localization.

Localization stems from the recognition that all media products, even those designed by global conglomerates, have to compete with a different and unique mixture of rivals in every local market. Consequently, global media organizations tend to delegate operations in each market to local decision-makers, who sometimes have a good deal of control over the production and distribution of content. At the same time, however, decision-makers at the parent company want to maintain some degree of brand consistency and quality across all markets. Different organizations solve this dilemma of how to retain consistency while providing enough "play" to remain competitive in numerous different markets in different ways. Disney, for instance, tends to run almost all decisions through headquarters before they are finally approved, even down to such details as how each of its characters will sound in each market, while MTV allows local executives in lucrative markets a fairly free hand in programming, talent selection, scheduling, and so forth.

At a minimum, however, most global media companies offer some degree of local control to decision-makers once they have been trained in the practices and cultures of the parent company. Fashion magazines, for instance, must of necessity localize their content because of fashion differences and different competitive mixes in each market, though some degree of global consistency in content and branding is also necessary to take advantage of global fashion trends and advertiser dollars. Before they are allowed to take the reins of the local version of the magazine, local editors of fashion magazines such as *Marie Claire*, *Elle*, and *Vogue* are sent to train at the magazine's headquarters, where they learn how to design photo layouts, stories, and overall issue themes that fit with the magazine's general brand. In addition, editors around the world participate in planning each new issue, again ensuring consistency across locally branded editions.

Localized versions of global fashion magazines offer good examples for exploring the patterns of similarity and difference in media content that localization strategies create. Fashion magazines feature a combination of fashion photo shoots, fashion-related articles, and news and gossip about the fashion industry, along with a large amount of advertising. The centerpiece of each issue is known as the "fashion well," which consists of about 40 to 50 pages of photo shoots, uninterrupted by advertising, featuring the latest fashion designs. Each photo layout is titled and themed to give it coherence. While this overall structure remains consistent across each local edition, local editors have some discretion over which specific photographs to use, how to lay them out on the page, and how to translate the sense of the theme and the title of each photo shoot. Meanwhile, both feature articles and fashion news include local content, as well as material that appears in other local editions. In other words, much of the *content* of the local version comes either from local fashion writers or from selections that local editors make from a range of foreign content options, while more senior editors and executives at the magazine's headquarters largely set the format.[11]

This replacement of imported forms with local content happens in other industries as well and is at the heart of what it means to "localize" media. In television, one of the most common ways that this localization happens is through **format sales**, such as the multiple national versions of the reality show *Big Brother*. In film and popular music, this phenomenon is less clearly directed by centralized institutions seeking to push their content abroad and more by media producers seeking to import formulas from foreign cultures. For example, musicians around the world have found rap music to be an effective vehicle for their own creative expression, and the adaptation of rap music cannot be dismissed as mere copying of foreign music. Still, the decision to import foreign cultural forms, such as rap, don't simply derive from producer's creative visions alone; instead, the distribution circuits of the global media industries brought rap music to these places in the first place, and only later were they adapted for domestic purposes.[12] To put it another way, there is a reason that, say, black Colombian music has not become the preferred format for youthful rebellion around the world the way that rap music has, and the reason for the discrepancy is that no global media industry exists to exploit black Colombian music. This interaction between coercion and choice when it comes to localizing foreign formats is crucial to understanding the cultural consequences of globalization, which we examine at the end of this chapter.

The situation of local adaptation of global formats is somewhat different in film as well. As with music, local creative talent tends to "pull" movie-making formulas from abroad to help with storytelling and visual engagement. In some instances, these directors, writers, and actors have trained in Hollywood and made their names there. For instance, the global blockbuster *Red Cliff*, produced and created in mainland China by successful Hollywood director John Woo, tells a distinctly Chinese story about one of the foundational historical myths in Chinese society. The story is told in such a manner (with clear villains and heroes, a climactic battle scene, and romantic overtones among male and female characters) and uses such a variety of visual techniques (including the Chinese and global cinema star system; the construction of elaborate, historically accurate sets; and the use of special effects and spectacular battles to grab the viewer's attention) that it is clearly identifiable as a global blockbuster, because it follows a formula that we have come to associate with those kinds of films.

Outsourcing

Each of these examples of strategies used by media industries to overcome the challenges of creating media for global audiences demonstrates how economic conditions have been altered by globalization and how these alterations have affected the practices of media distribution and production. When it comes to production, a related force—outsourcing—has also wrought profound changes. **Outsourcing** refers to the process whereby certain elements of production are completed somewhere away from the primary production in order to take advantage of cheaper labor conditions and government subsidies. For instance, in 2013, only 65 percent of Hollywood movies designed primarily for a US market were filmed in the United States.[13] Typically, only certain elements of production are outsourced, particularly those elements that require the greatest degree of labor and the slightest degree of creativity.

Much as in the general economy, outsourcing of media production has generated a good deal of heated debate in the United States. At issue are the loss of high-paying, unionized American jobs; the quality of production work done cheaply abroad; and human rights concerns about underpaid laborers in poor countries. Toby Miller et al., for instance, claim that global outsourcing has led to a "new international division of cultural labor," whereby Hollywood contributes to the disappearance of cultural diversity worldwide, as cultural workers abroad are forced to labor away on Hollywood projects rather than making their own, culturally distinct media.[14] Tinic, however, has discovered that television producers in Vancouver, one of the main locations of **runaway production**, use the money that they earn from working on Hollywood projects to tell their own stories that are distinct to the region. Still, it is quite apparent that outsourcing has weakened the positions of the various creative guilds and professional associations vis-à-vis media industry executives and management.[15]

MEDIA GLOBALIZATION IN THE GLOBAL SOUTH

Media globalization has largely been seen as a phenomenon dominated by large Western conglomerates working under commercial mandates. However, the spread of digital distribution—especially Internet distribution—has created opportunities for media produced outside of the global centers of power to gain audiences from around the world. In particular, media industries located in the Global South, or those nations and cultures that lag behind the developed nations in terms of wealth, life expectancy, and the availability of utilities and technology, might stand to gain from the cultivation of transnational digital markets that could help fund domestic media production. Most of these nations have traditionally been consumers rather than producers of modern media, but there are signs that the tides may be changing for these smaller media producers and distributors.

The circulation and consumption of media texts that are not driven by powerful global media conglomerates, or what we might call **alternative globalization**, takes place across all media industries, typically through informal, and sometimes illegal, channels. Popular music acts from Africa, for instance, have their recordings pirated and sold across South America and the Indian subcontinent. Meanwhile, alongside the legitimate and lucrative worldwide distribution of popular films produced in India (known as Bollywood), pirated copies are sold in informal marketplaces around the world. Because these transactions take place in illegal black and gray markets, they are usually not monitored or reported by any agency, making it hard to study or characterize them in any systematic way. However, as the example of Bollywood demonstrates, in many instances, in order for media industries from the Global South to gain a presence on the world scene, they must be built on strong, legitimate national media industries. Without such a base to support these industries, they cannot produce media in the first place.

One prominent example of the promises and perils of global, digital distribution for media industries in the Global South is the film industry in Nigeria, often referred to as "Nollywood." Based on the number of hours of film produced each year, Nollywood is the third-largest movie producer in the world, and its products, known as "video films," circulate around the globe, especially in the Global South where illegally pirated copies feature prominently in media stalls at large market bazaars. Nollywood producers have perfected a business and production model in which costs are contained by using extremely fast shooting schedules, usually one or two weeks, and cheap production techniques, such as shooting on video rather than film. Films are released on DVD for home viewing and in small viewing houses simultaneously, and they quickly spread through piracy throughout the country, the region, and the world. Only in the days and weeks before they lose control over the distribution of pirated copies can Nollywood producers make money, but this is enough to keep the industry afloat.[16]

Despite the popularity of Nollywood and the visibility it has received among industry insiders and academics, the business model is difficult to reproduce elsewhere because of its heavy reliance on domestic revenues. Still, the line between legitimate and illegitimate global media markets is somewhat fuzzy, and other media companies with varying degrees of legitimacy sit up and take notice of developments such as Nollywood as they seek to understand, organize, and exploit the markets that Nollywood video films have opened up. For instance, in New York and elsewhere in the United States, the US direct-to-home satellite service Dish Network has begun carrying Afrotainment, a digital channel built around the popularity of Nollywood films, and iRokoTV.com has begun a subscription streaming site dedicated to Nollywood videos that fans everywhere can sign up for.

What the Nollywood example makes clear is that digital *distribution* opens opportunities for media industries in the Global South to attract consumers from around the world. However, because many of those distribution outlets either work outside the legitimate economy or haven't yet developed viable business models, it is difficult for those industries to generate profits from abroad. Consequently, only the largest and richest nations in the Global South are capable, at present, of using media globalization to expand their commercial media industries.

THE COMMERCIAL AND SOCIAL CONSEQUENCES OF MEDIA GLOBALIZATION

Expanded Markets and Innovations

Imagine hundreds of millions of untapped Chinese media consumers. They have little access to media and entertainment, but their difficult life conditions make them ideal candidates for the kinds of escapist pleasures we associate with many media products. They may not have much money to spend individually, but, as a group, they represent a huge potential market. They are, in many ways, a media market yearning to be tapped. Such are the ideas—one might say delusions—that drive media organizations to seek new markets for their products, markets that can allow them to continue to exploit those products in more and more places for longer and longer periods of time.

However, as we have suggested, globalization of the media industries entails more than savvy salesmanship and bookkeeping: globalization is both an economic and a cultural process, and these two forces are just as often in conflict as they are in harmony. The early dreams of media moguls luring hundreds of millions of new consumers simply by setting up a satellite feed have been replaced by a range of institutional practices that work *with* the grain of cultural difference rather than against it. This has led to a growing variety of international opportunities for producers, distributors, and exhibitors of media content.

It has long been a truism that American media corporations exported a good deal to international markets but imported little. The exception to this rule is the popular music industry, which has long imported musical styles, talent, and recorded music from abroad. Generally speaking, however, American media imports have traditionally been quite low: foreign films have tended to show up only in specialty theaters, mostly in larger cities; television channels in the United States have typically imported only about 2 percent of their entire program schedules; and only a handful of foreign newspapers and magazines have generally been available, particularly those in languages other than English that are aimed at recent immigrants.

Today, however, all of this is changing, and television has been perhaps the most profoundly affected medium. Reality formats created in Europe and Australia have found their way onto cable channels and even prime-time network TV. The powerhouse program of the early 2000s, Fox Broadcasting's *American Idol*, for instance, is a format of the British series *Pop Idol*. Localized versions of scripted foreign series have become commonplace as well, including such well-known series as *The Office* and *Jane the Virgin*. Foreign production practices have also begun to show up in less obvious places such as the efforts in the mid-2000s by American soap opera producers to incorporate the storytelling techniques of Latin American telenovelas in an effort to attract both young and Latino audiences. In all of these instances, we see television producers trying to take advantage of innovations made elsewhere to create programming that is fresh and appealing.

Not only do today's television programs incorporate foreign styles and production practices, but they also are increasingly funded with foreign money, with overseas investors picking up distribution rights in their own markets and sometimes beyond. Media industries in other countries, meanwhile, have been dealing with these kinds of globalizing pressures for decades. Although innovation may be the positive side of this coin, the negative side has been characterized as the loss of one's distinct national culture and its replacement with a global commercial culture that values consumption over everything else. New media technologies such as satellite television, Internet distribution, and digitization in general have only sped up these processes of change, leading to a great deal of concern and speculation about the possible deleterious effects of media globalization among scholars, policymakers, and concerned citizens. From a practical standpoint, however, the media economies of the world's nations have now become so entangled that it would be extremely difficult to begin to pry them apart. In many ways, the genie of globalization is already well out of the bottle.

Cultural Imperialism Versus Hybridity

Concerns about the influence of foreign cultural values, particularly consumerism, have figured prominently in debates about media globalization, particularly in policy debates about limiting the import of American film and television programming, that have taken place across the globe. Such concerns about **cultural imperialism**, or the domination of local cultural values by imported American values, are common in academic and popular discussions about media globalization. These concerns are rooted in the worldwide dominance of Western media institutions, which, as we noted at the beginning of the chapter, goes back more than a century. In addition, concerns about the media industry have often formed against the backdrop of American military actions abroad, which until World War II was officially involved in conquering foreign territory, or imperialism.

Thus when people in other lands see children in China flocking to McDonald's for their birthday parties or poor workers in Nigeria foregoing food to buy Adidas shoes, it is no wonder that they worry about the serious negative consequences of exporting American media, its media system, and the values they contain. At the same time, the globalization of media points to and encourages other forms of cultural interactions that we might view more positively.

Hybridity, for instance, refers to a cultural process whereby different cultures interact and change over time. Rather than being anything destructive or new, hybridity theory suggests that all cultures are hybrids of prior cultural mixing going back centuries. In some versions of this theory, hybridity is seen as inherently positive: it is thought to make all of us less provincial, less xenophobic, and more open to encountering other people and points of view. On the other hand, many observers also point out that, while most of the world has to contend with large amounts of foreign media culture from America, Americans encounter little foreign media and very few challenges to their cultural insularity.

Hybridity, then, is not a simple mixing of equal parts of different cultures but occurs against the backdrop of significant inequalities among the nations of the world and their media industries. The cultural change that results is one in which certain elements of American or Western popular culture are integrated into the importing culture, while other elements are not. The children's television series *Sesame Street* is a good example of hybrid cultural change. It has been remade in more than 140 markets with local writers, producers, puppets, and stories that reflect the local culture and its values. At the same time, most versions of the series also advocate Western ideals of racial integration and tolerance, the importance of community, and the innocence of childhood that may not necessarily be indigenous to the local culture.

Connecting Dispersed Communities

Another consequence of media globalization has been the establishment and maintenance of **diasporic communities**, or groups of people, often defined by ethnicity or national origin, who live in various different countries but maintain cultural connections with one another. Chinese and Indian diasporas are probably the largest communities globally, and in country after country, one can find media outlets tailored to these communities, as well as a vibrant cultural exchange among them. Such media serve generations within the diaspora in different ways. Those who grew up in China or India before emigrating may embrace the international availability of media as a way to maintain connections with a familiar culture. Their children, however, who might have no firsthand experience with their parents' culture, might use media to learn about their parents' culture yet particularly embrace different media that give voice to their own experiences of negotiating among cultures.

Various changes in the media industries have altered the availability of media for diasporic communities. In the case of the Indian diaspora living in the United States in the 1970s, visual media were primarily circulated through film prints exhibited in community centers. This required the diasporic community to come together physically to enjoy familiar media. In the 1980s, these screenings gave way to videocassettes that were often circulated through South Asian grocery stores. In some places that had large diasporic communities, weekly public access television series were produced and distributed to other communities as well. In the 1990s, the availability of satellite television made it possible to receive packages of Indian television channels around the world. Also, late in the decade, the technology boom led to many India-related dotcom companies designed to aid members of the Indian diaspora who sought to connect with Indian culture. The Internet enabled real-time engagement with the films, songs, and controversies of the moment, eliminating the lag time of analog technologies. Thus shifts in technology that allow affordable international distribution and changes in industry practices that recognize the commercial value of diasporic and international audiences have reconfigured media content.

In addition, media globalization can allow groups that have little historical connection to imagine themselves as members of a larger diasporic community. Because of the widespread adoption of satellite and over-the-air television channels devoted to indigenous populations in various parts of the world, a small but significant international trade in indigenous television programming has developed. Though produced for a minority population within a single nation, indigenous programs sometimes are screened for viewers far across the world. According to some scholars, this kind of minority-to-minority communication, without the intervention of large Western institutions or industries, has the potential to increase cultural pride and political coordination for minority groups everywhere.

CONCLUSION

Undoubtedly, globalization has increased consumer choices in certain parts of the world, although access to media and communication technologies, as well as domestic and global media culture, are quite circumscribed around much of the globe. A good deal of debate exists, however, about the social and cultural consequences of those choices, particularly the degree to which those options merely increase consumerism around the world and undermine global cultural diversity and integrity.

Perhaps the most important thing to remember about globalization is that, in order to be profitable, globally circulated media must fit the demands of both the large corporations that push media abroad and local consumers who pull foreign media and consume them. As we have suggested throughout this chapter, large corporations try extremely hard to mold the desires of transnational consumer segments to fit their needs, but these efforts are only occasionally successful. Consequently, the contemporary media industries have developed a wide range of business practices designed to take advantage of, rather than destroy, cultural differences.

Finally, we have seen that significant debates exist about the social consequences of media globalization. Although some insist the globalization is destroying the world's cultural diversity, others claim it is preserving diversity. As with much we have discussed throughout these pages, we believe that such positions are too extreme. We do not want to dismiss or apologize for the power of massive media conglomerates to shape society and culture, but neither do we want to underestimate the resilience, adaptability, and stubbornness of cultural practices and traditions. Ultimately, the social and cultural consequences of media globalization vary among different countries, different groups within countries, and even different individuals.

QUESTIONS

1. Imagine that a major US media figure, such as Zac Efron or Taylor Swift, has hired you to help him or her appeal to more international markets in the future. What specific strategies might you recommend in order to localize his or her media content? Would certain aspects remain the same while others change based on different markets and why? Think about the different ways localization can occur in a variety of media industries and across a number of different media goods.

2. You are the president of a US television network and have the opportunity to purchase a hit Australian television show that has already been successfully sold in a number of different international markets. What factors would you need to consider and what changes might you have to make to help this show be successful for your network? For each change you identify, explain the reasons why you would make the change.

3. Try to identify two non–US-produced media goods that have achieved success in the United States. Your media examples can be from different industries and should include one that was successful without further translation (or adaptation), while the other may have been adapted for the US market. What factors do you think helped determine the relative differences in global movement for these two goods?

4. Discuss the advantages and disadvantages of a windowed release versus a simultaneous release, as discussed here and in Chapter 8. Think of a media good and then consider what a company might gain by staggering release dates around the world

instead of releasing it everywhere at the same time. What might be sacrificed with a simultaneous release—and vice versa? How does "buzz" factor into both strategies?

FURTHER READING

A wide range of books and articles exist on media globalization, only a fraction of which we can include here. For more on Western domination of world media markets, see Miller et al.'s *Global Hollywood 2* (London: BFI Publishing, 2008), and Daya Kishan Thussu's *International Communication: a Reader* (London: Routledge, 2010). For an example of globalization from below, see Moradewun A. Adejunmobi's "Nigerian Video Film as Minor Transnational Practice," *Postcolonial Text* 3 (2007). For studies of out-sourcing in the media industries, see *Global Hollywood 2* and Ted Tschang and Andrea Goldstein's "Production and Political Economy in the Animation Industry: Why Insourcing And Outsourcing Occur," DRUID Summer Conference, 2004, http://www .druid.dk/conferences/summer2004/papers/ds2004–92.pdf.

The breadth of work on globalization in the television and film industries is too numerous to do justice to here, but for news media see Daya Kishan Thussu's *News As Entertainment: The Rise of Global Infotainment* (Thousand Oaks, Calif: SAGE, 2007), and for the globalization of rap music see Tony Mitchell's edited volume *Global Noise; Rap and Hip-Hop Outside the USA* (Middletown, Conn.: Wesleyan University Press, 2001).

NOTES

1. The figures come from Kerry Segrave, *American Films Abroad: Hollywood's Domi-nation of the World's Movie Screens* (Jefferson, N.C.: McFarland & Company, 1997), and from the Motion Picture Association of America "Theatrical Market Statistics," 2013,http://www.mpaa.org/wp-content/uploads/2014/03/MPAA-Theatrical-Market-Statistics-2013_032514-v2.pdf (accessed September 10, 2014).
2. "Dominating the World Music Industry," *BBC Worldwide*, http://www.bbc.co.uk/ worldservice/specials/1042_globalmusic/page3.shtml (accessed September 17, 2014).
3. *Advertising Age*, May 4, 2015.
4. Uta G. Poiger, "Postwar German Popular Music: Americanization, the Cold War, and the Post-Nazi Heimat," in *Music and German National Identity*, ed. Celia Applegate and Pamela Potter (Chicago: University of Chicago Press, 2002), 134–150.
5. Timothy Havens, "Globalization and the Generic Transformation of Telenovelas," in *Thinking Outside the Box: Television Genres in Transition*, ed. Gary Edgerton and Brian Rose (University of Kentucky Press, 2005), 271–292.
6. Michael Curtin, "Murdoch's Dilemma, or 'What's the Price of TV in China?'" *Media, Culture & Society* 27 (2005), 155–175.
7. Phil Elliott, "Is Co-production the Future?" Gamesindustry.biz, June 1, 2009, http:// www.gamesindustry.biz/articles/is-co-production-the-future (accessed February 25, 2010).

8. Serra A. Tinic, *On Location: Canada's Television Industry in a Global Market* (Buffalo: University of Toronto Press, 2005).

9. Serra A. Tinic, "Between the Public and the Private: Television Drama Global Partnerships in the Neo-Network Era," in *Television Studies After TV*, ed. Graeme Turner and Jinna Tay (London: Taylor & Francis, 2009), 65–74.

10. Michael Zakkour, "China's Golden Week: A Good Time To Make Sure You Don't 'Bite The Wax Tadpole,'" *Forbes*, October 2, 2014, http://www.forbes.com/sites/michaelzakkour/2014/10/02/chinas-national-day-golden-week-a-good-time-to-make-sure-you-dont-bite-the-wax-tadpole/ (accessed February 16, 2015).

11. Brian Morean, "More Than Just a Fashion Magazine," *Current Sociology* 54 (2006), 725–744.

12. Tony Mitchell (ed.), *Global Noise: Rap and Hip-Hop Outside the USA* (Middletown, Conn.: Wesleyan University Press, 2001).

13. Adrian McDonald, "2013 Feature Film Production Report," FilmLA, 2014. http://www.hollywoodreporter.com/sites/default/files/custom/Embeds/2013%20Feature%20Study%20Corrected%20no%20Watermark%5B2%5D.pdf (accessed February 15, 2015).

14. Miller et al., *Global Hollywood* (London: BFI Publications, 2005).

15. Serra A. Tinic, *On Location: Canada's Television Industry in a Global Market* (Buffalo: University of Toronto Press, 2005).

16. Onookome Okome, "Nollywood: Africa at the Movies," *Film International* 5, no. 4 (2007), 4–9.

Glossary

Above-the-line Major personnel involved in the production of film and television; those seen as primarily responsible for the creative processes involved in production such as directors, actors, writers, and producers. Historically, Hollywood accounting forms used a line to separate these specialized creative costs from other technical and production costs, and the workers associated with these tasks came to be known as above-the-line workers. *See also* **Below-the-line**.

Access The ability, or right, to be able to connect to communications networks without undue costs or difficulties. Originally associated with cheap or free telephone service in home, the notion of access now extends to all forms of digital communication as well.

Advance payments A common tactic used by media industries to lure creative talent and to get the benefit of their services for a set time. These payments are often driven by the expectation this payment will enable the talent to complete the commissioned work, such as a script or album. It is intended to be remuneration for future work, and talent typically does not receive royalty or payment for the good until the label, studio, or publisher has earned profits equivalent to the advance.

Affiliates The individual television and/or radio stations that make up a broadcast network.

Agency The amount of control media industry workers have over how and what they do, allowing them to be meaningful actors in how their companies operate and in the creation of media products.

Aggregation/aggregators The activity/those involved in the process of making finalized media goods available for consumers, whether through a film theater, a television station, a radio station, digital download or stream, or a retail store.

A-list/B-list issue A peculiarity of the media industries that addresses the complicated decision-making necessary in hiring talent for media products. The financial benefits of selecting a well-known talent (A-list) to star in or make media productions over a lesser-known talent (B-list), who may offer just as good of a performance for a smaller salary, are not absolute or consistent, and choosing either option entails a high degree of risk.

Alternative globalization Forms of media globalization that take place outside the dominant players in the global media industries, especially nations with modest economies and media industries located in the Global South.

Analog media Media using a nondigital method of recording that stores signals in a manner that represents the message using a direct facsimile (copy) or an "analogy" of the original (e.g., audiotapes, vinyl records).

Antitrust regulations Laws, handled in the United States by the Department of Justice with the Federal Trade Commission, intended to prevent too much industry consolidation.

Ars longa Term used to highlight the longevity of media industry products due to the ability of these products to generate revenue for the studios/creators long after the original release/production date.

Art for art's sake An attitude pursued by many creative workers in the media industry whose primary incentive is not necessarily to make media goods that are likely to make money but to make the goods they are particularly inspired to produce.

Artificial scarcity Strategy employed by the media industries designed to control the availability of media texts in the hopes that demand will increase if the product is not readily available. Artificial scarcity includes practices such as **windowing** (see Ch. 8) and **price differentiation** that help determine where, when, for how long, and at what cost people may experience a media product.

Auxiliary practices The vast range of secondary roles necessary for the creation and distribution of media content. Although these media workers are not directly involved in the production and/or distribution of media content, they play a vital role in maintaining and supporting the infrastructure necessary for the smooth running of the media entity. Craft services, accounting, and legal services are some examples of the myriad roles that fall within this category.

Below-the-line Workers directly involved in the technical aspects of film and television production. Below-the-line personnel handle the day-to-day tasks of producing a movie or television show. Though below-the-line jobs are often overlooked when people consider creative professions in the media industries, they do involve creative practice. *See also* **above-the-line**.

Block booking A practice once used by film studios that required independent theaters to agree to take a block of studio-selected films (often films that were not very desirable) if they wanted to get the big new studio films with top talent.

Blockbusters High-budget media goods that are generally accompanied by lots of hype, extensive marketing, and promotion budgets and feature popular and well-known (A-list) stars. The term is most commonly used in relation to mega-spectacle films intended to generate huge sums at the box office; however, the concept of the "blockbuster" is relevant in other media industries as well. More often than not, blockbusters are also part of a movie franchise consisting of sequels, merchandising such as toys and other licensed agreements, books, and even amusement park rides.

Branded entertainment The practice of creating a media good that primarily serves as a promotional tool for a specific product or brand. It is an advertising strategy that weaves the product being advertised into the content of the good and helps to explicitly highlight the features of the product. The annual *Victoria's Secret Fashion Show* is a good example of branded entertainment on television; sometimes called "advertorial" content in print.

Bundling The practice of combining individual media goods and selling them together as a combined unit. In the music industry, the practice of selling albums containing multiple songs is one example of bundling, as is the method of cable providers selling packages of channels.

Business models Strategies that companies adopt with the objective of meeting income and profit goals. Revenue models help dictate the business policies that a company implements.

Casualization An increasingly common work arrangement where employees work on a project-by-project basis, rather than as year-round, full-time employees.

Circumscribed agency Perspective that assumes that the choices we make in our lives are not wholly our own, but neither are they simply imposed on us by outside forces.

Citizen journalists News audiences, armed with Internet access, search engines, etc., who dig up stories that mainstream media are not reporting, underreporting, or misreporting.

Closed hardware system Internal architecture of some technology products. Closed hardware systems are those that do not allow any modification from users and rely primarily on nonstandard software and parts that make adjusting those parts difficult. Closed hardware systems tend to be **proprietary**, with the manufacturer controlling most, if not all, of the technology and software of the product. The Apple iPhone is a good example of a closed system.

Commercial mandate When media industries are primarily driven by a profit-making objective. Companies operating within a commercial mandate place significant focus on obtaining high earnings and profits from their media goods, which in turn influences the decision-making within the organization and the type of media goods it produces.

Commercial media *See* **Commercial mandate**, Chapter 2.

Common carriers A legal term originally used to describe companies that were licensed to transport people or freight. In most cases, common carriers received exclusive licenses to operate such businesses and were thus subject to certain restrictions and regulations, such as the duty to transport people or goods without discrimination and at reasonable rates. The term was later expanded to include companies who provide public utility services (i.e., goods deemed to be essential to the public at large), such as electricity, gas, and telecommunications.

Company voice An advertising strategy aimed at advancing corporate image, rather than focusing on the attributes of the product. It was common during the sponsorship era of broadcasting.

Conditions The economic, regulatory, and technological realities that media industries operate within and that are larger than any individual entity or organization.

Conglomeration The combining together of several smaller business entities under a single corporate umbrella. Conglomeration is attractive to media companies because it allows for greater operational efficiencies, spreads risk, and reduces competition for the corporation. Conglomeration can involve companies working within the same industry or across different market sectors.

Consolidation of ownership The reduction of competitors to just a few media companies. Consolidation of ownership often leads to an **oligopoly** market.

Constructed audience An imaginary construct to describe the intended targets of media content. The constructed audience factors into whether a particular media good gets produced and into creative and distribution decisions throughout its development.

Content regulation The laws and guidelines that limit the type of content that can be broadcast to the general public. More specifically, these are regulations that seek to limit the broadcast of content that is deemed "obscene, indecent or profane."

Continuous media goods Media goods that are persistently produced. Continuous media goods are often supported by advertising or through a subscription to a bundle of goods.

Convergence A concept describing the new connections among media enabled by digitization. Connections include technical language, cultural and technological forms, media products, communication systems, and the media industries themselves.

Co-production A business arrangement in which production staff and creative workers from more than one country or organization work together on a project.

Copyright Legal protection for creators of original works (e.g., music, poetry, books) from those who might distribute others' work, passing it off as their own and profiting from it.

Cost plus A system used to finance the creation of television programs in which a producer brings an idea to a network, and, if the network wants to develop the idea, the network pays the cost of production plus a fee or profit to the producer.

Creative autonomy The degree of individual agency one can exercise in developing one's creative vision. The term applies mainly to creative workers in the media industries.

Creative commons (cc) A nonprofit movement, founded by Lawrence Lessig, responding to the possibilities for both sharing and producing digital media. Those who establish a Creative Commons license for their work waive some of their rights in order to more easily allow others to share and build upon their work while still maintaining some rights.

Creative practices The functions and roles of media workers directly involved in the creation of media content.

Creators The people who hold the guiding creative vision for a media good.

Cross-ownership regulation Rules that prevent the common ownership of companies in multiple media industries, such as owning a newspaper and broadcast station in the same city.

Cross-promotion A marketing strategy whereby a company markets the products of another company. Although cross-promotion can occur between two different corporate entities, media corporations most often rely on cross-promoting within the same corporate group (e.g., if 21st Century Fox, the parent company of 20th Century

Fox studio and the Fox television network used its television network to promote an upcoming movie from its movie studio).

Cross-subsidize Economic strategy of using profits from one business activity to cover losses in another, a common practice in media **conglomerates** (see Ch. 2).

Crowdfunding An emergent funding model for media (and other types of projects), in which creators propose projects and raise the funds to develop them by collecting money from a broad base of private individuals. These individuals, who are most commonly accessed through the web, often contribute fairly small amounts, but the large number of participants allows creators to raise enough money to finance production.

Crunch time A period of work, usually comprising a few weeks before the launch of a new media product, when employees regularly work long hours and weekends in order to finish the project on time.

Cultural determinism Belief that the cultural uses of a technology determine how that technology influences industry and society.

Cultural imperialism The theory that media globalization leads to the destruction of local cultural values, replacing them with those pervasive in media exported from other, typically more powerful, countries.

Cultural interventionist policy Policies that seek to encourage voices other than those of commercially motivated media and can take the form of content and structural regulations. These policies encourage the production of media believed to have some sort of prosocial effect.

Culture The artifacts of expressive culture that the media industries produce (e.g. films, newspapers) as well as to the specific social practices, values, and mores, associated with a particular group of people.

Deficit financing A television-industry process whereby production studios lose money in making series during the first few years—even if their show is a hit. While it loses money making the show, however, the studio (which licenses rather than sells the show to a network) maintains a possibility of other revenue streams through **secondary markets**.

Delivery technologies Technologies used in delivering media content to audiences.

Demographic A narrow subsection or segment of the entire population. *See also* **Niche** (Ch. 1).

Deterministic Term for approaches to studying media industries that try to explain their behavior in terms of a single aspect, such as the industry's mandate or technology. For example, those who view ownership as deterministic explain the behavior of media industries as entirely related to who owns the company. The Industrialization of Culture framework is deliberately nondeterministic. *See also* **Technological determinism** (Ch. 6).

Development costs The costs incurred during the initial stage in the industrial creation of any creative good. The development period includes all the activities and costs necessary to transform an idea into a working script (or the equivalent) that is ready to begin production.

Diasporic communities Groups of people, often defined by ethnicity or national origin, living in various different countries but maintaining cultural connections with one another.

Differential promotion The strategy of placing greater praise, attention, and money on a small fraction of the products, particularly those perceived to have the greatest potential to become hits.

Digital distribution The delivery of media content without the use of physical media (such as tapes, paper, CDs, DVDs, or film stock). Content streamed directly on the Internet is an example of digital distribution.

Digital divide Term used to describe the gap between those who have access to and facility with digital technologies (the "information rich") and those who do not (the "information poor").

Digital rights management (DRM) Technological enforcers of copyright that control use of media in many different ways (e.g., limiting the amount of time a digital file works, preventing printing or saving of files). Much of the legal support for DRM can be found in the Digital Millennium Copyright Act of 1998.

Digitization A broad technological change in the production and transmission of many goods and services. The process of digitization relies on converting media objects (sound, video, an image, text) into a digital code composed of discrete binary numbers (0s and 1s). Digitization leads to better efficiencies in the production and storage of these media objects and has rapidly overtaken older forms of production.

Direct pay A source of revenue generated from payment by audiences (e.g., film admissions, movie rentals, magazine purchases).

Disaggregation Unbundling media content from its traditional form of distribution and permitting it to circulate in other ways, such as taking songs from a CD and offering them for sale individually over an Internet music site.

Discerning savvy Term describing the awareness that media workers acquire through day-to-day interactions with their superiors and other workers. This savvy allows workers to successfully navigate the norms of the workplace and determine what is acceptable or not, simply through observation and familiarity with the workplace culture.

Distribution and aggregation practices The functions and roles of media workers and associated agents focused more on bringing the finished product to the audience. Thus distribution and aggregation practices include tasks such as marketing, **windowing**, and sales.

Distribution/distributors The process of transporting completed media goods from their sites of production to the places where they will be aggregated or retailed to audiences, as well as the range of business activities that this process entails.

Diversity of voices The goal of ensuring that media regulation fosters an environment in which audiences have the ability to access more, rather than fewer, voices and perspectives through media.

Dominant ideology Often thought of as "common sense" or just the way things are, dominant ideology describes systems of beliefs that are widely shared by a group or society at a moment in time. These ideas come to take on extraordinary power because they are normalized by everything from schools, to religious organizations, to the content of popular media such as television.

Downstream windows Distribution windows that occur later in the release of a media good. *See also* **upstream windows**.

Dual product market An economic concept referring to the two layers of sale that occur in media industries: a media company offers a media product (e.g., a radio playlist, a prime-time lineup) to an audience, although the economic transaction comes from selling the audience to an advertiser (also see Ch. 3).

Dual revenue streams Two sources of financial support for a media good industry, typically advertiser support and some subscription or direct payment by the media user.

Duopolies Ownership situation that occurs when two or more stations in the same market are owned by a common entity.

Economic norms A broad term that encapsulates the wide range of conditions that impact the financing and funding of media industries and media goods. Economic norms include the ways in which media goods are funded, how costs are recouped, the organizational structures surrounding production, and even the impact of macro-economic changes on the media industries.

Economies of scale The financial advantages that emerge from large-scale production of goods and services. Companies achieve economies of scale when the average cost of producing a good decreases as the number of units produced increases. Companies can achieve economies of scale with large-scale production because there are certain fixed costs that do not change irrespective of the number of units produced, so as production is ramped up, those fixed costs are spread over more units, leading to an overall lower production cost per unit.

Economies of scope The decreased costs of production that come from producing a wide range of products; the efficiencies can include sharing research and development costs across multiple products and taking advantage of integrated or related marketing campaigns.

Fair use Legal provision established by the 1976 Copyright Act that allows for limited copying or use of a product that is protected by copyright so long as it is in accord with a few key conditions, such as criticism, comment, news reporting, teaching, scholarship, or research.

Federal Communications Commission (FCC) Agency of the US government that is charged with enforcing the regulatory provisions that govern many media industries, particularly broadcast and cable television, telephony, and some aspects of the Internet.

Federal Radio Commission (FRC) Precursor to the Federal Communications Commission; regulatory agency that established the commercial norm of broadcasting by requiring broadcasters attain a license to use the airwaves.

Federal Trade Commission (FTC) Regulatory agency that assesses many aspects of the Internet and the advertising industry. For instance, along with the Department of Justice, the FTC oversees the competitive practices of all industries and evaluates mergers and acquisitions that diminish market competitiveness.

Financial Interest and Syndication Rules Set of rules imposed by the Federal Communications Commission in 1970 on broadcast networks, preventing these networks from having a financial stake in the shows they licensed for broadcast or in syndicated programming.

First-copy costs The costs of producing the first copy of a media good. It is an economic principle that highlights the cost to media companies of producing the original of any media good and that nearly all costs are tied up in producing the first good.

First-mover advantage The competitive advantage a company earns by being the first to enter a specific market. The advantage generally comes about through the opportunity to gain a strong-hold in the market and to establish brand loyalty.

Formal self-regulation Self-imposed rules enacted by an industry that limit or categorize content or behavior. Typically developed by an industry consortium, although often lacking a formal enforcement mechanism. For example, the Motion Picture Association of America's movie rating system.

Format sale Selling the particular features of a media good for production in another country. When a format is sold, a new version of the media good is produced. The premise, characters, and norms of the original are localized to fit the new setting. The creation of *American Idol*, which is based on the UK's *Pop Idol*, is a common example of a format sale.

Formatting A broad term that reflects the media industry's adoption of certain norms and rules that have been successful in the past as a prescription for future success. Established formulas include the use of known products (e.g. sequels), known talent (e.g., A-list stars), standard features (e.g., 30- or 60-minute television episodes) and "formats" (e.g., genres such as Top 40 radio, action-adventure movies, etc.). Note the use of specific "formats" and "format sales" are distinctive subcategories of this general strategy.

Fragmentation The breakdown of the mass-media audience into more targeted niche audience groups.

Freemium content Digital media content that is distributed free of charge to the consumer but that requires the consumer to pay for added features or functionality.

Genre Literary term used to describe media content that has similar characteristics such as the form, content, subject matter, and so on. It is a useful shorthand that can be used to distinguish what it is, and popular media content typically adheres to genre standards to help guarantee that it will find an appropriate and interested audience.

Geocultural markets Transnational media markets that are based on cultural rather than national boundaries.

Governmental regulation Rules imposed upon a media industry by an external body, typically the state.

Gross sales The total revenues a company makes prior to deducting costs of production, distribution, marketing, and overhead. This is not to be confused with net sales, which is gross sales with those costs subtracted out. For example, if a series "grosses" $200 million, and production, distribution, and promotional costs are $100 million, the "net" is $100 million. ($200m-$100m)

Hollywood accounting The creative reporting practices used by Hollywood studios to account for a movie's revenue. In most cases, the costs of producing and distributing the movie are inflated leading to a "loss" on the books for the movie.

Horizontal integration Another form of conglomeration in which companies merge with or acquire other companies engaged at the same level in the production process (e.g., a corporation owning several newspapers or multiple production studios is horizontally integrated); ultimate horizontal integration is the existence of a monopoly.

Hybridity A cultural process whereby different cultures interact and change each other over time.

Ideology The normative or common-sense ideas and worldviews that guide or inform every individual's understanding of society and the world in general. Ideologies are often shared by groups with common interests and often assume a taken-for-grantedness, thus they are rarely challenged and are often accepted uncritically. Most media scholars believe that the media are important purveyors of ideologies. *See also* **Dominant ideology**.

Indecent A legal distinction for a class of speech that is prohibited on the airwaves at certain times but that is not subject to prior restraint. The Federal Communications Commission defines indecency as "language or material that, in context, depicts or describes, in terms patently offensive as measured by contemporary community standards for the broadcast medium, sexual or excretory activities or organs."

Independent Term used to distinguish media created without support from the dominant production organizations (studios, labels, publishers) of a particular industry. Independent media creators often self-finance or solicit investors for the production of their media goods.

Industry lore "Common sense" ways of doing things among media industry executives and workers, including ideas about what consumers want, what trends are hot, etc. Typically industry lore is based more on perception and convention than on research.

Informal self-regulation Self-imposed narrowing of the universe of possible goods. These often come from **industry lore** (see Ch. 7) about what is or isn't profitable. Although fairly intangible, these are the most stringent regulations on media content.

Information and communication technologies (ICTs) Technologies that facilitate human communication through electronic means, as well as any application or device that takes advantage of such technologies. The term is more common outside the United States. The tendency to use the umbrella term ICT instead of older, medium-specific terms (like radio, satellite, Internet, videoconferencing) is indicative of the **convergence** (see Ch. 6) of communications technologies and applications due to **digitization** (see Ch. 1).

Information economy An economic system where the primary transactional good is intellectual property. Over the past 40 years, it has become the majority producer of gross domestic product in developed countries, as opposed to previous reliance on agriculture or manufacturing. Some examples of industries that make up the information economy include the IT and software industry, telecommunications industry, and creative industries such as media and fashion.

Intellectual property rights A legal guarantee that authors, inventors, researchers, and others keep the right to determine how their intellectual efforts get released to the general public and who gets to profit from them.

Intentional overproduction Involves deliberately producing more cultural goods than are likely to succeed in the hope that a few will become "hits" and make up for the financial losses of all the "misses." This is a strategy intended to manage the uncertainties in the marketplace.

Journalistic objectivity A core principle of journalistic ethics, journalistic objectivity advocates for journalists to remain neutral and unbiased in reporting news stories. It is often thought to be important for the proper functioning of democratic societies.

Just-in-time production A production process that minimizes the warehousing of physical goods. Instead, just-in-time production seeks to manufacture goods as close as possible to the time of sale to minimize the time between incurring costs of production and receiving revenue.

Known formats Broad characteristics that help establish the nature of media goods such as its genre, which helps to bracket off the type of content to be featured. Producing content that is a know format helps establish the overall concept behind a piece of media content and can be useful in identifying targeted audiences.

Known product The strategy of using intellectual property that has previously been successful in order to reduce uncertainty because known products have an established audience. Adaptations from other media, sequels, remakes, and spin-offs are some examples of using a known product.

Known talent The hiring of established talent as a selling tool for media products. The most obvious examples include the use of well-known stars in lead roles, but it also includes other strategies such as using a prominent star's voice in video games or know writers, directors, and producers.

Least objectionable programming A popular term used to refer to media content— usually television—that is considered to be acceptable to a wide array of audience members, though also not particularly desired by those audience members.

Legacy media industries Media industries, including newspaper, radio and television, broadcasting, music, etc., that existed prior to the widespread adoption of digital technologies and the Internet.

Libraries The collections of available goods that distributors have for sale, typically including goods from a range of producers.

Lobbyists Individuals who represent the interests of media industry sectors to the Federal Communications Commission and Congress. These associations, such as the Motion Picture Association of America, attempt to influence policy by using their funds to persuade the Federal Communications Commission and the legislature to make sure new policies help rather than hinder their businesses.

Localism A regulatory goal that guides the creation of media policies and regulation that enable media that originate from the community served.

Localize/localization The process of unmooring media goods from their immediate cultural surroundings and reproducing them in another locale. This includes translating the language, settings, and narrative techniques to fit the new location.

Long tail A concept coined by *Wired* magazine editor Chris Anderson that describes the value media industries can find outside of the blockbuster. Derived from **Pareto's principle**, earning revenue from the so-called long tail of media goods is made possible by the substantially reduced costs of digital distribution. In the era of brick-and-mortar retailers, there was insufficient space to sell most media goods. Digital retailers make it possible to monetize the many goods that may have only a few buyers, but a few buyers of many goods can introduce significant new revenue to media industries.

Loss leader A product that is sold below its production costs (i.e., at a loss) because of its potential to attract new customers or drive the sales of more lucrative products.

Magazine-format advertising An advertising strategy in which advertisers typically purchase 30-second spots in a portfolio of shows rather than paying for the entire production costs of a program (single sponsorship); replaced the single-sponsorship model as the norm on television.

Make-goods The industry term for additional advertising time or other remuneration made to an entity that does not receive whatever value was guaranteed for its purchase. For example, in the television industry, an advertiser is often guaranteed a certain number of viewers by the network. If the network doesn't deliver, it then gives the advertiser other spots to make up the deficit.

Mandate Frames the corporate mission or primary objective of the media industry entity. Corporations in the media industries can pursue a commercial mandate as a profit-driven entity or a noncommercial entity. Multiple mandates can exist in a single industry. Understanding a company's mandate can be useful in determining what sort of media good the firm produces and in understanding the company's strategies.

Marginal cost In economics, refers to those costs that are incurred in producing every incremental copy of a good or service. In media terms, this is the cost of reproduction for every additional good beyond the original.

Market (often **designated market area [DMA]** in Nielsen parlance): A geographical area reached by radio and television stations in the major city of the area.

Market research A category of research usually conducted prior to and during the development of products. Researchers take media products at various stages of completion and elicit responses from members of targeted demographic groups (through, e.g., surveys, focus groups, and other specialized techniques) in an effort to integrate audience preferences more into the final product, thereby increasing sales.

Marketing and distribution costs The costs incurred in getting completed media goods into the hands of audiences such as having films printed and shipped to theaters or having CDs made and shipped to stores, as well as the costs related to promoting media goods to distributors and consumers.

Mass customization A process that focuses on producing commodities that places a higher emphasis on tailoring goods to local market conditions. Although these commodities are still produced in factories for large numbers of people, in contrast to its predecessor, mass production, mass customization offers options for more individual tastes to take shape—though within very controlled parameters. Auto manufacturers offering customers the ability to tailor vehicles across a select number of prescribed options illustrates mass customization in practice.

Mass media Media goods designed to appeal to the widest group of consumers.

Mass production The use of systematic production techniques such as assembly-line modes of production or some form of rote mechanization for workers that yields large supplies of a good or product. Mass production leads to greater efficiencies and standardization in the production process, and the huge output generally leads to lower production costs per unit overall.

Media capital A major center for the transnational production and distribution of media content in the contemporary global economy, such as Los Angeles, London, Hong Kong, Tokyo, and Laos.

Media globalization Reflects both a cultural as well as an economic shift in emphasis in the production and distribution of a wide range of products including media goods. Although globalization has existed in one form or another for centuries, in its current form it entails a broader emphasis on cultural exchange and erosion of boundaries between nations alongside the more traditional focus on international trade.

Media text Any piece of audiovisual content that is produced for audience consumption. This is often defined as any media artifact that can be "read," meaning an object that is subject to interpretation and varied meaning-making. It is the actual output of the media industries. Examples of media texts range from advertising spots to video games, magazine articles, and film/television shows.

Mixed-mandate systems Contexts in which both commercial and noncommercial entities exist in the same media industry. For example, within the television industries of much of Western Europe, both noncommercial, public-mandate networks and commercial networks exist side by side.

Monopoly An organization that operates without competition in its industry, typically with governmental approval.

Multichannel networks Companies that work with online video content creators, providing funding, production, monetization, management, and audience development in exchange for a percentage of advertising revenue.

Multilateral governance model A manner of governing communications infrastructures where every member country gets a single vote.

Multi-stakeholder governance model A manner of governing communications infrastructures where member nations, civil society organizations, and businesses share decision-making.

Natural monopoly The concept that some industries can only operate efficiently and profitably if they are controlled by a single **monopoly** organization. They often receive greater regulatory oversight as a consequence.

Net neutrality The principle that Internet service providers not discriminate among messages or users, that they pass along all messages at equal speeds, and that users be able to access all web pages regardless of their service provider.

Niche audiences Smaller segments of the media population brought together by interests in media texts that do not appeal to the much broader mass population.

Nobody knows The perspective that speaks to the high degree of risk in predicting which media goods will be successful. Success depends on the whims and desires of consumers and there are no absolute rules to figure out what the audience wants. The type of product testing common in other industries has not proven similarly reliable in media industries.

Noncommercial mandate Occurs when media industry entities are motivated by something other than profit-making. The objectives of firms operating under a noncommercial mandate can vary based on the type of organization in play. Types of noncommercial mandates include public, community, alternative/DIY, and governmental mandates.

Obscene A legal distinction of a class of speech that doesn't enjoy free speech protection. Obscene works, as defined in the 1973 Supreme Court case *Miller v. California*, are those "which, taken as a whole, appeal to the prurient interest in sex, which portray sexual conduct in a patently offensive way, and which, taken as a whole, do not have serious literary, artistic, political, or scientific value." This ruling emphasized the idea that different communities are likely to have varying definitions of obscenity.

Oligopoly An industry that is dominated by a small number of companies that effectively block additional competitors from entering the market.

Outsourcing A labor practice that seeks to hire workers in the cheapest possible labor markets in order to save money. It has become more possible and more popular because of the rise of instantaneous, worldwide communications networks.

Overhead costs Expenses required to maintain media institutions. These costs are not isolated to a particular product but are required to maintain the infrastructure used by media entities such as film studios or record labels.

Overstocking Carrying a wider range and number of media goods than an organization expects to sell in an effort to manage risk.

Owned and operated station (O&Os) Individual stations, usually located in large cities such as New York and Los Angeles, owned by a network. Other stations are owned by other businesses and "affiliate" with the network. Affiliation is an agreement to trade advertising time and increasingly fees for programming. Historically, though, networks have paid stations to be affiliates.

Parallel economy An alternative term for what are often also described as a "shadow economy" or "black market economy." A parallel economy refers to the generally cash-only transactions that take place outside authorized or legal systems of exchange without any record keeping.

Paramount decree The outcome of *United States v. Paramount Pictures, Inc.*, a 1948 anti-trust case decided by the Supreme Court. It ended the vertical integration of the film industry by forcing the "Big Eight" studios to divest themselves of the theaters they owned.

Pareto's principle An economic principle that suggests labor, goods, and services work within an 80/20 rule, whereby 20 percent of a firm's resources produce 80 percent of its revenue. Chris Anderson adopted this principle in charting out his **long tail** theory that describes the shift in distribution practices created by digitization and the ability to monetize the 80 percent of goods that do not fall within the blockbuster category.

Payola Secret payment or incentive. Best-known case occurred in the music industry when distributors gave cash and other gifts to DJs in order to get them to play their songs and rave about them on the air.

Peer-to-peer network A network of computers whereby each computer on the network is able to directly "speak" to other computers on the network without the use of a central hub, also known as a server. Peer-to-peer networks allow for easy transmission of data between computers on the network.

Penny presses Cheap, commercially funded newspapers in the nineteenth century that began to reach a truly national readership and were read by a wide cross-section of the population, most notably working-class immigrants.

Pilot episode The initial episode of a television program, which serves as the test episode by which networks evaluate whether to develop the idea as a series and order additional episodes.

Piracy Buying and selling unlicensed copies of copyrighted media goods.

Platforms Broadly, any mode of delivering media content to consumers; these can be technological modes, such as streaming or broadcasting, or media forms, such as television, film, or gaming.

Point-to-point Media technologies designed to allow communication between two points, and thus facilitate interpersonal communication, rather than among institutions and audiences. Compare **mass media**.

Practices The day-to-day routines and standard operating procedures that media industry workers and organizations employ. Practices have been organized in this book as either creative or distribution and aggregation practices.

Price differentiation An economic term that explains the manipulation of a good's price depending on a set of circumstances. Within the media industries, the cost to see a movie or other media text is different depending on where and when you see it. For instance seeing a movie now in the theater is about $15, but it will only cost about $4 if you wait to rent it later.

Prior restraint The prevention of circulation of content. To protect free speech, the Supreme Court has ruled that prior restraint is only allowed if the content is **obscene**.

Private goods Goods that when consumed prevent others from consuming the same good. These goods often involve some ownership stakes for the consumer, hence the term "private."

Privately held companies Companies that do not trade on the stock market; although they may also issue shares or stock in the company, this is generally a private exchange done outside the purview of the stock market. Although privately held companies are not subject to the same disclosure requirements as publicly traded companies, each privately held company is restricted in the number of shareholders it can have (commonly no more than 50).

Product placement The advertising practice of inserting products into entertainment content as a form of advertisement.

Production costs All the expenses involved in the actual making of a media product.

Propaganda An effort to use the media to spread false or misleading information in an effort to influence or manipulate the public's opinion or persuade the public to take some sort of action.

Proprietary Term used to describe systems that are restrictive and often adopt stringent rules and regulations governing how the product can be modified. Often proprietary systems require all updates to the technology and its internal structure to be determined by the manufacturer or its exclusive agents and resellers.

Prosumer Term incorporating both the media "producer" and "consumer," which acknowledges that consumers are increasingly involved in the production process.

Public domain Content designated as "public property" because a copyright has expired and so one no longer needs to pay the originator for rights of use.

Public goods Goods or services that are not depleted or destroyed in the process of consumption. Unlike private goods, millions of people can consume a public good (e.g., watching a television show) without using it up or preventing others from doing so.

Public interest, convenience, and necessity The standard by which those entrusted with broadcast licenses in the United States are expected to perform.

Public sphere Coined by German theorist Jürgen Habermas to describe the social space where citizens could come together to discuss societal issues and through such rational debate inspire political action.

Publicly held companies Companies that trade on the stock market, offering the opportunity for anyone to purchase a stake in the company. Publicly held companies have a responsibility to stockholders to protect their investment (fiduciary duty) and are therefore subject to a number of security regulations such as the public disclosure of financial statements and holding an annual stockholders' meeting.

Publishers Primary industrial entity of single-goods industries. Publishers include publishers of books and video games, labels in the case of music, and studios in the case of film.

Real audience The tangible customers of a media good (i.e., those individuals who consume the media good after it has been created).

Recommendation algorithms Computer programs that collect information about our tastes and the tastes of people like us in order to recommend other media products we might want to consume.

Regulation The creation of laws, guidelines, and rules governing the operation of media industries (production, distribution, and exhibition) and the enforcement of those laws, which often requires the creation of specific regulatory bodies. Most media industries face two types of formal regulation: those that regulate either content or industry structure.

Regulations on industry structure Laws and guidelines that place restrictions on media industry governance such as regulations affecting media ownership or licensing agreements.

Remediation A process in which the characteristics of one medium influence the characteristics of another medium.

Reproduction costs Cost of making each additional good.

Rights period The contracted length of time that a distributor or aggregator can sell a media good.

Rights The contractual permissions that copyright holders give to other aggregators to sell their intellectual property.

Royalties Percentages of profits that media workers receive from the sale of media goods. Usually limited to **above-the-line** (see Ch. 7) workers.

Runaway production The outsourcing of media production, typically from Hollywood, to nearby nations.

Safe harbor The hours between 10:00 PM and 6:00 AM when broadcasters are allowed to air **indecent** content. The Federal Communications Commission established this practice because broadcasters can reasonably assume children will not be in the audience.

Secondary market The marketplace for the reselling of media goods. Secondary markets can be domestic, such as when a local affiliate purchases previously aired shows to rebroadcast on its station, or international, such as when studios sell shows to networks in other countries.

Segment-making media Joseph Turow's term for media that cater to niche audiences, or small slices of society. Segment-making media discourages one's likelihood of encountering diverse viewpoints and generally allows for reinforcing of existing beliefs. *Compare* **Society-making media**.

Self-regulation Rules and guidelines that are implemented outside of the purview of external and official regulatory bodies. These self-regulations can either be internal rules that a company adopts or may involve voluntary regulations that trade associations impose on their members.

Simultaneous release Synchronized worldwide distribution windows that allow media audiences in major global markets to consume the same goods at the same time.

Single media goods Media goods that are sold as stand-alone goods. Single media goods are generally purchased on a one-off basis, rather than as part of subscription package or advertiser-supported model in their initial distribution window. For example, purchasing books, songs or downloads, or attending a film's theatrical release.

Single sponsorship A means of advertiser funding in which one advertiser pays a show's production costs as well as fees to the network and advertising agency. In exchange, the advertiser is promoted as the show's exclusive sponsor. It was once the norm of the television industry.

Society-making media Term originally coined by scholar Joseph Turow to describe media that reach a broad cross-section of the general audience, creating the opportunity for these populations to "talk to each other" and gain access to a diversity of viewpoints. *Compare* **Segment-making media**.

Sponsorship model One-time norm of the television industry in which one advertiser was associated with a program, paying all the costs of production as well as fees to the network and advertising agency.

Standard features Commonly adopted conventions that have been incorporated into media production practices helping to create guidelines that normalize some level of consistency for the media industry.

Standards and practices The department responsible for ensuring that program content adheres to both network policies and legal regulations. This includes preventing content that could provoke legal action for reasons like defamation or indecency.

Star system The organization of many creative industries today, in which a small number of highly visible talents wield considerable power over the creative process. *Compare* **Studio system**.

Station group An entity that owns stations affiliated with various networks located in cities around the country.

Studio system The organizational model prevalent in the film industry from the 1920s through the 1950s, in which the major Hollywood studios controlled both the creative and business processes of the film industry. *Compare* **Star system**.

Subscription A form of payment in which a media user provides a source of revenue for the media outlet that typically involves buying access to a package of goods. Subscriptions may be a media entity's sole source of revenue (e.g., HBO) or may be paired with advertising support (e.g., most magazines).

Sunk costs An economic term that describes irrecoverable costs that are incurred in the production of goods and services. Media goods typically incur most of the production costs upfront, so these costs are "sunk" in the initial production process.

Surrogate consumers The role that aggregators play when winnowing down the thousands of media products that are available. As surrogate consumers, aggregators make decisions on the actual consumer's behalf.

Synergy A buzzword used to describe a belief that in conglomerating various media operations or companies, the combined value is greater than the sum of the individual parts due to the potential of cross-promotion. This value is enabled by owning multiple media outlets such as several different broadcast and cable channels.

Talent Media performers such as journalists, actors, and musicians who play a unique role in creating media goods.

Technological affordances The properties and capabilities of a technology.

Technological determinism The perspective that ascribes a significant amount of influence in technology's ability to shape society. It assumes that technology is the predominant force that helps change societal norms and behaviors. Compare **determinism** and **cultural determinism**.

Technological dystopianism The idea that technological innovation brings about a chaotic, undesirable human society on Earth.

Technological utopianism An overly optimistic and idealistic view of technology's ability to usher in progress that will help alleviate all of society's ills.

Technology An operating condition of the media industries. Refers to the mechanical and electronic means by which media content is created, distributed, and aggregated.

Telecommunications Act of 1996 The last major regulatory act, which lifted the limit on national ownership of radio stations and loosened other limits leading to a massive consolidation within media industries.

Unilateral governance model A manner of governing communications infrastructures where a single, powerful nation sets policy for the whole world.

Upstream windows Distribution channels that occur earlier in the release of a media good. Downstream windows occur later. For example, in film, theatrical distribution is upstream and prime-time network broadcast is downstream.

Vertical integration A competitive strategy companies use to establish complete control in producing a good or service. Vertical integration is achieved by acquiring other companies involved at each level of the production process. In the media industries, this means owning companies involved with both the production and distribution of media goods (e.g., the same corporation owning the television studio that makes a program and the network that airs it). Vertical integration is a form of conglomeration.

Windowing A distribution strategy that has historically been very important in film and television industries. It describes the practice of releasing media content on a staggered schedule for different platforms or countries. The staggered schedule is intended to build excitement about media products and encourage consumption in earlier windows, which typically are more profitable for media companies. Digital distribution and the easy simultaneous release it allows are leading many industries to reconsider the extent to which they use it.

Credits

Index